Jesus Christ for
Contemporary Life

Jesus Christ for Contemporary Life

His Person, Work, and Relationships

DON SCHWEITZER

CASCADE *Books* · Eugene, Oregon

JESUS CHRIST FOR CONTEMPORARY LIFE
His Person, Work, and Relationships

Unless otherwise noted, all biblical quotations and references are taken from
the New Revised Standard Version Bible, copyright 1989, Division of Christian
Education of the National Council of the Churches of Christ in the United States of
America. Used by permission. All rights reserved.

Cascade Books
An Imprint of Wipf and Stock Publishers
199 W. 8th Ave., Suite 3
Eugene, OR 97401

www.wipfandstock.com

ISBN 13: 978-1-55635-107-5

Cataloging-in-Publication data:

Schweitzer, Don

Jesus Christ for contemporary life : his person, work, and relationships / Don
Schweitzer

x + 308 p. ; 23 cm. Includes bibliographical references.

ISBN 13: 978-1-55635-107-5

1. Jesus Christ—Significance. 2. Jesus Christ—Person and offices. 3. Jesus Christ—
History of doctrines. I. Title.

BT301 S395 2012

Manufactured in the U.S.A.

Dedicated to Leslie, Simon, and Ian

Contents

Preface

CHRISTIANS TODAY LIVE IN a cosmopolitan world. Previous boundaries of nation, ethnicity, culture, class, gender, and race have become porous. Yet many injustices of the modern world remain, exacerbated now by the rise of an empire that enforces them ruthlessly and without compunction. Joined to this are the environmental crisis and a sense of the limitations and fallibility of all moral codes and religious traditions, Christianity included. Christian discipleship in this time requires an identity bound to an emancipatory vision yet open to others and capable of self-critique. Such an identity requires strong moral sources to sustain it.

This book presents an understanding of Jesus Christ in a Trinitarian perspective that tries to provide these moral sources and identity. It argues that Jesus Christ communicates the beauty and goodness of God in a way that can empower people to further express this in their own lives, even in confrontation with the forces of empire and their own failings, and is open to celebrating other traditions and receiving from them. It draws upon the quest for the historical Jesus and from New Testament, patristic, and contemporary Christologies to argue this. It presents this understanding by examining first the person of Jesus Christ, then his saving significances, and finally his relationships, to the church and to others.

Many people and institutions played a role in the writing of this book. Tatha Wiley encouraged me to begin. Various editors at Wipf and Stock have patiently waited for it to be completed. Mallory Wiebe, library technician at St. Andrew's College, helped me obtain books and articles from other libraries in the Saskatoon Theological Union. Melanie Schwanbeck helped me when I had computer troubles. The interlibrary loans staff at the University of Saskatchewan also helped me access materials. Teaching sessions at Bishop's College in Kolkata, Serampore

College in Serampore, United Theological College in Bangalore, and Kerela United Theological Seminary in Trivanandrum, India, and visiting HanShin Graduate School of Theology in Seoul, Korea, all helped broaden my thought. Rev. Deborah Shanks and Rev. Gord Waldie, former students, and Dr. Harold Wells, a long-time colleague, read drafts of the chapters and made valuable suggestions. Many of the students who took the course "Jesus Christ and the Quest for Wholeness" in the years I taught it have also helped improve the ideas presented here. I thank all of the above and any others I have forgotten to name for their help with this book.

Introduction

T HIS BOOK PRESENTS A Christology developed in a Canadian/North Atlantic context. A Christology is an understanding of Jesus Christ; who he was and is, what his saving significance is, and how he relates to the church, other religions, and other forms of knowledge and experience. Christologies are usually developed by interpreting the biblical witness to Jesus Christ in relation to one's context, the time and place in which one lives. This involves (a) interpreting present experience, (b) interpreting Scripture, and (c) a way of bringing the two together. The criteria of a Christology are the adequacy of its interpretations of Scripture and the present, its systematic coherence, and its performance, how well it illuminates the reality of Jesus Christ in its context. At present there are various ways of doing (a), (b), and (c) that have a relative validity and integrity, but there is no one way that is adequate in every respect and superior to all others.[1]

Ultimately it is difficult to disentangle a reading of Scripture from a reading of one's context, to say which came first or where one should begin. The two always mutually influence and interpenetrate each other. Both are also always influenced to some degree by preceding traditions of christological reflection. A Christology is always contextual, related to its time and place. Yet in seeking to understand Jesus Christ no one begins from scratch. If every speaker is "a respondent to a greater or lesser degree,"[2] this is particularly true of those who write Christologies. Every Christology is a response to others that have preceded it as well as to one's context. Ultimately, each is a response to what God has said and done through Jesus Christ and in the Holy Spirit.

1. Schweitzer, *Contemporary Christologies*, 133–34.
2. Bakhtin, *Speech Genres*, 69.

SCRIPTURE

This Christology interprets Scripture by drawing upon it on three levels. First, it works from what can be known about Jesus and the movement that gathered about him through the quest for the historical Jesus. In doing so it recognizes that there is more to Jesus as the crucified and risen Christ than what the quest for the historical Jesus can discern. Drawing upon what can be known about Jesus historically, without being limited to this, is intended to keep this Christology grounded in history and historically concrete in its references to Jesus. Recognizing that there is more to the risen Christ than can be known by the quest for the historical Jesus, this Christology also draws upon various Christologies found in the New Testament, primarily in the Synoptic Gospels and in the writings of Paul. Finally, the metaphysical framework of this Christology is drawn from the Johannine understanding of Jesus as the Word of God. A word is always addressed to someone. Jesus as the incarnate Word communicates the radical transcendence of God's love and the aseity of God's being, yet is not complete without an audience who receives this love and then seeks to further communicate it in their own lives.[3]

THE CANADIAN/NORTH ATLANTIC CONTEXT

This Christology is written from a Canadian context characterized by a diffuseness or lack of concentration in the issues it presents that a Christology must take up. For a white, middle-class, heterosexual, anglophone male like myself, there is no one issue or crisis in this context that predominates over all others. To be such in this context is to have a complicated moral identity. One is at least implicated in oppressions, yet also threatened by issues like the environmental crisis. To relate efficaciously to this kind of complicated identity, Christ must have more than one saving significance.

Theologians interested in the world have noted the diffuse nature of issues in this context for some time. Gregory Baum argued in 1975 that the North American context was characterized by "a complex intermeshing of technocratic depersonalization and immobility, economic domination and exploitation, racial exclusion and inferiorization, and other forms including the subjugation of women."[4] To this list one

---

3. Brown, *Epistles of John*, 555.
4. Baum, *Religion and Alienation*, 218–19.

should add today the threat of the environmental crisis, the struggles of First Nations peoples for liberation and of Quebec and francophones in Canada for recognition. Baum argued that as a result of this diffuseness, "the analysis of social sin in North American will inevitably be complex," and that in this context "the commitment to justice and human emancipation, to which Christians are summoned, cannot be expressed by identification with a single movement."[5]

This diffuseness of issues remains, but is now joined by a new development, the rise of empire. Empire designates "massive concentrations of power that permeate all aspects or life and that cannot be controlled by any one actor alone."[6] An empire not only exerts control through its massive power, but also uses this "to extend its control as far as possible"[7] in every conceivable domain. In the early 1980s a new economic, cultural, political constellation of empire began to emerge "that protects the interests of the developed nations, regulates the flow of money all over the world, controls oil and other natural resources," and pacifies "the unruly by military force."[8] This "contemporary empire is a more dispersed reality"[9] than previous imperial regimes. It "is embodied in various dependencies maintained through less visible ties."[10] But its power and presence are no less real. It is centered in the boardrooms and political offices of developed North Atlantic nations. Canada is one of the developed nations whose economic interests this empire protects. Therefore it seems more accurate to describe the Canadian standpoint of this book as located within a North Atlantic rather than a North American context. This North Atlantic context at present is characterized by both a diffuseness of issues and the presence of empire.

Writing in 1990 in the shadow of this emerging empire and responding to the diffuseness of the issues facing Christologies here, Mark Lewis Taylor identified a postmodern trilemma of three demands that Christian theologies must simultaneously respect: "to acknowledge some

---

5. Ibid., 219.

6. Rieger, *Christ and Empire*, 2.

7. Ibid.

8. Baum, *Religion and Alienation*, 2nd ed,, 225.

9. Rieger, *Christ and Empire*, 3.

10. Ibid.

sense of tradition, to celebrate plurality, and to resist domination."[11] His analysis remains accurate.

The first trait of this trilemma, the need "to acknowledge one's tradition,"[12] runs two ways. First, one needs to acknowledge the reality and importance of tradition for human life, how it can authorize and guide one by articulating transcendent moral sources that identify the good, critique evil, and empower and sustain resistance to evil. Second though, one needs to acknowledge the limits of one's tradition, the evils and injustices it has been involved in, and the privilege it may be accorded and the power it may have in contemporary society. Part of acknowledging one's tradition is owning up "to where you are, whoever you are and however complex your located self and group identities may be."[13] For Christians it is the moral values articulated in the confession of Jesus Christ that demand this acknowledgement and openness to critique.

The second trait is the need to celebrate and embrace plurality. This needs to happen in three ways. First there needs to be a recognition of the religious and cultural pluralism of the present; that it is not going away, and that Christian theology must be able to live within this as a force for peace and justice for all. Second, there needs to be a recognition of the functional value of pluralism. Dialogue with the other can lead to insights about one's self and one's context that cannot be had in any other way. Finally, there needs to be a recognition that traditions and cultural heritages other than Christianity are a good in and of themselves, and hence worthy of respect. The celebration and embrace of pluralism requires an openness to the other.

The third trait is the need to resist domination. Again, this needs to happen in a number of ways. Domination can be exercised along lines such as race, religion, gender, sexual orientation, and class. It also comes in different forms. It may be the domination of hegemony which suppresses ideas and voices so that only those of a certain group are heard or deemed legitimate. It may be domination by violence and military force. It may be economic or cultural domination. Resistance to domination requires different kinds of power. The one Christ empowers people to resist different forms of domination in several different ways.

---

11. Taylor, *Remembering Esperanza*, 23.

12. Ibid., 31.

13. Ibid., 31–32.

What makes these three traits a trilemma is the necessity and difficulty of addressing all three at once. Taylor argues the necessity of this as follows:

> First, a program of resisting domination, without the other two postmodern emphases, easily fails to actualize its own envisioned strategies for achieving justice and freedom from oppression. Without developing a sense of plurality, the struggle to be free from domination can founder on the divisiveness that springs up among agents for change who work with different visions of "the just" and from different experiences of oppression. Moreover, without a sense of tradition (some tradition of myth and ritual, at least, not necessarily the established Traditions), the struggle is impoverished, lacking the resources of communal memory and symbolic heritage that often provide some minimal dialogical consensus for marshalling critique and action.[14]

Second, it is difficult to do all three at once. Acknowledging tradition has frequently been seen as denying an embrace of pluralism. Resisting domination for many has meant a critique of tradition(s). Celebrating pluralism sometimes leaves one without a substantive basis for resistance to evil. Still, difficulty does not equal impossibility. This trilemma can present a possibility. The complexity of the present and its diffuseness of issues can be an opportunity to discover the complexity of the New Testament witness to Jesus Christ, the many different saving significances it attributes to him, and the ways in which they can be appropriated in the present.

THE STRUCTURE AND ARGUMENT OF THIS BOOK

This book is structured according to my own interpretation of Taylor's trilemma. The need to acknowledge tradition issues in part I, which focuses on the person of Jesus Christ. The need to resist domination issues in part II, which looks at Jesus' saving significance. The need to embrace and celebrate plurality issues in part III, which looks at some relationships of Jesus Christ, to those within the church and to others. This division into parts is a matter of focus, not an airtight compartmentalization. The three demands of acknowledging tradition, celebrating plurality, and resisting domination are present to some degree in each section. The acknowledgment of tradition in part I provides a metaphysical framework

14. Ibid., 41.

that informs how domination should be resisted and plurality celebrated, and is also present in other ways in parts II and III. Conversely, the needs to celebrate plurality and resist domination inform the way tradition is acknowledged in part I.

Modern Christologies have often been divided into two parts, studying Jesus Christ in terms of (1) his person and (2) his work. In one sense this is a false distinction. If one follows the guidelines of the Chalcedonian Definition, Jesus' person as the Christ is also his work as such. Jesus saves by being the Christ. Yet the modern distinction between person and work in Christology remains a useful heuristic for focusing discussion. The structure of this book maintains this division for this reason but extends it by adding a third category, that of relationships. This third category has been developing in recent decades as a result of the emphasis of feminist and process theologies on relationality and the increased recognition of religious pluralism.

The argument of this book is that Jesus Christ can be understood from a Trinitarian perspective as the incarnation of the Word of God. This incarnation happens to further communicate the goodness and beauty of God in time and space. As this occurs it brings a relative but still real increase to the being of God in the "person" of the Holy Spirit. Here the Johannine notion of Jesus as the Word is taken up into a Trinitarian perspective derived from the thought of Jonathan Edwards as interpreted by Sang Hyun Lee.[15] Part I develops this understanding by following what Karl Rahner called an ascending and then a descending Christology.[16]

Part II turns from the person of Jesus Christ to his work. The saving significances of Jesus,[17] as articulated in various atonement theories, are here understood as what Charles Taylor calls "moral sources."[18] They are articulations of the saving significance of Jesus that move people to communicate in their own lives the goodness and beauty of God that Jesus incarnated in his, and that sustain them in doing so in spite of opposition to this and their own failures. This understanding of Jesus'

---

15. Lee, *Jonathan Edwards*.

16. Rahner, *Foundations of the Christian Faith*, 177.

17. The book works with a total of six saving significances or atonement theories: Gustav Aulén's three; the Christus Victor, substitutionary, and moral influence theories, as well as a notion of Christ as revealing the nature of God (part I), Christ as working to reconcile humanity to God through his teaching (chapter 5), and Christ as the center of history (chapter 10).

18. Taylor, *Sources of the Self*, 91–93.

saving significance reflects the influence of modern liberalism, which is concerned with life in history as opposed to eternity,[19] and a development within the past several generations of Christologies that has ancient roots that sees Jesus as a source of salvation for all.[20] In light of this, that Jesus "saves" people in eternity is taken as a given. The question then becomes, what is his saving significance for people within history?

Part III focuses on some relationships of Jesus Christ to others. As the Word of God, Jesus Christ exists in history dialogically, giving shape and orientation to Christians' lives, yet also being shaped by their needs and concerns, faithfulness, and creativity. As the Word, Jesus provides a center for Christians in history, but a center that exists in dialectical relationships to other religions and social movements, as a result of values that Jesus incarnates. Finally, part of Jesus' saving significance is the influence he can have on a person through prayer.

This study of Jesus' person, work, and relationships does not claim to be exhaustive. As John 21:25 indicates, no Christology can be. What it does claim is that understanding Jesus as the Word of God, grounded in what can be known historically of Jesus and informed by subsequent reflection upon him, can give Christians an identity characterized by what Serene Jones calls "bounded openness."[21] This is an identity bounded by what is revealed of God in Christ, yet open to the world. This Christology seeks to acknowledge Christian traditions so that they empower Christians to seek justice and resist evil, in a way that is open to critique and reformulation. At the same time it claims to find in Christ reasons for openness to others.

19. The modern liberal concern for life within history itself arose partly through the influence of the Reformation's "affirmation of ordinary life as more than profane, as itself hallowed and in no way second class." Ibid., 218.

20. Moltmann, *Coming of God*, 235–55.

21. Jones, *Feminist Theory*, 170.

Part I

Introduction to Part I

THE FOLLOWING FOUR CHAPTERS that comprise part I primarily seek to understand the person of Jesus Christ. The first three do this by following an ascending Christology, beginning with what can be known about Jesus historically and following the development of Christology in the early church and patristic era up until the Councils of Nicaea (325 CE) and Chalcedon (451 CE). An ascending Christology seeks to show the legitimacy of the affirmations of these councils as ways of understanding Jesus by showing the continuity between what they state and what can be known about Jesus historically and what was affirmed about him by the early church in the New Testament

Chapter 1 offers a portrait of Jesus drawn from the quest for the historical Jesus. Faith in Jesus Christ does not usually begin with what can be known historically about Jesus and it is not based upon this. But this study of Jesus Christ begins here for the following reasons. The Gospels interpreted the history of Jesus each in a different way in light of his resurrection, the early church's experiences of the Holy Spirit, and the concerns and insights of the church communities they originated from. The quest for the historical Jesus attempts to discern the historical figure of Jesus amidst this interpretation. The results of this quest are never final. But historical knowledge of Jesus can provide a check on the human imagination's temptation to fashion images of Jesus determined by self-interests and can also help keep an understanding of Jesus historically concrete, showing how and where Jesus located himself amidst the social conflicts of his day. From this we can gain a sense of where one should follow Jesus and expect to encounter him in the present.

Chapter 2 examines New Testament descriptions of Jesus' resurrection and its meaning for Christian faith. It is necessary to study Jesus' resurrection in order to understand who Jesus Christ is and the nature of his saving significance. It was as a result of Jesus' resurrection that he was proclaimed as the Christ and became the center of what became a new religion. In the course of this Jesus' resurrection triggered a far-reaching doctrinal development that eventually helped transform the Christian understanding of God.

Chapter 3 traces the course of this transformation, examining the development of the patristic church's understanding of Jesus Christ that culminated in the decisions of the Councils of Nicaea and Chalcedon. These decisions did not end christological inquiry. They are interpreted here as providing guidelines for understanding Jesus Christ. In tracing this development this chapter also notes some gains and losses it involved for the early church's understanding of Jesus Christ.

Chapter 4 reverses the direction of inquiry and presents a descending Christology. Chapter 3 traced and critically accepted the developments leading to the affirmations of Nicaea and Chalcedon. This chapter seeks to understand Jesus Christ and God in light of them. Given that Jesus is the Christ, the incarnation of the second person of the Trinity, how should the Trinity be understood? What was the reason for the incarnation? By answering these questions, this chapter provides a metaphysical framework for the understanding of Jesus' saving significance and relationships that follows in parts II and III.

1 The Historical Jesus: His Message and Person

The gospels differ among themselves in regards to historical details about Jesus[1] and in their overall interpretations of him. These differences, along with the extraordinary claims the gospels make about him, raise the question, what can be known historically about Jesus? In a society where historical inquiry is an accepted form of knowledge this question cannot be avoided. This is the starting point for the quest for the historical Jesus, which can be traced back through various stages to Hermann Samuel Reimarus (1694–1768).[2] This quest is usually undertaken with some purpose related to the Christian faith.[3] It has theological importance. Historical inquiry is one source of knowledge about Jesus. It can help assess the continuity and discontinuity between what faith claims about Jesus Christ and the life he lived.[4] It can also give historical concreteness to one's understanding of Jesus, showing how he was situated amidst the social conflicts of his day.

The quest has produced numerous contradictory images of Jesus. These often betray an ideological bias in relation to cultural, political, and religious conflicts of the present. Yet understandings of Jesus produced by the quest cannot be simply dismissed as expressions of current

1. For instance, the day on which he died; Meier, *Marginal Jew*, 1:390.

2. For an overview of the history of the quest for the historical Jesus that unfortunately omits the Jesus Seminar, see Keating, "Epistemology and Theological Application," 19–21.

3. Elizabeth Johnson divides approaches to the quest into three often concurrent trajectories: one that seeks to debunk or drastically reformulate Christian faith, one that repudiates the relevance of the quest for Christian faith, and one that sees the quest as having a theological importance on the grounds that it provides knowledge about the person that Christians claim in the Christ; see Johnson, "Word Was Made Flesh," 147–49.

4. Haight, *Jesus*, 38–40.

ideologies. Research into the historical Jesus needs to be critically evaluated in terms of whose interests it serves. But it remains a potential source of knowledge about Jesus that has emancipatory power. The presence of ideological distortions in historical claims about Jesus can only be demonstrated through further historical inquiry. Therefore this inquiry needs to continue.[5] What can be known historically about Jesus, like any historical knowledge, is always subject to correction or refutation by further research. It is not the basis of faith in Jesus Christ. This faith is based on experiencing the proclamation of Jesus Christ as true in a compelling way. But knowledge about Jesus gained through the quest can and should inform this faith.

This chapter presents a description and interpretation of Jesus' message and person drawn from the work of people engaged in the quest for the historical Jesus. Subsequent chapters will return to the historical Jesus in relation to particular questions. This chapter has a broader focus: Jesus' proclamation of the coming reign of God and how this was intertwined with his person. Who Jesus was and how he lived was a medium for his message. Conversely this message and the way he proclaimed it made an implicit claim about his person, which eventually led to his death.

THE SETTING

Apart from one or more trips to Jerusalem, Jesus lived and worked in Galilee. He probably first became publicly active between 26 and 29 CE. His death outside Jerusalem probably occurred in 30 CE. These dates cannot be certain, partly because of the nature of the evidence in the gospels, and partly because of the time and place in which he lived.[6] Galilee was a hinterland to Jerusalem. Jerusalem was a hinterland to imperial Rome. Jesus had no significant impact on the Roman Empire during his lifetime. From a Jewish perspective he was only one of a number of charismatic leaders of messianic movements who were killed by Roman forces or by Herod, their client-king.[7] In relation to the political and cultural centers of his time, he lived and died in almost complete obscurity. Consequently, little exists in the way of records or historical references independent of the New Testament or related literature like

---

5. Schüssler Fiorenza, "Jesus of Nazareth in Historical Research," 41.

6. Meier, *Marginal Jew*, 1:372–409.

7. Jaffee, *Early Judaism*, 114.

the *Gospel of Thomas*[8] by which a more precise dating of his activities could be obtained.

Galilee in Jesus' time was experiencing deep social tensions along religious, cultural, political, and economic lines. Hellenism had been challenging and interacting with Judaism for several centuries. Taxation from Roman and subordinate regional authorities was pushing many peasant families into permanent debt. The divide between rich and poor was growing. Local and family authorities frequently had difficulty coping with the erosion of social values[9] caused by these cultural, economic, and political forces. This helped create an openness to successive eschatological renewal movements led by charismatic figures like John the Baptist and Jesus. These movements in turn created tensions between themselves, more established forms of Jewish religion, and Roman and Jewish political authorities.

Jesus was a first-century Jew. He lived in the period known as Second Temple Judaism.[10] It was a time of religious ferment and divergent movements within Judaism, to the extent that some suggest speaking of Judaisms rather than Judaism in this period. The gospels all describe Jesus as having an understanding of the Jewish religious traditions and practices sufficient to present himself as an authoritative interpreter of these and to defend his views in debate with other Jewish religious leaders. Evidence in the gospels suggests that he came from Nazareth in Galilee, a rural village off the beaten track yet close enough to the city of Sepphoris that he might be exposed to broader cultural currents.[11] Jesus was a layperson with no official qualifications or group affiliation to fall back on when resistance rose up against him. By all accounts he remained unmarried. His public ministry began after his baptism by John the Baptist, a charismatic Jewish religious leader preceding him. Jesus' relationship to John was in some ways analogous to his relationship to the institutions and traditions of Second Temple Judaism. Jesus accepted many of the teaching of both, yet he also creatively interpreted these and departed from them in significant ways. In doing so, he helped

---

8. For one study of the *Gospel of Thomas* and other non-canonical literature that some use as a source of historical knowledge about Jesus and the development of the New Testament, see Crossan, *Four Other Gospels*.

9. Freyne, *Jesus*, 46, 136.

10. For an overview of Second Temple Judaism, see Cohen, *From the Maccabees*.

11. Crossan, *Historical Jesus*, 18–19.

give rise to one of the covenantal renewal movements[12] that were part of Second Temple Judaism.

JOHN THE BAPTIST

John the Baptist was a preacher of eschatological renewal whose message centered on the theme that all people, even those considered righteous and good, needed to repent to escape God's impending judgment. Jesus went to John to be baptized. The significance of this can be summarized as follows:

> By doing this Jesus acknowledged John's charismatic authority as an eschatological prophet, accepted his message of imminent fiery judgment on a sinful Israel, submitted to his baptism as a seal of his resolve to change his life and as a pledge of salvation as part of a purified Israel, on whom God (through some agent?) would pour out the holy spirit on the last day.[13]

Being baptized by John positioned Jesus as implicitly criticizing other Jewish religious authorities and institutions, as these were included among those addressed by John's call to repentance. It is crucial though to note that John's and Jesus' at times radical criticism of other Jewish movements and institutions came from within Second Temple Judaism. Both John and Jesus were Jews. Neither departed from underlying assumptions shared by the divergent movements within Second Temple Judaism[14] and thus by the other Jewish religious leaders and institutions they criticized. Their criticisms and denunciations were part of an inner-Jewish debate at that time about the nature and purposes of God. They were in no way a criticism of Judaism per se.

A CONTEMPORARY DEBATE

Jesus has recently been at the center of a debate between those who interpret him as having been an eschatological prophet of Jewish renewal, acting in expectation of a dramatic new action by God,[15] and those who

---

12. Sanders, *Jesus and Judaism*, 335–40.

13. Meier, *Marginal Jew*, 2:116.

14. For a discussion of these, see Sanders, *Jesus and Judaism*, 335–37.

15. Ibid., 319. This understanding is typical of scholars participating in what is frequently called the "third quest" for the historical Jesus.

downplay the presence of eschatological expectation in Jesus' teaching, preaching, and symbolic activities, or who argue that this does not indicate an expectation on his part of an imminent action by God, and who tend to see the apocalyptic elements in the Gospels as later additions to traditions that grew up about Jesus after his death.[16] The debate is partly about how diverse Second Temple Judaism was and where Jesus should be located within this. Both sides have emphasized that Jesus belongs within this milieu and have enhanced contemporary understandings of Second Temple Judaism. Jesus' baptism by John and the presence and importance of eschatological expectation in Jesus' message, widely attested "in many different gospel sources and literary forms,"[17] suggests that he too was an eschatological prophet who shared John's expectation that God was about to dramatically intervene in history. Eschatological expectation is present to the same degree in every tradition about Jesus. Jesus probably made varying impressions on different social groups so that different kinds of traditions arose about him.[18] But eschatological expectation does seem to have given decisive shape to Jesus' message and public activity as a whole.[19] A non-eschatological Jesus looks odd situated between his baptism by John and the eschatological orientation of the early church after his death. "The origin of Jesus' activity in the apocalyptic movement of John the Baptist, the known events of his life, and the apocalyptic movement initiated by his followers after his death suggest that Jesus understood himself and his mission in apocalyptic terms."[20]

---

16. Crossan, *Historical Jesus*, 238, 243–60. This position is often found in the work of scholars associated with the Jesus Seminar.

17. Meier, "Present State of 'Third Quest,'" 460.

18. As Michael Welker notes, "we must consider the likelihood that Jesus had a different impact on the rural population of Galilee than he did on the urban population of Jerusalem . . . that those who wished to hold high the Mosaic law or the Temple cult in the face of the Roman occupation perceived Jesus differently than did those who wanted to embrace Roman culture . . . that the testimony of those whom Jesus met with healing and acceptance must differ from the testimony of those whose main impression of Jesus was drawn from his conflicts with Rome and Jerusalem" (Welker, "'Who Is Jesus for Us?,'" 140.

19. John Meier, "Elijah-Like Prophet," 46.

20. Collins and Collins, *King and Messiah*, 171.

JESUS' MESSAGE: THE COMING REIGN OF GOD

The gospels describe Jesus' baptism by John as connected to the beginning of Jesus' own ministry, which had significant differences from John's. While John's ministry was located on the banks of the Jordan River, Jesus circulated among villages in Galilee, preaching, teaching, healing, casting out demons, and having table fellowship with those considered sinners. Whereas people came to John, Jesus went to people. This basic difference is also reflected in Jesus' message. Like John, Jesus preached that God was about to decisively intervene in history and that people needed to repent and recommit themselves to God in light of this. But the focus of Jesus' proclamation was not so much the threat of judgment as the possibility and joy of salvation and reconciliation with others.[21] If John with his prophecies of coming judgment, "came across to the people as a grim ascetic, . . . as a sort of dirge, . . . Jesus . . . [came] across as a song!"[22] In Jesus' public work, the gracious initiative of God was extended to people as they were, before they repented. In his parables and public activity Jesus proclaimed that God's coming brought a possibility of salvation that was of surpassing value and available to all as a gift.

This message, exemplified in his eating and drinking with tax collectors and sinners, relativized many moral norms as a means or barrier to being accepted by God. Even flagrant sinners and the wicked were told that through God's forgiving grace they too could enter the coming reign of God. Yet this also created new divisions around the acceptance or rejection of Jesus and his message. At the heart of Jesus' message was the claim that peoples' hope lay ultimately not in what they did, but in the gracious initiative of God.[23] This emphasis on the reign of God as a gift, a feast to which all were invited, was central to Jesus' preaching and teaching. Aspects of this scandalized some other Jewish religious leaders and helped create opposition to him. What was scandalous though was not so much the idea that God's grace came as a gift, but Jesus' claim that it was extended through his person to those considered unrighteous and that people would be judged in accordance with their response to him.

Jesus proclaimed the coming reign of God to be a state of salvation that would embrace the whole person and potentially all creation. Its

---

21. Tilley, *Disciples' Jesus*, 121.

22. Schillebeeckx, *Jesus*, 139.

23. Becker, *Jesus of Nazareth*, 79–80.

coming in fullness would include past generations as well as the present through the resurrection of the dead.[24] It was of surpassing value, worth more than anything else a person might have. It would involve a renewal of Israel and the fulfillment of God's long-standing promises of salvation. Its coming would establish "the wholeness and integrity of creatures"[25] through overcoming all forms of suffering and evil.

The reign of God was to have an egalitarian nature. Leaders were to be servants of others. While Jesus' preaching often seems to have lacked the critical focus on sinful social structures characteristic of the Hebrew prophets, his proclamation had a politically and socially revolutionary dimension.[26] The powerful would be cast down and the poor and oppressed lifted up. This clearly implied that Rome was not eternal and that its rule would soon end.[27] The reign of God was to be free from oppression of all kinds. No one would be dependent upon the influence and power of others.[28] As all are children of God, all were to be equal. Jesus' message was also culturally revolutionary. Some women found a new open space around him as members of his following.[29] Social and religious conventions were declared not binding if they hindered people from responding to his call. Jesus understood this reign of God to be already present to some degree in his healings, exorcisms, table fellowship with sinners, and in the community of those who accepted his message.[30] Though still to come in fullness, it was already initially present in his work and the movement gathered around him.

According to Jesus, the nature of the reign of God as salvation, its coming into history, and its character as a gift result from God's goodness. It is God's nature to give good things to people, to bring the reign in which all life will flourish. Thus present in Jesus' preaching is the idea that there is a dynamic quality to God's being. God's goodness moves God to act, to bring the reign of God. This reign comes as a gift but it is not

24. Meier, *Marginal Jew*, 3:438–39, 443.
25. Becker, *Jesus of Nazareth*, 138.
26. Schüssler Fiorenza, *Jesus*, 110–11.
27. Horsley, *Jesus and Empire*, 103.
28. Crossan, *Historical Jesus*, 262, 298.
29. Becker, *Jesus of Nazareth*, 29; Theissen and Merz, *Historical Jesus*, 220–24.
30. Matt 11:2–6; Wright, *Jesus*, 193–94.

peripheral to God. Its coming will bring an increase to God's joy. It issues from a "relationship of God to history" that is intrinsic to God's being.[31]

However, this reign of God is an embattled reality within history. It broke into the present in deeds of saving power that were part of Jesus' ministry, yet it was also contested and opposed. There were times when Jesus could do no miracles. There were many who spurned his invitation to the reign of God. This points to an important paradox about Jesus and his message. Jesus claimed the power of God was at work in his ministry and manifest in his healing miracles and exorcisms. These helped authentic him as doing the work of God. In keeping with Jewish tradition Jesus proclaimed God as having ultimate power over the final destiny of all creation. Yet he did not claim that God was the sole power in creation or that God intended to be such.

JESUS AND POWER

The reign of God that Jesus proclaimed was contested on several levels. Its fundamental conflict was with the power of evil. Jesus described this power as being overcome on a metaphysical or mythic level[32] through the exorcisms and healings he and others did in his name, and through his message being preached to the poor. His healings, exorcisms, and table fellowship were signs that the reign of God was initially present and a source of hope that it would soon come in fullness. Yet Jesus did not present the reign of God as breaking or ending the power of people. In relation to other people, the coming of the reign of God occurred through their being won to it. Jesus called people to follow him but he had no direct power to force them to do so. He had to move people to seek to enter the reign of God that he proclaimed. The coming of the reign of God did not break the power of people who entered into it. It increased it.

In his healings and exorcisms, Jesus did things for people that they were not able to do for themselves. This was also true of his preaching and table fellowship. Here Jesus mediated God's acceptance and grace to people in ways that they could not do for themselves. However, people could only enter the reign of God through the exercise of their own power and volition. The power revealed in his healing miracles and exorcisms

---

31. Sobrino, *Jesus the Liberator*, 68.

32. Wright, *Jesus*, 451–54.

is portrayed at times as subordinated, even dependent, upon his ability to win their hearts and minds. The inbreaking of the reign of God was happening not through people being subdued but through their power being enhanced and reoriented.[33] The reign of God was coming through God empowering people and attracting them to it. As they entered it, it in turn empowered them.

This combination of power and powerlessness was reflected in Jesus' relationships to the political and religious institutions of his day. The ability of Jesus to frame powerful sayings and draw large crowds made him a concern to Roman officials and Jewish religious and political authorities. At the same time he was vulnerable to critique and violence from these. He announced the coming of the reign of God in a powerful way, in part through his miracles and exorcisms, but he did so in a "defenceless form,"[34] leaving people free to reject his message and himself.

Thus the reign of God that Jesus proclaimed was characterized by a strange mix of power and vulnerability, as was Jesus himself. While it broke into the present through healings and exorcisms and in teaching and preaching that many experienced as authoritative and compelling, it was without any direct means of enforcement. It was supposed to gain subjects non-violently.[35] As a result, Jesus frequently appeared to be powerful in relation to metaphysical evil, yet vulnerable in relation to people. This vulnerability was most profoundly expressed in Jesus' death on the cross.

THE GOD JESUS PROCLAIMED

In proclaiming the coming of God's reign, Jesus spoke of God. He shared central convictions of Second Temple Judaism that God is one, unique, radically transcendent, good, powerful, active, calls people to do justice, and had entered into a special covenant with Israel.[36] God was the sovereign Creator, the giver of life and a source of hope in the face of death. Yet Jesus also described this transcendent God as compassionate and standing in a personal relationship to people, who were to speak to God with the familiarity and confidence of a trusting child speaking to

33. Theissen, "Ambivalence of Power," 26, 28.

34. Käsemann, *Essays on New Testament Themes*, 43.

35. Theissen, "Ambivalence of Power," 28.

36. Theissen and Merz, *Historical Jesus*, 146.

a loving parent. The active and compassionate nature of God required that God be spoken of in anthropomorphisms. Jesus did speak of God as constant, ultimate, steadfast, certain, and trustworthy. But he also spoke of God in dynamic terms; as experiencing joy, as giving daily bread, as hearing and answering prayer. Jesus often used an image familiar to his listeners, that of "the well-to-do landowner and paterfamilias of rural Galilee,"[37] to describe God as directly approachable, able to help and standing in a personal relationship to those presenting petitions.

There were significant tensions in Jesus' proclamation of God. A first relates to the nature of the power associated with the reign of God, mentioned above. On the one hand, Jesus proclaimed God as all-powerful, all-knowing, and constantly present. Yet he also described people as having freedom in relation to God, and God as having desires and intentions that depended to some extent on human freedom for their fulfilment. While Jesus proclaimed God as having ultimate power, he did not proclaim God as having the only power, or as desiring to be the only one with power.

A second tension in Jesus' proclamation was around God's mercy and judgment. While Jesus spoke of God's mercy and forgiveness, he did claim that those who spurned his message or who failed to show compassion for others would experience judgment. This reflects a tension running throughout the Hebrew Bible and the New Testament between the moral demand of God for righteousness and the mercy of God which extends to sinners. This can be described as the tension between the moral and the transmoral dimensions of God.[38] A fundamental affirmation of Second Temple Judaism shared by Jesus was that there is a moral dimension to God and human life. Jesus' preaching of judgment for those who rejected his message emphasized this. Human choices can have a deep impact on God's creation and make a difference to God. Yet in Jesus' words and actions overall, the weight given to human choice and action was outweighed by God's grace, which is able to create new beginnings for even the worst sinners. Though sinners deserve judgment, forgiveness and new life are made freely available to them. God's love is transmoral in doing this in that it goes beyond what morality requires, without obviating it. According to Jesus' teaching there is always a transmoral element to God's love, in that God always gives people

---

37. Vermes, *Religion of Jesus*, 146.

38. For the notion of "transmoral," see Tillich, *Morality and Beyond*, 80–81.

more than they deserve. God does not give because people are deserving, but because God is good and cares for all of God's creation.[39]

In Jesus' proclamation the moral and the transmoral aspects of God's nature stand in tension but they have a common source. The goodness of God demands to be reflected in human conduct. This is the source of the moral demand of the law. Yet this goodness that demands moral action and so judges also reaches out to the fallen and the wicked to reconcile and redeem. It impels the endless searching for the morally lost that will not cease until they are found. Thus the goodness of God that gives rise to judgment when life is destroyed or injured also gives rise to God's gracious initiative to save the lost. The standard of God's judgment in Jesus' preaching is God's infinite goodness,[40] which stands behind the coming of God's reign and the hope of God's graciousness for all. In proclaiming the threat of judgment for those who spurned his message of the coming of God's reign, Jesus was expressing the significance and urgency of God's gracious initiative present in his own person and work. To spurn God's grace was in effect to sin against it, to injure oneself and others. If Jesus' proclamation of judgment on those who do this is interpreted as expressing the significance of the grace arising from God's goodness, God's judgment remains ultimately subordinate to God's love. Jesus proclaimed a God who judges by high standards, but a God whose infinite goodness is always a source of assurance and hope for those judged.

At the heart of Jesus' proclamation was "the conviction that the eternal, distant, dominating and tremendous Creator is also and primarily a near and approachable God."[41] This nearness and approachableness took on a particular emphasis in Jesus' preaching and activity, which was characterized by a constant turning towards and openness to the marginalized and oppressed.[42] While Jesus' message and work were directed to all of Israel and potentially beyond it, they were directed first to the poor and marginalized. In this way he proclaimed God as having a preferential option for the poor. Through his words and actions, Jesus depicted God as judging reality from the perspective of the poor and

---

39. Freyne, *Jesus*, 169.

40. Theissen and Merz, *Historical Jesus*, 272–74.

41. Vermes, *Religion of Jesu*, 180.

42. Sanders, *Jesus and Judaism*, 179; Meier, *Marginal Jew*, 3:528.

marginalized and as standing in solidarity with them. Jesus' death on the cross was the ultimate expression of this.

JESUS HIMSELF

Jesus proclaimed the coming reign of God, not himself. Yet his proclamation was deeply intertwined with his person in two ways. First, through symbolic actions like his table fellowship with sinners, his person became a medium for his message, a way of expressing and actualizing it.[43] As this happened, his person became caught up in his message and became identified with it. Second, implicit in much of Jesus' preaching and teaching, in his relationship to the Scriptures and the traditions of Second Temple Judaism,[44] in his symbolic actions such as the gathering of twelve disciples, and in his healings and exorcisms was a claim about himself. The public and symbolic actions that Jesus deliberately undertook expressed a sense of what he was trying to do and of how he saw himself.[45] They indicate that he "had a sense of eschatological authority. He saw the dawn of a new world in his actions."[46] Just as John's preaching of the imminent judgment implicitly gave him a high status as the herald of this, so Jesus' preaching and public activity signalled that in and through him God's reign was breaking into the present. His public activity thus made a "monumental though implicit"[47] claim that he was the "climatic and definitive fulfiller of the hopes of Israel,"[48] the one through whom God's reign was being ushered in. Thus implicit in his proclamation was a claim that his person was uniquely important in salvation history and that he had a key role to play in the coming of God's promised redemption. In his entry into Jerusalem at Passover and in the "cleansing" of the temple he made this claim explicit in a dramatic fashion that led to his death.

---

43. Schillebeeckx, *Jesus*, 213.

44. Kasemann, *Essays on New Testament Themes*, 42.

45. Meyer, *Aims of Jesus*, 151–53.

46. Theissen and Merz, *Historical Jesus*, 513. See also Fredriksen, *Jesus of Nazareth*, 249–50.

47. Meier, *Marginal Jew*, 2:144.

48. Meyer, "Jesus' Ministry and Self-Understanding," 352.

JESUS' DEATH

That Jesus died on a Roman cross is generally accepted as one of the "few indisputable facts"[49] that can be known about him. Crucifixion was "a tortuous death reserved" by the Romans "for provincial rebels as well as slaves."[50] That Jesus died in this way indicates that the Roman governor Pilate had him executed as a threat to Roman rule. This probably happened as a result of three actions on Jesus' part.

The first was his going to Jerusalem at the time of the Passover. The crowd of pilgrims flooding into Jerusalem and the temple at this time tended to create a tense atmosphere in which unrest fuelled by religious convictions could break out against the Roman occupation.[51] The nature of the gospels as theological interpretations of Jesus' history do not enable the construction of a detailed chronology of his activity between his baptism by John and his last days in Jerusalem.[52] But it can be surmised that by the time Jesus arrived at Jerusalem for the Passover celebration at which he died, he had become a public figure whose message and presence in Jerusalem at this time would have concerned Pilate and probably the temple authorities as well.[53]

Upon arriving at Jerusalem Jesus is reported to have staged two symbolic actions: his entry into Jerusalem and his cleansing of the temple. Both are well attested enough in the New Testament traditions to be accepted as historical in some form. His entry portrayed him as the Son of David, a messianic characterization that had definite political overtones.[54] The cleansing of the temple suggested that the reign of God he proclaimed would "spell an end to the present system of temple worship."[55] In these two symbolic actions the claim about himself that had been implicit in his proclamation was dramatically portrayed in a confrontational way, exacerbating tensions between himself and religious and political authorities in Jerusalem. These two actions can be seen as leading to Pilate's acting against him and to the accusation that he had claimed to be the king of the Jews.

49. Fredriksen, *Jesus of Nazareth*, 268.

50. Horsley, *Jesus and Empire*, 129.

51. Fredriksen, *Jesus of Nazareth*, 15.

52. Meier, "Elijah-Like Prophet," 70.

53. Fredriksen, *Jesus of Nazareth*, 240–41.

54. Meier, "Elijah-Like Prophet," 68–69.

55. Ibid.

The conflict that came to a head here between Jesus, other Jewish religious leaders, and Pilate was over who spoke for God.[56] It was Pilate who had Jesus crucified, but Jesus' conflicts with other religious groups and authorities likely contributed to his death as well.

> The death of Jesus is the consequence of tensions between a charismatic coming from the country and an urban elite, between a Jewish renewal movement and alien Roman rule, between someone who proclaimed cosmic change which was also to transform the temple and the representatives of the status quo. Religious and political grounds cannot be separated.[57]

Jesus himself was to some extent responsible for his death, in that it seems to have been the confrontational nature of his final symbolic actions that provoked others to act against him. He must have known that he was risking death in acting as he did and that his lack of institutionalized power left him open to the violence of those who opposed his message. His last symbolic actions made a claim to truth that Pilate contested by putting him to death. The death of Jesus thus had an aspect of a trial about it, a testing of the truth of his claim versus others' authority. In his symbolic actions Jesus claimed to be speaking for God and declaring that God was the ultimate power in creation. In crucifying him, others denied the first claim. Pilate may have been denying the second as well. The death of Jesus was intended to refute his claim about the coming of God's reign and about his person. It seems to have initially shattered the movement that had formed around Jesus. But this movement was soon reconstituted around a new understanding of Jesus in light of his resurrection.

CONCLUSION

We will return in later chapters to what can be known historically about Jesus and his message and work. Here we have simply sketched his message, the claim about his person implicit in his preaching, and the relation of this to his death on the cross. Jesus, as a charismatic leader, had a vision of the coming reign of God that he pursued, though not a clearly defined timetable or detailed blueprint of how it would come or what it would look like. His healing miracles, exorcisms, symbolic actions,

---

56. Sanders, *Jesus and Judaism*, 281.

57. Theissen and Merz, *Historical Jesus*, 466–67.

teaching and preaching—all combined to present an implicit claim about his person. He seems to have symbolically portrayed himself as the Son of David in his entry into Jerusalem, but even then he lacked some of the trappings expected of such a figure.

The grand nature of Jesus' claims about the coming of God's reign, the significance of his ministry and himself, combined with his vulnerability to physical violence, made putting him to death a way to decisively refute him. Shortly after his death, some of his former followers came to believe that Jesus was risen from the dead and had appeared to them. They were soon joined by others, such as James and Paul, who had not been Jesus' followers but who also had experiences in which he appeared to them as risen from the dead. Jesus' resurrection was interpreted by those who believed in it as the final word in the trial about the truth of Jesus' person and message. In raising Jesus from the dead God had vindicated Jesus and his claims about himself. Jesus was also seen to have been exalted by God to a uniquely divine status. These beliefs, coupled with the experience of the Holy Spirit by those who gathered to worship in Jesus' name, triggered dramatic developments in the way Jesus was understood. The next chapter will trace some of these, examining how Jesus, who proclaimed the message of God's coming reign, came to be at the center of a new and very different message: that he is the Christ.

2 Jesus' Resurrection

The messianic expectations that Jesus aroused and the movement gathered about him were shattered by his death.[1] But after a few days some of his followers and later others claimed he had been raised from the dead. The New Testament does not support any theory that this belief arose after his death as a matter of course in light of Jewish teachings current at that time about the resurrection of the righteous. By all accounts Jesus' resurrection was experienced by his followers as a second interruption, as unexpected and difficult to assimilate in terms of their expectations as was his death. In light of Jesus' resurrection, the hopes and beliefs about him, broken by his death, were reformulated into new understandings of him as the Christ. These reformulations were also stimulated by the belief that the risen Jesus had been exalted to a unique status in relation to God and by the experience of salvation, a new experience of the Holy Spirit, associated with faith in him. All this helped transform the movement Jesus had begun within Judaism into what eventually became another religion, sharing much with Judaism, but distinct in the belief that Jesus is the Christ.

THE BELIEF IN RESURRECTION IN SECOND TEMPLE JUDAISM

Those who first claimed that Jesus was risen from the dead were Jews. They made use of Jewish beliefs in the resurrection to understand what they claimed to have experienced. The exact origins of these beliefs are difficult to discern. The notion of resurrection from the dead is found explicitly in Daniel 12:2 as an answer to the question of theodicy, presumably in relation to the sufferings of faithful Jews during the Maccabean Revolt.[2] The belief expressed here that the dead would

1. Becker, *Jesus of Nazareth*, 345, 354; Theissen and Merz, *Historical Jesus*, 428.
2. Albertz, *History of Israelite Religion*, 2:575–97, 592.

be resurrected at the end of time, "some to everlasting life, and some to shame and everlasting contempt" (Dan 12:2), was part of the apocalyptic tradition within Second Temple Judaism, which formed the matrix of Jesus' ministry and Christian faith.[3] While explicit statements of belief in the resurrection are not common in the Hebrew Bible or Old Testament, the belief is not foreign to it. The notion of resurrection fits with the understandings of God's righteousness, creative power, and faithfulness found therein, as a fulfillment of God's justice and promises to Israel.[4] It can be seen as an outgrowth of these themes.

The concept of resurrection was at hand then, during Jesus' ministry and after his death. Jesus seems to have endorsed a belief in it.[5] He may have looked forward to his own resurrection in some way. But the New Testament gives little evidence that Jesus' resurrection as experienced by his disciples and others was expected to follow his death. Predictions that he would die and rise again, such as Mark 9:31, are generally seen to have been produced by the early church after Easter, rather than being statements made by Jesus during his ministry. Like Paul's statement that Jesus had died and risen in accordance with the Scriptures (1 Cor 15:4), these were attempts to make sense of the scandal of his death on the cross and are expressions of faith that it was God who had raised him to new life. Descriptions of Jesus' resurrection in the New Testament suggest that there was a dialectical relationship between predominantly Jewish notions of resurrection and the encounters that people had with Jesus after his death. These experiences were such that the early church used notions of resurrection to describe what had happened to Jesus, and in doing so, transformed these notions. What can be known historically about the events that gave rise to this?

WHAT CAN BE KNOWN HISTORICALLY ABOUT JESUS' RESURRECTION?

To begin with, Jesus' resurrection is not described in the New Testament as a historical event on par with others, but as a uniquely transcendent event that began a new age of salvation. It is presented as an eschatological event impinging upon history in subsequent appearances of the

3. Ibid., 597.

4. Levenson, *Resurrection and Restoration*, 200.

5. Meier, *Marginal Jew*, 3:438–44.

risen Christ, the empty tomb, and the continuing witness of the early church. Here an event expected at the end of history happened to one person in the midst of it. The end of history, the destiny of creation, became partially present or was anticipated in the one person of Jesus, ahead of time as it were.[6] The occurrence of Jesus' resurrection is never portrayed in the New Testament. Instead it is presented as beyond the reach of human power and explanatory reason to describe. This has implications for what can be known about it. Technical or explanatory reason must be used to interpret the New Testament accounts of Jesus' resurrection and to assess and interpret the belief that he is risen. But explanatory reasoning cannot prove that Jesus' resurrection occurred in the way that a historical event can be proven to have taken place. This is partly because of the fragmentary nature of the accounts of it and partly because of its transcendent nature. The New Testament traditions indicate that the risen Christ remains transcendent to those who believe in him.[7] Attempting to prove the facticity of Jesus' resurrection clashes with this by effectively trying to reduce the risen Jesus to an object that can be manipulated. Even the appearance accounts found in the Gospels of Luke and John, which stress the palpable nature of the body of the risen Jesus, also emphasize that he is not an object subject to human manipulation. One can bear witness to Jesus' resurrection,[8] but one cannot prove its occurrence.

Descriptions of Jesus' resurrection in the New Testament can be categorized into a formula tradition of brief summary or kerygmatic statements, and a narrative tradition of more extended accounts of appearances of the risen Christ or of the empty tomb.[9] The formula tradition includes brief summary statements like "God raised Jesus from the dead" (Rom 10:9), which may have been one of the earliest expressions of faith in Jesus' resurrection.[10] Such statements are also combined with others about Jesus' death, as in Peter's speech in Acts 2:23–24, and

---

6. Pannenberg, *Jesus*, 67.

7. Williams, "Between the Cherubim," 91–92.

8. The narrative accounts of the empty tomb and appearances of Jesus should be not be understood as objective accounts but as testimonies or witness to "a concrete singular event" that they invest with an absolute character (Schüssler Fiorenza, *Foundational Theology*, 30).

9. Theissen and Merz, *Historical Jesus*, 482; Perkins, *Resurrection*, 19.

10. Theissen and Merz, *Historical Jesus*, 483.

sometimes with statements about the risen Christ's exalted state, as in Ephesians 1:20. This formula tradition includes the list of those to whom the risen Christ appeared that Paul gives in 1 Corinthians 15:5–8, as well as statements that the Son of Man will be killed and then rise again, found in passion summaries such as Mark 8:31 and 9:31.[11] It is generally regarded as older than the narrative tradition. Examples of it such as Acts 2:32 indicate that the belief that God raised Jesus from the dead probably formed the center of the earliest Christian faith and preaching.

The narrative tradition includes accounts of the empty tomb and appearances of the risen Jesus that conclude the Gospels, and accounts of Paul's conversion in Acts. These typically present dramatic descriptions of the basic message found in the formula tradition. They can be subdivided into narratives of appearances focusing on the risen Jesus giving a command or instruction (Matt 28:9–10), narratives in which the risen Jesus appears incognito and then is recognized (Luke 24:13–35), and narratives about the empty tomb (Mark 16:1–8).

Various degrees of commonality exist among these summary and narrative traditions. All describe Jesus' existence as being transformed through his being raised from the dead. Apart from the brief summary statements (Rom 10:9; Mark 9:31), most describe Jesus as appearing to some of his followers after his death.[12] Those that give a time frame to these appearances locate the first as happening on "the third day" following his death, though Paul's list in 1 Corinthians 15:5–8 indicates that appearances of the risen Jesus may have continued for several years.[13] Traditions describing appearances typically portray Jesus as revealing himself to those to whom he appeared and as appearing in a transformed existence continuous with and yet different from his human form before death. His appearances frequently involve a commissioning to some task, usually connected with his resurrection. Finally, all accounts are embedded in discourses in which Jesus' resurrection is seen to have saving significance for others.

There are irreconcilable differences among these accounts. To whom did Jesus appear? Paul speaks of Jesus appearing first to Peter,

11. Ibid.

12. Carnley, *Structure of Resurrection Belief*, 224. While Mark's Gospel does not describe an appearance, knowledge of a Galilean appearance seems implied in Mark 16:7 (Theissen and Merz, *Historical* Jesus, 494).

13. Jeremias, *New Testament Theology*, 301.

then to the Twelve, then to more than five hundred "of the brothers," then to James, then to all the apostles, and last of all to himself (1 Cor 15:5–8). This list includes appearances that the narrative accounts lack (those to the five hundred, to James and to Paul), and omits appearances to Mary Magdalene (John 20:14–17), to the women (Matt 28:9), and "to seven disciples by the Lake of Galilee" (John 21: 2) that the narrative traditions include. Paul's account does not mention the empty tomb or the body-like form of the risen Christ, which some narrative accounts stress. The narrative traditions also differ among themselves as to which women went to the tomb, when they went, what they saw, what they found and were told there, what they did next, where the risen Jesus appeared (Jerusalem or Galilee), and who saw him first.[14] These differences are such that the various accounts of Jesus' resurrection cannot be harmonized with each other. This has been seen as evidence against their historical reliability.

Some of these differences can be attributed to these accounts being written so as to establish the authority of specific people in the early church and to express the theology of an early church community or New Testament author. Raymond Brown argues that as the narrative accounts convey both a report of an occurrence and an interpretation of this, the differences between these accounts should be seen as expressing different interpretations of the underlying occurrence and not as evidence against its historicity.[15] But the question then arises, where do the underlying events end and interpretations begin? The question "Did something happen?" becomes "What happened?"

The accounts of Jesus' resurrection do not point to any one event as the source of the belief in Jesus' resurrection. Instead they describe or mention a number of appearances, in which the form of the risen Jesus may not always have been the same. Also, these accounts are too fragmentary, contradictory, and bear evidence of too much reshaping to enable one to construct a coherent account of the events lying behind them. Attempting to determine the historicity of details in the narrative accounts of Jesus' resurrection does not yield much in the way of firm results. For example, the empty tomb is only explicitly mentioned in narrative traditions concluding the Gospels. This suggests that it is a late development, probably an interpretation of Jesus' resurrection

14. Wedderburn, *Beyond Resurrection*, 24–25.

15. Brown, *Introduction to New Testament Christology*, 169.

originating in the early church.[16] But why would anyone invent a story in which women were the chief witnesses in a patriarchal culture where their testimony was disvalued? This suggests that these accounts may have a historical basis. Also, it is unlikely that the message of Jesus' resurrection could have survived in Jerusalem if his body could be shown to still be in the tomb or a grave.[17] This also suggests that the empty tomb is historical. All three arguments are insightful but none can be conclusive. The accounts of the empty tomb have a symbolic character. They "dramatize" the faith of the early church in Jesus' resurrection.[18] But historical inquiry cannot determine the historicity of what they relate.

One can gather that a few days after Jesus' death some of his followers, and later others who had not been followers, like James and Paul, had experiences leading them to believe that God had raised Jesus to new life. The appearance of the risen Christ to the disciples or the Twelve is implied in Mark 16:7 and narrated in Matthew 28:16–20; Luke 24:36–49; and John 20:19–23. These accounts of this appearance, though similar in many respects, do not seem to be dependent on each other. Paul also gives what appears to be an independent version of the same appearance in 1 Corinthians 15:5, 7.[19] The relative independence of different accounts of the same appearance, combined with the agreements between them, is sufficient to infer that a real event lies behind them.[20] There is also Paul's testimony that the risen Christ appeared to him, one of several appearances that he speaks of in addition to this to the Twelve. Thus, while one cannot claim to know much in the way of details about Jesus' resurrection, one can conclude that his disciples and others did have experiences in which they believed Jesus had appeared to them after his death, in a transformed existence, and that they concluded from this that he had been resurrected from the dead by God.

Modern historiography has typically used two criteria to assess the historicity of reported events like this. One is critical and the other constructive. The critical criterion requires that past events be similar to the historian's own experience.[21] For an event to be accepted as historical it

---

16. Segal, "The Resurrection: Faith or History?," 134.

17. Pannenberg, "History and the Reality of the Resurrection," 68–70.

18. Haight, *Jesus*, 135.

19. Theissen and Merz, *Historical Jesus*, 496.

20. Ibid.; Dunn, *Christianity in the Making*, 1:861–62.

21. Collingwood, *Idea of History*, 239–240.

"must be analogous to other events within the human world."[22] By this criterion it is difficult to accept the resurrection of Jesus as historical even though there is sufficient evidence to claim that the appearance of the risen Christ to the Twelve did happen. What the resurrection accounts describe is too unique, too unlike what is generally experienced by most people, to be "integrated into the world of modern convictions."[23] Yet in the clash between this criterion and the New Testament there is also agreement. The New Testament also characterizes the resurrection of Jesus as utterly unique and without analogy in history. The uniqueness of this event is part of the proclamation of it. The resurrection of Jesus was a scandal to the expectations and experiences of Paul's time (1 Cor 1:23) as well as being a scandal to the expectations of the present.

This criterion that only events similar to present experience can be accepted as historical has been questioned. To do justice to an event like the Holocaust one must speak of it as incomparable,[24] as lacking analogy in important respects to present experience. If the criterion of analogy is pressed too far it can become imperialistic towards others and make one's own experience a confining prison. Yet even if there can be incomparable events in history, Jesus' resurrection still remains contradictory in significant ways to modern experiences and expectations. It clashes with the experience of most that the dead do not rise and that incalculable suffering and injustice frequently find no answering miracle.

But there is also resonance between contemporary experience and Jesus' resurrection. Globalization has made every person a potential neighbor to others, so that there has been in many contemporary societies a "colossal extension of a Gospel ethic to a universal solidarity,"[25] extending to every corner of the earth and, in light of the environmental crisis, beyond the human community. The belief that this striving for justice is meaningful implies a belief that in the end the executioner will not triumph over their victim.[26] This is analogous to faith in Jesus' resurrection. In this respect Jesus' resurrection is analogous to one of the underlying presuppositions of contemporary Western experience. It does not fit with the contemporary experience of history in which

22. Schüssler-Fiorenza, *Foundational Theology*, 31.

23. Theissen and Merz, *Historical* Jesus, 504.

24. Ricoeur, *Memory, History, Forgetting*, 332.

25. Taylor, *Secular Age*, 695.

26. Moltmann, *Crucified God*, 223–24.

innocent victims often perish unaided, yet it does fit with some of the beliefs about the meaningfulness of life that structure the contemporary experience of many.

A second general criterion for historical inquiry is that of constructive or imaginative interpolation. This involves postulating as historical what is not stated but nonetheless implied by the accepted evidence in terms of modern experience.[27] For example, if historical sources describe a person as assembling ingredients for making a pie, and then later as eating a pie made from these ingredients, the analogy to present experience dictates that the historian must postulate that someone made these ingredients into the pie that was eaten in order to construct a coherent history based on these sources. Without this kind of imaginative construction there can be no coherent account of history.[28]

This second criterion has led many to argue that some causal event must be posited to account for the rise of faith in Jesus' resurrection after his death.

> [The Easter faith] could not have been self-generated, nor could it have arisen directly from Jesus' proclamation of the advent of the kingdom. If the only sequel to that proclamation was the crucifixion, then that proclamation would have been demonstrably false. Jesus had proclaimed the coming of the kingdom and it had not come. Instead, his message had ostensibly been utterly discredited by the crucifixion.
>
> The very fact of the church's kerygma therefore requires that the historian postulate some other event over and above Good Friday, an event which is not itself the "rise of the Easter faith," but the cause of the Easter faith.[29]

Also, it is not simply faith in Jesus' resurrection that must be explained, but the way preceding notions of resurrection were substantially modified by the early church.[30]

The concept of resurrection has a significantly different position in the New Testament compared to its place in Second Temple Judaism. The idea was present in the Jewish religious traditions that formed the

27. Collingwood, *Idea of History*, 240.

28. Ibid., 241.

29. Fuller, *Formation of Resurrection Narratives*, 169.

30. Wright, *Resurrection of the Son*, 477; Leon-Dufour, *Resurrection and the Message*, 22.

matrix for Jesus' activity and the life of the earliest churches. But it did not figure in any movement in Second Temple Judaism as prominently as Jesus' resurrection does in the New Testament. The notion of resurrection and more specifically Jesus' own resurrection also was not prominent in the teachings of Jesus. Yet in the New Testament one finds a "confident and articulate faith in which resurrection has moved from the circumference to the centre."[31] Jesus' resurrection seems to have provided the "decisive impulse"[32] for this and for the development of most theologies in the New Testament.

All of this suggests that what happened after Jesus' death was dramatic enough and sufficiently tied to Jesus' person that his followers invoked the notion of his being resurrected and exalted to describe it. The resurrection of Jesus thus appears to have been an interruption that affirmed his public ministry and yet transformed its meaning and his person. It is this kind of circumstantial evidence that led to the conclusion of Martin Dibelius that between the death of Jesus and the rise of faith in his resurrection the historian has to posit "something" that precipitated this change in his disciples.[33]

Such evidence cannot prove the historicity of Jesus' resurrection. The faith of the disciples "even with all its distinctiveness, could have resulted as well from an equally distinctive illusion as from a distinctive fact,"[34] though it is unlikely that different witnesses like Paul, James, Mary Magdalene, and the disciples would all have suffered the same delusion. Still, though the belief in Jesus' resurrection was necessary for the early church to come into being, it could have been a mistake.

In conclusion, the historical evidence for Jesus' resurrection is enigmatic. One can know historically that the shattered community was transformed, moving from despair to hope and joy, and in the structure of its beliefs. One can also discern formal evidence sufficient to argue for the historicity of some of the reported appearances of the risen Jesus. But the substance of what the witnesses convey is so unique that it cannot easily be accepted as historical. It clashes with contemporary experience and convictions in significant ways even as it resonates with them in others.

31. Evans, *Resurrection and the New Testament*, 40; Perkins, *Resurrection*, 84, 102.

32. Pokorný, *Genesis of Christology*, 108.

33. Dibelius, *Jesus*, 141–44.

34. Carnley, *Structure of Resurrection Belief*, 169.

As noted earlier, the nature of Jesus' resurrection also affects how it can be known. Jesus' resurrection cannot be explained in terms of empirically deduced principles or its historicity proven by critical inquiry, yet it can be understood, received as testimony, as a revelation of God. Understanding is a form of knowledge different from explanation.[35] The two are always related and intermingled but nonetheless distinct. Explanatory knowledge is technical in nature; it seeks to grasp reality in terms of law-like principles and is not tied to personal experience. While explanatory knowledge is necessary to know the basic parameters of an event like Jesus' resurrection or the Holocaust, there is a dimension to the meaning of each that goes beyond what can be ascertained by technical reason and that can only be conveyed by testimony. Understanding such testimony always has "an identity cost"[36] because understanding is a self-involving form of knowledge. To understand the meaning of Jesus' resurrection is to have one's identity changed. The appearance narratives in the New Testament all portray that to come to believe that Jesus is risen is to undergo a conversion.

Thus the nature of Jesus' resurrection is such that there can be no binding logical argument leading from empirical inquiry to faith in it.[37] In this all are contemporaries of those who first believed that Jesus was risen. There is evidence that supports their witness but it can never be conclusive. At some point one finds oneself moving from unbelief to faith, or one doesn't. Not everyone makes the journey and those that do aren't morally superior to those who don't. While one can give reasons for one's faith, one cannot finally prove or demonstrate its truth.[38] Jesus' resurrection is something that one bears witness to, but not something one can prove. Furthermore, belief in Jesus' resurrection has never rested on the reports of his appearances as risen alone. It was and continues to be based also on experiences of the Holy Spirit associated with faith in his resurrection.[39]

Though faith in Jesus' resurrection is intellectually defensible, it has several "in spite of" qualities so that it always remains subject to doubt and question. One must believe in Jesus' resurrection in spite of the limi-

35. Schweitzer, "Dialectic of Understanding," 252–55.

36. Taylor, "Gadamer on Human Sciences," 141.

37. Niebuhr, *Meaning of Revelation*, 83.

38. Schüssler-Fiorenza, *Foundational Theology*, 33.

39. Carnley, *Structure of Resurrection Belief*, 260–61; Haight, *Jesus*, 144.

tations of our cognitive faculties, which are unable to master or grasp it with "scientific certainty."[40] One believes in Jesus' resurrection in spite of the Holocaust and other events of suffering and evil that make Jesus' resurrection impossible to assimilate to present experience.[41] Consequently faith in Jesus' resurrection is easily mocked. It also displaces one. It makes one a pilgrim in this world, journeying towards the coming universal redemption that Jesus' resurrection promises.[42] The ambivalence of contemporary experience to Jesus' resurrection depends partly on one's social location and situation.[43] Its eschatological nature means that it can never be domesticated. It is a revelation of the otherness of God, which is both a source of hope and joy and also of judgment. It presses towards the coming of a new heaven and a new earth, when evil and sin will be no more. It can be a powerful moral source that engenders resistance born of hope and love against oppression, suffering, and evil. It is not meant to be proven, but to be celebrated, lived, and proclaimed.

THE NATURE OF JESUS' RESURRECTION

During the twentieth century a debate has raged in Western Christian thought over the nature of Jesus' resurrection. This is related to the question of its historicity. One position, exemplified in the work of Willi Marxsen and popularized by John Shelby Spong,[44] interprets Jesus' resurrection as a subjective event happening in the minds and hearts of his disciples and those who accept their message. Jesus is risen as people continue to live in his name. Opposed to this interpretation are others that stress the objectivity of Jesus' resurrection, arguing that he appeared in bodily form as some appearance accounts portray him.[45] Between these two poles lie a host of positions concerning the nature of Jesus' resurrection. Marxsen's subjective interpretation avoids the cognitive difficulty associated with affirming Jesus' resurrection as an objective event. But the danger is that it empties the event of its objective content, which the New Testament insists on and which is crucial to its meaning.

40. Marion, "'They Recognized Him,'" 145, 150–51.
41. Moltmann, *Crucified God*, 173.
42. Moltmann, *Way of Jesus Christ*, 32–33.
43. Baum, "Reflections," 13.
44. Marxsen, *Resurrection*; Spong, *Resurrection*.
45. Wright, *Resurrection of the Son*.

Elisabeth Johnson affirms the objective reality of Jesus' resurrection but declares it "an unimaginable event enveloped in the mystery of God"[46] and focuses instead on its salvific meaning.

It is important to note that the New Testament offers different images of the risen Jesus. The Gospel of Mark as included in the biblical canon does not depict the risen Jesus after his death but relies instead on the empty tomb and the angel's words to describe and interpret Jesus' resurrection. Paul affirms that the risen Christ has a spiritual body but does not describe what this looked like when the risen Jesus appeared to him. Some scholars argue that in the resurrection appearances "Jesus appeared as a blinding light rather than as a human body."[47] Luke and John on the other hand stress the palpable nature of the body of the risen Christ.[48] In attempting to describe the nature of the risen Christ at this point in time, when there is renewed confidence in some quarters in the truth claims of religion in relation to other forms of knowledge and experience like the natural sciences, it is important to heed Johnson's emphasis on the mystery of Jesus' resurrection. All the New Testament witnesses affirm that Jesus' resurrection included his body. But an emphasis on the physicality of the risen Jesus that forgets his transcendent nature can easily lead to absurdity and worse.[49] It is not possible to develop an understanding of the appearance of the risen Jesus that harmonizes with every detail of every account of it in the New Testament. The body of the risen Jesus is palpable in some accounts. Yet in Mark's Gospel it is simply absent.

Still one can discern certain commonalities among the accounts of the risen Jesus in the New Testament. A first is the emphasis on the continuity and discontinuity between the risen Jesus and Jesus of Nazareth. The risen Jesus is continuous with Jesus who was crucified. This affirms that Jesus' death was really overcome in his resurrection. Second, this continuity is crucial to locating the presence of the risen Christ. The risen Christ is present in preaching, prayer, praxis, worship (especially in the Eucharist), and fellowship that is in continuity with the public ministry of Jesus of Nazareth. The risen Christ is also present where Jesus of Nazareth was present: among the poor, the oppressed, and the

---

46. Johnson, *She Who Is*, 163.

47. Robinson, "Very Goddess and Very Man," 119.

48. Catchpole, *Resurrection People*, 96, 134.

49. Tillich, *Systematic Theology*, 2:155–56.

suffering. The risen Christ meets people today in the faces of victims. Finally, the risen Christ in present in movements for peace and justice that have continuities with his public ministry.

Jesus' resurrection does not simply restore him to life, but transforms him to new life. The risen Jesus is more than Jesus of Nazareth was. Jesus of Nazareth proclaimed the coming of the reign of God. The foundation of this new reality is constituted through his resurrection. As the foundation of God's coming reign, the risen Christ is objectively present to history as the otherness of God that makes possible a struggle for justice, an acceptance of one's self, and an affirmation of one's humanity in inhumane situations.[50] Within history the risen Christ is not confined to one place as Jesus of Nazareth was, but is present as a pneumatological reality throughout history in the faces of victims, in the struggle for peace and justice, and in the worship of the church. Jesus of Nazareth was male, but once risen Jesus is present in and imaged by women and children as well.[51] Finally, the risen Jesus is the fulfillment of Jesus of Nazareth. Jesus' resurrection is partly the culmination of the incarnation, the final yes of God to the life and humanity of Jesus and to the goodness of creation. Thus the risen Jesus is both continuous and discontinuous with Jesus of Nazareth.

Second, the resurrection of Jesus has both subjective and objective dimensions. Purely subjective accounts such as those of Marxsen fail to provide an adequate explanation for the rise of faith in Jesus' resurrection but do attend to an essential dimension of it: the subjective response of those who believe in it. Jesus' resurrection presents people with a call to mission and enables them to live it out. If people did not answer this call, part of the purpose of Jesus' resurrection would have remained unfulfilled. Similarly, Paul in Romans 4:25 describes Jesus' resurrection as occurring for the sake of peoples' justification. This purpose is only realized when people come to believe that Jesus is risen and that they are reconciled to God through this.[52] Throughout the New Testament Jesus' resurrection is presented as a saving event that has "occurred and yet is quite without effect except as it is subjectively appropriated by individuals."[53] The resurrection of Jesus thus includes the creation of a community that

---

50. Cone, *God of the Oppressed*, 114, 130–31.

51. Johnson, *She Who Is*, 161–162.

52. Käsemann, *Commentary on Romans*, 129.

53. Perkins, *Resurrection*, 318.

gathers and lives in his name. Without this, it would leave no trace "in the world to which its message was addressed."[54] Regardless of how Jesus' risen form is conceived, his resurrection is seen to have been an event intended to find further expression in the lives of others.

> What is at issue is an appearance that we can say is "grounded in reality." At the same time the life of the risen Christ is now lived in self-revelation to other human beings. That life is carried out in comforting them, in strengthening them, and in sending them forth. What is at issue is thus an appearance that we can say "grounds reality," because the appearance brings itself to bear as the strengthening, gathering, commissioning, calling, and sending of human beings.[55]

In sum, Jesus' resurrection has an inherently subjective dimension. It would be incomplete without those who believe in it.

However, the New Testament traditions do not describe Jesus' resurrection as happening only in the minds and actions of his disciples, but as an eschatological event that initiates a new era in salvation history. The eschatological framework in which it is interpreted varies. But in general the resurrection expected at the end of time is seen to have already happened in the person of Jesus. This is the beginning of a new creation that will embrace the whole earth.[56] In the New Testament traditions it is the objective nature of this event that empowers the believing response of individuals. While Jesus' resurrection is not complete without peoples' subjective response, it cannot be reduced to it. In Jesus' resurrection a victim is raised up from death, so that the executioner does not triumph over him. A part of creation is rescued from annihilation and elevated into the glory of God, as a foretaste of the destiny that awaits the rest. The resurrection of Jesus transcends the dichotomy of subjective and objective dimensions.[57] As a saving event his resurrection has a relational dimension and a purpose that is not complete without its subjective appropriation by those who have faith in it. Yet this appropriation is a response to something that has happened apart from their response to it.

---

54. Ibid., 317.

55. Welker, "Resurrection and the Reign," 8.

56. Schillebeeckx, *Jesus*, 395–96.

57. Kelly, *Resurrection Effect*, 15–16, 126–27.

As Jesus' resurrection has objective and subjective dimensions, it is both an event, an objective reality and a symbol expressive of its meaning, a promise that points beyond itself. It was an event before it became a symbol. Yet the transcendent nature of this event is such that it could only be interpreted in "metaphoric and mythic categories."[58] It is a symbol based on a real event,[59] but its symbolic power is not limited to what historical inquiry can establish.[60] Because it is based on a real event, it is a promise that presses towards its fulfillment, when what it symbolizes will become fully real. One can speak of it as a saturated event full of multidimensional and inexhaustible meaning[61] that reshapes one's worldview and continually presses towards new and further expressions of its excess of meaning. It presents an ultimate newness[62] that can empower struggles for justice, acts of compassion, mercy, forgiveness, and reconciliation.

Yet if the "in spite of" character of Jesus' resurrection is forgotten it can become a source of imperialism and religious oppression.[63] The meaning of Jesus' resurrection is intrinsically tied to his cross. Jesus' resurrection did not obliterate this, but stands in a dialectical relationship to the continuing realities of what his cross symbolizes, such as suffering from oppression, the tyranny of empire, and injustice. When the historical concreteness of Jesus' cross is remembered, his resurrection becomes an expression of God's preferential option for the poor. This is a transcendent principle.[64] As the face of evil changes from age to age, Jesus' resurrection calls for solidarity with and liberation of the new poor, who, depending on the time and place, may be Jewish, Islamic, or atheist.

The "in spite of" character of Jesus' resurrection also relates to the church. The risen Jesus is still on the way to the fulfillment of what is promised in his resurrection and remains transcendent to the church, which always needs to learn new aspects of the truth of his resurrection. As a result the risen Jesus frequently confronts the church as a stranger and in judgment. Accompanying this, one of the key meanings of Jesus' resurrection is forgiveness. The risen Jesus may confront the church

58. Perkins, *Resurrection*, 318; see also Theissen and Merz, *Historical Jesus*, 508.

59. Tillich, *Systematic Theology*, 2:154.

60. Taylor, *Executed God*, 103.

61. Kelly, *Resurrection Effect*, 33, 59.

62. Moltmann, *Theology of Hope*, 179.

63. Ruether, *Faith and Fratricide*, 246–51.

64. Baum, "Afterword," 143.

through the voices of other religions. This difference between the risen Jesus and the church creates a dialogical situation between Christianity and Judaism[65] and, by extension, between Christianity and other religions. Aspects of the meaning of the symbol of Jesus' resurrection can be revealed through dialogue with the symbols and teachings of other world religions.

THEOLOGICAL AND SOTERIOLOGICAL DIMENSIONS OF JESUS' RESURRECTION

Jesus' resurrection has theological and soteriological trajectories of meaning. Both summary and narrative traditions interpret it as God's vindication of Jesus' person and ministry over against the repudiation of both in his crucifixion. An early and permanent meaning of this, picking up the apocalyptic understanding of resurrection, was that here God's love triumphed over evil in a definitive way that points towards a final overcoming of evil. As Jesus' resurrection was a vindication of his person and message, it was also, for those believing in it, a revelation of God. It affirms the characterization of God in Jesus' ministry and reaffirms the Jewish belief in God as a source of hope for the final overcoming of evil. It reveals God to be ultimate (Rom 4:17), yet also living,[66] active in history in specific events and new ways and doing new things. The similarity of the grammatical structure of some early expressions of Easter faith such as "God raised him from the dead" (Rom 10:9) to some summary statements of faith in the Hebrew Bible such as "God brought Israel out of Egypt" (Deut 8:14) points to how the Easter faith of some parts of the early church was "an innovation within Judaism" that could regard "the Easter experience qualitatively as on the same level as God's classical act, the Exodus of Israel from Egypt."[67] The resurrection of Jesus was thus seen by some as a defining event in the life of God.

Jesus' resurrection was also interpreted as the exaltation of his person into the presence of God.[68] This led to him being portrayed in the New Testament as the key figure and his coming as the decisive event in the history of salvation. The transformation of Jesus' person here was

---

65. Moltmann, *Way of Jesus Christ*, 32–33.

66. Collins, *Birth of the New Testament*, 55.

67. Becker, *Jesus of Nazareth*, 362.

68. Perkins, *Resurrection*, 318.

also seen to affect the Holy Spirit and Jesus' relationship to it. Through his resurrection and exaltation, Jesus went from being inspired by the Spirit during his earthly life to becoming the giver of the Spirit as the ✓ risen Christ.[69] The Holy Spirit was experienced as present in a new way through faith in Jesus and became identified in the early church as the Spirit of Christ. Jesus' resurrection was thus interpreted as part of a theological event that included his ministry and crucifixion and the pouring out of the Holy Spirit. Through these events God became present in history in a new way.

This experience and interpretation of Jesus' resurrection, combined with the idea of his exaltation into God's presence, led to worship of Jesus in significant portions of the early church, soon including prayer and praise directed to him. This created a dialectical relationship between the early church's communal memory of Jesus and its inherited understandings of God, so that throughout the New Testament "given concepts of God are used to interpret what happened to Jesus and what occurred within the Christian church and its mission, and faith in God is in turn shaped by faith in Jesus and related events."[70] Jesus' resurrection thus had a far-reaching effect on the early church's worship and theology.

Jesus' resurrection was interpreted as revealing that God's love is greater than sin and evil, so that it came to be seen as a source of hope against various forms of suffering and alienation. As God's vindication of Jesus as a victim of violent injustice, Jesus' resurrection revealed that God's love is ultimately greater than forces of oppression that bear down on people from without. Interpreted as involving forgiveness for those who deserted him,[71] Jesus' resurrection also shows God's love as able to overcome the damaging effects of one's own actions to one's identity. The saving significance of Jesus' resurrection also extends beyond history and human relations. For Paul it promises the coming of a transformed existence in which sin and death are no more (1 Cor 15: 22). Its eschatological character "makes it an event of significance not only for Jesus' person but for the whole of reality."[72] Theologians concerned with the environmental crisis have seen in the resurrection of Jesus' body a promise of salvation

---

69. Dunn, "Towards the Spirit of Christ," 13–14.
70. Dahl, *Jesus the Christ*, 180.
71. Schillebeeckx, *Jesus*, 391.
72. Johnson, "Resurrection and Reality," 1.

for the whole creation[73] and a call for faithfulness to the earth. As the cross symbolizes all that negates God's presence and alienates people and creation from their divine destiny, Jesus' resurrection is a source of an all-embracing hope.[74] Its soteriological meaning reaches out to encompass virtually every form of alienation, suffering, and evil.

Jesus' resurrection by itself has indeterminate meaning in relation to particular social conflicts within history. It only becomes concrete as a source of hope through the memory of his public activity that led to his death. The memory of his public ministry, which was vindicated by his resurrection, gives definition to its saving significance,[75] so that Jesus' resurrection brings hope to the poor and oppressed for liberation. More generally, it brings hope for a life beyond death to creation as a whole.

CONCLUSION

As an eschatological event with objective and subjective dimensions, Jesus' resurrection does not have any one fundamental meaning. It has many. It receives a different interpretation in each of the Gospels and throughout other books of the New Testament. These share themes and emphases, but they cannot be reduced to one common denominator. Jesus' resurrection formed a dynamic center of meaning in conjunction with preceding Jewish traditions, the memory of his ministry and death, and subsequent experiences of the Holy Spirit. It gave rise to the faith, after his death, that he is the Christ. In the next chapter we will examine how this faith developed over the subsequent centuries, so that this Jewish "rabbi" came to be affirmed by Gentile Christians as the Son of God, the second person of the Trinity, at once fully human and fully divine.

73. Moltmann, *Way of Jesus Christ*, 258–59.

74. Moltmann, *Theology of Hope*, 211.

75. Käsemann, *New Testament Questions*, 63.

3 From Risen Christ to Second Person of the Trinity

THE TRANSITION OF THE EARLY CHURCH FROM BEING A SECT WITHIN JUDAISM TO A GENTILE RELIGION

In the centuries following Jesus' public ministry and the rise of faith in his resurrection, the Christian church grew in numbers and spread throughout the Roman Empire. Though Christian faith was persecuted at times, it came to permeate Roman society. Constantine, who became sole ruler of the Roman Empire in 323 CE, was "in all practical respects" a Christian.[1] He and Licinius granted Christianity legal equality with other religions of the empire in 313 CE. Christianity, originally a sect within Judaism, had become an influential and well established religion in the empire. The church was now a significant institution with its own internal politics. When it was rent by doctrinal debates, Constantine and emperors after him attempted to restore its unity, as disunity in the church undermined the unity of the empire.

There were cultural dimensions to this transition. Second Temple Judaism, from which Christianity emerged, had long been influenced by Hellenistic culture. This influence is evident in varying degrees throughout the New Testament. But as the church became a Gentile religion a deeper encounter occurred between the gospel and Hellenism. The cultural and religious background in terms of which Paul understood Jesus was Hellenistic Judaism. As the church grew in numbers, fewer and fewer members had this kind of background. More and more, the church came to be formed of Gentiles who tried to understand the gospel in relation to the values and practices of their predominantly Hellenistic ethos.

This brought a gradual shift in the questions occupying Christian intellectuals. From roughly 120 to 200 CE Christian theologians asserted

1. Walker, *History*, 101.

45

that Jesus was both divine and human, but did not ponder at length how Jesus' person was related to God, though the question was raised. As Christian theologians began to consider this, a fundamental axiom of their thinking deriving in part from their Hellenistic ethos was that the divine is absolute and impassible.[2] This was both a presupposition of and a central problem for developments in Christology occurring in the first five centuries of church history and the ecumenical councils of Nicaea (325), Constantinople (381), Ephesus (431) and Chalcedon (451).

APPROPRIATING NICAEA AND CHALCEDON TODAY

Of these four councils, the declarations of Nicaea concerning the triune nature of God and Jesus' relation to the first person of the Trinity and those of the Chalcedonian Definition regarding the presence and relationship of divine and human natures in Jesus' person have been particularly influential for subsequent Christologies. Until the Enlightenment these provided the basic presuppositions for many Christologies. Even today they are affirmed officially by most churches. Yet the differences between the Gospel portrayals of Jesus and the technical terminology of these affirmations and the equally great difference between their terminology and content and contemporary thought[3] make them controversial and subject to wide-spread criticism.

The understandings of Jesus promulgated by the councils of Nicaea and Chalcedon are part of the legacy of the church's first centuries as it struggled to understand Jesus and his saving significance. The questions wrestled with here are partly posed by the variety of Christologies in the New Testament,[4] which require subsequent generations to determine their own. This means that the questions of Jesus' relationship to God and the nature of Jesus' person have to be asked and answered in every age. These kinds of questions and the diversity of New Testament answers to them make theology necessary.[5] Part of answering them in the present is critically appraising the answers given to them in the past. The affirmations of Nicaea and Chalcedon were given partly as guides to how the New Testament, particularly the Gospels, should be read. They

2. Pelikan, *Christian Tradition*, 1:229.

3. These differences are summarized in Haight, *Jesus*, 273–74.

4. Dünzl, *Brief History*, 6, 9–10.

5. Williams, *Arius*, 236.

offer guidelines as to how an interpretative framework for understanding Jesus as the Christ should be formulated. These guidelines do not end theological discussion. Instead, they open it up by raising further questions that continue to challenge theologians today.

The questions wrestled with here were also partly posed by the challenge of inculturating the gospel in a Hellenistic milieu, a process necessitated by the church moving from being a Jewish sect to a Gentile religion. In this particular process of inculturation there were gains and losses. The inculturation of the gospel is part of the history of revelation, through which its truth continues to be revealed and appropriated. While this particular inculturation is finished, the inculturation of the gospel continues today as the church moves into new cultural contexts in the course of history.[6] Western churches have now entered into a cultural context of postmodernity. Within this context two contrasting demands meet. One demand is for critical inquiry and recognition of the genuine humanity of Jesus.[7] This requires that all truth claims about Jesus' divinity be critically investigated and acknowledged as open to revision. The other demand is for recognition of the transcendence and otherness of God in relation to human finitude.[8]

What follows will examine the christological developments leading to the affirmations of Nicaea and Chalcedon, tracing their roots, noting their continuities and discontinuities with what can be known historically about Jesus and with the early church's faith in him as the risen Christ. The conclusion will examine how the process leading to Nicaea is continued in a theological development begun by Karl Barth, in which the affirmations of Chalcedon became a basis for rethinking the nature of God in light of Jesus Christ.

THE IMPACT OF JESUS' RESURRECTION
ON HOW JESUS WAS UNDERSTOOD

Jesus' resurrection and experiences of the Holy Spirit connected to it led some Jewish-Christian groups to interpret his person in light of passages like Psalm 110:1, with the result that Jesus was seen to have a unique relationship to God and a divine status in relation to creation and salvation

6. Niebuhr, *Meaning of Revelation*, 81–90, 114–20.

7. Johnson, "Jesus and Salvation," 2.

8. Tracy, *On Naming the Present*, 40–44.

history.[9] Through his resurrection Jesus was seen to have become God's Son.[10] The worship of these Christians became "binitarian" in that they began to worship Jesus as the risen Christ along with God.[11]

> Jesus did not really "become a god." Instead, he was given devotion that expressed the distinctively Christian recognition that Jesus was God's unique emissary, in whom the glory of the one God was singularly reflected and to whom God "the Father" now demanded full reverence "as to a god."[12]

Within two decades of Jesus' resurrection this kind of reverence seems to have become widespread within the early church.

This reverence for Jesus was also expressed through titles such as Wisdom or Sophia, Christ and Lord. Some early Christians continued to view Jesus more as a martyred prophet who had been inspired by the Spirit and vindicated by God.[13] Even within groups viewing Jesus as having become the Son of God there were variations in how this was understood.[14] In the New Testament generally, this understanding of Jesus as having a special status and relationship to God did not displace others, such as interpretations of him as an eschatological prophet. Instead it functioned as an overarching metaphor that could be enriched and made concrete by these, but which in turn expressed a fuller understanding of Jesus' relationship to God in light of his resurrection. This relationship is the basis of his ultimate saving significance.[15] Tensions remain between these various Christologies. For the early churches that produced the writings making up the New Testament, Jesus had been inspired by the Holy Spirit. But through his resurrection he had become more than an inspired prophet and teacher. As the risen Christ he was the basis of a new relationship to God and a new experience of the Holy Spirit was available through him. Titles such as Lord, Wisdom of God, and Son of God were used to express this sense of Jesus' transcendence and ultimate saving significance that reached beyond what notions of Jesus as an inspired teacher or prophet could express.

9. Hengel, *Studies in Early Christology*, 225.

10. Dunn, *Christology in the Making*, 36.

11. Hurtado, *One God, One Lord*, 122–23.

12. Hurtado, *How on Earth*, 30.

13. Dünzl, *A Brief History*, 7–8.

14. Dunn, *Christology in the Making*, 59–60.

15. Schnackenberg, *Jesus in the Gospels*, 312.

Developing in the first two decades after Jesus' resurrection, this affirmation of Jesus' distinction from and yet closeness to God sowed seeds that, through sustained debate over Jesus' relationship to God, would eventually culminate in the doctrinal affirmations of Nicaea and Chalcedon. It was the Johannine understanding of Jesus as the pre-existent Word that particularly provided impetus for this development. Here the understanding of Jesus as the Son of God and the personification of divine wisdom blossomed into a notion of Jesus' pre-existence as the Word of God. While notions of Jesus' pre-existence may be found elsewhere in the New Testament, Johannine Christology was a dramatic development in the clarity and emphasis with which this was expressed.

> [Here] the word of God is identified with a particular historical person, whose pre-existence as a person with God is asserted throughout. Now the Christian conception of God must make room for the person who was Christ, the Logos incarnate.[16]

The notion of Jesus as becoming Son of God in his resurrection has continuities with what can be surmised about Jesus' sense of himself and his calling. But the Johannine notion of Jesus as the pre-existent Son of God goes beyond this.[17] There is no evidence that Jesus ever thought of himself in this way. Yet there is continuity between the understanding that Jesus became God's Son through his resurrection and the Johannine understanding of Jesus as the pre-existent Word. Throughout the New Testament Jesus is understood to bring a new era of salvation and a new relationship with God. How is this possible? Already in the New Testament this question was raised and answered through Christologies like those identifying Jesus as God's Sophia or Son.[18] The Gospel of John went further by equating the creative love that appears in Jesus with the being of God and the being of Jesus. Jesus is able to be the basis for a new era of salvation because he is both one with God and distinct from God (John 1:1, 18). This radicalizes the understandings of Jesus as divine Wisdom and as God's Son and takes them further, but not in a different direction.[19]

The understanding that Jesus became God's unique child through his resurrection and the Johannine understanding of Jesus' pre-existence

---

16. Dunn, *Christology in the Making*, 250.

17. Ibid., 253–54.

18. Schillebeeckx, *Jesus*, 549.

19. Schnackenberg, *Jesus in the Gospels*, 315–16.

as the Word of God make distinct affirmations. Christian theology needs to recognize both.[20] The first sees Jesus becoming something more through his death and resurrection than he had been in life. The events of his life, death, and resurrection have a real significance for his person, and beyond that for God and God's creation. Jesus as eschatological prophet and Jesus as the risen Christ do not fit into the world as it is, but call for and promise its transformation. The second understanding affirms the radical transcendence of God's Word to creation, yet also that this radically transcendent Word became incarnate in Jesus, experienced the human condition, suffered, died, and rose again. In this way God has already entered into a new relationship with creation that is the basis of what the first understanding promises. Both understandings are oriented to Jesus' special status and relationship to God, not his gender. This relationship and status can also be expressed through the feminine image of Sophia, divine Wisdom.[21]

The decision made in the early church to understand Jesus in this way rather than simply as inspired by God is one that has to be rethought in the present generation. Some argue that this was a departure from Jesus of Galilee, a mystification that helped enshrine a patriarchal worldview in the church and that lost sight of Jesus' prophetic practice.[22] There is some truth in this.[23] Notions of Jesus as God's Son or as fully human and fully divine need to be made concrete by recurrence to accounts of Jesus' life in the Synoptic Gospels,[24] and at times subjected to an ideological critique. But conversely, notions of Jesus as a moral exemplar need to be undergirded by understandings of his ultimate saving significance that mediate the courage to love in the face of radical sin and evil.[25] Understandings of Jesus as the Son or Wisdom of God can do this, and also express how the risen Christ is continuous with but not restricted to Jesus' historical particularity.[26]

20. Dunn, *Christology in the Making*, 267–68.

21. Johnson, *She Who Is*, 151–61.

22. Ruether, "Can Christology Be Liberated?," 8–16, 23.

23. For a brief examination and correction of distortions the patriarchal worldview of the Greco-Roman world introduced into Christology and Christian anthropology, see Johnson, *She Who Is*, 151–56.

24. Sobrino, *Christ the Liberator*, 286.

25. Moltmann, *Crucified God*, 334–35.

26. Cahill, "Christology, Ethics, and Spirituality," 202–4.

The early Christian experience of salvation in Jesus was one of in-spiring example and authoritative teaching, but also of reconciliation to God and others despite one's sin, hope for a new heaven and a new earth, and for life after death. These different aspects of salvation can conflict, but they also remain unfulfilled without each other. The salvation Jesus brings, like the Reign of God he preached, includes all aspects of the person and creation. Christologies have to offer an adequate explana-tion of how Jesus can mediate this kind of radical salvation.[27] As only God can save and if salvation is experienced through Jesus, Jesus must in some way have a unique relationship to God. The divinity of Jesus is inferred from the experience of his saving significance.[28] Affirmations of this and Jesus' ultimate saving significance can become mystifications distracting people from urgent tasks within history that Jesus calls them too. But these can also be powerful moral sources enabling people to oppose radical evil without becoming fanatical in the quest for justice or falling into contempt for those they care for.[29] Understandings of Jesus as God's Sophia or Son explain how Jesus is able to mediate this kind of salvation[30] and by doing so be this kind of moral source.

FROM BINITARIAN WORSHIP IN THE NEW TESTAMENT TO TRINITARIAN FAITH AT THE COUNCIL OF NICAEA

There are passages in the New Testament that speak of Jesus Christ, God, and the Holy Spirit (2 Cor 13:13) or of the Father, the Son, and the Holy Spirit (Matt 28:19), and a Trinitarian understanding of God can be discerned "retrospectively" within John's Gospel.[31] But the full doctrine of the Trinity as affirmed at the council of Nicaea is not present in the New Testament. In hindsight one can say that its roots are present there. A number of New Testament passages are "functionally Trinitarian."[32] They speak of how salvation is mediated to humanity from God through Jesus Christ in the Holy Spirit. But the council of Nicaea was

---

27. Haight, *Jesus*, 183.

28. Tanner, *Christ the Key*, 56.

29. Taylor, *Secular Age*, 695–703.

30. Haight, *Jesus*, 208–12.

31. Watson, "Trinity and Community," 183–84.

32. Fee, *God's Empowering Presence*, 839. See also Schweizer, *Good News according to Matthew*, 533.

concerned not only with Jesus' saving function, but also with what enabled him to fulfill this, the nature of his person and relationship to God. In this respect the council of Nicaea said things about Jesus that the New Testament does not. Through the process of inculturation that led to this council, the church attained greater metaphysical precision in its understanding of Jesus.

The church's journey from the New Testament to Nicaea was a search for an understanding of God adequate to certain aspects of the gospel.[33] It was "a process of trial-and-error,"[34] influenced by political, religious, ecclesiastical, and personal factors. It did not end at Nicaea. What follows will sketch some of the stages of this development.

As the church took shape as an institution in the second century CE, ecclesiastical writers sought to harmonize the disparate teachings of the New Testament.[35] At roughly the same time Christian theologians entered into a prolonged dispute with Gnosticism, which saw Jesus as representing a higher divinity over against a lesser divinity who had created the world. This controversy led the early church to emphasize the oneness and sovereignty of God,[36] which in turn raised the question of Jesus' relationship to God. Use of the formula "Father, Son, and Holy Spirit" became increasingly common in Christian worship and was used by theologians like Irenaeus of Lyons (c. 135–200) to understand the dynamics of salvation history. By the late second century Christian theologians were asking about Jesus' relationship to God.[37] The term "the Logos"[38] was seized upon by some to describe Jesus' relationship to God in opposition to a theological movement known as Monarchianism, which more sharply distinguished the two. This term was chosen because of its use in the Gospel of John and its resonances in Hellenistic culture. By this time Christian theologians had begun to seek greater clarity in their understanding of the gospel through the use of Hellenistic philosophy. This produced various ways of understanding Jesus' relation to God

---

33. This is R.P.C. Hanson's description of the process of doctrinal development that went on in the Arian controversy (Hanson, *Search*, xviii–xx).

34. Ibid., 873.

35. Dünzl, *Brief History*, 6–7.

36. Ibid., 9.

37. Ibid., 18–19.

38. McGuckin, "Logos Theology," 207–8.

that led to the affirmations of Nicaea and Chalcedon[39] and made them necessary as part of defining the theological parameters of Christian faith in the Hellenistic world.

Early in the third century, in dispute with the Monarchian Praxeas, Tertullian (c. 160–225) developed the first explicitly Trinitarian understanding of God. Tertullian developed an economic[40] theory of the Trinity, concerned with how God acts and is experienced in history. Subsequently Origen of Alexandria (c. 186–255) went further, describing God as existing in three hypostases. This term "hypostasis" became important in subsequent Trinitarian discussion. In this usage it means concrete reality, individual entity or subsistence.[41] Origen also argued that the divine Logos was united to Jesus' human soul as the heat of fire infuses a piece of iron placed in it. In arguing this Origen stated a principle that became central to christological teachings judged to be orthodox at Nicaea and Chalcedon: those elements of human nature which are not assumed by God in the incarnation are not saved.[42] Origen was a highly significant and transitional figure to the subsequent Arian debate.[43] Both sides followed trajectories of interpretation influenced by his attempt to understand the person and work of Jesus Christ within a Neoplatonic worldview.

Neoplatonism was a prevalent philosophy within the Roman Empire that Christian theologians used along with Aristotelianism to develop their understandings of the gospel. A key assumption of both philosophies was that the divine is immutable. As the divine was thought to be perfect it was understood to be unchangeable, existing in eternity beyond the fluctuations of history. This notion of divinity underlay what is known as the Arian controversy, named after Arius, whose teachings helped instigate it. Theologians on both sides of this controversy assumed God to be immutable. Arians argued that Jesus who suffered on the cross could not be fully divine because the divine was unchanging and so could

39. Grillmeier, *Christ in Christian Tradition*, 40.

40. The "economic" Trinity refers to God as experienced in salvation history. The "immanent" Trinity refers to God as existing in eternity.

41. In Origen's time it could also be translated in Latin as "substance," but in the course of the development of Trinitarian theology the former became its technical meaning (McGuckin, "Hypostasis," 174).

42. Grillmeier, *Christ in Christian Tradition*, 171.

43. For an overview of Origen's theology, its ambiguities and subsequent influence in this regard, see Ayres, *Nicaea and Its Legacy*, 20–30.

not "become" something. The Word that became incarnate in Jesus was therefore a lesser god,[44] created by a higher and greater divinity that was unchanging and fully divine. The Word mediated between this fully divine God and creation but did not share God's nature.[45] Athanasius' contrary argument was based on the same premise but determined by soteriological concerns. Only God whose existence is unchanging and beyond the power of sin and death is able to save humanity from these. In order for Jesus to save he must share this divine nature. For Athanasius, only if human nature is assumed by the radically transcendent God through the Logos becoming incarnate in Jesus is humanity saved from sin and death. Therefore Jesus as the mediator of salvation could not be a lesser divinity, but must be fully divine, one with the God whom Jesus called "Father" in John's Gospel, where the two are said to be one (John 10:30).

The New Testament could not be decisive in this debate because it was a source for both sides. Resolving this question of the nature of Jesus' person and relationship to God involved developing doctrine that went beyond explicit statements of Scripture. The Arian debate was not about what the Bible said but about how its witness should be interpreted.[46] This question became pressing partly because the notion of divine immutability was so deeply embedded in Hellenistic thought and culture.[47] The biblical witness describes God as absolute and immutable. But it also describes God as living and, to a certain extent, internally related to creation.[48] Understanding these two affirmations in a coherent way is one of the greatest challenges of Christian theology. In the Arian debate both sides were sure that God was absolute and unchanging. But if Jesus was fully divine, God also has to be understood as living and able to act in new ways. The way the church found to understand God as both living and absolute was the doctrine of the Trinity. It was the experience

44. Hanson, *Search*, 121.

45. Ibid., 102–4.

46. Ibid., 848.

47. Paul Gavrilyuk disputes this, arguing that "there was no consensus philosophorum amounting to an affirmation of divine indifference and non-involvement" among Hellenistic philosophers (Gavrilyuk, *Suffering of the Impassible God*, 35–36). However, a page earlier he admits that it "is true that among educated pagans, whose philosophical views tended towards later Platonism, the divine impassibility did acquire the status of a universally shared opinion" (ibid., 34).

48. Tillich, *Systematic Theology*, 1:242.

of salvation mediated through Jesus Christ and a sense of God's radical transcendence that compelled the church to understand God in this way.

The Arian controversy that led to the council of Nicaea began about the year 318, when a priest named Arius objected to the teachings of his bishop Alexander that the Son was always with and eternally generated from the Father.[49] At this time there was no consensus or explicit church teaching on what was orthodox in this regard. Arius' dispute with his bishop "ignited a fire waiting to happen."[50] It began a wide-ranging controversy involving church polity as well as doctrine. Bishops lined up for or against Arius and his teaching. Lay people became caught up in the debate. In its later stages Gregory of Nyssa complained about the extent of this.

> If you ask for change, the man launches into a theological discussion about begotten and unbegotten; if you enquire about the price of bread, the answer is given that the Father is greater and the Son subordinate; if you remark that the bath is nice the man pronounces that the Son is from non-existence.[51]

These were issues that moved church members and so concerned the Emperor.

In order to restore unity to the church Constantine convened the council of Nicaea in 325, which he paid for and presided over. Between 250 and 300 bishops attended, most from the Eastern church.[52] The results of their meeting can be summarized as follows:

> The council issued a creed which said that the Son was generated "from the essence of the Father" and was hence "homoousios" (the same thing or being or essence) with the Father. The creed also condemned anyone who said that the Son was from an ousia or hypostasis other than that of the Father. Arius was condemned and exiled.[53]

Arius himself soon ceased to be important to the controversy, which continued until shortly before the council of Constantinople in

---

49. Ayres, *Nicaea and Its Legacy*, 430.

50. Ibid., 20.

51. Quoted from Hanson, *Search*, 806.

52. Ibid., 156.

53. Ayres, *Nicaea and Its Legacy*, 430.

381.[54] Part of the reason it went on so long was that theologians were developing technical terms like hypostasis and homoousios to conceptualize Jesus' relationship to God. In effect, they were developing a new understanding of God under the impact of Christology. The result was the doctrine of the Trinity affirmed at Nicaea, but only subsequently conceptualized more fully by the Cappadocians[55] in the East and Augustine in the West.

The doctrine of the Trinity affirmed at Nicaea expresses the otherness and freedom of God in relation to creation.[56] God is not an aspect of the universe or even its highest element. Rather, God is able to become present in history in a new way, and in so doing bring the promise of a future beyond the limits of created life as presently experienced. The doctrine as eventually worked out by Augustine and the Cappadocians affirms that God is one in nature (ousia) but exists in three persons (hypostasis). The affirmation that Jesus was of one nature, homoousios with the first person of the Trinity meant that the divine being was essentially and eternally Trinitarian. Tertullian and others had understood God as Trinitarian in terms of God's relationship to history. But Nicaea pushed beyond this to affirm that God was Trinitarian in eternity, before and apart from creation. This remarkable innovation in church teaching[57] led to the development of a distinction between the immanent Trinity, God in eternity apart from creation, and the economic Trinity, God as revealed and active in history.[58] This problematic but important distinction helped the church understand how God could be living, involved in history, and radically transcendent to it. The affirmation of the Trinitarian nature of God at the council of Nicaea was in effect a new beginning that came to provide the framework for Christian understanding of God and Jesus Christ in centuries to come.[59]

---

54. For a brief overview of the history of the Arian controversy, see ibid., 430–35.

55. Hanson, *Search*, 676–737.

56. Ibid., 873.

57. Ibid., 167–68.

58. Studer, *Trinity and Incarnation*, 113.

59. The focus at Nicaea was on the relationship of Jesus Christ to God the Creator and Redeemer, with little attention given to the Holy Spirit. Only later at the council of Constantinople in 381 CE was the divinity of the Holy Spirit given explicit attention.

FROM NICAEA TO CHALCEDON

The council of Nicaea did not end the Arian controversy. Decades of debate and polemic followed until roughly 360,[60] although Arianism continued to be present in the church long afterwards and still is today. However, after 360 the focus of controversy shifted from Jesus' relationship to God to the nature of Jesus' person. The questions now became, given that Jesus was fully divine, was he also fully human and if so to what extent, and how were his human and divine natures related? Disputes over these questions led to the council of Chalcedon in 451 and continued afterwards.[61]

These issues first surfaced at the synod of Alexandria of 362 in connection with the Christology of Apollinaris.[62] Athanasius had argued against Arians that the Logos, which came to be known as the second person of the Trinity, assumed flesh. Appollinaris carried this Logos/*sarx* Christology further to the point of denying that Jesus had a human soul. In this way he wanted to exclude any possibility of there being a conflict between Jesus' human and divine will, "thus safeguarding the sinlessness of Christ, without which there was no redemption from sin."[63] But opposition soon arose on the grounds that if the Logos did not assume a fully human nature, then that which was not assumed was not healed. To be human is to be subject to change. As the divine was understood to be immutable, the two seemed mutually exclusive.[64] How could Jesus be both at once? Yet it was only by their coming together in the one person of Jesus that salvation in its fullest sense had been effected. For most theologians involved in this debate, the fundamental saving significance of Jesus lay in the appearance in his person of a new reality in which God and humanity were united while still distinct.[65] In the Christ event, which included Jesus' ministry, death, and resurrection, the new reality promised in his preaching of the kingdom of God became present in his person. The presence of this in his person is the basis of the hope for its coming in fullness in the future.[66] The question was, how did this

60. Ibid., 193.

61. For an overview of this, see Norris, *Christological Controversy*, 1–31.

62. Studer, *Trinity and Incarnation*, 194.

63. Ibid.

64. McGuckin, *Saint Cyril of Alexandria*, 138.

65. Daley, "'He Himself Is Our Peace,'" 173.

66. Moltmann, *Way of Jesus Christ*, 149.

come about and how was it to be understood? Three major positions developed in this regard: the schools of Antioch and Alexandria in the East, and the Western tradition influenced by Augustine, which found expression at Chalcedon through Pope Leo the Great.

The greatest theologian of the Antioch school was Theodore of Mopsuestia, bishop of Antioch for 36 years until his death in 428.[67] Theodore emphasized Jesus' full humanity against Apollinaris. The Logos was not subject to Jesus' human limitations. It became incarnate in Jesus by uniting itself to him at his conception and indwelling his person. This indwelling of the Logos in Jesus was continuous with the inspiration experienced by prophets and others before him but distinct in degree. Jesus' resurrection revealed that the Logos and his person had always been a functional unity.[68] For Theodore this was a moral unity occurring in the conjunction of their wills. The second person of the Trinity became incarnate in Jesus through Jesus continually choosing to follow the former's inspiration. This was made possible by the special indwelling of the Logos, but it only happened through the decision making of the human being Jesus. Theodore's focus was on the particular life and achievement of the individual Jesus who at times struggled to overcome temptation and follow God's will. This was essential to his triumph over sin and evil. The whole of Jesus' life and public ministry has redemptive significance. It culminates in his resurrection, in which the power of sin and death are broken in principle as a result of his moral obedience, achieved through the indwelling of the Logos and the "active agency" of Jesus' humanity.[69]

Theodore insisted against Apollinaris that Jesus was only able to effect salvation because he had been fully human and lived a genuinely human life. But Theodore's account of the unity of the Logos with Jesus' humanity remains problematic. For Theodore and others in the school of Antioch there seem to be two subjects in the one person of Jesus Christ. The Logos inspires Jesus and identifies with him in his resurrection, but this was a functional unity. The danger here is that Jesus becomes only a moral hero rather than the person in whom a new reality appears within history, in which God and humanity exist in a reconciled and new state of differentiated unity. Jesus can only be the Christ if he

---

67. Walker, *History*, 133.

68. Norris, "Introduction," 25.

69. Pelikan, *Christian Tradition*, 1:236.

is a moral exemplar. But as the Christ he is not simply a great person but a new person, in whom a new reality is present in which others can participate through faith and in him. Theodore and the school of Antioch celebrated the arrival of this new reality in Jesus but had difficulty conceptualizing the unity of his person.

The leading theologian of the Alexandrian school was Cyril of Alexandria (378–444), bishop of Alexandria for 32 years. Cyril followed the Logos/*sarx* way of understanding Jesus' person[70] but insisted on the fullness of Jesus' humanity. The unity of Jesus' person is central for Cyril. For him the "Gospels bear witness that there is one subject or person in Christ."[71] This person resulted from the Logos uniting itself to a human nature so that the two became one concrete reality. This happened through the initiative of the Logos. For Cyril Jesus is fully human but not simply human. He is a divine person, the second person of the Trinity, who chose "to live in the human condition."[72] The line of interpretation he follows stresses the newness and uniqueness of Christ[73] and the freedom of God to act creatively to rescue humanity from sin and evil. With Jesus the Logos has entered history in a new way, becoming incarnate in Jesus' person. The Logos did not change in this but did something new. It became the active subject of a human life.[74] The result was an "indissoluble union"[75] of two distinct natures, an ontological rather than a functional or moral unity. Cyril conceives it as occurring more on the level of being than will.

How was this union effected? This was a mystery.[76] But Cyril conceived it as the paradigm of the salvation it effects. Cyril understood salvation as divinization, the transformation of humanity through union with God so as to no longer be vulnerable to sin and death. This was effected by Christ taking "what was ours to be his very own so that we

---

70. Wilken, *Judaism and the Early Christian Mind*, 106–7. For Cyril, the council of Nicaea endorsed this approach by placing "Christ entirely on the side of the creator" (Studer, *Trinity and Incarnation*, 114).

71. Weinandy, "Cyril and the Mystery," 35.

72. McGuckin, *Saint Cyril of Alexandria*, 210.

73. Wilken, *Judaism and the Early Christian Mind*, 104–10.

74. For Cyril, the humanity assumed "belonged so intimately to the Logos that there was actually only one subject or subsistent reality in Jesus" (Norris, "Introduction," 28).

75. St. Cyril of Alexandria, *On the Unity of Christ*, 77.

76. Ibid.

might have all that was his."[77] The incarnation happens by the creative power of the Logos healing the humanity it took on as it assumed it, so that the two were able to become one in Jesus' person while remaining distinct. As a result Jesus' person becomes the paradigm of the fullness of humanity. By assuming human nature the Logos is able to experience the human condition, including suffering. Cyril is careful to affirm that Jesus suffered in his human nature. The divine Logos did not change even while experiencing suffering through being incarnate in Jesus.[78] The Logos experienced sin and death in the humanity of Jesus and, by virtue of its impassible divine nature, overcame these in the resurrection.[79] The transformation of this one concrete instance of humanity, revealed in Jesus' resurrection, reveals the transformation that as a result will be the future of all humanity. Salvation is "an ontological rescue of the race,"[80] effected by the Logos becoming incarnate.

Cyril took seriously "what Christ had done as man"[81] during his ministry and death, but the danger in the Logos/*sarx* approach he followed is that while the full humanity of Jesus is affirmed in principle, it tends to be curtailed by the emphasis on the Logos as the sole subject of his person. It is difficult to find room in this understanding for the fear and temptation that the Gospels report Jesus suffered.

The schools of Antioch and Alexandria both affirmed that in Jesus' person the Logos and Jesus' humanity were united in a unique way that has saving significance for all people. Each approach has contemporary representatives. Karl Rahner and Roger Haight follow Theodore

---

77. Ibid., 59. This is known as the communication of attributes or communication idiomatum. It states that "there obtains between God's eternal Word and the human reality of Jesus a unity . . . such that the attributes of Jesus' human reality can be predicated of the eternal Word—the Word has become a human being, the eternal Word has suffered, the Son of the Father died, and so on. And, vice versa, wherever Jesus' human reality is grasped in its definitive concretion, in which it may be no means be thought of as existing in separation from God, divine attributes can be predicated of Jesus—Jesus is God, and so on" (Rahner, *Love of Jesus*, 30–31).

78. Cyril likens this to the soul of a person, the nature of which remains unchanged even as it experiences the suffering of the body it is in, which is changed by the suffering (Cyril of Alexandria, "Scholia on the Incarnation," 301). But while the soul of a person may remain unchanged even as it experiences suffering in a formal sense, experiences of great suffering do leave a mark upon the soul of a person.

79. McGuckin, *Saint Cyril*, 203–4.

80. Ibid., 187.

81. Wilken, *Judaism and the Early Christian Mind*, 200.

in emphasizing that the incarnation occurred through the indwelling of the Word in Jesus' person.[82] Cyril's emphasis that in Jesus the Logos experienced human suffering was radicalized by Jürgen Moltmann in his theology of the cross.[83]

The controversy leading directly to the council of Chalcedon began through a clash between Nestorius, a leading representative of the school of Antioch who became bishop of Constantinople in 428, and Cyril of Alexandria. Nestorius attempted to enforce what he saw to be doctrinal orthodoxy, particularly around devotion to Mary as Theotokos, mother of God. For Nestorius Mary was the mother of Jesus, not of the Logos. But for Cyril and others following the Logos/*sarx* approach, the Logos had been present in Mary's womb. In 429 Nestorius gave a series of sermons attacking this and related notions. As opposition to Nestorius' teaching and person increased Cyril began to attack Nestorius' views and promote his own in letters circulated throughout Egypt. The dispute was enflamed by the personalities of both. It was also about ecclesiastical primacy: Constantinople versus Alexandria and Rome. But it was primarily driven by each side's belief that they were fighting for the truth of the gospel.[84] Because their struggle threatened the unity of the empire, Emperor Theodosius called what became the council of Ephesus in 431. In 444 the dispute reignited. Theodosius II convened another council at Ephesus in 449, which was tainted by violence. Pope Leo I addressed the issue with his *Tome* (449), directed against the position of Eutyches, who developed an extreme version of Cyril's early emphasis on the unity of Christ's person. Leo's *Tome* introduced the Latin tradition into the christological debate.

For Leo, "Christ was born of God and Mary and therefore possessed a divine and a human nature, and accordingly possessed both divine and human characteristics and ways of acting."[85] Leo followed Nicaea in seeing Jesus as originating from God. The presence of divine and human natures in Jesus' person were not symmetrical. But it was only by becoming incarnate that the Logos could effectively communicate salvation to humanity, and it was only as Jesus was the Son of God that he could effect salvation.

---

82. Rahner, *Love of Jesus*, 54–60; Haight, *Jesus*, 285–97, 445–66.

83. Moltmann, *Crucified God*, 227–49.

84. Sellers, *Council of Chalcedon*, 7.

85. Studer, *Trinity and Incarnation*, 208.

The traditions of Alexandria, Antioch, and the Western or Latin tradition that would play influential roles at the council of Chalcedon each had different emphases:

> The Alexandrine tradition emphasizes the unity of subject of the whole existence of Christ, the Antiochene the integrity of the nature of the man Jesus (of the homo assumptus), and the Latin the double solidarity with God and humankind.[86]

In 450 the Empire was threatened by external armies as Pulcheria and Emperor Marcian assumed power. They convened another council to restore unity to the church. It met at Chalcedon in October of 451. Their representatives insisted on the formulation of a new statement of faith that would end the christological controversy. The bishops reluctantly agreed and began by reading first the creed from the council of Nicaea, then subsequent documents, including the *Tome* of Leo.[87] The creed of Nicaea was accepted by all as the "master text"[88] defining orthodoxy. To answer the question of how the unity of divine and human natures in Jesus was to be understood, the bishops, under imperial pressure, finally produced the Chalcedonian Definition.[89] This represented a genuine consensus among them, intended to make explicit what they believed Nicaea implied.[90]

The Definition affirmed that Jesus Christ was fully divine and fully human: "as to his humanity, being like us in every respect apart from sin."[91] These positive statements were balanced by four negative ones. In Jesus both natures were present "unconfusedly, unalterably, undividedly, inseparably . . . , the character of each nature is preserved and comes together in one person and one hypostasis."[92] While the Definition followed Cyril's emphasis on the unity of Jesus' person,[93] it tried to affirm a position beyond the three alternatives[94] that included the strengths of

---

86. Ibid., 210.

87. For an account of the proceedings of the council of Chalcedon, see Slusser, "Issues in the Definition," 63–65.

88. Ibid., 64.

89. For the full text see Norris, *Christological Controversy*, 155–59.

90. Norris, "Chalcedon Revisited," 141.

91. Norris, *Christological Controversy*, 159.

92. Ibid.

93. Norris, "Toward a Contemporary Interpretation," 75.

94. Pelikan, "Chalcedon after Fifteen Centuries," 930.

each: Cyril's emphasis on the unity of Christ's person and that the Christ event was a saving act of God, Theodore's emphasis on the full humanity of Christ, and Leo's emphasis that both must be stated simultaneously and clearly.[95] It did not so much state an understanding of Jesus' person as a way in which Jesus should be understood, a "grammar" that Christologies should follow, "based in the last resort on the logical form of traditional confessional statement about Christ."[96] Its combination of positive and negative affirmations can be seen as presenting a framework for developing an understanding of Jesus' person.[97]

THE LEGACY OF CHALCEDON AND NICAEA

The Chalcedonian Definition did not provide the doctrinal unity the emperor desired. Further christological controversies resulted after its promulgation, which lasted another two centuries.[98] Yet it became and continues to be an important guideline for how Jesus can be understood as the Christ. While the language used and the questions answered by the Definition are different in many respects from those that occupied New Testament authors, it is concerned with a similar central theme: how to understand Jesus in light of the experience of salvation in and through him. In accordance with the Gospels the Definition affirms that Jesus is fully human and that his public ministry required the use of his human faculties and creativity. Jesus experienced the human condition of struggling to know and follow God's will and of being inspired by God's Spirit. Like the Gospels and the rest of the New Testament, the Definition also affirms that in Jesus the divine became present in history in a new way. This resulted from the inspiration of the Holy Spirit, but more fundamentally from a new initiative of God in the second person of the Trinity. Jesus' person thus has a unique relationship to God and an ultimate saving significance. In arriving at this, the doctrinal development culminating in Nicaea and Chalcedon brought a new metaphysical precision to the understanding of Jesus as the Christ. If adopted as guidelines for understanding Jesus' person, Nicaea and Chalcedon prevent the radical transcendence of God in Jesus from being domesticated.

95. Ibid., 932.

96. Norris, "Toward a Contemporary Interpretation," 76.

97. Coakley, "What Does Chalcedon Solve?," 161.

98. Norris, "Chalcedon Revisited," 140.

A Christology developed along these lines will point beyond the present to a greater reality in which sin and death have been overcome, inviting and empowering people to participate in this.

Yet this doctrinal development also involved significant losses. In emphasizing the uniqueness and transcendence of Jesus the theologians of this era "forgot that Jesus himself proclaimed a coming Kingdom of God."[99] The hope for liberation within history was forgotten and a repressive orientation towards Judaism developed.[100] In order to be faithful to Jesus and create space within Christian consciousness for Judaism and other religions, Christian theology must reclaim Jesus' proclamation of the coming reign of God, remembering that he looked to the coming of a reality that he prefigured, which includes more than the church and himself. The search for metaphysical concreteness in understanding Jesus also brought a loss of concern for Jesus' historical concreteness,[101] for understanding where and how he located himself within the social conflicts of his day, and with this came a loss of Jesus' preferential option of the poor. Christology was assimilated to a patriarchal worldview and began to function "as a sacred justification for male dominance."[102]

However, the Christology of Nicaea and Chalcedon also has liberating potential. The central principle of this Christology, "the unassumed is the unhealed,"[103] suggests that what is salvific about the incarnation is not that Jesus was male, but that he assumed a human nature. If what he assumed does not include women's nature then Jesus cannot be their savior. This principle thus undermines patriarchal distortions of Christology.[104] It also has liberating potential in relation to the environmental crisis. In the incarnation and resurrection of Jesus, Jesus' body, a piece of creation, was taken up into the glory of God. This transformation of one piece of nature "pledges a joyful future beyond death" for the rest.[105] From this expectation can come a new understanding of nature in the context of the environmental crisis, as destined for glory and to be respected as such. The emphasis in Alexandrian and Antiochean

---

99. Wilken, *Judaism and the Early Christian Mind*, 230.

100. Ruether, *Faith and Fratricide*, 246–48.

101. Ruether, "Can Christology Be Liberated?," 23.

102. Johnson, *She Who Is*, 151.

103. Gregory of Nazianzus, *On God and Christ*, 158.

104. Johnson, *She Who Is*, 153.

105. Johnson, "Passion for God," 121.

Christologies that Jesus reveals the fullness of humanity also has liberating implications when Jesus' historical concreteness is recovered.[106] In a world plagued by sin and evil, Jesus reveals that the fullness of humanity is to be found in the struggle for justice.

Finally, Jesus proclaimed a radically transcendent God, yet a God who rejoices over the salvation of sinners (Luke 15:10), a God responsive to human need. The Johannine interpretation of Jesus also portrays God as radically transcendent to creation, yet as living and finding fulfillment through people receiving Jesus' message and living in light of it.[107] In the doctrinal development leading to Nicaea and Chalcedon, this living aspect of the divine nature was formally encoded in the doctrine of the Trinity. But substantively the Hellenistic notion of divine impassibility that Christian theologians used to understand God meant that God was no longer conceived as living in this way. This made it difficult to understand how Jesus' divinity could be present in his suffering on the cross. The doctrine of the Trinity affirmed at Nicaea emphasized the radical transcendence of God and the freedom of God to do new things in history. But its emphasis on the living aspect of God's being was undercut by the fundamental assumption that the divine being was immutable. In this respect the search for a Christian doctrine of God that led to Nicaea remains unfinished.

CHALCEDON AS A STARTING POINT FOR
A DESCENDING CHRISTOLOGY

The Chalcedonian Definition bequeaths Christian theologians the task of striving to understand how the second person of the Trinity and Jesus' humanity are united in his one person.[108] In this respect Chalcedon represents the end of a long process of doctrinal development. But as a guideline for how the person of Jesus Christ should be understood it also presents a starting point for further reflection.[109] Swiss theologian Karl Barth (1886–1968) understood this in a particular way.

---

106. Schüssler Fiorenza, *Jesus*, 92–94.

107. Brown, *Epistles of John*, 555.

108. This can lead to very elaborate understandings of Jesus' person, as in the later theology of Karl Barth (Jones, *Humanity of Christ*, 117–50).

109. Rahner, *Theological Investigations*, 1:150.

The outbreak of World War I, the fact that many of Barth's liberal theology professors supported German participation in the war, and Barth's reflections on Scripture in light of this led him to argue that humanity exists in a state of alienation from God and can only have authentic knowledge of God through God's self-revelation in Jesus Christ.[110] Following a progressively developing approach informed by the Chalcedonian Definition, Barth went on to argue that Jesus did not simply embody what could be known of God from elsewhere, but that all Christian concepts of God must be developed in light of Jesus Christ.[111] In keeping with this Barth undertook a far-reaching revision of the idea of God that was formulated during the period of Nicaea and Chalcedon.[112] Theologians influential at these councils insisted on God's otherness and understood this in terms of God's absoluteness and immutability. But Barth argued that when Jesus Christ becomes the starting point for understanding God this conception is not enough. The immutable absolute is other to sinful humanity, but it is not the otherness of God. According to Barth, understanding God in light of Jesus Christ requires that one recognize a second otherness to God. God is not only absolute; God is also living. God's being is moved and dynamic,[113] at once radically transcendent yet also capable of entering into relationships with creation and humanity. The true otherness of God is only revealed in the freedom and love of God revealed in Jesus Christ. Barth's demand that the doctrine of God be developed in light of Christology has been widely influential in recent Western Christian theology.[114]

In this way Chalcedon presents a starting point for what Karl Rahner called a descending Christology. This chapter and the two preceding it have attempted an "ascending Christology," beginning with Jesus and seeking to understand the experience of salvation through him.[115] But if an ascending Christology concludes with finding the conditions of possibility for this in Jesus being the incarnation of the second person of the Trinity, then this in turn calls for a descending Christology that seeks to understand God in light of Jesus. An ascending Christology begins with

---

110. McCormack, *Karl Barth's Dialectical Theology*, 245–50.

111. Barth, *Church Dogmatics*, IV/1:129.

112. Schweitzer, "Karl Barth's Critique," 231–44.

113. Jüngel, *Doctrine of the Trinity*.

114. Johnson, "Christology's Impact," 161 n. 9.

115. Rahner, *Foundations*, 177.

Jesus and studies the continuities and discontinuities between what can be known of him and the confession of him as the second person of the Trinity. A descending Christology reverses this direction of inquiry. It takes up Barth's challenge to understand God in light of Jesus Christ. It begins with God understood as triune in light of Jesus. It then seeks to understand Jesus, his person and work, in light of what he reveals about God. At the same time it seeks to understand God in light of Jesus as the Christ. It asks, what must God be like if Jesus is the Word of God? For instance, if the second person of the Trinity became incarnate in Jesus, then God must be absolute and immutable, yet also capable of change in the sense of becoming incarnate.[116] In this way a descending Christology seeks to provide a more consistently "Christian doctrine of God,"[117] and with that a metaphysical framework for understanding Jesus and what it means to have faith in him. The next chapter will present a descending Christology of this kind.

116. Ibid, 219–23.

117. Moltmann, *Crucified God*, 200.

4 Jesus Christ—the Word of God

WHY DEVELOP A DESCENDING CHRISTOLOGY?

A descending Christology seeks to understand Jesus in terms of the Trinitarian life of God. The preceding chapter traced how reflection on the experience of salvation in Jesus Christ led to the conclusion that God is eternally triune and that Jesus is the incarnation of the second person of the Trinity. This concept of God then becomes the starting point for a descending Christology that asks what it is about God that makes God's being triune and leads to the incarnation of Jesus Christ. The answers to such questions are necessarily speculative and seek to describe the ineffable, so as "to speak in some way about that which we cannot fully express in any way."[1] The basis for pursuing these questions lies in the experience of salvation through Jesus. This experience of salvation is also a commissioning to speak of God as encountered in Jesus as best one can, even though God remains mysterious, ultimately incomprehensible and so can never be finally known.[2] Any understanding of God remains a work in progress and the limits of human knowledge have to be respected.

Yet a descending Christology is necessary because talk of God never takes place in a vacuum. It is intrinsic to humanity to exalt something or someone. People live within moral horizons that inevitably esteem some values over others, investing some with ultimate concern.[3] Some form of at least a minimal theology seems intrinsic to human life.[4] Though God is ineffable, still one's ultimate concern or vision of God is expressed in

1. Augustine, *Trinity*, 229 (7.4.7).
2. Haight, *Jesus*, 489.
3. Tillich, *Systematic Theology*, 1:11–15.
4. De Vries, *Minimal Theologies*, 616.

one's life. Talk of one's ultimate concern or concept of God is inevitable in examining the vision one lives by. The question is not whether one has an ultimate concern, but what it is. If one claims God as one's ultimate concern the question is which God one believes in. A descending Christology seeks to develop a consistently Christian understanding of God.

A descending Christology is speculative. It asks about what has not been directly experienced, the nature of God in eternity, on the basis of what has been experienced of God in Jesus Christ and the Holy Spirit. Such speculation is inevitable in any discussion of God or ultimate concern. It is not empty speculation if it proceeds on the basis of revelation as witnessed to in Scripture and with due attention to other forms of knowledge and experience. Without this inquiry the task of Christian theology to test the congruence of the church's understanding of God with what it believes about Jesus remains unfulfilled. A descending Christology is a form of discernment,[5] an attempt to understand God as best one can in light of what one has experienced in Jesus Christ.

GOD AS LIVING AND ABSOLUTE

Christian theologians reflecting on Jesus' relationship to God in the era of the council of Nicaea (325 CE) understood God's being in terms of the Hellenistic axiom that the divine is absolute and impassible. This axiom developed partly through Plato and Aristotle's critique of the depiction of the gods in the literature of Homer and Hesiod.[6] In taking over this axiom Christian theologians internalized this critique of anthropomorphic understandings of God and affirmed God's transcendence to humanity. Homer depicted the gods as the highest of beings, but as beings much like humanity in being subject to moral temptations and conflicts. Plato and Aristotle argued that God was beyond this. As the absolute, God was not a projection of humanity but the standard by which humanity should live. Patristic theologians took up this critique and in principle went beyond it, affirming God's absoluteness, but also that God is living; able to do new things and moved by love to redeem creation.[7] For the patristic theologians, God was not subject to temptation, but God was

---

5. LaCugna, *God for Us*, 230.

6. Plato's critique is summarized in Despland, *Education of Desire*, 130–33.

7. Abraham Heschel found a similar movement in the thought of the Hebrew prophets (Heschel, *Prophet*, 2:48–58).

living. This last affirmation was undercut by their adoption of the axiom of divine impassibility. This axiom did not fit with the biblical notion of God as living,[8] for life involves change and the actualization of potential. Adopting this axiom made it difficult to say why God created the world or acted to redeem it. The notion of God as absolute and therefore immutable expressed the power of God's being in relation to sin and death, describing God as transcendent to both and so able to save humanity from them. But it cannot express the nature of God's being as moved by love.[9] This requires a more dialectical understanding of God's relationship to creation, in which God is absolute but also internally related[10] to it.

The Hellenistic notion of God as absolute and immutable gave rise to a conception of God known as classical theism, in which God does not change, has no need of the world, and receives nothing from it. This notion of God as having no real relation to the world is deeply entrenched in Western Christian thought, but has been accurately criticized as inadequate on the basis of Christology,[11] its inner incoherence, and its effective history, particularly in relation to women.[12] Yet the idea of God as radically transcendent to creation, acting freely in relation to it, out of love but not out of ontological necessity, needs to be preserved for the doctrine of God to be adequate to the biblical witness and contemporary experience.[13] One way to do this is to understand God's being as an expression of God's goodness.

THE SELF-DIFFUSIVE NATURE OF GOD'S GOODNESS

Central to Jesus' preaching was an emphasis on the goodness of God as absolute and determining God's actions in history.[14] St. Francis of Assisi (c. 1181–1226) made celebrating God's goodness central to his understanding of Christian life. This had an influence in Franciscan theology.

---

8. Pelikan, *Christian Tradition*, 1:52.

9. Barth, *Church Dogmatics*, II/1:496.

10. To be internally related to something is to be affected by it, such that one's being would be different in some way without it.

11. Moltmann, *Crucified God*, 214–17.

12. Johnson, *She Who Is*, 225.

13. Ibid, 226.

14. Gnilka, *Jesus of Nazareth*, 91–102.

According to Anselm (c. 1033–1109 CE), God is absolute as that "than which nothing greater can be conceived."[15] Bonaventure (c. 1221–1274 CE), a Franciscan, applied this to God's goodness. The good that is self-diffusive, that communicates and further expresses itself, is greater than the good that does not. God's goodness, as "that than which nothing better can be thought," must therefore be "supremely self-diffusive."[16] It must also be fully actual, as the good that is actual is greater than the good that is not. According to Bonaventure, the self-diffusion or communication of divine goodness occurs eternally in the generation of the second person of the Trinity and the spiration of the third. Through this God's goodness is infinitely diffused and fully actual. Thus "the supreme communicability of the good demands necessarily that there be a Trinity of Father, Son and Holy Spirit."[17] Yet while God's goodness is absolute in being supremely self-diffused in the Trinity in eternity, it remains open to further diffusion in time and space through creation and redemption,[18] for the self-diffusive nature of the divine goodness is fulfilled in the eternal generation of the Word and spiration of the Holy Spirit but is not limited by this. Consequently it is open to further expression through the economic Trinity in creation and redemption. For Bonaventure the divine nature does not need this further communication and it adds nothing to God's already infinite being. But creation and redemption are fitting and appropriate further expressions of God's self-diffusive goodness.

Jonathan Edwards would develop this understanding God's relationship to the world further, arguing that while God's being is absolute it is also open to a relative but still real increase through the further communication of God's beauty and goodness in creation and redemption.[19] This understanding of God's absoluteness is more coherent with Jesus' proclamation of the reign of God than classical theism, for in Jesus' proclamation the final reality is not simply God, but God and the reign of God, or God and the redeemed creation.[20] In the gospels God is

---

15. Anselm, *Basic Writings*, 8.

16. Bonaventure, *Itinerarium Mentis in Deum*, 123.

17. Ibid, 125.

18. Keane, "Why Creation?," 112–15.

19. For Edwards' understanding of God's relationship to he world, see Lee, *Jonathan Edwards*. For a comparison of Bonaventure and Edwards on this issue, see Schweitzer, "Aspects of God's Relationship," 5–24.

20. Sobrino, *Jesus the Liberator*, 68–69; Schillebeeckx, *Jesus*, 68.

depicted as radically transcendent to creation yet also internally related to it.

THE FRANCISCAN INNOVATION IN CHRISTOLOGY

The spiritual vision of St. Francis with its focus on the goodness of God led to another innovation in Franciscan theology that had precedents in patristic theology. In much of Western theology from Athanasius to Anselm, the main reason given for the coming of Christ was to save humanity from sin. However in patristic theologians like Gregory of Nyssa, the ultimate vision of the purpose of the incarnation is not simply overcoming the alienation of humanity and creation from God introduced by sin, but rather the deification of created beings, their entry into an eternal communion with God, "so that 'God may be all in all.'"[21] Here the reason for Christ's coming is ultimately not to save humanity from sin, but to gather a community about God. Medieval Franciscan theologians took this idea further.

In the 1200s Robert Grosseteste and others argued that Christ would have become incarnate even if humanity had not fallen into sin. These theologians saw Jesus to be the perfection towards which all of creation was oriented. Even had there been no sin he would have still come to express God's goodness, power, and wisdom.[22] This idea found its fullest expression in the Christology of Franciscan theologian John Duns Scotus (1265/66–1308). For Scotus Jesus Christ is the culmination or perfection of creation. If the main reason for Christ's coming was to save humanity from sin, the "best thing God does in creation would be motivated by the worst thing that creatures do."[23] Scotus considered this view irrational. Goodness, not sin, must be the primary reason for Christ's coming. Accordingly Scotus argued that the three persons of the Trinity together desire others to join in the praise, joy, and love that they share. Christ became incarnate so as to become the head of "a vast community of created co-lovers . . . destined for the beatific intimacy of sharing in the Trinitarian love-life."[24] Christ's atoning work is a means to this more fundamental end. Creation is oriented towards the coming of

21. Lossky, "Redemption and Deification," 241.

22. Adams, *What Sort of Human Nature?*, 25.

23. Ibid, 70.

24. Ibid, 69.

Christ and is fulfilled in and through him. Aspects of this understanding the reason for the incarnation can also be found in the theologies of Friedrich Schleiermacher, I. A. Dorner, and Karl Barth,[25] and in the more recent Christologies of Jürgen Moltmann and Marilyn McCord Adams.[26]

Noting these developments, we turn to understanding the place of Jesus Christ in the truine life of God and the reason for his coming. To do this, we first discuss the relationship of the economic and immanent Trinity.

THE RELATIONSHIP OF THE IMMANENT AND THE ECONOMIC TRINITY

The affirmation of the Council of Nicaea that God must be understood in Trinitarian terms implicitly affirmed a difference between the economic Trinity, God as encountered in history in Jesus Christ and the Holy Spirit, and the immanent Trinity, God in eternity prior to creation and redemption.[27] The latter is the basis of the former. What God is eternally in the immanent Trinity determines what God does in creation and redemption. The latter is a further expression of what is present in the former. The unity of the two must be maintained as Jesus can only mediate salvation if God becomes personally present to humanity and creation through him.[28] Yet over centuries the connection between the two weakened in Western Christian thought until the renewal of Trinitarian theology in the twentieth century, when Karl Barth and Karl Rahner insisted that the doctrine of the Trinity was an explication of what was revealed of God or of the experience of salvation in Jesus Christ. According to Rahner, "the 'economic' Trinity is the 'immanent' Trinity"[29] and vice versa.

However, this necessary emphasis on the unity of the immanent and economic Trinity must not obscure an equally necessary distinction between them. The two are not identical, for through "the incarnation the second divine person exists in history in a new way."[30] The second

25. For Schleiermacher, Dorner, and Barth, see van Driel, *Incarnation Anyway*.

26. Schweitzer, *Contemporary Christologies*, 128.

27. Studer, *Trinity and Incarnation*, 96–97.

28. Haight, *Jesus*, 484.

29. Rahner, *Trinity*, 22.

30. Kasper, *God of Jesus Christ*, 275.

divine person is not crucified in the immanent Trinity, but only after becoming incarnate in the economic Trinity. The distinction between the two developed in order to preserve the radical transcendence of God to sin and evil.[31] It remains necessary if Jesus' crucifixion is to be taken seriously and God is still to be a source of hope for the final overcoming of evil.[32]

A second reason for preserving this distinction lies in the New Testament's emphasis that in Christ a new reality appeared that has created a new divine/human situation.[33] The new is by definition different in some respect from that which preceded it. John 1:14 indicates that in the incarnation "the divine life of the Logos itself underwent something decisively new."[34] As Karl Rahner argued, while God is immutable in the sense of not being subject to change in God's self, the incarnation did involve God being "subject to change in something else."[35] The incarnation was a new event in the life of God involving a "becoming"[36] on the part of the second person of the Trinity. This cannot be denied without undermining the New Testament claim that in Christ God has done a new thing. Once this is acknowledged the economic and immanent Trinity can no longer be understood as simply identical. Because the second person of the immanent Trinity exists " in history in a new way" through the incarnation, the economic Trinity needs to be distinguished from it as well as internally connected to it[37] in order to preserve divine transcendence and do justice to what is new here in relation to the immanent Trinity. Both the transcendence of God and the reality of God's actions in history are at stake in bringing the unity and the distinction between the immanent and economic Trinity to expression.

How can this unity and difference be maintained? The doctrine of the Trinity as a whole seeks to conceptualize what is perceived of God in Jesus Christ.[38] The economic Trinity conceptualizes the experience of

---

31. Studer, *Trinity and Incarnation*, 75.

32. LaCugna, *God for Us*, 216–17.

33. Moltmann, *Religion*, 10–11.

34. Lincoln, "I Am the Resurrection," 126. Other NT passages such as Phil 2:5–11 suggest this as well.

35. Rahner, *Foundations*, 220.

36. Ibid.

37. Kasper, *God of Jesus Christ*, 275.

38. Moltmann, *Crucified God*, 240–41.

Jesus Christ and the Holy Spirit in history, in God's economy of salvation. The immanent Trinity is a theory "about the eternal ground and intrinsic structure"[39] of the economic Trinity. It conceptualizes the eternal being of God; what must be presupposed in light of what is experienced in the economic Trinity. Following Karl Barth and others, one can say that in the economic Trinity the immanent Trinity "reiterates,"[40] repeats, or further expresses itself in time and space. In this repetition, the unity of the economic and immanent Trinity is maintained. The goodness of God proclaimed and enacted by Jesus is the same as is shared and celebrated within the immanent Trinity, only now expressed in history. Conversely, this further communication of God's goodness in time and space is new and different in its form, as it happens now in history, in the context of a fundamentally good creation distorted by sin. It also makes a difference to God as it brings into being an additional reality that did not exist before: the reign of God. As it does this it brings a relative but still real increase to God's being. To conceptualize this we begin by sketching an understanding of the immanent Trinity.

THE IMMANENT TRINITY

The centrality of God's goodness in the preaching and practice of Jesus suggests that it be taken as the primary divine attribute. This goodness, God's agape or self-giving love, is also beautiful, so that one can speak of God's goodness and beauty together. Following Bonaventure one can take the self-diffusive goodness of God as a key to understanding God's Trinitarian being. Intrinsic to God's goodness and beauty is a disposition, an energy and tendency, to further communicate itself. This disposition is fulfilled in the life of the immanent Trinity. It is actualized eternally through the free and creative assent of the first "person"[41] of the Trinity.[42] This assent is also key to understanding the Trinity. The self-diffusive energy of the divine goodness and beauty connects with a corresponding eros in the divine will for its further expression. This eros is not simply desire for something lacking, but also a productive will

---

39. LaCugna, *God for Us*, 230.

40. Jüngel, *Doctrine of the Trinity*, 103–6.

41. While the term "person" is used analogously here for want of a better term, its use is rooted in what was revealed in Jesus Christ (Schillebeeckx, *Jesus*, 660–66).

42. Gilson, *Philosophy of St. Bonaventure*, 163.

arising from joyful ecstasy in the divine goodness.[43] At this point this eros is partly a desire for something lacking, for the self-diffusive nature of the divine goodness would not be fulfilled if it did not find eternal expression in the immanent Trinity. This rejoicing in divine goodness, assent to its further expression, and the actualization of it are characteristic of the divine life.

The will of the first person of the Trinity reflects on the divine goodness and beauty and rejoices in it, saying yes to its further expression. The conjunction of this assent with the self-diffusive nature of divine goodness and beauty leads to the eternal generation of the second person of the Trinity, the Word of God. This generation of the Word is necessary for the fulfillment of the self-diffusive nature of God's goodness. Yet it does not happen mechanically. It occurs through the freedom and creativity of the divine will, so that it gives rise to the second "person" of the Trinity who is "other" to the first. The "persons" of the Trinity are one in nature yet distinct from each other. The Word of God infinitely expresses the divine goodness and beauty with love and rejoicing. The first person of the Trinity loves and rejoices in this expression of its goodness and beauty. From their combined love and joy in each other proceeds the Holy Spirit, the third "person" of the Trinity,[44] the bond of love uniting the other two.

The goodness and beauty of God are unendingly and immeasurably communicated and shared in the expression and celebration of love and joy that characterize the life of the immanent Trinity. This fulfills the need of God's goodness and beauty to communicate itself. The self-diffusive nature of God's goodness is thus fulfilled within the immanent Trinity. God has no ontological need of creation or anything else for this to happen. In this sense, God is absolute, eternal, unchanging. Even when God enters into relationship with creation, God remains transcendent to it.[45] What God does in creation and redemption is only a further expression, a repetition, of what is already fully actual in the immanent Trinity.

However, while God has no ontological need of anything else, God is open to communicating and sharing God's goodness and beauty with

43. According to Bernard McGinn, this second view of eros is first found in the theology of Pseudo-Dionysius (McGinn, "God as Eros," 200–202).

44. This Augustinian way of conceptualizing the Trinity does not account for the personhood of the Holy Spirit. To account for this personhood, the model being used here would need to be supplemented by another. For the personhood of the Holy Spirit, see Hilbreath, "Identity through Self-Transcendence, 278–85.

45. Fretheim, *God and World*, 16.

others. Jesus reveals God to be the giver whose nature is to freely communicate goodness to others, to share with them and enter into communion with them.[46] God's self-giving nature is fulfilled in the immanent Trinity, but not restricted or limited by it. The expression and celebration of love and joy in God's being is infinite not only in being immeasurable and unending, but also in being free from external limitation. Though nothing is lacking in the divine being, still eros for the further communication of God's goodness and beauty continues to arise from God's exuberant joy in it.[47] This divine joy leads God to create others so as to communicate and share God's goodness and beauty with them. To this end God created the world and became incarnate in it. Here the eros that gives rise to the further communication of God's goodness and beauty does not arise from a lack, but rather from an ecstatic joy in God's own goodness. Joy in the good is sufficient in and of itself to give rise to desire to see the good further communicated and shared. As God communicates divine goodness and beauty out of joy and not out of a lack or need to share it, God is able to give it as grace, a gift.

This further communication of God's goodness and beauty in creation and redemption involves Jesus' death on the cross. This provides the basis for the further celebration of God's beauty and goodness among the redeemed, but it is not a part of that celebration itself.[48] In the encounter with sin and evil, the communication of God's goodness and beauty takes on the particular form paradigmatically revealed in Jesus' ministry, death, and resurrection. The love revealed here is already fully present in the immanent Trinity but in a different form, as suffering is not part of the life of the immanent Trinity. The basis for arguing this is Jesus' resurrection, which reveals that God's being is greater than suffering and evil.[49] This transcendence of God's being in the immanent Trinity to suffering and evil is the source of hope for its final overcoming. The suffering God takes on in the Word and Spirit in history is not

---

46. Schillebeeckx, *Jesus*, 666.

47. "The divine longing is Good seeking good for the sake of the Good. That yearning which creates all the goodness of the world preexisted superabundantly within the God and did not allow it to remain without issue. It stirred him to use the abundance of his powers in the production of the world" (Pseudo-Dionysius, *Pseudo-Dionysius*, 79–80).

48. Moltmann, *Theology of Joy*, 50–51.

49. Johnson, *She Who Is*, 268–69.

intrinsic to God's being but a moral excellence,[50] something God freely takes on out of love for creation. In this sense Jesus' suffering is rooted in God's love, for when this love encounters sin and evil it acts to reconcile and redeem. Yet this suffering is not ontologically essential to the goodness and beauty of God's love.

This points to a second aspect of God's relationship to creation. While God creates the world out of exuberant joy that gives rise to a desire to share God's goodness with others, there is an element of moral necessity to this. Creation is essentially good. As God is good and always does what is good, and as God is able to create the world, there is an element of moral necessity in God creating and redeeming it, grounded in God's own nature and being. As God is living, there is a character to God's being, a disposition to goodness and beauty. It is the beauty and goodness of God's nature and the power or transcendence of God's being that makes creation and redemption morally necessary for God. Moral necessity differs from ontological necessity. If something is ontologically necessary to a person, they cannot exist without it. If something is morally necessary to a person, they can exist without it, but they are not the same in terms of their identity and character. God is not a person, but God is not less than personal. God is always greater than humanity and so is able to enter into an I-Thou relation to persons. God is not an "it," but both the basis of creation and able to relate to it in moral terms. In this sense, God is "supra-personal," as Paul Tillich once wrote.[51] As such God can be said to have a moral character.[52] Morally necessary acts are carried out freely in that one chooses to do them without external necessity to do so. But they are not arbitrary, in that the basis for one's choice lies in one's own character, moral disposition, or worldview. It is God's own character as loving, God's being able to create and redeem, and the goodness and beauty of creation and redemption that makes these actions morally necessary for God. The suffering God undertakes in the cross is also a further expression of God's goodness and beauty. It is a moral excellence, done out of moral necessity and love, but not out of joy. There is joy in what Jesus' cross helps attain, but no joy in the experience of the cross itself.

50. Ibid., 266.

51. Tillich, *Theology of Culture*, 131.

52. Hanson, "New Challenge to Biblical Theology," 454–58.

The moral dimension of creation and redemption points to how God is internally related to creation. God's creating and redeeming the world is grounded in God's nature and being. It also brings an increase to it.[53] This happens in several ways. First, the further expression of God's goodness and beauty in creation brings joy to God, as God reflects upon it. Second, as the parables of the lost coin and the lost sheep indicate, the redemption of a sinner brings joy to God.[54] Third, as people live in light of their faith in Jesus and express this in praise to God and love for others, God's own love reaches its goal of further expression in history.[55] As people give thanks to God for the beauty of creation and love one another, they experience a fulfillment of their being as persons. Their fulfillment brings an increase to God's being as well.

God's nature is already fulfilled in God's own being in the immanent Trinity. The self-diffusive nature of God's goodness and beauty is fully actualized here. Yet it remains capable of further self-diffusion through creation and redemption. In conjunction with this, God's being is capable of increase in the particular person of the Holy Spirit. As the bond of love that unites the other two "persons," the Holy Spirit can be increased by others joining in the praise and celebration of God's goodness and beauty. Qualitatively the Holy Spirit as fully divine cannot be increased. It already includes an unending and immeasurable joy. But quantitatively the Holy Spirit can be increased through others coming to share this joy. As they do so, the Holy Spirit comes to be present in places where previously it was not. This brings an increase to its being, and thus to the being of God. The infinite is qualitatively different from the finite, but still capable of relative quantitative increase by it.[56] Though it is relative, this quantitative increase is real. As people perceive the goodness and beauty of God manifested in creation and redemption, above all in Jesus Christ, and give thanks to God, they participate in the "circle of love"[57] that is the triune life of God. The Holy Spirit abides in them and they in it. The bond of love that is the Holy Spirit now includes them as well, which it did not do before. This brings a relative but still

---

53. This understanding of God's relation to the world here and in what follows is substantially drawn from Lee, *Jonathan Edwards*, 170–231.

54. Fitzmyer, *Gospel according to Luke X–XXIV*, 1071, 1075.

55. Brown, *Epistles of John*, 555.

56. Oppy, *Philosophical Perspectives on Infinity*, 55–56.

57. McDonnell, *Other Hand of God*, 180.

real increase to the being of God.[58] Furthermore, wherever there is love
that resembles that revealed in Jesus Christ, there is God,[59] and wherever
such love is expressed in time and space, there is a relative but still real
increase to the being of God in the person of the Holy Spirit.

THE ECONOMIC TRINITY

In the economic Trinity, the triune being of God is reiterated, repeated,
or further expressed in time and space. Creation has to exist for this to
happen and is the first work of the economic Trinity. Creation is also, in
itself, a further expression of God's beauty and goodness. As the Word
of God in which this is goodness is infinitely expressed in the immanent
Trinity, Christ is the foundation of creation, the basis of it and the goal
it is oriented towards. Creation is brought into being through the Word
and Spirit working together. The Word provides its basis, structure, and
goal. The Spirit provides the energy, life, and motivation for it.[60]

Creation is fundamentally good, yet distorted and perverted by the
fall or original sin. Augustine argued at one point that no efficient cause
exists for evil.[61] No ultimate rational explanation can be given for its
existence, for if there were such an explanation evil, sin, and suffering
would ultimately be good. As it is they exist in contradiction to God,
as something God permits but that in principle should not be.[62] In the
context of creation distorted by the fall, the Holy Spirit is present as
an unpredictable power, coming upon people in contexts of communal distress, effecting deliverance from evil by restoring a community's
solidarity and capacity for action.[63] The Holy Spirit is also present in a
more constant way in social and religious institutions and traditions. Its
inspiration and the record of its activity can become a Word addressing
humanity, a Word that judges and inspires, confirms and directs, promises and calls. Experiences of the Spirit frequently have an eschatological
nature, pointing beyond themselves to an as yet unrealized future. They

58. Lee, *Jonathan Edwards*, 206–10.

59. Bulgakov, *Comforter*, 337.

60. Johnson, *Women, Earth and Creator Spirit*, 42.

61. Augustine, *City of God*, 477–80 (12.6.6–7).

62. Barth, *Church Dogmatics*, III/3:351–52.

63. Michael Welker discerns this way of the Holy Spirit acting in what he describes
as the earliest reliable testimonies to the Holy Spirit's activity (Welker, *God the Spirit*, 53,
52–62).

are also frequently ambiguous and require discernment. This led to a crisis in the religious life of Israel in the sixth century BCE, as conflicting claims and predictions by prophets, all claiming inspiration by God, led to a breakdown in prophetic authority and questioning of the intentions and ethical character of the God who was claimed to have inspired them.[64] In Christian perspectives, Jesus Christ is the ultimate answer to this need for discernment.

The Synoptic Gospels present Jesus as standing in a long line of teachers, prophets, and healers inspired by the Holy Spirit. They also present Jesus as the culmination of this line, as the messianic human being who was born "from the Spirit" and in whom the Spirit is continually present.[65] As such his presence marks the inbreaking of the reign of God in history. Jesus is not only inspired by the Spirit. Through his ministry, death and resurrection, the Holy Spirit becomes present in history in a new way[66] and Jesus himself becomes a figure by which the Holy Spirit inspires others and by which the presence of the Holy Spirit in others can be discerned.

The Synoptic Gospels proclaim Jesus as unique among those inspired by the Holy Spirit in terms of the qualitative difference of the Spirit's presence in his life. To fully account for this uniqueness, in light of his resurrection and the subsequent experience of salvation mediated by him, some New Testament authors and subsequent theologians interpreted Jesus by a different logic, as not only inspired by the Spirit but as the incarnation of God's Wisdom or the Word. These two logics, parallel to the later approaches to understanding Jesus' person of the schools of Antioch and Alexandria, reflect different aspects of the experience of Jesus as recorded in the Gospels. These describe Jesus as inspired by the Spirit like other persons, only to an extent surpassing all others. Yet the salvation experienced through him was not the work of an inspired person, but the result of an initiative of God. In a sense, these two logics mirror those of an ascending and a descending Christology. The initiative of God in the incarnation is the basis of Jesus' person as the Christ. But he is not the Christ without the response of his humanity to the

64. Blenkinsopp, *History of Prophecy*, 157–60.

65. Moltmann, *Way of Jesus Christ*, 78, 86, 92.

66. The "newness" of the presence of the Holy Spirit linked to faith in Jesus Christ has rightly become a contentious issue, as it easily becomes a warrant for religious imperialism (Schweitzer, "Holy Spirit," 30–31).

initiative and inspiration of God. This pattern is then replicated in Jesus' own relationship to others. Jesus himself was inspired by the Holy Spirit, and became incarnate, for the sake of others, that they might receive through faith in him the continual presence of the Holy Spirit as well.[67]

Jesus, inspired by the Holy Spirit, announced and enacted the coming reign of God. Yet what came instead was his death and resurrection, which shed new light on his person and relationship to God. But the coming reign of God to which his ministry was oriented remains outstanding. Jesus gives the Spirit for the sake of its coming. His resurrection is not the conclusion of his story but a new beginning. It too is oriented towards the fulfillment of life, the final overcoming of sin and death, variously expressed as the last judgment or the coming of the reign of God. The Holy Spirit does not simply inspire Jesus. It also works to actualize in the lives of others the new reality that was present in him and towards which his life was oriented. The work of the Holy Spirit thus surrounds that of Jesus as the Word. The Holy Spirit prepares the way for Jesus' coming, over the centuries and in the lives of individuals. It also works to actualize in peoples' lives the new reality that Jesus is oriented towards and that is present in his person.

As the culmination of a long line of prophets, teachers, healers, and leaders inspired by the Holy Spirit, Jesus is not the end of this line but becomes, through his death and resurrection, the basis for discerning the presence of the Holy Spirit in the lives of others. As the Word of God or the Logos, Jesus expresses the meaning and purpose of life to be the celebration and communication of God's love, and helps others to experience and express this in their own lives. However, as Jesus' own experience of ministry and his death show, this is an embattled meaning; fragile, easily distorted, and contested on many fronts. In Jesus' ministry, death, and resurrection the goodness and beauty of God find definitive expression in a beautiful but needy world. Through this definitive expression and the continued presence of the Holy Spirit, in and outside of the church, this goodness and beauty finds further expression in the lives of others. It also finds new expression, for as the face of evil changes in the course of history, the Holy Spirit works to lead people to new understandings of Jesus as the Christ,[68] and to new ways of expressing God's goodness and beauty appropriate to changing contexts. As the Word of God, Jesus is

67. Moltmann, *Way of Jesus Christ*, 94.
68. Baum, *Religion and Alienation*, 188–200.

definitive but not static. In a context defined by white racism and a new sense of African-American identity, Jesus is black.[69] In the context of a patriarchal society and church and a new feminist consciousness, Jesus can be represented by the statue of a crucified woman.[70]

The economic Trinity works towards the coming of the reign of God. Through its working towards this the beauty and goodness of God finds further expression in time and space. This is the reason for the incarnation. Jesus came to further express God's goodness and beauty, and so that it could find further expression again in the lives of others. As this happens, a community of love also grows, which rejoices in the goodness and beauty of God's love and its further expression, and which, in this rejoicing, shares in the inner-Trinitarian joy of God.

Creation is both the context in which this takes place and a further communication of God's goodness and beauty itself. This has a particular relevance in the present ecological crisis. Overcoming this crisis requires not only action, but also a new moral framework that will help engender a greater sensitivity to environmental degradation and destruction,[71] without falling into an anti-humanism. Understanding creation as an expression of God's goodness and beauty that has meaning and purpose apart from human use of it can help provide this. Creation is not simply a means to an end. As an expression of God's goodness and beauty, it fulfills a purpose in the economy of salvation by itself.[72] As previously noted, the resurrection of Jesus suggests that creation too is included in the scope of redemption. The concept of God developed through a descending Christology can thus make a contribution to ecological theology.

JESUS AS THE WORD AND THE WAY

The descending Christology developed here sees Jesus as the goal towards which creation is oriented, as he is the definitive expression of God's goodness and beauty. Yet as the Word of God Jesus points beyond himself to the community of the church, for a word exists to be heard. Jesus would not be the Christ without the church, those who receive him

---

69. Cone, *God of the Oppressed*, 114.

70. Johnson, *She Who Is*, 264.

71. Rasmussen, *Earth Community, Earth Ethics*, 344–48.

72. Lee, "Edwards on God," 25–44.

as such.[73] He also points beyond himself to the reign of God, for the sake of which he came. Jesus is the Word that seeks to be further expressed in peoples' lives, in the way societies are structured, in the relationships between generations, and in the relation of humanity to creation. As the one who proclaimed the coming of God's reign, he is also a way to it. He is a way[74] that his followers must take as they seek to express in their own lives the goodness and beauty of God that Jesus expressed in his. His explicit followers are not the only ones to follow him. As the Word of God Jesus expresses the meaning of creation and life and the goal towards which God tends it. As the meaning he expresses is contested and costly, people need to be empowered in order to follow the way to it. Jesus also provides this. He is the Word of God, a way to that which the Word proclaims, and a source of the empowerment that people need to follow it. The next section will examine in more detail the way of Jesus, what the goodness and beauty of God look like in his ethical teaching. It will then examine how his person, particularly his death and resurrection, empower people to communicate this to others through their own lives.

73. Tillich, *Systematic Theology*, 3:149.
74. Moltmann, *Jesus Christ for Today's World*, 47.

Part II

Introduction to Part II

H AVING DEVELOPED AN UNDERSTANDING of Jesus' person in part I, we turn to examine his saving significance in part II. Part I concluded that Jesus became incarnate in order to further communicate God's goodness and beauty in time and space. Part II begins in chapter 5 by looking at how that goodness and beauty was defined by the way of Jesus,[1] his ethical teaching and praxis. This way was and is characterized by high moral standards and ideals. Chapters 6–8 then each examine a different kind of atonement theory, looking at how each articulates Jesus' saving significance as a strong moral source that empowers people to follow the way of Jesus and/or sustains them in this when they fail to live up to its ethical ideals. Chapter 6 looks at the moral influence theory of atonement. Chapter 7 looks at the Christus Victor theory. Chapter 8 looks at the substitutionary theory of atonement.

Each of these theories addresses a particular form of sin, evil, or suffering. Each can do a particular saving work in relation to these that the others cannot. Each is also liable to distortion that the others can correct. These three kinds of atonement theory are thus shown to supplement and correct each other. Each is necessary in its own way, yet each needs the others. No single theory can adequately express the fullness of Jesus' saving significance, or address the different forms of sin and evil that afflict people who have complicated moral identities as both victims of some forms of sin and perpetrators of others.

Given that, the saving significance of Jesus needs to be unfolded in various ways, beginning with the way Jesus provides an orientation by which these can be coordinated. As moral sources, the understandings of Jesus' saving significance articulated in each atonement theory serve to empower or sustain people as they follow the way of Jesus. As they do so, people participate in the further communication and celebration of the goodness and beauty of God revealed in Jesus.

1. I have taken this term from Moltmann, *The Way of Jesus Christ*, 33-34.

5 The Way of Jesus

The previous chapter developed an understanding of Jesus as the incarnation of the Word of God, who repeats in history in and with the Holy Spirit the beauty and goodness eternally expressed in the immanent Trinity. For Christians, Jesus' ministry, death, and resurrection give definitive and concrete expression to God's beauty and goodness. The salvation Jesus brings is the ultimate beauty and goodness in a world of many beauties and competing goods.

The ministry of Jesus was oriented towards the coming of the reign of God. Jesus through his ministry modeled what this reign looks like and the way that those who seek it must follow. Throughout the New Testament it is repeatedly emphasized that what Jesus revealed and offered should find further expression in his followers' lives through their imitation of him.[2] Jesus came to effect a change in the world. What he is and what he brings is something that people, as they receive it, are to further express in their own lives. Jesus reconciles people with God so they can participate in the further expression of God's own goodness and beauty. The human heart is restless until it finds its rest in God.[3] But having found this, it needs to celebrate and further express what it has found. This chapter will examine the way of Jesus, how he instantiated the reign of God in his ministry and exemplified the goodness and beauty that Christians should seek to further express in their own lives.

JESUS AS GUIDE

There is continuity between Jesus and the present. He told parables about lost coins, prodigal children, and hidden treasure that still resonate today. The salvation he brings remains relevant. Yet if Jesus is to define

---

2. Schillebeeckx, *Jesus*, 222.

3. Augustine, Confessions, 21 (1.1).

God's goodness and beauty it is important to remember his otherness.[4] Jesus and his way are non-contemporary, "distant from and alien to the present."[5] This distance can lead people to posit false dichotomies, such as choosing between trusting in Jesus' healing power or undergoing contemporary medical treatment. This kind of dichotomy makes Jesus an idol demanding the sacrifice of aspects of human nature. It conflicts with the way he is portrayed in the New Testament. Here he is described as the Messiah who offers humanity fulfillment and salvation (Matt 11:2–6). The Chalcedonian Definition described Jesus as fully human, redeeming all of human nature, not just parts of it. Suggesting that people have to choose between Jesus and contemporary ways of aiding humanity contradicts who he was and is.

An understanding of Jesus' relationship to the present should be based on who he was and what he did in his public ministry. Jesus promised a reality better than the present. He and his way represent an "unfinished past"[6] that is non-contemporary in that the future he promised is still outstanding. The reign of God Jesus proclaimed includes the reconciliation of God and humanity, God indwelling creation fully, and creation and humanity experiencing fulfillment. The non-contemporaneity[7] of Jesus becomes productive when it serves the coming of this future, when it challenges not contemporary medicine and natural science, but the mythologies these are used to buttress, which tend to sacralize contemporary social structures and power relations, masking or hallowing their injustices.

For example, writing in the late 1960s and early 70s, James Cone noted how the achievements of the natural sciences and a sense of cultural progress over the past led white theologians in the United States to interpret New Testament references to "cosmic powers" and "spiritual forces of evil" (Eph 6:12) as outmoded mythological expressions that must be abandoned. Cone argued that in the United States at that time, the debate between liberal and conservative theologians over demythologizing the gospel diverted attention away from the gospel's clash

---

4. Keck, *Who Is Jesus?*, 161–62.

5. Bloch, *Heritage of Our Times*, 108.

6. Ibid., 113.

7. "Non-contemporaneity" is Ernst Bloch's term for traditions, cultural artifacts, institutions, or practices from the past that seem outdated but that reflect critically on the inhumanity of the present (ibid., 104–12).

with the oppression of the poor.[8] The non-contemporaneity of Jesus' conflict with Satan and the powers and principalities of evil needed not to be dismissed or simply opposed to contemporary forms of knowledge and experience, but productively related to the presence of these powers and principalities in the racist actions and mythology of white society,[9] which used its scientific achievements to bolster its sense of superiority in which its racism was entrenched.

This productive understanding of the otherness or non-contemporaneity of Jesus distinguishes between what is unfinished in his past and what is not. Determining this depends partly on one's context. As the face of evil changes from age to age,[10] different aspects of Jesus' person and ministry will become productively non-contemporary. When the worldview mediated by modern natural sciences enjoyed a near "monopoly on truth in the marketplace of ideas,"[11] the idea that the resurrection of Jesus included a transformation of his physical body was sometimes deemed unnecessary and possibly an unproductive impediment to faith.[12] Now when this monopoly has become insecure and fragmented partly under the impact of the environmental crisis, the resurrection of Jesus' body is seen to be productively non-contemporary, a promise of salvation for the natural environment,[13] giving creation an intrinsic value that must be respected. What is unfinished in the past depends partly on the sufferings of the present.

Respecting the otherness of Jesus also means he cannot be taken simply as a new lawgiver whose teachings and examples are to be followed literally. In some instances this may be appropriate. However, the risen Christ is continuous with but not limited to the earthly Jesus.[14] Jesus' past activity is "a pointer to what he is doing now"[15] and where he is present in the Spirit as the risen Christ. Christians today do not live in the Galilee of Jesus' time. This means that following him must

---

8. Cone, *God of the Oppressed*, 77–81.

9. Ibid., 232.

10. Baum, *Religion and Alienation*, 188–90.

11. West, *Prophesy Deliverance!*, 28.

12. Soelle, *Theology for Skeptics*, 104–8.

13. Johnson, "Passion for God," 121.

14. Welker, "Wright on the resurrection," 471.

15. Cone, *God of the Oppressed*, 224.

be a matter of creative fidelity;[16] adaptation, improvisation, and at times negation of aspects of what Jesus modeled. The way Jesus is remembered in the Gospels, through a process of interpretation and emendation, is itself an indication of how the church's memory of him should function to define the beauty and goodness Christians celebrate and seek to express.[17] While this is exemplified in Jesus and his relationships with others through his ministry, death, and resurrection, still the concrete form that it should take in any given context is something that has to be "negotiated again and again."[18]

Also, Jesus called people to follow him in a variety of ways.[19] With unity in Christ comes diversity in the Holy Spirit. What Jesus exemplified is capable of multiple forms of further expression. These often mutually reinforce, complement, and sometimes correct each other. The way of Jesus has definition and identity markers. The concrete instructions of Jesus found primarily in the gospels help provide these,[20] as do his characteristic activities and relationships. But there are different ways of following the one way, depending on one's gifts and circumstances. The way of Jesus must also be followed on different levels and in different spheres of life, and in relation to different forms of alienation.[21] For example, reconciliation needs to be sought on the level of nations and peoples, yet also between individuals in conflict. Concern to provide fellowship for prison inmates who want it needs to be matched by concern for the prison conditions of all inmates, concern for the justice of the legal system, and concern to reduce social causes of crime.[22] The converse is also true. Concern for social justice needs to be matched by concern to follow the way of Jesus in one's personal life. For example, in the midst of the Confessing Church struggle, Dietrich Bonhoeffer took the time to ask a member of his community to hear his confession.[23] Individuals and groups will take on specific tasks within the diversity of needs to be

---

16. Tilley, *Disciples' Jesus*, 129–30.

17. Schüssler Fiorenza, *Jesus*, 94–95.

18. Ibid., 96.

19. Catchpole, *Jesus People*, 61.

20. Gnilka, *Jesus of Nazareth*, 237.

21. Moltmann, *Crucified God*, 329–37.

22. Placher, *Jesus the Savior*, 155–56. While some are attending to the concerns of prisoners, others need to attend to the needs of victims of crime. Rarely can one person do both.

23. Bethge, *Dietrich Bonhoeffer*, 465.

addressed depending on their circumstances and gifts. Still, the way of Jesus needs to be followed in all spheres and on all levels of life.

The way of Jesus is also open-ended. Jesus is the way his followers must take, but that way is further exemplified by others who follow him.[24] Through followers like Francis of Assisi and Oscar Romero, or the art of Almuth Lutkenhaus-Lackey,[25] the person and way of Jesus finds new shape and definition that gives its truth original and unforeseen expression. However, regardless of where one is or the particular way in which one is following Jesus, there is always a need to return again and again to the New Testament, particularly to the gospels, to consider the way of Jesus himself and how it confirms or critiques one's own expression of what he modeled. Jesus can function to empower and guide the moral life in a variety of ways.[26] These do not all focus on what can be known of his public ministry. Yet the church, primarily through the Gospels, remembered the way of Jesus in order to remain faithful to him. As Jesus brought the reign of God to those immediately present in his ministry, he also defined it for those who came later. In doing this he was "working" for our salvation as well.[27] We turn now to examine his way.

THE REIGN OF GOD

The reign of God was Jesus' cause, what he lived and died for. An examination of the way he practiced and proclaimed it, through his teaching, preaching, healings, exorcisms, table fellowship with the despised, and symbolic actions, leads to the conclusion that the reign of God includes the well-being of humanity[28] and creation. It involved characteristic practices of healing, teaching, table fellowship, and mutual forgiveness.[29] It extended into the political sphere. Jesus was baptized by John the Baptist, who was executed by order of a political ruler, and Jesus himself died on a Roman cross. His ministry evoked political expectations.[30]

---

24. Heyward, *Saving Jesus*, 3.

25. Lutkenhaus-Lackey created the sculpture *Crucified Woman*. For a discussion of this see Dyke, *Crucified Woman*.

26. Gustafson, *Christ and the Moral Life*.

27. Placher, *Jesus the Savior*, 62.

28. Schillebeeckx, *Jesus*, 213.

29. Tilley, *Disciples' Jesus*, 188.

30. Theissen, "Political Dimension," 229–30.

While Jesus may or may not have had a program for social reform,[31] the reign of God he proclaimed and practiced entailed freedom from domination[32] and resistance to the empire of his day. It was thus a comprehensive symbol for a "highly positive reality . . . critical of the bad and unjust present."[33]

It is important to note that the way of Jesus and the symbol of the reign of God are themselves open to false interpretation and misuse. For instance, stories of Jesus' healings are sometimes told in ways that reinforce social stereotypes and cultural norms denigrating people with disabilities.[34] Anything that has saving power is also potentially dangerous and open to being consciously or unconsciously used in damaging ways. When a practice or characteristic of Jesus is abused in this way, the centering of the symbol of the reign of God on a vision of the well-being of humanity and creation needs to generate a critique of how Jesus and his way are being misappropriated.

The way of Jesus can be summarized as the intertwining of love of God and love of others. This gives it both definition and openness.[35] Definition comes from the concrete directives and actions recorded of Jesus.[36] The meaning of love finds paradigmatic expression in these. Yet the way of Jesus is open to new forms of relationship in changed circumstances. Jesus called people to give him and the reign of God absolute priority in their lives. In the religiously pluralistic context of the present these two aspects of Jesus' proclamation sometimes collide. The demand for absolute commitment to Jesus can become a warrant for religious imperialism, even violence, in contradiction to his teaching of love for others. Jesus was not a religious pluralist, nor was he interpreted as such throughout the New Testament. Yet, in a context of religious pluralism, his teaching of love of God and others becomes a warrant for dialogue with and openness to other religions.[37] Again, Jesus and his way are open

---

31. Richard Horsley affirms that he did (Horsley, *Jesus and Empire*, 14); Leander Keck argues that he did not (Keck, *Who Is Jesus?*, 156).

32. Schüssler Fiorenza, *Jesus*, 92.

33. Sobrino, *Jesus the Liberator*, 71.

34. Betcher, *Spirit and the Politics of Disablement*, 78–79.

35. Gnilka, *Jesus of Nazareth*, 246.

36. Ibid., 237. These are supplemented and illuminated by the traditions of the Hebrew Bible.

37. Cobb, *Transforming Christianity*, 71.

to being wrongly used. But there is within them the basis for a critique of this when it happens.

In keeping with this, one may note that in the Gospels, along with the proclamation of God's reign there are also frequent denunciations of other Jewish religious leaders and institutions, such as those found in Matthew 23. Over time these have often become stereotypes of Judaism per se, helping give rise to untold suffering. These critiques of other Jewish groups attributed to Jesus are not accurate descriptions of Judaism. But they can be read productively as denouncing a social pathology, a degeneration that can be present in all religions, including Christianity, when religious people and institutions prioritize the maintenance of their position and power over the central themes of their tradition and mission.[38] The way of Jesus was "to serve and realize the reign of God."[39] When the church departs from this and becomes self-serving it must be subject to critique in the name of what it claims to serve. The way of Jesus includes resistance to evil and prophetic denunciation of sin and injustice at home and abroad. With this must come an openness to self-critique,[40] a willingness to stand under the symbol of the reign of God as a universal principle of justice and allow one's self and community to be judged by it.

The way of Jesus includes celebrating God's goodness and beauty as well as seeking to further express it. The Gospels record numerous instances of Jesus eating and drinking with his disciples and with "sinners and tax collectors."[41] The latter meals instantiated the welcome of all to the reign of God. Together with the former, they were also celebrations of God's reign for its own sake. Such meals, "a fundamental trait" of the historical Jesus,[42] point to an aesthetic dimension intrinsic to his way. The goodness and beauty of God calls for celebration. Jesus' public ministry, like all public behavior, was partly a performance and as such a celebration of particular values and realities.[43] Then as now, the experience of God's beauty and goodness, a foretaste of the coming fullness of the reign of God, leads those who seek it "to go dancing."[44]

38. Baum, *Credibility of the Church*, 76.

39. Tilley, *Disciples' Jesus*, 188

40. Taylor, *Religion, Politics*, 29–30.

41. Moltmann, *Way of Jesus Christ*, 115.

42. Schillebeeckx, *Jesus*, 218.

43. Goffman, *Presentation of Self*, 35–36.

44. Taylor, *Executed God*, 160.

There is a dialectical tension between these moral and aesthetic dimensions of the reign of God. The moral dimension demands that resources be devoted to alleviating suffering and not squandered in celebration. Yet justice also demands that the good and beautiful be recognized and celebrated. For this reason moral struggles frequently conclude in acts of celebration or mourning. Resources given to celebration cannot go to feed the hungry. Yet aesthetic celebration of the moral good can awaken, empower, and sustain moral passion.[45] Though the two are in tension, they are intrinsically connected to one another and need each other. The way of Jesus includes celebration and thanksgiving, fundamentally in worship and the Eucharist, but beyond that as well. As experiences of the goodness and beauty of God give rise to celebration and thanksgiving to God, the circle of Trinitarian love is repeated in time and space.

Finally, as the way of Jesus aims at overcoming injustice, it is by nature fraught with controversy and conflict.[46] The reign of God is an embattled reality, constantly threatened by the fallibility and moral weakness of those who seek to serve it and by external forces that oppose it. It comes as a gift, yet it requires sacrifice, struggle, and perseverance. This means that prayer is an essential part of the way of Jesus.[47] This way demands the full exercise of all the gifts that people have. Yet one can persevere in it only through constant reliance on God.

THE COMING OF GOD'S REIGN

"Jesus welcomed everyone."[48] The way of Jesus was marked by a radical inclusivity. The socially despised were accepted into his company. While he seems to have oriented his mission mainly towards Jews, the gospels record instances of his being open or becoming open to include others in his concern.[49] This is supported by the observation that the movement Jesus started within Judaism "came to see the Gentile mission as a logical extension of itself."[50] How Gentiles were to be included was

45. Schweitzer, "Place for Aesthetics," 3–4.

46. Moltmann, *Way of Jesus Christ*, 97.

47. Copeland, "Cross of Christ," 182. This theme is further elaborated in chapter 12 below.

48. Placher, *Jesus the Savior*, 74.

49. Freyne, *Jesus*, 89–90.

50. Sanders, *Jesus and Judaism*, 220.

contentious in the early church, but not that they should be. The way of Jesus included judgment and critique of religious institutions other than his own movement, but no categorical exclusion of others. It was marked by a radical inclusivity.

This inclusivity gave the way of Jesus a definite orientation amidst the conflicts of his time, signaled in the Gospel of Luke by the "Nazareth Manifesto"[51] (Luke 4:16–21). Here Jesus' mission is portrayed as bringing liberation to the oppressed, freedom from material want to the poor, and inclusion to the marginalized. The concern to include all necessarily involves a program of social change, for if the exclusionary practices and structures of society remain unchanged the poor and marginalized will continue to be excluded from fullness of life. Jesus' concern for the poor thus follows from his inclusivity and concern for the wholeness of the human community.[52]

The way of Jesus was thus characterized by what is known as a preferential option for the poor.[53] Jesus interpreted society in light of the experience of the poor and showed public solidarity with them. The "poor" in Jesus' time were "the sick, demoniacs, epileptics, blind, as well as people who are unable to realize their life to the full and hence need assistance . . . those who have become debtors, tax gatherers, suspicious, despised, marginalized, who foundered in life, who do not see a way out, who are despairing."[54] Their lives were characterized by a lack of the essentials of life, powerlessness to change this condition, and at best lack of recognition of their personhood and belonging to society or at worst a status of being despised. The poor suffer from their own sins, but much more from the sins of others, from oppressive external forces. The reign of God comes through their liberation from both, particularly from want and denigration to enjoying abundance of life and mutual respect.

Who are the "poor" today? There is no one form of oppression in North America that is the root of all others.[55] The "poor" today are many and diverse. No attempt to list them can be comprehensive. But there are social trends that need to be mentioned. In Canada, many First Nations

---

51. Nirmal, "Towards a Christian Dalit Theology," 227.

52. Catchpole, *Jesus People*, 212–13.

53. Sobrino, *Jesus the Liberator*, 81.

54. Gnilka, *Jesus of Nazareth*, 176.

55. Baum, *Religion and Alienation*, 218–20.

peoples remain excluded from Canada's economic well-being.[56] Blacks experience prejudice "qualitatively different" from that experienced by other minority groups.[57] Francophone Quebecers and Aboriginal peoples tend to be alienated from the rest of Canada.[58] On a broader scale, since the horrific events of September 11, 2001, "prejudice and discrimination against Muslim citizens in Western countries have greatly increased," and in some ways are legitimated by antiterrorist legislation.[59] Economically and in terms of political power, all over the world societies of exclusion are being formed in which the working poor and unemployed, including a high percentage of women and children, are denied economic security, access to opportunity, and an effective voice in shaping social policy.[60] This amounts to a gigantic depredation of impoverished peoples around the world. The desperate needs this creates and the excessive consumption by the middle and upper classes contributes to the growing environmental crisis.[61] Today creation itself and plant and animal species must be included among the "poor," those threatened by external forces beyond their control. These are some of the poor and marginalized today. The reign of God comes through their liberation.

The liberation of the poor and marginalized aims towards their inclusion in society but not their homogenization. The liberation of the oppressed must proceed along the lines of social power and privilege, primarily in terms of economic and political power and opportunity for education, meaningful employment, and health care. But liberation must also proceed along the lines of social status, so that it includes recognition[62] on various levels and acceptance of difference. The radical inclusivity of Jesus does not mean that everyone becomes the same. The early church was characterized by the inclusion of others, notably Gentiles, who did not have to become Jewish to follow Jesus.

Jesus' preferential option for the poor requires understanding society in terms of the conflicts within it between social groups. One has

56. Banting et al., "Conclusion," 658.
57. Ibid., 656.
58. Ibid., 661.
59. Baum, *Signs of the Times*, 18.
60. Ibid., 160.
61. Moltmann, *God for a Secular Society*, 92–95.
62. Taylor, *Philosophical Arguments*, 232.

to ask of social institutions, policies and practices, whom do they serve? Given Jesus' preferential option for the poor, where is the risen Christ to be found in the conflicts of the present? The risen Christ is ubiquitous but not present everywhere in the same way. He is to be found in the church, where he, his work, and the reign of God are proclaimed and celebrated. He is present among the poor and the marginalized and in struggles for their liberation and inclusion. He is also to be found among the threatened natural species. Finally, he is to be found in the future, when the promises of his unfinished past will be fulfilled.[63]

EMANCIPATION AND RECONCILIATION

Jesus' preferential option for the poor creates a tension in his way between reconciliation and emancipation, forgiveness and enforcing the right, and love of self and others versus love of enemies. Striving for liberation of the poor often involves conflict and struggle. On occasion it may involve violence. Such struggles may implicate one in injustice.[64] All this stands in tension to Jesus' call to be reconciled to others and to forgive those who have wronged one. As noted earlier, Jesus' stance of radical inclusivity demands justice for the excluded and oppressed. To call for reconciliation and forgiveness and neglect or ignore the need for liberation in the midst of injustice and violence is to exclude the victims of society from fullness of life. Jesus and the movement around him modeled a primacy of liberation over reconciliation.[65] For these reasons seeking liberation for the oppressed and marginalized should be the priority in following the way of Jesus.

However, the struggle for liberation and seeking reconciliation are not simply opposites. Both are grounded in Jesus' welcome of all and his call to seek justice, forgive those who have wronged one, and love one's enemies. They exist in a dialectical tension. Reconciliation of enemies can be both part of the "path leading to justice and the result of achieving justice."[66] For example, in the liberation struggle to overcome apartheid in South Africa during the 1980s, Nelson Mandela, a key leader in the opposition to apartheid, entered into secret talks with F. W. de Klerk,

63. Moltmann, *Church*, 123.

64. De Gruchy, "Dialectic of Reconciliation," 25.

65. Taylor, *Remembering Esperanza*, 180.

66. De Gruchy, "Dialectic of Reconciliation," 22.

the leader of the apartheid regime, to seek a peaceful end to the violent struggle against apartheid. Mandela realized that seeking reconciliation with the oppressors while maintaining the struggle for liberation could be a way of providing the oppressors security that would enable them to relinquish their power. In this situation reconciliation could be a means to liberation.

> It had become abundantly clear to him [Mandela] that there was no alternative. Neither the state nor the liberation movement had the capacity to achieve a decisive victory, and the prolonging of the vicious stalemate could only spell disaster for the country as a whole. Seeking reconciliation was, paradoxically, an instrument of the struggle to end apartheid and establish a just social order. The path of reconciliation was not only the goal of liberation but a means to achieve that end.[67]

When one should pursue a conflictual approach of seeking liberation, and when working for reconciliation in the midst of injustice can be a strategic move creating possibilities for liberation, is a practical judgment that can only be made in the context of the struggle.[68] In the example above, the liberation struggle continued even as the offer of reconciliation presented the possibility of an alternative future. Without its continuation this offer would have had a very different moral quality.

Liberation and reconciliation are two sides of the reign of God. Liberation has a primacy, as authentic reconciliation presumes liberation of the oppressed. Yet a "will to embrace"[69] the oppressor must constantly inform every struggle for liberation. Reconciliation between peoples in conflict must be its final goal. In the way of Jesus, once liberation is achieved then work towards reconciliation between former enemies must begin. Seeking reconciliation without liberation is a betrayal of the oppressed. Yet liberation without reconciliation is unfinished.

---

67. Ibid., 18.

68. James Cone's analysis of the different roles played by the "uncompromising militancy" of Malcolm X and the commitment of Martin Luther King Jr. to nonviolence and the goal of eventual reconciliation with whites shows how these two emphases functioned in a constructive way to correct and complement each other in the black freedom struggle in the United States during the 1950s and 60s. At times both are needed. Cone, *Martin & Malcolm*, 262–71.

69. Volf, *Exclusion and Embrace*, 215.

FORGIVENESS AND ENFORCING A RIGHT

A similar tension exists in the way of Jesus between forgiveness and enforcing a right. The liberating praxis of Jesus is a call to uphold the rights of victims. In a religiously pluralistic world, this call is expressed by churches through support for human rights and, more recently, the rights of creation.[70] Yet the way of Jesus also includes a call to forgive others, thus relinquishing one's right and claim upon them.[71] This tension is not absolute. Like reconciliation, forgiveness can be a way towards liberation in some instances. In the example of Nelson Mandela noted above, "Mandela . . . saw the need to take the first step towards reconciliation, the step of forgiveness, as a means to restoring justice."[72] Forgiveness can be a creative act that victims take to reclaim their agency and dignity, a step towards liberating themselves from the indignity they have experienced.[73] Acts of violence degrade both victim and perpetrator, denying the dignity of both. Forgiveness can be an assertion of dignity on the part of a victim, when it is freely given by their own choice. At the same time it recognizes the image of God in the oppressor, their human dignity that their actions betrayed. Forgiveness, when freely given and freely accepted, can re-establish the dignity of both, creating the basis for a renewed relationship and a new future between the two. In a situation where oppression is increasingly costly for the oppressor, as it presents the possibility of a different future in which the status and power of oppressor and victim are changed so that they become partners rather than opponents and the dignity of both is preserved, forgiveness can create an opening to a future preferable to the present for both. In this way it can be a step towards liberation.

Yet forgiveness and reconciliation cannot take the place of liberation. While forgiveness can "interrupt the cycle of violence" between persons and peoples, if it leaves the conditions of oppression intact "it enables violators to continue to violate," and so "violates the gospel law of love."[74] For reconciliation to occur, there must be both liberation from oppression and then, hopefully, forgiveness of the wrongs that were

70. Moltmann, *On Human Dignity*, 19–35.

71. Gruchy, *Reconciliation*, 172.

72. Ibid., 179.

73. Baker-Fletcher, *Dancing with God*, 112.

74. Keller, *On the Mystery*, 116.

done. While forgiveness is an integral part of the way of Jesus, it cannot be demanded of someone and does not necessarily free the perpetrator from the consequences of their action.[75] While justice is something one is due, forgiveness is something one is given. As forgiveness is given in spite of the suffering a perpetrator has caused, and as it is received as a gift that could not be demanded, forgiveness mirrors the justice of God.

In the way of Jesus justice is not simply retributive or distributive, but creative and transformative.[76] The justice of God exemplified in Jesus meets people where they are and moves them to where they should be. Forgiveness fulfills this justice when it preserves the dignity of both victim and oppressor and yet effects reconciliation between them. Forgiveness goes beyond the justice that can be demanded, but must never obviate it.

Finally though, people may forgive those who have wronged them, regardless of how their forgiveness is received or if their situation as changed, because out of faithfulness or love for Jesus they do not wish to hold what they have suffered against the perpetrator. This becomes morally wrong if it leaves the perpetrator free to continue their violence. But in situations where a victim has little power in regards to those victimizing them, forgiveness can be an act of dignity and liberation, a way of asserting that one belongs ultimately to God rather than to one's victimizers, and a way of releasing oneself from fixation on them and what they have done. As such it maintains the tension between God's justice and the injustice victims suffer. Justice and forgiveness are both essential components of the reign of God and any lasting human relationships. Forgiveness is crucial in the reconciliation of enemies. It is also essential in any lasting friendship or working relationship.

LOVE OF SELF AND ENEMIES

A parallel tension between what is due to one's enemy and what is due to one's self and others exists in Jesus' call to love even one's enemies. This call is part of the radical inclusivity of Jesus' way. The commandments to love God and one's neighbor are central to this way.[77] Jesus' himself becomes the paradigm of this love, which is the measure by which all

75. Baker-Fletcher, *Dancing with God*, 114.

76. Tillich, *Theology of Culture*, 144.

77. Schillebeeckx, *Jesus*, 253.

actions are to be assessed.[78] Jesus sharpened the commandment to love by replacing neighbor with enemy, so that all persons, "equally and without exception," are to be objects of love.[79] The image in Matthew 5:45 of the sun rising "on the evil and on the good" indicates that love is to be oriented towards the "universal creation to which all of God's creatures belong."[80] The way to the reign of God, the community in which all peoples live together in justice and peace, and in peace with creation, is love, particularly of enemies. The command to love one's enemies is part of the intensifying and relaxing of the teachings of Torah that is characteristic of Jesus' teaching.[81] This was intended to consolidate the community's identity as one of love and enable the integration of the marginalized and excluded into it.[82] It is by practicing this that one becomes fully human, for the fullness of one's own humanity is bound up with the fullness of the humanity of others. As "'all life is interrelated,' justice for the others is—in spirit and in truth—a mode of self-care."[83]

Love for others, particularly for enemies, is not static or necessarily innocent. It may begin with charity, acting to preserve or save the life of the other. But if genuine it must move from acting for the other to openness to the other. Love involves openness even to the otherness of the enemy. In seeking reconciliation with them, it involves hearing their story and their understanding of oneself. This openness to others "stretches" one,[84] changing one's self-understanding and notions of truth and goodness. Yet while love involves a radical openness to the other, it also has boundaries, leading it to become resistance to injustice and refusal to acquiesce in abuse. To urge the humiliated, persecuted, and vulnerable to love their enemies without such boundaries is not loving towards them. The call to love others, even enemies, must have some guidelines so that it does not trap people in passive acceptance of abuse and injustice.

In Matthew's Gospel, Jesus is recorded as stating that the law and the prophets are summarized in the teaching "do to others as you would

78. Gnilka, *Jesus of Nazareth*, 242.

79. Becker, *Jesus of Nazareth*, 256, 255–56.

80. Ibid., 256.

81. Theissen and Merz, *Historical Jesus*, 361.

82. Ibid., 395.

83. Keller, *On the Mystery*, 116.

84. Ibid.

have them do to you" (Matt 7:12). The guiding principle here is that "self-love is the standard measure of love for neighbor."[85] Love of self here is meant to stimulate the ethical imagination by leading one to think of oneself as in the other's place. By this criterion, letting abusive or unjust actions towards oneself go unchallenged is not loving towards the abuser or oneself. Love involves respect for "the otherness and mystery of the beloved."[86] This respect for the other must become resistance to their actions when these violate their own essential personhood and that of others. The call to love one's enemies is intended to broaden the call to love others. It includes the call to love the vulnerable, which may include oneself.[87] It is violated when it leads to a refusal to resist injustice and evil.

In considering this it is important to note that acts of love rarely occur in a one-to-one relationship involving only oneself and another person. As people always exist in relationships, there are almost always others indirectly involved in any act of injustice besides the perpetrator and their victim. How actions will affect third parties must always be considered, as love is to extend to them as well. There will always have to be contextual and pragmatic judgments about what should be accepted and what resisted. When love becomes resistance to another, it must always be accompanied by openness to them as part of the "will to embrace." When sufficient liberation is achieved it must then lead to work towards reconciliation.

Jesus' call to love others may involve self-sacrifice even to the point of death. The twentieth century has seen a number of Christian martyrs unequaled since the persecutions of the early church.[88] Many of these were brought on by the martyrs' faithfulness to Jesus' call to love others in murderous situations. For some perhaps such death comes as a fulfillment of their person, a yes to God in a context demanding radical discipleship. Yet most twentieth century martyrs died as victims of murder, often murder sanctioned by the state. While their faithfulness is exemplary and moving, their murders were crimes that should have been prevented. Martyrdom should never be deliberately sought, for this violates love of oneself and others. Love inevitably involves sacrifice of

85. Gnilka, *Jesus of Nazareth*, 243.

86. Craigo-Snell, *Silence, Love, and Death*, 94.

87. Ricoeur, *Oneself as Another*, 339.

88. Moltmann, *Way of Jesus Christ*, 197.

some kind. But love that disregards the value of what it sacrifices violates Jesus' call to love others as oneself.

CONCLUSION

For many middle- and upper-class Christians in North Atlantic nations, the greatest challenge of the way of Jesus is not to love their enemy, but to love the poor, those whose lives have little value in the globalized economy. Their lack of power and the insensitivity of the middle and upper classes render them invisible,[89] though their sufferings are real. Though compassion has become a prominent value in Western societies, it is often a compassion of charity, not a compassion that seeks justice. The way of Jesus demands the latter, and this requires a restructuring of the global economy. For the middle and upper classes of North Atlantic nations, the greatest threat facing them lies in the damage to the environment wrought by their own civilization and lifestyle. In the context of the environmental crisis we are our own worst enemies. The call to love our enemy here is a call to love ourselves through repentance and conversion to solidarity with the poor and to a sustainable lifestyle. Such love involves genuine sacrifice, but sacrifice for the sake of a deeper and a richer life together.

The way of Jesus is life-giving, according to Jesus and many who have followed him. Yet it is also very demanding. Jesus' teaching involved a heightening of ethical demands such that "the imitation of God usually required of kings and the powerful is called for in the form of generosity and renunciation of power on the part of those who are powerless, persecuted and humiliated."[90] With this heightened demand comes a heightened status: those who follow Jesus are sons and daughters of God. As such they should act with confidence befitting those who know that their future as members of the royal family is secure. Heightened ethical norms can be sustained, however, even in principle, only if they are accompanied by strong moral sources.[91] In the ethical teachings of Jesus in the gospels a radicalized ethic is often juxtaposed with a realistic ethic. This juxtaposing seems to reflect an awareness of the difficulty of fulfilling the radical ethic. This awareness gives rise to the need for

89. Sobrino, *No Salvation outside the Poor*, 28.

90. Theissen and Merz, *Historical Jesus*, 393.

91. Taylor, *Secular Age*, 695–703.

a realistic ethic, but also to the recognition that those who follow the way of Jesus need grace[92] and ethical empowerment. This came in part through Jesus' death and resurrection. The next three chapters will study three classic ways of understanding the saving significance of Jesus' death and resurrection, examining how they function as strong moral sources empowering people to live in his way.

92. Theissen, *Religion of the Earliest Churches*, 30.

6 Jesus' Moral Influence and Its Saving Significance

Jesus is to many an attractive figure who gives joy, ethical guidance, and spiritual comfort. But as Jesus gives to people he also calls them to follow him. The gifts Jesus gives contain this call. These gifts are not contingent on people following him, but they are only fully experienced as people do, and they are the means by which he empowers people to do so. In a sense his call is one of his gifts.

The way of Jesus that he calls people to follow has its attractions but is challenging and demanding. People need grace and empowerment to follow it. Jesus provides this through what has traditionally been called his work of atonement. The doctrine of the atonement traditionally describes how Jesus saves people from sin and reconciles them to God. Through his atoning work Christ moves people from a state of alienation or separation from God to union with God. In looking at (1) Jesus as the word of God and (2) the way of Jesus, we have already ventured into this topic. As the word of God, Jesus saves by revealing God's presence and nature, thus overcoming a lack of awareness or a false image of the divine that can separate people from God. Through his ministry Jesus saves by showing people how to live, so that their lives become more in accord with God's will. As "the multiplicity of images used in the New Testament to describe the atonement suggests,"[1] Jesus saves in more than one way and from more than one kind of sin or evil.

Jesus' followers are also not all the same.[2] They come from different cultural backgrounds and live in different social locations. They face different challenges in following Jesus, have different resources at their disposal, and need different kinds of empowerment. Moreover, those who seek to follow Jesus frequently have complex identities. They may

1. Stroup, *Why Jesus Matters*, 67.
2. Fulkerson, *Changing the Subject*, 356–57.

be oppressors to some, oppressed by others, and icons of encourage-
ment to others. No one understanding of Jesus' saving significance can
adequately address the whole of the human condition or even all the
challenges of one person's life.

Consequently people need different kinds of empowerment to follow Jesus. Some need their hardness of heart removed and their moral
vision expanded. Others made fragile by sufferings need to be strengthened.[3] Some need hope. Others need forgiveness. The one Jesus works in
different ways to provide these different kinds of empowerment.[4] Each
way is articulated through a different type of atonement theory. Though
one may be most appropriate in a particular context, these different
theories can complement, correct, and enhance each other.[5]

This chapter and the next two will each analyze a different way of
understanding Jesus' saving significance. These are sometimes referred
to as the moral influence, the Christus Victor, and the substitutionary
theories of atonement.[6] Each will be studied in terms of the kind of evil
or sin they address, the way they address it, and how they can correct
and supplement each other as moral sources empowering people to follow Jesus. A moral source is something that moves one to do what is
good. Each of these theories presents a distinctive understanding of how
Jesus does this.

THE MORAL INFLUENCE THEORY OF ATONEMENT

This chapter studies the moral influence theory of atonement, often associated with the medieval theologian Abelard (1079–1142).[7] We begin
with it because it focuses on how Jesus moves people to follow him. The
primary concern of Abelard and contemporary theologians like Carter
Heyward[8] who emphasize the saving significance of Jesus' moral influence is with how Jesus empowers people to follow him by awakening

3. Keller, *On the Mystery*, 97.

4. Schmiechen, *Saving Power*, 331.

5. Ibid., 340.

6. This typology is frequently attributed to Gustav Aulén's influential book *Christus Victor*. Aulén acknowledges the distinctive focus of Abelard's atonement theory here but devotes little space to it (ibid., 112–13).

7. For an overview of Abelard's understanding of Jesus' saving significance, see Weingart, *Logic of Divine Love*.

8. Heyward, *Saving Jesus*, 8.

within them an eros, a desire and energy, to express in their own lives the love of God that they see in him. This is one of the ways in which Jesus empowers people to follow him. The saving significance of Jesus extends beyond what he moves people to do, yet this is a crucial part of it.[9] People cannot be reduced to their actions. But if our lives are not changed by Jesus, "we can drop the christological question."[10]

Each atonement theory studied in this chapter and the next two focuses on Jesus' death or death and resurrection. But there are precedents in his public ministry to what each sees the saving significance of his death to be. According to the Gospels Jesus spent much of his ministry wooing people for the reign of God, telling parables and teaching about it so as to move them to seek it. In examining the moral influence theory of atonement, we begin by looking at how Luke presents Jesus attempting to impart his moral vision through telling the parable of the Good Samaritan. We then look at how this "teller of parables" became "for those who have ears to hear and eyes to see, the parable of God."[11]

WHY DID JESUS TELL PARABLES?

Reading through the gospels one finds Jesus encouraging and empowering people to seek the reign of God and instructing them in this through telling parables. Luke 10:25–37 is an example of this. In this passage a lawyer asks Jesus what he must do to inherit eternal life. Jesus answers by asking what is written or taught in Jewish law, the Torah or Pentateuch, the first five books of the Hebrew Bible or Old Testament. The lawyer responds by quoting what is known as the Shema, found in Deuteronomy 6:5, the command to love God with all one's heart, soul, strength, and mind; and Leviticus 19:18b, the command to one's neighbor as one's self (Luke 10:27).[12] Jesus is shown as affirming the correctness of this answer drawn from Torah. The joining of these two commandments as a summary statement of how one should live subsequently became normative for Christianity.

---

9. Placher, *Jesus the Savior*, 131.

10. Soelle, *Thinking about God*, 103.

11. Keller, *On the Mystery*, 155.

12. Fitzmyer, *Luke X–XXIV*, 880. In Matthew it is a lawyer (Matt 22:34–40) who asks Jesus this question and in Mark it is a scribe. Jesus replies with the answer attributed by Luke to the lawyer.

It is important to note that from the perspective of the Lucan Jesus here there is nothing deficient or pernicious about Judaism. The Lucan Jesus responds to the lawyer, "You have given the right answer; do this, and you will live" (Luke 10:28). Though the parable of the Good Samaritan that follows has often been a springboard for anti-Semitism, Jesus as described here affirms the opposite: the teaching and resources of Judaism are sufficient for salvation.

The lawyer then asks, "Who is my neighbor?" (Luke 10:29). Jesus answers with a story, the parable of the Good Samaritan. Assuming the narrative unity of this passage as found in Luke's Gospel,[13] one can ask, why did Jesus answer this question with a story, and not a statement of principle? One might answer that the parable of the Good Samaritan "unmasks the lawyer's effort to justify himself," through illustrating that it is not proximity to someone that makes one their neighbor, but actions of love that create relations of neighborliness.[14] But why did Jesus tell a story when he could have given a more brief and direct answer, as the lawyer did to him?

The parable of the Good Samaritan may have been joined to the incident of the lawyer's question by the author of Luke. But Jesus did tell parables and stories, like many other religious leaders before him and since. Why did he do this? On one level, the answer lies in studying the historical Jesus, the movement gathered around him, and the Jewish matrix of both. But many parables of Jesus are still recounted today. They still awaken eros for the kingdom and inform people's moral views. This points to another answer deriving from the nature of moral sources or goods and how they are perceived.

A moral source or good is something that moves one to act morally. People are only moved by these as they become present to them through being articulated in some way.[15] The power of a moral good to move someone depends not only on what it is, but also on how it is articulated or presented. A particular moral good articulated in a certain way will resonate more with some people and less with others, depending on their social location, worldview, and personal characteristics.[16]

13. Only Luke has joined the parable of the Good Samaritan to this exchange (Fitzmyer, *Luke X–XXIV*, 882–83).

14. Ibid., 884.

15. Taylor, *Sources of the Self*, 91.

16. For a study of this in a congregational setting, see Fulkerson, *Places of Redemption*, 92–125.

Moral goods like justice or compassion can be articulated discursively, through summary statements, analytical concepts, and explanatory reasoning; or artistically, through drama, painting, parables, and such. These two kinds of presentation are distinct yet intertwined. There is an aesthetic dimension to any discursive reasoning and there is always discursive reasoning at work in any artistic endeavor. Yet a story is different from a concise definition such as the lawyer gave in answer to the question of how one should live (Luke 10:27). A story like the parable of the Good Samaritan calls for the kind of interpretation that a definition provides. What a story narrates or presents may exemplify what terms like "love" or "neighbor" define, but its presentation is less direct. It must be interpreted by those to whom it is addressed. This requires activating one's own convictions, powers of observation, and reasoning in order to arrive at its meaning. The identity of the person addressed is thus involved in discerning the truth of a work of art, so that understanding the meaning conveyed by this form of presentation is more self-involving for those addressed by it than a concise definition. A definition can be given to a person. But interpreting a story or work of art is a self-involving process that "always has an identity cost."[17] King David is reported to have discovered this through interpreting the prophet Nathan's story (2 Sam 12:1–13).

An artistic presentation can articulate a moral good in a way that a concise definition cannot, and vice versa. The two supplement each other. The moral good presented in a story like the parable of the Good Samaritan needs conceptual definition so that its meaning can be summarized and applied in other domains. Yet the meaning of a story like that of the Good Samaritan can never be exhaustively expressed in abstract terms. In some ways its meaning is bound up with its form of expression.[18] This intrinsic relationship between form and content in a work of art means there is a surplus of meaning in the parables of Jesus such that their meaning is never exhausted in the best of interpretations. They continue to stimulate thought and the ethical imagination, so that people return to interpret them again and again. This characteristic of religious symbols and stories is classically expressed in the phrase, "the symbol gives rise to thought."[19]

---

17. Taylor, "Gadamer on Human Sciences," 141.

18. Fulkerson, *Changing the Subject*, 178.

19. Ricoeur, *Symbolism of Evil*, 348.

Returning to the question of why Jesus and other religious leaders tell parables and stories, we can answer that, first of all, this kind of communication is often able to articulate the beauty of a moral good in a way that a concise statement of principle cannot. By presenting the beauty of the good, an artistic articulation can awaken eros for it. The parable of the Good Samaritan illustrates this. The beauty of the moral good depicted in this parable has moved many to express its meaning in their own lives despite obstacles in their way. The desire this parable can awaken can create an energy for the moral life that previously was not present. As well, through its surplus of meaning a story like the parable of the Good Samaritan can become a permanent stimulus to one's ethical imagination. The moral influence of Jesus functions in much the same way.

The gospels and other New Testament writings tell the story of Jesus in part so as to move people to follow him. Through their accounts, Jesus the teller of parables has become part of a story told by others, a figure who can awaken an eros to follow him, to express in one's own life the love of God that he expressed in his. This was Abelard's emphasis in his understanding of Jesus' saving significance:

> Through this unique act of grace manifested to us—in that his Son has taken upon himself our nature and persevered therein in teaching us by word and example even unto death'—he has more fully bound us to himself by love; with the result that our hearts should be enkindled by such a gift of divine grace, and true charity should not now shrink from enduring anything for him.[20]

Through his public ministry and death Jesus demonstrated the beauty of God's love. His demonstration can move people to seek to express this love and beauty in their own lives. In this way Jesus exercises a moral influence that can move people to follow him.

Carter Heyward describes the effect of this influence when she writes of how "something about Jesus seemed to make me glad simply to be alive and part of something much larger than myself."[21] Mark Lewis Taylor notes how the story of Jesus, as narrated in Mark's Gospel, has the power to move people to resist the powers of empire.[22] James Poling offers a case study in which the story of Jesus provided a moral framework and impetus for a nine-year-old boy who witnessed school yard bullying.[23] Dorothee Soelle and Luis Schottroff write of how Jesus "changes the consciousness of people," giving them hope, moral insight, and the courage to act.[24] These are all examples of how there is an aesthetic power in the story of Jesus as recorded in the Gospels that enables it to exercise a moral influence on people. This power has not diminished with time.

LOVE AND SUFFERING IN THE MORAL EXAMPLE OF JESUS.

A persuasive argument has been made for a broadening the focus of the moral influence theory to Jesus' life, rather than restricting it to just his death.[25] This is necessary as Jesus' ministry also functions as a powerful moral influence. This broadening also clarifies that what Jesus exemplifies is the beauty of love that enhances the well-being of peoples' lives. But it is not a case of choosing between Jesus' ministry and his death on the cross, because there was an intrinsic relationship between the two. Jesus' ministry was a significant factor leading to his death.[26] The love of God for humanity demonstrated in his public ministry was also demonstrated in his willingness to die for his proclamation of the reign of God. Jesus' demonstration of God's love for humanity culminates in his death in terms of what it cost him. It is not suffering that is glorified here, but love that is willing to endure suffering for the beloved.[27] Suffering per se is not part of the moral good of God's love that Jesus demonstrates, though it can be confused with it. For this reason the eros Jesus awakens, like any eros, needs to be accompanied by careful moral discernment.[28]

The image of Jesus' suffering love has enabled people to see meaning in their suffering resulting from service and care for others. This can be empowering when such suffering must be accepted. But seeing meaning in suffering can function as an opiate if it leads people to accept what should be resisted.[29] Jesus demonstrated the love of God that seeks justice in an unjust world. This provoked resistance leading to his death

23. Poling, "Cross and Male Violence," 55–60.

24. Soelle and Schottroff, *Jesus of Nazareth*, 140.

25. Young, "Beyond Moral Influence."

26. Theissen and Merz, *Historical Jesus*, 466–68.

27. Love, "In Search of Non-Violent Atonement," 211–13.

28. Sands, "Uses of the Thea(o)logian," 21.

29. Kyung, *Struggle to be the Sun*, 54.

on the cross. However, it cannot be pointed out too often that this suffer-ing was a consequence of his love and struggle for justice, not the goal or purpose of it.[30] Suffering is intrinsic to love in a world of injustice, but it is never something to be sought or celebrated for its own sake.

Still the danger remains that Jesus' cross can be seen as presenting suffering as something necessary or good, because through his resurrec-tion it has become "a two-edged symbol—at once a symbol of the human capacity for violence and a symbol of God's power in Jesus Christ to over-come evil, hatred, and suffering."[31] As Jesus' cross symbolizes both, there is always the danger that these two meanings may become confused. Jesus' public ministry can function as an essential safeguard against this. When Jesus called people to take up their cross he was not affirming suf-fering as a good in itself, but urging them to join him in seeking God's reign. The suffering Jesus calls people to in taking up their cross is a con-sequence of their choice to join him. It is provoked by their resistance to evil, not inflicted on them as passive victims. The intention behind taking on this suffering is that by doing so one works to deliver others from oppression that causes them suffering and, following that, to help effect reconciliation between former victims and oppressors.[32] Understanding Jesus' death as a consequence of his public ministry should prevent him from becoming an image that makes suffering in itself holy.

Recognizing that attributing saving significance to Jesus' cross can sacralize violence, legitimate abuse, and encourage passive acceptance of it, some theologians have attempted to develop nonviolent theories of atonement that do not see Jesus' suffering as having saving signifi-cance.[33] This will be discussed more fully in chapter 8. Here it must suffice to note that though Jesus' cross has sometimes been claimed to legitimize suffering as something to be embraced and accepted, still a moral or spiritual source does not necessarily become invalid if it has been misappropriated in ways that lead "to suffering or destruction."[34] Even though Jesus' cross has been misappropriated in destructive ways, it at the same time has been and continues to be a powerful moral influ-ence moving people to express the love of God for others in their own

30. Heyward, *Saving Jesus*, 138.
31. Baker-Fletcher, *Dancing with God*, 97.
32. Jennings Jr., *Transforming Atonement*, 106–8.
33. Love, "In Search of Non-Violent Atonement," 197.
34. Taylor, *Sources of the Self*, 519.

lives. The misuse of Jesus' cross to legitimate suffering calls not for its dismissal as a moral source, but for a retrieval of its context within Jesus' public ministry and his proclamation of the reign of God,[35] so that these help clarify its meaning and prevent its misuse.

The attempt to rid one's religious tradition of bias and morally objectionable elements is part of the task of Christian theology. But demanding innocent moral sources that cannot have destructive consequences is a mistake, as it is doubtful if such exist. A moral source by its very nature is powerful. Wherever there is power there is the danger of misuse and destructive consequences. Destructive misappropriations of Jesus' cross and moral example need to be critiqued. But critics who only see Jesus' cross as a destructive moral source should also attend to how it has frequently empowered and sustained victims of oppression.[36]

The search for an innocent moral vision can itself be destructive as it can lead to the removal of so many moral sources that the human spirit is stifled.[37] The result may be human communities with high moral standards but without moral sources to sustain them. Without such sources, high moral standards can collapse or become perverted.[38] Though one must continually strive for a better understanding of one's moral sources, there is no escape from the ambiguity of the human condition, which affects all moral sources and appropriations of them. Instead of seeking an innocent moral source, it is better to draw upon several to mutually strengthen and correct each other. In relation to Jesus' cross, this can be done by relating Jesus' cross and resurrection to his public ministry and his proclamation of the coming reign of God.

THE LOCATION AND FORM OF THE SIN AND EVIL THAT JESUS' MORAL EXAMPLE OVERCOMES

Atonement theories describe how Jesus effects a change that has saving significance. The change Jesus' moral influence effects is located initially in the human mind and will, in terms of what one knows and loves. Changing this changes how a person acts. The figure of Jesus as portrayed in the gospels and in hymns, sermons, liturgies, movies, and

35. Carbine, "Contextualizing the Cross," 105.
36. Terrell, "Our Mothers' Gardens," 45–47.
37. Taylor, *Sources of the Self,* 520.
38. Ibid., 516.

books presents the good news that God is love, frequently in ways depicting its beauty. This does three things. Jesus' revelation of God's love through his actions remedies ignorance or fear of God. The beauty of his example creates a desire in people to express God's love in their own lives and empowers them to do so. His example models the nature of love and the meaning of life.

What Jesus' ministry and death exemplify is a moral good of a higher order, a "hypergood" that provides the standpoint from which other moral goods are "weighed, judged, decided about."[39] An essential feature of such is that as one recognizes it for the surpassing moral good that it is, one is moved by it.[40] The recognition of its surpassing nature awakens a desire and energy to participate in it and express it in one's own life. To know Jesus as the Christ is to be moved to follow him. To recognize the love of God exemplified in his life is to be moved to express it in one's own. It is through moving people to follow him that Jesus as a moral influence liberates them from self-enclosed worlds, from idols, demonic loves, false self-images, and apathy lodged in one's heart and mind.

This liberation is essential because human beings have a tendency to overvalue themselves and what they love. In a world of scarce resources this leads people to seek the well-being of themselves and the people and things they love "at the expense of other life."[41] As well, in order to function as human beings people need a horizon of values, some notion of the good that gives them guidance and direction. This need creates an openness for the heart and mind to be captured by false images like those promoted by the marketing forces of globalized capitalism or the propaganda of empires. No heart is free of the tendency to overvalue one's self and one's own, or untouched by the powerful images of a consumer or imperial culture. Conversely, one may be afflicted by a lack of will or love, a lack of vision and a failure to recognize one's own potential, resulting from socialization or other factors, leading to a failure to exercise one's potential to do the good.[42] The potential to contribute may

39. Ibid., 63.

40. Ibid., 73. Taylor argues that it is necessary to add that we are moved by hypergoods "'in a complex way,' because we never think of these things entirely on our own and monologically" (ibid.). One's culture, social location, and personal characteristics inevitably influence the way and extent to which one is moved by Jesus and how one seeks to follow his way.

41. Niebuhr, *Nature and Destiny*, 1:182.

42. Plaskow, *Sex, Sin, and Grace*, 167–68.

be present, but for whatever reason, one does not see it or one lacks the will to actualize it. Both the strong will that misdirects one's potential and the weak will that fails to actualize it can be transformed by Jesus' moral influence.

The liberation Jesus offers as a moral influence is a transformation of one's heart and mind that one cannot effect by one's self. Yet this liberation takes effect through the exercise of one's freedom. While the human will is free to choose, its choices are always constrained and directed by what it loves and believes. It may love more than one thing and be conflicted between several loves. But one's choices are always determined by what one loves and believes. Moral influence theories of atonement focus on how Jesus overcomes sin or disorder internal to human hearts and minds by changing what one loves and what one believes to be possible. The transformed mind and heart continue to function as before, but now are guided more by an eros to express in one's own life the love of God demonstrated by Jesus. One acts freely, but one's freedom has been enlarged and redirected by the love Jesus awakens within one.

The condition of sin that Jesus' moral influence saves one from is limited in scope. Jesus' moral influence only directly affects one's will. Still the disorder of one's will can be multifaceted. It can be ignorance, a wrong or distorted love, apathy and a false self-image, or a combination thereof. As a result of any or all of these false loves and misperceptions, one's potential is not exercised or is exercised in harmful ways. Jesus liberates one from this condition by his demonstration of God's love, which corrects one's misunderstanding of love and awakens a desire to express God's love in one's own life.

The moral influence theory of atonement is often criticized for restricting the scope of Jesus' saving significance to the human mind and will.[43] Jesus' moral influence alone is insufficient to effect the fullness of salvation. Abelard did not restrict Jesus' saving significance to only this, but this is what he emphasized. What Abelard's theory highlights is how Jesus effects a particular kind of salvation in a particular but very

---

43. In reviewing the use of this atonement theory in neo-Protestant Christology in Europe, Wolfhart Pannenberg notes "the modesty of its soteriological interest. The neo-Protestant theologians are concerned only with making possible the humanness of life on earth. They are no longer concerned with the conquest of death and with the theme of resurrection, and they deal with the question of the forgiveness of sins only in the sense that the possibility for every individual's overcoming sin derives from Jesus" (Pannenberg, *Jesus*, 45).

significant part of creation: human minds and hearts. Though the locus of the saving effect of Jesus' moral influence is limited to this, it offers a liberation essential for human fulfillment. The transformation of one's heart and mind is indispensable for salvation.

The distinctiveness and importance of this locus in which the moral influence of Jesus has its effect is illustrated by the following quotation from Martin Luther King Jr.:

> Desegregation will break down the legal barriers and bring men together physically, but something must touch the hearts and souls of men so that they will come tougher spiritually because it is natural and right. A vigorous enforcement of civil rights will bring an end to segregated public facilities, but it cannot bring an end to fears, prejudice, pride and irrationality, which are the barriers to a truly integrated society. These dark and demonic responses will be removed only as men are possessed by the invisible inner law which etches on their hearts the conviction that all men are brothers and that love is mankind's most potent weapon for personal and social transformation. True integration will be achieved by men who are willingly obedient to unenforceable obligations.[44]

As King notes, the external force of law can affect peoples' actions, but it cannot by itself bring an end to the inner disorder giving rise to racism. This is where the moral influence of Jesus has its effect. The mental state of an individual is always shaped and affected by the values and order of the society they live in. But as King notes, there is a distinction between the two. People are always influenced by the values and ideals of their social milieu, but they are not completely trapped by these. The moral influence of Jesus can dislodge one from the biases of one's upbringing and society, leading one to oppose these.

Changing a person's mind and heart requires a form of power different from the external force that can change social institutions.[45] This can be described as aesthetic power, the power of a parable, a painting, or a song to transform from within one's sense of self what one loves and one's energy to pursue it. Aesthetic power has distinct roles to play in the drama of redemption. It can help communicate a truth claim, help envision a more just social order, enliven and restrain a passion for justice,

---

44. King, *Where Do We Go*, 118.

45. Hall, *God and Human Suffering*, 95–103.

and serve as a means of resistance to evil when others are not available.[46] As a form of aesthetic power, the moral influence of Jesus goes where other aspects of his saving significance cannot reach. It does a crucial work that these others cannot do.

The holy strives "to include within itself the whole of life."[47] The whole of life includes the space within a person, their will and moral imagination, their heart and mind, which are as big in their own way as the space outside of them. Sanctification includes the making holy of these. In Christian terms the holy tries to include these inner spaces in part through Jesus' moral influence. The sanctification of the moral vision and will within a person also works towards the sanctification of the space outside of them.

The effect Jesus' moral influence can have on human minds and wills can lead to derivative changes in human cultures with far-reaching effects on the lives of others. The influence of stories such as that of Jesus on individuals can lead to these stories and their symbols gaining a formative status in the life of a community. For instance, while Canada is officially a multicultural country and no longer "Christian," Christianity continues to exercise a powerful influence on Canadian society.[48] Stories like that of Jesus can become "representative facts of a particular culture,"[49] having a paradigmatic function within them, helping define the moral nature of reality and moving people to act. In this way stories can become formative realities helping shape the societies in which they hold a key place.[50] Though they are only stories, in this way they can come to have an objective cultural reality.

Every person, people, and society lives by some stories or myths. What these are is an important question. Equally important is how they are lived out.[51] The cultural presence of Jesus, like that of every hypergood, is inherently ambiguous. Its meaning depends partly on how it is appropriated. This requires scrutiny, particularly in light of the experiences of society's vulnerable members. The figure of Jesus can be

46. Schweitzer, "Place for Aesthetics," 1–5.
47. Buber, "God and Man," 571.
48. Bramadat and Seljak, "Toward a New Story," 224.
49. Tracy, *Blessed Rage for Order*, 216.
50. Baum, *Religion and Alienation*, 241–49.
51. Ruether, "What I Have Learned from Buddhism," 148, 186.

appropriated in ways that are baneful[52] or that are a blessing. One task of Christians is to see that it is more of the latter than the former.

Within history Jesus' sanctifying influence on peoples' inner space is never complete. This means that people need not only to be empowered by Jesus' moral example but also to be restrained by it from following the eros of destructive pleasures. Jesus urges people to break some boundaries,[53] as in his parable of the Good Samaritan, which teaches that the breadth of one's responsibility to care for others "is, in principle, unlimited."[54] But his moral influence should also check people from breaking boundaries that maintain the dignity and safety of themselves and others.

The self and the culture surrounding it remain sites of struggle between the influence of Jesus and those like him and influences leading elsewhere. The figure of Jesus also remains a site of struggle over what kind of personal and cultural influence he will exercise. The continuing nature of this struggle points to the insufficiency of the moral influence theory on its own to empower people to follow Jesus, for it leaves the outcome of Jesus' work uncertain. The history of the twentieth century does not suggest that human potential alone, enlivened and guided by the influence of Jesus and others, can achieve a fully meaningful life. The struggle for justice cannot be sustained by love alone. It also requires hope of an ultimate fulfillment. This means that the limited scope of the moral influence theory needs to be supplemented by the Christus Victor theory, which articulates how Jesus brings this hope. We turn to this in the next chapter.

PARTICULAR CONTRIBUTIONS OF THE MORAL INFLUENCE THEORY TO UNDERSTANDING JESUS' SAVING SIGNIFICANCE

The moral influence theory of atonement makes a particular contribution to understanding Jesus' saving significance in its emphasis on Jesus' demonstration of God's love and how he moves people to love themselves and others in response to this. This theory states more clearly than others that the goal of Jesus' saving work is the communication of God's love

52. Davies, *Crucified Nation*, 109–14.

53. Heyward, *Saving Jesus*, 139–41.

54. Metz, *Love's Strategy*, 170.

and its further expression by those who receive it. It understands salvation as humanity finding fulfillment in expressing love for one another, for God, and for creation. In this theory justification and sanctification blend together because the change Jesus effects is in the way people act. This blending can be a weakness unless this atonement theory is complemented by others emphasizing that God justifies and accepts people in spite of their sin. But this weakness is also a strength. It shows that justification is incomplete without sanctification. The two need to be distinguished but they should never be separated. Justification is oriented towards sanctification even when sanctification fails to appear.

The moral influence theory also lifts up the relational nature of Jesus' person and work. Because of its orientation towards the effect Jesus has on people, the way he changes lives, the moral influence theory highlights the intrinsic connection between Jesus being the Christ and those who receive him as such. Jesus is not a hero who saves while others watch. He does do things for people that they cannot do for themselves, but the dynamics of his moral influence make clear that his saving significance only becomes fully effective through the exercise of the freedom of those who receive him. There are dialogical and relational aspects intrinsic to Jesus' identity as the Word of God. In the end Jesus does not fully save without the assent of those he seeks to save. In this particular respect, the hope of salvation rests on a particular aspect of the power of God's love: its beauty.

7 Jesus as a Source of Ultimate Hope

Throughout the New Testament there sounds a note of joyful assurance. Paul expresses this at the close of Romans 8 when he writes,

> Who will separate us from the love of Christ? Will hardship, or distress, or persecution, or famine, or nakedness, or peril, or sword? As it is written "For your sake we are being killed all day long; we are accounted as sheep to be slaughtered." No, in all these things we are more than conquerors through him who loved us. For I am convinced that neither death, nor life, nor angels, nor rulers, nor things present, nor things to come, nor powers, nor height, nor depth, nor anything else in all creation, will be able to separate us from the love of God in Christ Jesus our Lord. (Rom 8:35–39)

Here in "a jubilant hymn of praise to the love of God in Christ Jesus, Paul notes how victory has been gained for humanity over all things that might conceivably oppose it."[1]

The joyful assurance Paul writes of is expressed in the mode of hope. What Paul experiences in the Holy Spirit gives rise to testimony in words and actions, but it cannot be demonstrated through empirical analysis or laboratory tests. As this passage indicates there is an "in spite of" quality to this hope. Paul is confident that nothing can separate him or other Christians from God's love because of what God has done in Jesus Christ, despite the agonies, frustrations, and anxieties he experiences in daily life. Both are real. But Paul's overwhelming conviction is that the former is greater and that the latter will eventually give way to it. The suffering and injustices of life and their ultimate causes will pass away when creation becomes transformed into the new reality that has been promised in Jesus Christ. This hope is expressed in the midst of a struggle between God's love and the "rulers" and "powers." These terms

1. Fitzmyer, *Romans*, 529.

denote cosmic forces of evil, sin, and death[2] that take historical form in conquering armies, plagues, and disaster, in social or structural sins,[3] as well as in personal sins and afflictions.[4] This hope is cosmic in extent and eschatological in nature. It looks forward to the transformation of the existing world into a new creation in which sin and sorrow will be no more. This future can be experienced in the present through faith, so that even the worst experiences cannot separate one from God's love.

Paul is confident from what God has done in Jesus' death and resurrection that this ultimate future will come to be. A similar conviction is expressed elsewhere in the New Testament.[5] This conviction confers a new identity based upon God's love upon those who receive it. As this love has proved in Jesus' resurrection to be more powerful than sin and death, no created power can take this identity away. It comes as a gift from God, "won by Christ alone."[6] In turn it creates a moral necessity for those who accept it, to work towards the realization in history for themselves and all others of the freedom and well-being that they now know in faith. Faith in the ultimacy of God's love empowers one to love in the present.

The previous chapter noted that struggles for justice, the desire to live a moral life, cannot be sustained by eros or love of the good alone. As desire for the good encounters persistent, powerful, and destructive forms of radical evil and deeply entrenched sin, it can turn into despair, desperation, or contempt for those it claims to love. It is doubtful if compassion and resistance to evil can be sustained unless people believe themselves to be empowered by a transcendent moral source that gives meaning to their efforts even when these are unsuccessful. Otherwise their compassion is likely to degenerate into resentment and violence towards others, even those they claim to serve.[7] For this reason the moral influence of Jesus needs to be supplemented by another understanding

---

2. Ibid.

3. "Structural sins, then, are institutional realities, such as colonialism and imperialism, that create an unjust distribution of wealth, power, and recognition, and thus push a section of the population to the margin of society where their well-being or even their life is in danger" (Baum, "Structures of Sin," 112).

4. Russell, *Household of Freedom*, 78–89.

5. Matt 28:18–20; John 16:33.

6. Käsemann, *Romans*, 248.

7. Taylor, *A Secular Age*, 695–99.

of his saving significance that focuses on the ultimacy of his person and work. This is known as the Christus Victor theory of atonement.

The Christus Victor theory is associated with Gustaf Aulén, who championed it in an influential book by that name.[8] According to Aulén this theory has several essential features.[9] It understands the work of atonement as something that God has done for humanity and creation and that God alone could do. It involves a dramatic action on God's part. God enters into creation in a new way, encounters the forces of sin and evil and decisively overcomes them. This model conceives the world in the dualistic terms of a struggle between ultimate good and evil and salvation as the final victory of good over evil. We turn now to explore its strengths and weaknesses.

JESUS' PERSON AND WORK AS A DECISIVE EVENT

Christus Victor theories insist that an event of decisive significance took place involving Jesus' person. As Jesus' saving significance is bound up with what happened in his history, it can only be described by narrating this.[10] Theologically speaking, Jesus' history has its beginning in the self-diffusive nature of God's love and the assent of God's will to this being actualized. Jesus became incarnate in order to give God's goodness and beauty further expression in history. As he did so he inevitably came into conflict with sin and evil. This conflict is waged on personal and social levels in every society. According to the New Testament it occurred decisively in the public ministry, death, and resurrection of Jesus. From what can be known historically about Jesus' words and deeds, it seems he saw himself as "God's last emissary" whose actions would be instrumental in bringing in God's kingdom.[11] His public ministry took place in Galilee, a region fraught with social tension between (a) the upper and lower classes and (b) the Roman forces of occupation and resident Galileans. These tensions did not often irrupt into overt violence in Jesus' time, partly because of the severity of the threat that the dominant forces posed to any challengers. Jesus' charismatic religious authority also created tension between himself and more institutionalized Jewish

---

8. Aulén, *Christus Victor*.

9. Ibid., 50–51.

10. Barth, *Church Dogmatics* IV/3.1:165–66.

11. Sanders, *Historical Figure of Jesus*, 248.

authorities, particularly those in charge of the temple in Jerusalem. His public ministry put him on the side of the oppressed in the social conflicts of his time. His conflicts with the Roman and temple authorities resulted from his proclamation of the reign of God, for it left "no place for the rule of the temple aristocracy and the Romans."[12]

Jesus seems to have seen these conflicts occurring on the level of history as part of a more encompassing metaphysical conflict between God and the cosmic forces of evil, sin, and death.[13] These conflicts, historical and metaphysical, led to Jesus' death. Pilate had Jesus crucified to remove the threat he posed to the established social order. Jesus' resurrection was experienced by those who believed in it as God's vindication of Jesus' person and ministry.[14]

This series of events is interpreted in various ways throughout the New Testament. One early and continuing interpretation emphasized Jesus' resurrection as God's victory over suffering and death.[15] In Jesus' resurrection God overcame the cosmic powers of sin, evil, and death that Jesus had struggled with and inaugurated a new era in salvation history. This line of interpretation highlights the conflict between God and the forces that killed Jesus. It also tends to see the events of Jesus' ministry, death, and particularly his resurrection as effecting a change in reality that determines the ultimate destiny of every person and all creation.

In the patristic period of Christian theology these themes were prominent in various versions of what Aulén called the Christus Victor theory of the atonement, developed by theologians like Irenaeus, Origen, and Gregory of Nyssa. According to Aulén this understanding of Jesus' saving significance was superseded in the Middle Ages through the influence of Anselm's theory of vicarious substitution. In the modern era many theologians have favored versions of the moral influence theory of atonement. But versions of the Christus Victor theory of atonement have never been completely absent. These typically interpret the meaning of Jesus' death and resurrection in relation to metaphysical questions about the ultimate nature of reality. According to Paul Tillich, they address the anxiety of meaninglessness and emptiness arising from the threat of nonbeing, which is ever present in the transitory and contingent nature

12. Theissen and Merz, *Historical Jesus*, 467.

13. Wright, *Jesus*, 449.

14. Schüssler Fiorenza, *Jesus*, 112.

15. Schillebeeckx, *Christ*, 729.

of human life.[16] This anxiety surfaces whenever virtue and love fail to have effect and the meaningfulness of life is undermined by the threat of nonbeing. This anxiety can only be constructively born and love's meaningfulness realistically affirmed in the face of this threat on the basis of a power of being greater than one's own.

The Christus Victor theory attempts to articulate how this threat of nonbeing was overcome in principle through Jesus' death and resurrection. "In principle" means that while the destructive powers of sin and evil remain present and active, a decisive event has occurred that will lead to their disappearance. The Christus Victor theory of atonement affirms that this decisive event took place in the public ministry, death, and resurrection of Jesus Christ. It acknowledges the realities of sin, evil, and death but states that in Jesus' resurrection God's love was revealed to be ultimately more powerful than these. It affirms the meaningfulness of life and that the meaning of life is love. God's self-affirmation in the resurrection of the crucified Jesus reveals the ultimate power of God's love in relation to sin and death. This can give people a hope and assurance that makes possible their self-affirmation. It can give people joy in life and the courage to love. It reveals that events in history and daily life can have a lasting meaning.

The event-character of Jesus' death and resurrection is intrinsic to the Christus Victor theory's affirmation of life and history as ultimately meaningful, despite the destructive power of sin and evil. This theory uses mythical and symbolic terms to express the ultimate nature of what occurred in Jesus' death and resurrection, but it claims to interpret historical and eschatological events. Jesus' death and resurrection is not a metaphor for what always happens, but an event that did happen. The meaningfulness of life and love that this theory affirms is not presented as a myth or wishful idea, but as something revealed in the events of Jesus' death and resurrection and experienced in faith by those who accept Jesus as the Christ. In recent decades the Christus Victor theory has been developed in two different ways.

16. Tillich, *Courage to Be*, 47–51.

A MODERN TYPE OF THE CHRISTUS VICTOR THEORY

The Christus Victor theory has a predominantly "objective" emphasis.[17] Its focus has traditionally been on the resurrection of Jesus, an act of God that the New Testament reports but never attempts to describe. This was an event external to people that brought something new into reality. This event is not simply objective.[18] It has a subjective dimension: it reaches its goal as it empowers people to proclaim and follow Jesus. This event has occurred and is perceived and received now in faith, but will come to full effect in the future. The eschatological nature and cosmic scope of this hope mean that it can only be expressed in symbolic and mythological terms. With the rise of modern Western culture, in which "philosophy granted science a monopoly on truth in the market place of ideas,"[19] the idea of this kind of change and the mythological and symbolic ways in which it is expressed were discredited as unbelievable[20] or having no discernible reference to objective reality. Karl Rahner (1904–1984) and John Cobb Jr. (b. 1925) responded to this by developing a modern type of Christus Victor theory of atonement.

Karl Rahner

One of the aims of Rahner's theology was to bridge the chasm that had opened up between Roman Catholic Church teaching and the daily experience of Western Roman Catholics, to show how Christian faith could be credible within the worldview characteristic of Western modernity. What Aulén called the "classic" or Christus Victor theory of atonement was typically premised upon an Alexandrian understanding of the incarnation. The Word became incarnate by assuming human nature in the person of Jesus and in him encountered sin and death in a decisive way. Rahner acknowledged that this understanding of the incarnation belongs to the "Catholic Christianity's deposit of faith."[21] But he thought it did not sufficiently maintain the distinction of divinity and humanity in Jesus' person that the Chalcedonian Definition insisted on.[22] He

---

17. Tillich, *Systematic Theology*, 2:171.
18. Kelly, *Resurrection Effect*, 128–29.
19. West, *Prophesy Deliverance*, 28.
20. Bultmann, "New Testament and Mythology," 2–3.
21. Rahner, *Love of Jesus*, 55.
22. Ibid., 56.

also thought that its description of the incarnation had a mythological character that was a barrier to its intelligibility in the modern era.[23]
Rahner developed instead a modern understanding of the incarnation
reminiscent of Antiochene Christology's understanding of Jesus as the
second Adam.

According to Rahner, the history of the world is a history of God's
self-communication to creation, ultimately to humanity, and of humanity's response to this. Jesus was the human being in whom this process
reached its goal, through his unconditional solidarity with other human
beings and his "pure obedience to God."[24] This led to his death. Jesus
proclaimed his message as God's definitive self-communication to humanity. Jesus' resurrection was God's affirmation of this claim and Jesus'
faithfulness to it in dying on the cross.[25] In Jesus' unique faithfulness to
God and God's affirmation of this faithfulness in Jesus' resurrection, the
hypostatic union of God's Logos and Jesus' person occurred. With this
occurrence the hope of humanity for meaning in life that is not thwarted
by sin and death was answered in a final way, as God's salvific will became definitively expressed in history in Jesus' person, ministry, and
resurrection as "victorious and irreversible."[26] The hypostatic union of
God and humanity that took place in Jesus' person is the decisive event[27]
that gives to Christian faith assurance of salvation and the presence of
God's love that Paul celebrates in Romans 8.

John Cobb Jr.

John Cobb Jr. also sought to develop an understanding of Jesus' saving
significance that would be credible within the worldview of Western modernity. His early theology argued the legitimacy of faith in Jesus Christ
by showing how the structure of contemporary Western existence could
be traced to Jesus' proclamation of the coming reign of God and the

23. Rahner, "Jesus Christ," 196.

24. Rahner, *Love of Jesus*, 58. For Rahner this solidarity and obedience are intrinsically related (ibid., 71–72).

25. Rahner, *Foundations*, 266. At an earlier stage in his Christology, Rahner fol-
lowed a more Alexandrian understanding of the incarnation, arguing that the fate of
Jesus' person as one part of creation necessarily affects the fate of all the rest (Burke,
Reinterpreting Rahner, 138–39).

26. Rahner, *Foundations*, 255.

27. Ibid., 181.

experience of the Holy Spirit through faith in him.[28] Then the late 1960s brought a new awareness of the complicity of modern Western cultures in human oppression and environmental degradation and with this a new demand for meaningful images of hope.[29] Cobb drew upon the process philosophy of Alfred North Whitehead[30] to argue that the future is an indeterminate flux of possibilities in relation to the present. Within this flux the Logos of God, "the transcendent ground of order," presents a lure to humanity to realize a potential that goes beyond the present in terms of the beauty and goodness it makes actual.[31] The lure that the Logos offers makes possible a creative transformation of the present. "Christ" designates the incarnate Logos,[32] the presence of the Logos in events or persons in which its lure to a higher reality has been actualized to some extent and remains a continued invitation and stimulus to further transcendence. As nothing exists without incarnating the Logos to some degree, Christ is present in all things. Jesus though is the person who was so attentive and responsive to the Logos that it co-constituted his person together with his human self, so that he is *the* Christ.[33]

Writing in the aftermath of the 1960s, Cobb argued that the ambiguity of Western culture and Christian existence meant that both must be creatively transformed towards greater justice and peace.[34] The unity of Jesus' person with the divine Logos was grounds for hope "that what we now experience is not the final possibility for humanity."[35] The achievement of this unity in his person created a force field of attraction that still draws people to follow him. As people worship Jesus as the Christ, he becomes their point of orientation, their inspiration and guide in responding to the lure of the Logos in the present. As a source of the hope that people can respond to the Logos and that creative transformation is

28. Cobb, *Structure of Christian Existence*.

29. Cobb, *Christ in a Pluralistic Age*, 179–82.

30. For Cobb's overview of Whitehead's process philosophy, see Cobb and Griffin, *Process Theology*, 13–29.

31. Cobb, *Christ in a Pluralistic Age*, 75. This kind of lure is extended to every actual occasion.

32. Ibid., 142.

33. Ibid.

34. Ibid., 183–84.

35. Ibid., 184.

possible, Jesus gives meaning to human existence and empowers people to seek creative transformation in the present.

Both Rahner and Cobb see the self-communication of God or the Logos to be at work in all dimensions of reality. They also do not hold optimistic visions of history. Jesus is a source of hope despite the sins and sufferings of humanity and the travail of creation. But both argue that in Jesus' person the ambiguity of human existence was overcome in principle. Here a new unity was achieved between God and humanity. This decisive event is a source of hope for the rest of creation. It points to a final fulfillment and meaningful future yet to come and empowers people to love others, accept themselves, forgive those who wrong them, and work for peace and justice.

THE EVENT-CHARACTER OF JESUS' RESURRECTION

For Rahner and Cobb the decisive event that is a source of ultimate hope happens in the person of Jesus and his influence on others. In emphasizing what happens in Jesus' person they follow patristic theologians who pioneered the Christus Victor theory of atonement. These too tended to see salvation as "the union, the living interpenetration of God and humanity that is first fully realized"[36] in Jesus' own person. This union is the basis of the ultimate hope that Jesus brings. But this hope comes not just from what Jesus was in himself, but from the things he did and that happened to him. The union of divinity and humanity in Jesus' person has saving significance because of his public ministry that it gave rise to and the events of his death and resurrection that his person was involved in. The event-character that the Christus Victor theory celebrates is not confined to the interaction within his person between his will and God's. It has its basis in the unity of these in his person. But Jesus' ministry, death, and resurrection were not just events through which this unity occurred in his person. They were also events that happened through and to his person.

The Christus Victor theory of atonement is about the conflict between God's love and the cosmic powers of sin, evil, and death. This conflict takes place within people, in their struggles to be faithful to God. But it is not confined to there. These powers are not only present within people's minds. They are also objective factors in reality that press down

36. Daley, "'He Himself Is Our Peace,'" 173.

upon people from without, holding them captive. For instance, white racism, against which James Cone developed a Christus Victor interpretation of Jesus' saving significance,[37] can enter into the minds of people, becoming something they must struggle against internally. But it does not exist only in peoples' minds. It is also an objective social factor that no amount of virtue or effort on the part of individuals can overcome.

Objective social factors like poverty, racism, anti-Semitism, or homophobia affect the lives of those upon whom they press down. The conflicts between God and the historical equivalents to these present-day social factors in Jesus' time were played out not only in Jesus' mind and soul, but also on his body and on those of others. Jesus' death was not simply a trial in which he proved faithful to God. It was also a shattering of his person,[38] mentally, spiritually, and physically. His resurrection was not simply God's affirmation of his perfect obedience. It was "above all a liberating action"[39] on God's part, in which God liberated the victim Jesus from the power of death. The cosmic powers of evil, sin, and death which Jesus saw himself to be opposed to are seen in the New Testament to be overcome partly through his faithfulness, but moreover through God's faithfulness to him in raising him from the dead. Jesus is a source of ultimate hope because of what happened in him, but also because of what happened to him, first in his undergoing crucifixion and then in his being liberated through resurrection to new life. Both are essential to his being a source of ultimate hope.

The threat of nonbeing is overcome for Christians through the event of Jesus' death and resurrection, the meaning of which is perceived in faith. While the meaning of this is received and takes effect subjectively within a person, its meaningfulness depends upon its character as an event. The moral character of the individual Jesus was crucial to the meaning of this event. It was Jesus who was vindicated through resurrection by God, not Pilate. Jesus' resurrection vindicates the moral values that his person embodied in conflict with the power of Rome. But crucial to the vindication of Jesus is the objectivity of what happened to him in his resurrection. Jesus did not simply rise in the faith of his followers who continued his mission despite his death. The assurance that Paul describes in Romans 8 is not simply an expression of determination on his

37. Cone, *God of the Oppressed*, 232.
38. Johnson, *She Who Is*, 158.
39. Sobrino, *Christ the Liberator*, 80.

part to continue the work of Jesus. It is first of all a celebration of what God has done, apart from Paul and anyone else, in raising Jesus from the dead. This act of God in turn empowers action on Paul's part. Paul's assurance was based on what he believed to be an event that happened apart from him, equal to creation out of nothing and definitive of who and what God is (Rom 4: 17). This event was also done for him and all others. These two aspects of Jesus' resurrection are fundamental to the Christus Victor theory of atonement.

The objectivity of Jesus' death is not in question. The objectivity of his resurrection is impossible to prove and remains open to doubt in light of its uniqueness and the continuing presence of sin and evil in the world. Jesus' resurrection was not a historical event in a strict sense, but an eschatological event that impinged upon history, leaving traces of its occurrence in the worshipping community. Jesus is a source of ultimate hope because in his death and resurrection the forces that threaten creation with nonbeing were undergone and overcome, not in thought, but in an actual event. They were only overcome in his death and resurrection "proleptically,"[40] that is, in principle and as the anticipatory appearance of a new reality that heralds their full overcoming in the eschatological future. Still this one event illuminates the many partial overcomings that occur in history and radiates hope for more.

People live by convictions, beliefs, and ideas. These are only meaningful as they have some reference to reality. Jesus' resurrection is only meaningful as it refers to two events. Both can be illuminated by studies in the humanities and the natural sciences, but neither can be firmly demonstrated or denied by these. The first event is Jesus' resurrection. The second is the experience of this as meaningful, as empowering one to love, and as mediating joy, courage, and hope in the present.

In a famous essay calling for the demythologization of the New Testament message, first published in Germany during the early 1940s, Rudolf Bultmann argued that the rise of modern science and the passage of time since the first Easter meant that the objectivity of Jesus' resurrection can no longer be affirmed in a meaningful way. Jesus should be understood as risen in the faith of the first disciples and those who continue to believe in him as such.[41] In effect, Bultmann was reducing the reality referent of Jesus' resurrection to the experience of

40. Pannenberg, *Jesus*, 108, 157.
41. Bultmann, "New Testament and Mythology," 42.

its proclamation as meaningful. Bultmann's views were based partly on the belief that Western societies had reached an intellectual maturity surpassing that of previous eras. Progress in human knowledge and the use of modern technology were seen to have produced a mythless understanding of the world that was a permanent achievement and that made any talk of Jesus' resurrection as an objective event a barrier to faith. For many the clash between a modern Western understanding of the world and the uniqueness of Jesus' resurrection that Bultmann articulated remains a barrier to affirming it as an objective event.

Others interpret the narratives of the empty tomb and the appearances of the risen Jesus in the Gospels as primarily symbolic but affirm that these express the meaning of an eschatological event, an initiative of God's grace that the first witnesses perceived in faith.[42] The meaningfulness of Jesus' resurrection does not depend on the historicity of the details in the resurrection accounts, but on the reality of the eschatological event involving Jesus' person that gave rise to these accounts. This is true to a large extent for the Christus Victor theory of atonement as well. Its meaningfulness depends upon the reality of this eschatological event, not the historicity of the details in the accounts of it.[43] Its clash with Western modernity lies partly in what can be affirmed about the event character of Jesus' resurrection, but equally in what can be hoped for on the basis of it.

The belief that Western modernity represented an intellectual and moral maturity surpassing that of previous eras, in principal beneficial to all, implied an eschatology in which the future would not be fundamentally different from the present. This meant an end to transcendent hopes for a radically different future in which suffering, alienation, and oppression would be overcome.[44] This belief was an ideology that expressed the self-interests and legitimated the power and authority of privileged elites within Western societies, and with this the domination of Western nations over others. If myth is defined as "an ill-founded belief held uncritically especially by an interested group,"[45] this ideology

---

42. Haight, *Jesus*, 141–46.

43. While all the NT accounts affirm the "event character" of Jesus' resurrection, the nature of the Gospel accounts themselves suggests caution regarding what can be affirmed as historical in terms of details (Placher, *Jesus the Savior*, 167).

44. Gouldner, *Dialectic of Ideology*, 261.

45. "Myth," *Webster's New Collegiate Dictionary*, 1975 ed.

of the finality of Western modernity was as much a myth as anything in Scripture.

Contemporary Western societies are permeated with aspirations for the well-being of all, for compassion and respect for others, for peace with the environment, for the fulfillment of all forms of life. Mingled with these aspirations and undergirding them is the desire to be part of something that time and death do not sweep away. But while these aspirations remain, the hopes that they could be achieved through human virtue and effort have been dashed.[46] The eschatological hope that the Christus Victor theory articulates now sits in an ambiguous relationship to these aspirations and ideals of Western societies. On the one hand, these require a transcendent moral source such as the Christus Victor theory to sustain them. On the other hand, the notions of a God who acts in history and of sin and evil as cosmic forces that permeate people's lives are foreign in many respects to the notion pervasive in Western societies that people's lives are "self-authorized,"[47] that people choose and actualize the meaning of their lives themselves, and have their dignity in doing so.

The resurrection of Jesus was an event in which actuality and meaning cohere. It is difficult to affirm it in a neutral or unmoved way. To affirm that Christ is risen is to experience a call to bear witness to this in one's own life. Part of the meaning of Jesus' resurrection as articulated by the Christus Victor theory is that in the end, our lives are not fully self-authorized. We are not our own. We belong to God. The meaning of our lives and our ultimate destiny are not finally determined by ourselves or anyone else. In an ultimate sense these rest with God and have been already secured in Jesus Christ. One of the main difficulties in affirming an objective dimension to Jesus' resurrection in modern Western societies lies here. The historical evidence alone regarding the event character of Jesus' resurrection is inconclusive, either way.

However, the relationship between Western modernity and the Christus Victor theory is not simply antagonistic. For many people the claims of Western modernity to finality are a barrier to the self-affirmation and well-being of themselves and others, for this seems to entrench patriarchy, racism, massive poverty, and colonialism as permanent realities. For some of these people it is precisely the ultimate significance of Jesus' death and resurrection that empowers them to take up Western

---

46. Taylor, *Secular Age*, 616.

47. Ibid., 582–89.

aspirations to compassion, universal well-being, and self-affirmation. In recent decades this finality of modernity has become the hegemony of empire headed by the United States.[48] Jesus' resurrection can serve as a basis for demythologizing the claims to finality of American empire and the permanence of its social exclusions.[49] The unilateral way in which empires act implies a claim to ultimate power and authority. The Christus Victor theory of atonement can be a powerful way of articulating how these claims and the violent power used to reinforce them encounter a different and greater power and authority in the resurrection of the crucified Christ. In this way Jesus' resurrection and the Christus Victor interpretation of it open up a horizon of expectation in which Western aspirations to universal solidarity and human dignity, critically reconfigured, can be meaningfully pursued by the poor, the marginalized and colonized, and by those who seek to be allied with them.

A SECOND MODERN TYPE OF THE CHRISTUS VICTOR THEORY

The ideology of Western modernity has had an unintended effect.

> [It] generated a dynamic civilization that could not but expand. This means that it also joined in expanding the influence of the West by colonialism, a highly ambiguous development. Ironically, it not only exploited weaker civilizations but transferred to them a desire for the fruits of this civilization: technology, democracy, human rights, urbanization, corporate capitalism, professional excellence and, eventually, aspects of a redefined family life and cuisines, clothing styles, musical styles, etc. What is ironic about these developments is that precisely these "powers, principalities, and authorities" also became key resources for overthrowing colonialism, often in alliance with nationalism and socialism.[50]

A similar inversion occurred within Western societies and irrupted in the 1960s, as oppressed peoples and social groups began to appropriate Western ideals as a basis for critiquing Western modernity, demanding liberation from patriarchy, Western colonialism, white racism,

---

48. Rieger, *Christ and Empire*, 314.

49. Griffin, "Resurrection and Empire," 153–57; Taylor, *Executed God*, 102–4.

50. Stackhouse, "'All Things to All People,'" 260.

and economic and cultural oppression.[51] Through their experiences of oppression, many women, Latin Americans, Canadian francophones, African Americans, First Nations peoples and others recognized the profound irrationality of modern Western societies, in terms of the gap they experienced between Western ideals and the oppressions that Western modernity engendered and legitimized. A renewed Christian-Marxist dialogue also developed in the 1960s, and in New Testament studies a new appreciation of the significance of eschatology and apocalyptic in the New Testament.

Karl Barth had already broken with the restrictions that Western modernity placed upon the meaningfulness of the biblical message, reclaiming the transcendence of God as witnessed to in Scripture as a basis for a thoroughgoing critique of society. Following Barth but influenced by some of the developments noted above, Jürgen Moltmann appealed to the event character of Jesus' resurrection as a basis to demythologize Western modernity and its claims to finality in his book *Theology of Hope*.[52] Here Moltmann argued that Jesus' cross and resurrection were two contradictory and interrelated events that together created a dialectic that will be resolved only in the overcoming of all sin and evil, with the transformation of the present world into a new creation.[53] The hope radiating from Jesus' resurrection sets in process a mission seeking to overcome all that his cross represents, all that denies and destroys the goodness of life. Here the finality of Jesus' resurrection and the Christus Victor affirmation of it were recast as the basis of a critical social theory that related Jesus' cross and resurrection critically to the sinful social structures of contemporary societies. Bultmann's program of demythologization restricted the meaning of Jesus' cross and resurrection to what is meaningful in terms of the experience of Western middle-class people.[54] As the new form of the Christus Victor theory pioneered by Moltmann was picked up by Latin American, black, and feminist theologians, the meaning of Jesus' cross and resurrection was understood in relation to the experiences of the "nonpersons, the poor of today,"[55]

---

51. For an account of this from a Canadian perspective, see Hall, "Christianity and Canadian Contexts," 18–26.

52. Moltmann, *Theology of Hope*.

53. Ibid., 201.

54. Moltmann, *Theology Today*, 87.

55. Gutiérrez, *Truth Shall Make You Free*, 24.

whose sufferings and oppression are frequently a byproduct of Western middle-class affluence.

This form of Christus Victor theory understands Jesus' resurrection to be the basis of a transcendent principle of expectation for the overcoming of the injustices and sufferings of the present. Jesus' death and resurrection reveal God's love to be that than which "nothing greater can be conceived."[56] In light of this,

> The human struggle can go forward in hard-won hope against hope that the compassion of God will overcome chaos and death and set limits even to the unfathomable mystery of evil. Speech about the suffering God points forward: in the end all will be well, and so energy to resist despair arises.[57]

Key to this form of the Christus Victor theory, as in Alexandrian Christology, is the presence of God in Jesus' death on the cross. Guiding both is the soteriological principle of the communication of attributes. Through becoming incarnate in Jesus and dying on the cross, God assumes the depths of human suffering, taking on human attributes of suffering, despair, and susceptibility to degradation and death.[58] Through God experiencing this in the person of Jesus and overcoming these in Jesus' resurrection, humanity and creation receive from God the hope of eternal life, and from this peace, joy, and the courage to love. In the death of Jesus the divine nature experiences death. Its overcoming of this in Jesus' resurrection creates a horizon of expectation for all creation that empowers resistance to injustice, exclusion, denigration, and death in whatever forms these take.

WHAT HAPPENED IN JESUS' DEATH AND RESURRECTION?

The overcoming of the power of sin, evil, and death occurs through the encounter of the divine nature with these in Jesus' death. Patristic theologian Gregory of Nyssa conceptualized this in terms of an image of fishing. According to Gregory, Satan held humanity in bondage. When Christ appeared as the fullness of humanity, Satan could not resist exchanging the souls he held in bondage for this one.[59] But Satan saw only

56. Johnson, *She Who Is*, 268.
57. Ibid.
58. Moltmann, *Crucified God*, 276–78.
59. Gregory of Nyssa, *Great Catechism*, 493.

the human or fleshly nature of Jesus and not his divinity. The humanity of Jesus was to Satan like bait or an attractive lure to a fish. The divinity of Jesus, hidden in Jesus' humble vulnerability, was like the hook. God became incarnate in order to deceive Satan in this way, so that

> as with a ravenous fish, the hook of the Deity might be gulped down along with the basis of flesh, and thus, life being intro-duced into the house of death, and light shining in darkness, that which is diametrically opposed to light and life might vanish; for it is not in the nature of darkness to remain when light is present, or of death to exist when life is active.[60]

This image as a way of conceptualizing how God in Christ overcame the power of sin and death in principle was widely used by patristic theologians "from the mid-fourth through the seventh centuries and beyond."[61] Though frequently ridiculed and criticized then and now, it serves to illustrate several aspects of how Jesus' person effects salvation from sin and death as objective forces that humanity and creation are vulnerable to and cannot overcome.

As Gregory makes clear, it is through the encounter that occurs in Jesus' death between the divine nature and sin and death that the latter are overcome. Here the power of God's love decisively affirmed itself over against the destructive power of sin, evil, and death, overcom-ing them in principle. This overcoming is an eschatological event that promises that what happened here will in the future become fully actual everywhere. The deception of the devil is a device by which Gregory defended the incarnation of God in the suffering and humiliated person of Jesus against Arian critics.[62] For many the idea of God stooping to deceive the devil is ridiculous, but for Gregory this was the decisive act in a cosmic struggle, and divine deception was justified by the unprin-cipled nature of the foe and the great end that this achieved. In his view this great act will ultimately lead to the redemption of Satan, after which even Satan will find it to have been just and beneficial.[63] Though imaged as the catching of a fish, the victory of good over evil here is not finally attributed to violence. As Gregory explains, it is the appearance of God's

60. Ibid., 494.

61. Constas, "Last Temptation of Satan," 146.

62. Ibid., 161.

63. Ibid., 157.

own being in Jesus in creation and the subsequent participation of God's incarnate love in creation's suffering and fate, culminating in Jesus' death on the cross, that overcomes the forces of evil, sin, and death. The love of God overcomes sin and death in principle through its greater power of being.

Gregory's fishing image conveys other themes. Evil is ultimately self-destructive through overreaching itself, biting off more than it can chew. The goodness of God's love is something that sin and evil cannot really recognize or understand. Evil feeds off the good, destroys instances of it, but can never finally overcome it because the "negative lives from the positive, which it distorts."[64] The converse of this is that the good is always greater than evil in its power of being, even if not in its actualized being. The Christus Victor theory asserts that regardless of what form sin and evil take, Christ is always greater.

This means that there is always a surplus[65] in the resurrection of the crucified Christ that exceeds the power of sin and evil, that creates hope in the face of it and empowers love to resist it. The finality of Jesus' person, his eschatological significance, makes Christian hope expansive, so that it is not a fixed doctrine but "much more a way and a moving forward, in the discovery of 'the always greater Christ.'"[66] There is always more to Jesus' saving significance than people have discovered. As new forms of evil and sin arise, like the environmental crisis, people discover new saving significances in Jesus and relate the ultimate hope he brings to the sin and evil of the present in ways that empower faithful action.

This ultimacy of Jesus Christ is something that can only be conceptualized in symbolic and mythic terms. There is always a mythic dimension or element in every person's worldview, in which they express what they hold to be ultimate or what they exalt. Through mythic descriptions of struggle the Christus Victor theory seeks to articulate both the reality of sin and evil and the ultimacy of Jesus. Modern versions tend to prescind from the images and mythic descriptions that patristic theologians used, such as Gregory's fishing image, and adopt simpler paradoxical expressions.[67] The Christus Victor theory is inevitably paradoxical because

---

64. Tillich, *Systematic Theology*, 2:171.

65. Rieger, *Christ and Empire*, 315–16.

66. Moltmann, *Way of Jesus Christ*, 275.

67. Johnson, *She Who Is*, 268–69.

it affirms two opposing truths: (a) the goodness and power of God and
(b) the reality of sin and evil. Today the destructive power of sin and evil
is real and all too apparent; in the sufferings of the poor, in the devastat-
ing effects of patriarchy, among the victims of AIDs, in the indifference
or hostility of Western elites to the sufferings and cries for justice of the
oppressed in their own countries and around the globe. Yet the love of
God revealed in Jesus' death and resurrection can bring hope and empower faithful love, even in the face of these.

Like Gregory's articulation of the Christus Victor theory of atonement, the second modern version found in liberation theology and
some feminist and black theologies understands sin and redemption in
expansive terms, in which sin and evil, in their small or immense mani-
festations, are understood as powers that hold people in bondage, captive to meaningless and despair.[68] However, these versions are distinctly
modern in several respects. Like Gregory, all see the ultimacy of Jesus'
saving significance to be a source of empowerment for love and faithfulness to God and creation. But feminist, liberation, and black theologies
understand this love and faithfulness through a modern social imagi-
nary that sees societies not as givens, but as social projects, constructed
through peoples' joint decisions and actions.[69] Furthermore, they tend
to see that an understanding of society must begin with an analysis of
the conflicts in it between the victims of society and those who oppress
them, intentionally or otherwise. Finally, they take up the Marxist challenge that theory should not seek so much to understand the world as it
is as to change it for the better.

THE DANGER OF MORAL DUALISM IN THE
CHRISTUS VICTOR THEORY

A major criticism of the Christus Victor theory is that its dualistic outlook tends to locate the causes of people's sufferings outside of themselves and may lead to identifying these with other races, social classes,
or groups in a way that demonizes these.[70] This dualistic outlook can
become a dangerous reduction and oversimplification of moral reality
that "bypasses the complexity and subtlety of evil . . . , feeding illusions

68. Ray, *Deceiving the Devil*, 131.
69. Baum, "Cultural Causes," 49–51.
70. Hall, *God and Human Suffering*, 100.

of purity and innocence, on the one hand, and permitting the demonization of those people and groups viewed as unclean or damaged, on the other."[71] President George W. Bush's rhetoric during his regime's "war on terror" exemplified this in a deliberate and extreme way.[72] However, in relation to social injustices like those created by globalized capitalism in the present,[73] there is also the danger of failing to tell the truth about the conflictual nature of reality in light of Jesus' preferential option for the poor.

There are "soft" and "hard" approaches to social justice.[74] The soft approach tends to view society as an organic whole. It sees that as people grow in love for God and one another they will work together for a more just society. It speaks of evil, sin, and injustice in general terms and typically seeks the reform of society, not structural change. This approach is not very effective in relation to systemic oppression and radical evil. Because it fails to acknowledge these realities that are a deeper cause of people's suffering and lack of love, the strategies it suggests to address the latter tend to remain superficial, regardless of how well-intentioned or well-carried-out they are. The hard approach "names the systemic causes of human misery"[75] and the social classes, institutions, cultural ethos, and even the individuals who perpetuate them.[76] It condemns these and demands their replacement with more just social structures and institutions. Because it seeks to be concrete in its understanding of a situation of systemic injustice, it tends to be dualistic in its understanding of society.

Both approaches have validity, but they cannot be applied simultaneously and their efficaciousness depends partly on the nature of the context in which they are applied.[77] The Christus Victor theory of atonement may tend to demonize peoples or social groups when it is applied

---

71. Ray, *Deceiving the Devil*, 126.

72. Taylor, *Religion, Politics*, 30.

73. "[I]n our present day we are basically still involved in a civilization of capital, which generates extreme scarcities, dehumanizes persons, and destroys the human family: it produces impoverished and excluded people and divides the world into conquerors and conquered" (Sobrino, *No Salvation*, 37).

74. For what follows see Baum, *Theology and Society*, 8–11.

75. Ibid., 10.

76. For an example of this, see Cone, *God of the Oppressed*, 232.

77. Baum, *Theology and Society*, 10–11.

in a hard fashion to specific social injustices, as it has been in some black and liberation theologies. But the other danger that theologies face in these contexts is that of failing to fully and concretely articulate the evils and demonic nature of the injustices there. Christian theology has to operate on the ontological, historical, and ecclesiastical levels. The Christus Victor theory can apply to sin and evil on both the ontological and the historical levels. On an ontological level all people and all of creation are held captive by the cosmic forces of sin and death.[78] As the author of Ephesians put it, "our struggle is not against enemies of blood and flesh, but against . . . cosmic powers " (Eph 6:12). But on the historical level, these forces can take shape in specific regimes, social institutions, and customs. Then a hard approach to liberation and a certain dualism may be warranted.[79] As noted in a previous chapter, this hard approach on the level of history needs to be balanced by recognition of the ontological inclusivity of Christ's redemptive work, which generates a will to embrace the other.

A second critique of the Christus Victor theory of atonement, as it appears in Moltmann's *Theology of Hope*, is that the hope it inspires can function to bless the status quo of an officially optimistic society,[80] thus functioning as a soft approach to liberation when a hard approach would be more appropriate. But feminist, liberation, and black theologies that see Jesus' resurrection as a source of hope emphasize that Jesus' resurrection was the resurrection of a victim.[81] The hope it gives rise to has a radical ethical content through Jesus' preferential option for the poor. When linked to the historical particularity of Jesus in this way, Jesus' resurrection does not support the official optimism[82] of North Atlantic

78. "When the crucifixion of God's Messiah is seen as the event of God's apocalypse, the forces of oppression and dehumanization which cause our world to remain unredeemed are not to be explained by identifying them with any discrete group of human beings" (Martyn, *Theological Issues*, 286).

79. An example where it was would be James Cone's approach in Cone, *God of the Oppressed*, 232, cited previously. In his study of Martin Luther King Jr. and Malcolm X, Cone studies the question of the appropriateness of what have here been termed "soft" and "hard" approaches to liberation, and notes their strengths and weaknesses, and also how they may both be necessary and can complement each other (Cone, *Martin & Malcolm*, 244–71).

80. Hall, "Theology of Hope," 376–90; Rieger, *Christ and Empire*, 249–50.

81. Sobrino, *Christology at the Crossroads*, 244.

82. Hall, *Thinking the Faith*, 164.

societies. It is a call to these societies to repent of their contributions to the plight of the global poor, the destruction of the environment, and their indifference to both. It is also a source of hope for the victims of these societies.

"BUT THANKS BE TO GOD, WHO GIVES US THE VICTORY THROUGH OUR LORD JESUS CHRIST"[83]

If in Jesus' resurrection God's love has overcome in principle sin, evil, and death, what does this entail? Its immediate meaning is generally one of exhortation to mission.[84] Also, as Jesus' resurrection gives meaning to life and acts of love it is a source of joy that must be celebrated. Yet this victory remains eschatological. It is not yet historical. The Christus Victor theory of Jesus' saving significance has to acknowledge the Jewish insistence that the world is not yet redeemed.[85] It is an eschatological hope that affirms the resurrection of Jesus in spite of the unredeemed state of the world. But such hope "becomes false and cheap when it is divorced from the reality of suffering."[86]

The hope that the Christus Victor theory articulates is for a great justice and peace in history.[87] But it also looks beyond history to a transformation through which the present world will become a new creation. The new that Christ brings is not simply a rescue or restoration of the old, purified from sin. It will be something more, a new reality in which sin and death will have no place. But this future new reality is to be sought in the present through faithfulness to the earth in its ecological sufferings, through love that seeks justice and peace, through forgiveness and acts of reconciliation.

If the Christus Victor theory is not linked to Jesus' devotion to the coming of God's reign and is celebrated in a triumphalistic way, it can give rise to oppression of Jews and others who refuse or are unable to acknowledge Jesus as the Christ.[88] But if the hope that Christ brings is

83. I Cor 15:57.

84. William Placher summarizes the message of the resurrection accounts as follows: "Go. Tell. Be witnesses. Proclaim. Feed my Sheep" (Placher, *Jesus the Savior*, 181).

85. Moltmann, *Way of Jesus Christ*, 28–33.

86. Beker, *Suffering and Hope*, 85.

87. Sobrino, *Christology at the Crossroads*, 242.

88. Wells, *Christic Center*, 146–47.

given ethical orientation from Jesus' ministry, its assurance of Christ's ultimacy can be a source of openness to other religions and solidarity with them. The assurance that the Christus Victor theory articulates can mean that Christians do not need to be aggressively defensive towards others who do not accept him or who are critical of Christian faith. This ultimate assurance can become a source of openness to criticism and to dialogue with and learning from other religions.

CONCLUSION

The Christus Victor theory has some typical features, particularly its assertion of an intrinsic opposition between God's love and the suffering and destruction of human life and creation that sin and evil bring. But like other Christian doctrines its typical themes have an inherent polyvalence. They can be appropriated in various ways. The Christus Victor theory can empower one to act. It can also enable one to accept difference, suffering, and death in the knowledge that, despite these, life and love are still meaningful. The Christus Victor theory can thus be a source of peace; not peace in the sense of complacency in the face of evil, but peace in the faith that evil and sin will not have the last word on creation. In this way it enables one to accept one's mortality in the present. It gives one consolation and hope in times of grief. It does not diminish the pain of loss and sorrow over death. But it does enable one, in the midst of this pain and sorrow, to look beyond it in hope to a different future. The Christus Victor theory speaks to the anxiety that evil and sin cause concerning the meaning of life and the meaningfulness of love. It can be a source of revolutionary patience and consolation, for it affirms that death does not have the last word on us, on those we love, or on anyone else. That last word belongs to God, and it has already been spoken in the resurrection of Jesus Christ.

The will that is moved to love by the moral example of Jesus can be strengthened by the Christus Victor theory of atonement. This states that the love to which Jesus moves us is never in vain. Though it meets resistance, though it fail to achieve its goals, though those it loves be taken by death, still such love has an ultimate meaning. Conversely, the moral influence of Jesus gives ethical focus to the hope and will for the future that springs from the Christus Victor theory.

But people who are moved by Jesus to love and given hope by his resurrection often fail to act out of this and sin intentionally. Or they find that their actions done out of love have caused others harm, sometimes irreparably. Guilt means that one's identity has been irreparably compromised by involvement with sin and evil, the very forces that Christ rose to overcome. The next chapter will examine the theory of substitutionary atonement, which seeks to understand how Jesus Christ saves in relation to this.

8 Jesus as the Basis of Reconciliation

We have examined the way of Jesus, how people need empowerment to follow it, and how the moral influence and Christus Victor theories of atonement provide this. We now come to Gustav Aulén's third type of atonement theory, which he called the Anselmian or Latin type.[1] It too can function as a strong moral source, but its destructive potential has recently been much criticized. For this reason it requires more prolonged study.

The New Testament is permeated by interpretations of Jesus' death as a sacrifice that reconciles people to God,[2] on the basis of which people should be reconciled to one another. This way of interpreting Jesus' death has been part of the Christian tradition since its inception. Anselm made it central to his understanding of Jesus' saving significance, as did Luther, Calvin, and many others up into the modern era. It gained renewed prominence in the thought of Karl Barth, Paul Tillich, Dietrich Bonhoeffer, and Reinhold Niebuhr. Penal satisfaction, vicarious substitution, sacrifice; all name versions of this way of interpreting Jesus' death. These can be named substitutionary theories of atonement because they focus on how Jesus dies in the place of sinners. But as we shall argue, the meaning of "place" here needs redefining. Typically these understandings portray people as standing under God's judgment for their sin. In dying on the cross Christ takes the sinner's place, paying the debt they owe to God's honor (Anselm) or suffering the punishment due them (Calvin). In these understandings Christ suffers vicariously, representing or substituting for people so that their sin might be forgiven.

Forgiveness of sin is only part of what these theories are about. Most see that through Christ's death on the cross God creates a new

1. Aulén, *Christus Victor*, 17–19.
2. Dalferth, "Christ Died for Us," 302–3.

reality in which peoples' identities and relationship to God are secure regardless of what they do, how others view them, or what happens to them. At heart substitutionary theories of atonement are not about Jesus paying a debt or suffering punishment, but about how he creates for us a new relationship to God, to one another, and to ourselves. In light of this new relationship, if we want to know who we really are, we don't judge by what we see in the mirror or in our conscience. We don't measure ourselves by what others say of us. We look at Jesus Christ. He is the truth of who we are.[3] As we enter into this new identity of being "in Christ"[4] we are to relate to others in light of it. They too have an identity in Christ that cannot be destroyed by anything they have done to us, to others or themselves, and that cannot be taken away by anything that has been done to them or by how society views them.

In the past thirty years this way of understanding Jesus' saving significance has been at the center of "one of the most heated conflicts in contemporary theology."[5] It is said to be morally dangerous and religiously unacceptable because it portrays God as violent, Jesus as modeling acceptance of abuse, and suffering as intrinsically good. It is claimed to be irrational to contemporary understanding[6] and to sacralize the kind of surrogacy, having their bodies put at the service of others, that black women in the United States have been forced to endure, thus encouraging what should be overcome.[7] It is said to drive "a huge and misleading wedge between how we experience God's love and suffering and how we experience our own love and suffering."[8] These critiques have prompted restatements of substitutionary atonement that stress the incarnation of God in Jesus and the Trinitarian nature of the event of his cross and resurrection. At the same time numerous theologians and church leaders have also stressed its ethical importance in the aftermath of violent conflicts and histories of oppression[9] and its spiritual importance in the lives of Christians and the church.

3. Barth, *Church Dogmatics* IV/1, 92.

4. 2 Corinthians 5: 17.

5. Duff, "Atonement and the Christian Life," 22.

6. For a summary of these critiques see Finlan, *Problems with Atonement*, 96–108.

7. Williams, *Sisters in the Wilderness*, 161–67.

8. Heyward, *Saving Jesus*, 171.

9. De Gruchy, *Reconciliation*, 58–63.

Substitutionary understandings of atonement challenge reductionist rationalities that refuse to acknowledge how sin complicates human identities and creates tension between God's justice and God's mercy.[10] Their interpretations of Jesus' death will always be potentially dangerous. Yet they can also be life-giving, morally empowering in several ways, and authentic interpretations of one aspect of Jesus' saving significance. This way of understanding Jesus addresses guilt and issues around marginalization and spoiled identities. It has an important role to play for those who wish to repent of their former ways, but also for sustaining those who have been moved by the beauty of Jesus' moral example and empowered to follow him. Christians inevitably violate Jesus' teaching, example, and meaning, irreparably compromising their identities. The greatest saints know themselves to be the greatest sinners. Moreover, all moral codes create exclusions and require reformulation at times. The meaning of Jesus' death that substitutionary theories of atonement attempt to communicate can help Christians face their failings constructively. It can create a space in which Christians, churches, and their teachings can be open to critique and reformation. Jesus addressed issues of marginalization and spoiled identities in his public ministry. Christians have also believed that these were addressed in a final way through his death and resurrection. When Jesus' role in substitutionary atonement is seen as something he did for others that he voluntarily undertook out of love, it does not model "passivity before undeserved suffering, but instead urges active resistance to it in the power of the Spirit."[11]

FORGIVENESS AND ACCEPTANCE IN THE MINISTRY OF JESUS

There is a tension running throughout the Hebrew Bible between God's judgment and God's mercy, both of which are aspects of God's love. This tension surfaces acutely in Hosea 11:8–9:

> How can I give you up, Ephraim? How can I hand you over, O Israel? . . . My heart recoils within me; my compassion grows warm and tender. I will not execute my fierce anger; I will not again destroy Ephraim; for I am God and no mortal, the Holy One in your midst, and I will not come in wrath.[12]

10. Schmiechen, *Saving Power*, 119.

11. Gilliss, "Resurrecting the Atonement," 135–36.

12. The text is uncertain but clearly expresses tension between God's judgment on sin and God's mercy.

The same tension is present between the moral and transmoral dimensions of Jesus' ministry. In being baptized by John, Jesus endorsed John's proclamation of moral judgment. Yet Jesus' ministry, as noted in chapters 1 and 5 above, also featured a transmoral acceptance of people publicly characterized as sinners. In light of his resurrection this can be seen to have begun with his baptism by John. Here Jesus not only endorsed John's message of coming judgment. He also identified with those needing to repent and stood in their place.

Jesus' public ministry was characterized by rigorous moral teaching. His followers were to display a higher righteousness. Yet he also sought out and included in his company and table fellowship people publicly characterized as sinners. Forgiveness of sin was readily available to these people through Jewish religious practices. What was scandalous about Jesus' inclusion of them was that he "offered companionship to the wicked of Israel as a sign that God would save them, and he did not make his association dependent on their conversion to the law."[13] This questioned the adequacy of Jewish law as the basis of people's relationship to God.[14] Jesus offered trust in himself and his message in its place as the basis for this. In doing so he presented himself as renewing Judaism, not departing from it.

Alongside his behavior that called aspects of Jewish law into question, Jesus also radicalized some of its moral teachings.[15] This and his offer of companionship to the wicked moved in opposing directions but had an inner unity. His radicalized ethic "potentially turns into a recognition of the inadequacy of all human beings—and this recognition is in turn the basis of a radicalized preaching of grace."[16] Conversely, the radical message of grace enables one to hold on to high ethical demands even when one fails to fulfill them. Jesus' radical moral teaching and transmoral acceptance of people regardless of their moral failings are both rooted in the transcendent goodness and beauty of God's love. For Jesus, the resolution of the tension between his radical ethical teaching and his transmoral acceptance of sinners lay in the transformation that would be effected by the coming reign of God.

13. Sanders, *Jesus and Judaism*, 207.
14. Ibid., 255.
15. Theissen, *The Religion*, 27–31.
16. Ibid., 30.

This did not come as Jesus may have expected. Instead, following his death and resurrection, and his followers' experiences of the Holy Spirit connected to this, there arose the early churches from which the New Testament was produced. Here Jesus' death and resurrection were interpreted along these two trajectories that characterized his public ministry. Jesus' death was seen to present a radical moral demand. Christians were to take up their crosses in imitation of Jesus and follow him (Mark 8:34). Yet Jesus' death and resurrection were also seen as a basis of God's unconditional acceptance of sinners in spite of their sin (Rom 4:25). Thus, from early on Jesus' resurrection gave his cross multiple meanings. It was (1) "a symbol of human sin and violence"[17] that Christians must oppose and be willing to face in following him, (2) a symbol of the power of God's love in Jesus Christ to overcome cosmic powers of sin and evil, and (3) a symbol of God's love which accepts and values people unconditionally, regardless of their status before society or God's law. The inclusion of these different interpretations of Jesus' cross in the New Testament indicates a recognition of the complexity and ambiguity of the human condition, which is always present, though one aspect may be predominant in a given context for certain groups or persons. It also recognized that Jesus saves in different ways depending on whether one is a victim, oppressor, guilty bystander, or all three at once.

SUBSTITUTIONARY THEORIES OF ATONEMENT

Anselm of Canterbury (1033–1100) developed a classic expression of substitutionary atonement in his book *Cur Deus Homo*.[18] Here he sought to show why it was necessary for God to become incarnate in Christ and die on the cross.[19] According to Anselm each person owes perfect obedience to God. As God is infinite, sin creates an infinite debt to God's honor, which no finite person can repay. Every person sins and so all owe God this infinite debt except Jesus Christ, who was sinless. As he was fully human he was able to take our place. As he was fully divine he was able to pay the infinite debt that each person owes

---

17. Baker-Fletcher, *Dancing With God*, 97.

18. Anselm of Canterbury, *St. Anselm: Basic Writings*, 171–288.

19. Ibid., 177. For a discussion of Anselm's intellectual context, see Colish, *Medieval Foundations*, 167–70. For a summary of Anselm's theory of atonement, see Haight, *Jesus*, 227–30.

through sacrificing his life. No one else was able to do this and so Christ "preferred to suffer, rather than that the human race should be lost."[20] Love for a fallen creation and desire to save humanity from the harmful consequences of their own actions motivated Jesus' willingness to die. These motives were shared by the first and second persons of the Trinity. Sin had disrupted the triune God's original intention for the world. Jesus died so that God's original intention might be fulfilled and people experience salvation.

What Anselm describes as the honor due to God represents respect for the moral meaning of life and the beauty and order of creation.[21] This moral meaning arises from the same divine love that moves Jesus to redeem humanity. Opposition to evil and sin is inherent in God's love. Without this and the power to act on it God's love becomes mere sentimentality.[22] Love is lacking where justice is not upheld. For this reason Anselm insisted that God could not simply overlook sin.[23] This inherent opposition between God and sin makes God a basis of hope for suffering humanity. Yet it makes God an object of fear when one perceives oneself to be a sinner. This perception also alienates one from oneself. As sin ruptures the moral meaning of life, it also ruptures the moral basis of one's own identity and the moral fabric of one's community in a way that one cannot repair.[24] The alienation created by sin is threefold: from God, from others, and from oneself. In arguing that the sinner cannot repay the debt they owe Anselm is describing how a sinful act creates this condition of alienation. A person's sin leaves a stain spoiling their identity that they cannot remove.

According to Anselm, Jesus sacrificed himself in order to uphold the moral dimension of God's love and the moral meaning of life while redeeming those who have irrevocably violated it, thus repairing the rupture sin has caused. His death on the cross creates a new transcendent reality of reconciliation to God in which people participate by faith. Through this they receive a new identity independent of their own actions or moral qualities that becomes the basis for their life. Anselm thus portrays Jesus' death as having a transmoral meaning. It gives a gift,

20. Anselm, *Anselm: Basic Writings*, 196.
21. Haight, *Jesus*, 228.
22. Tillich, *Systematic Theology* Vol. II, 172.
23. Anselm, *Anselm: Basic Writings*, 235.
24. Volf, *Free of Charge*, 128–29.

more than what is morally required. Through it sinners who deserve judgment are offered reconciliation with God. There are many versions of this kind of atonement theory,[25] but for our purposes this sketch of Anselm's will suffice.

A first criticism of this kind of theory is that, as the death of the innocent victim Jesus is needed to satisfy the wrath of God, violence is portrayed here as intrinsic to God's character and receives divine sanction.[26] In acquiescing to this violence Jesus models and sanctifies passive acceptance of abuse. Many substitutionary theories of atonement are guilty of portraying God as a merciless judge and Jesus as a passive victim, thus obscuring how God's judgment and mercy are both aspects of God's love.[27] In attempting to explicate the transmoral dimension of Jesus' death they end up portraying God and Jesus as submoral from a Christian perspective. When God is depicted as a demanding judge who requires Jesus' death to satisfy the requirements of divine justice, the first person of the Trinity does "appear as a vindictive deity, who requires the death of an innocent person as retribution for the sins of the world,"[28] and Jesus models the surrogacy that has been a major form of oppression for, in particular, black women in the United States. Some aspects of Anselm's theory, such as his insistence that the infinite debt owed to God's honor must be repaid, portray God and Jesus in this way. Other aspects do not, such as Anselm's stress on the unity of wills between the first and second persons of the Trinity in the act of redemption, and that both will this out of love for humanity.

Theories of substitutionary atonement like Anselm's correctly see that sin creates a tension between God's love for the sinner and God's opposition to sin.[29] But they often fail to sufficiently articulate that God never ceases to love the sinner. Humanity's sin does not change God's basic disposition of love. It is sinful humanity that has to be reconciled to God,[30] not God to humanity. Justice and opposition to sin are inherent in God's love, but these never cause God to cease loving humanity and creation. As humanity has fallen into sin it is unable to transform

25. For a survey of some of these see Schmiechen, *Saving Power*, 20–119.
26. Weaver, "The Nonviolent Atonement," 338.
27. Schmiechen, *Saving Power*, 110.
28. Ibid., 40.
29. Schmiechen, *Saving Power*, 110.
30. Pannenberg, *Systematic Theology* Vol. 2, 415.

its sinful condition on its own.[31] For this transformation to occur, God's enduring love must create the possibility of sinful humanity being reconciled with God, and the human heart must be transformed, brought into line with God's disposition to goodness and beauty. Substitutionary models of atonement try to articulate how Jesus creates a new relationship to God in which humanity is embraced and valued regardless of its sinful condition or actions. This provides a permanent identity within which the moral influence of God's love and the hope Jesus brings can work to transform the human heart. One may be moved first by the moral influence of Jesus or the hope he brings. But eventually one needs the assurance of God's love that Jesus brings as well.

The fullness of redemption includes justification and sanctification. Justification is God's acceptance of the sinner in spite of their sin. Substitutionary theories of atonement try to articulate how this happens. Justification has an eschatological goal, the coming of God's new creation and provides the foundation for sanctification that works towards this. Justification serves sanctification partly by creating a relationship to God that is not dependent upon sanctification, in which sanctification can continue even though it has been jeopardized by sin.

As Nancy Duff notes, the "way images function, whether in compliance with original intention or not, has a powerful impact, which must be taken seriously."[32] Symbols of God influence human thought and behavior.[33] Substitutionary theories of atonement that see Jesus' death as in accordance with the will of God's will always be in danger of portraying God as inherently violent and acquiescing to this as exemplary. Numerous critics of substitutionary atonement have done churches and humanity a service in highlighting how these theories can distort the gospel.[34] But many of these critics tend to argue as though their critiques completely refute this kind of atonement theory as a way of communicating a salvific

---

31. Heschel, "A Hebrew Evaluation of Reinhold Niebuhr," 404–5.

32. Duff, "Atonement and the Christian Life," 26.

33. Johnson, *She Who Is*, 4.

34. Duff, "Atonement and the Christian Life," 21–26. As Peter Schmiechen notes, a central problem of penal substitution theories of atonement is that they eliminate the tension between God's love and God's justice by "affirming justice as the only significant and functional divine attribute," Schmiechen, *Saving Power*, 110. This is a reductive solution because God's justice is always an expression of God's love, which remains in force, even as it expresses itself as judgment. To reduce God's love simply to judgment is precisely what Hosea 11:8–9 portrays God as refusing to do.

meaning. In doing so they make two mistakes. First, they typically leave issues around guilt and spoiled or marginalized identities inadequately addressed. This leaves the violence of the guilty still in force,[35] fostering resentment and desire for revenge among the victims, and self-hatred among many of the guilty. A failure to adequately address issues of guilt and spoiled identities is itself dangerous. Second, symbols are usually multivalent. They rarely portray only one meaning or function in only one way. How a symbol functions depends very much on the background theories and context in which it is interpreted. Critics of substitutionary theories of atonement often argue as if it must be an invalid understanding of Jesus' saving significance if it has led or might lead to destructive consequences. If that was all these theories did these critics would be right. But a potentially destructive understanding of Jesus can still communicate important aspects of his saving significance.[36] To throw substitutionary theories of atonement away because of their potential or past destructive consequences when they still have a significant efficacious potential is to rob the Holy Spirit of some of the means it needs to do its work.[37] Yet failing to attend to valid criticisms of substitutionary theories of atonement also quenches the Spirit.[38]

A similar dilemma has surfaced in feminist theology around the maleness of Jesus. This has functioned as a means of patriarchal oppression. Yet many women have found faith in Jesus Christ to be life-giving. The solution for many was not to abandon this faith but to rethink the background theories and context in which Jesus had been interpreted so that an oppressive and false emphasis on his maleness could be overcome and his being as the Christ could assume an "emancipatory gestalt" once more.[39] Christian theology needs to respond to critiques of substitutionary theories of atonement in this way. It needs to be aware of their dangerous aspects, how they have been misused or misconstrued, and supplement them with the symbols of the reign of God, the moral influence and the Christus Victor theories of atonement, all of which

35. Milbank, *Being Reconciled*, 52–55.

36. Charles Taylor argues this in terms of moral ideals in Taylor, *Sources of the Self*, 519–20.

37. Womanist theologian JoAnne Marie Terrell discusses the importance of this efficacious potential in Terrell, "Our Mother's Gardens," 46–49.

38. 1 Thessalonians 5:19.

39. Johnson, *She Who Is*, 156, 154–56.

stress God's will for human flourishing and the fulfillment of life.[40] Christian theology also needs to reformulate substitutionary theories of atonement in ways that acknowledge how Jesus' cross represents the execution of a prophet of justice and that correct distortions in traditional formulations of this theory that these critiques have identified.

Significant New Testament texts that interpret Jesus' death in terms of substitutionary atonement do not present God as passive, waiting for and demanding the sacrifice of an innocent victim. Instead they emphasize that God was active in Christ to save humanity and that Christ's death was an act of love for humanity on God's part.[41] Reinterpreting substitutionary atonement along these lines can "do justice"[42] to the criticisms outlined above and help unfold the rationality of this atonement model so that it can be an effective, though always potentially dangerous, understanding of Jesus' saving significance for the church.

ATONEMENT AS A REPETITION IN HISTORY OF GOD'S ETERNAL BEING

Theories of substitutionary atonement go wrong when they portray Jesus as making atonement for humanity to God. What they should portray is how God in Jesus creates a new relationship to humanity in which peoples' identities as loved and valued by God are secure regardless of their sin, the sins of others, or natural evil. The reconciling and redeeming work of God finds its focal point in the person, ministry, death, and resurrection of Jesus Christ. This remains the decisive event in salvation history. But it was not something Jesus was or did alone. The work of Christ is always surrounded by that of the Holy Spirit, which prepares the possibility of what Jesus does and is and which works to further actualize this in the lives of others. Jesus' atoning work is a repetition in history of the communication of God's beauty and goodness that characterizes the life of the immanent Trinity. Substitutionary theories of atonement attempt to articulate how God's goodness and beauty are further expressed in history through Jesus establishing the basis of a new relationship of God to humanity in which people are justified by grace.

---

40. Cahill, "Quaestio Disputata," 424.

41. Schmiechen, *Saving Power*, 40.

42. Tanner, *Christ the Key*, 247.

This expression of God's goodness and beauty has the goal of enabling people to further express it in their own lives.

The distinctiveness and saving ultimacy of Jesus rests upon God's unique presence in him, as expressed in the Chalcedonian Definition of Jesus as fully human and fully divine, the two natures united in his one person. In light of this Jesus' journey to the cross needs to be read on two levels. On the first, it is the story of a person whose love of God and others is so strong that he is willing to risk death for them. On this level the Gospels "tell the story of a brave frightened, lonely young man who is killed by powerful people and institutions in his society."[43] But as Jesus' resurrection reveals him to be the Christ, his death must also be understood on a second level; as "the suffering and death of the Christ of God,"[44] as something God underwent for the sake of humanity and creation. "Through Jesus, God participates in the situation of those oppressed by every kind of sin and evil."[45] This happens most profoundly in Jesus' death on the cross.[46] On this second level of what God experiences through the second person of the Trinity becoming incarnate, one aspect of God's goodness and beauty can be seen to have been decisively expressed in Jesus' death. His death was not beautiful. Yet something beautiful happened in it. Through Jesus' death God entered irrevocably into the situation of all who believe themselves to be cut off from God, by their own action or that of others,[47] in order to establish a communion with them that cannot be broken.

Jesus' death resulted from the encounter of God's love with sin and evil. God did not will Jesus' death directly. But God does will to enter into communion with those who have become separated from God, through their own actions or those of others. As God's goodness and beauty are expressed in history they encounter human sin and the cosmic powers of sin and death. In the ministry, death, and resurrection of Jesus God's love struggled with these powers and decisively overcame them.[48] Jesus' suffering and death were a crucial part of this. Through this God entered into the hell on earth that humanity creates for itself and others. In doing

43. Placher, *Jesus the Savior*, 115.
44. Moltmann, *The Crucified God*, 182.
45. Fiddes, *Past Event and Present Salvation*, 56.
46. Tanner, *Christ the Key*, 260.
47. Moltmann, *In The End—The Beginning*, 74.
48. Barth, *Church Dogmatics* IV/1, 47.

so God was faithful to Godself, further expressing God's goodness and beauty where sin and evil seemed to have blocked the way.

At this point we need to distinguish three types of alienation addressed by substitutionary theories of atonement. A first is the experience of godforsakenness, feeling abandoned by God as a result of suffering. The second is the experience of guilt, of having one's identity spoiled through one's own sin. The third is that of a spoiled or marginalized identity that is not one's fault. Substitutionary atonement addresses each of these in slightly different ways.

GODFORSAKENNESS

There are experiences of suffering in which people seem forsaken by God. Out of these often comes the cry, "God, where are you?" In suffering death on the cross Jesus entered into this kind of experience, dying in isolation, seemingly abandoned and forsaken by the first person of the Trinity.[49] Through dying in this way Jesus as the second person of the Trinity brings God's presence into such situations. Looking at his cross, those who seem godforsaken can trust that they are not alone, that God is near, that God shares and knows their sorrow and pain.[50] In Jesus God suffers death, the death of the godforsaken, sharing their experience so that they are no longer separated from God. Through this there occurs what is sometimes called the communication of attributes or the joyful exchange. God in Christ experiences godforsakenness so that the godforsaken can know that God is with them and gain a transcendent hope that their suffering will be overcome. God in Christ takes on the attributes of suffering humanity, so that in faith suffering humanity can receive peace, love, even joy, and the promise of wholeness that are attributes of God. Here the word "substitutionary" can be misleading, for in relation to godforsakenness Jesus does not take someone else's place but brings God's presence into the situation of those who are suffering. In relation to godforsakenness, substitutionary theories of atonement work in conjunction with Christus Victor theories. The former articulate how God is with those who seem godforsaken, even in their worst experiences, through Christ's suffering. In turn, Christus Victor theories articulate how Christ brings hope for the overcoming of their suffering.

49. Moltmann, *The Crucified God*, 235–49, 267–78.
50. Johnson, *She Who Is*, 264.

DIVINE SUFFERING

Jesus cannot enter into the situation of those who suffer without suffering himself. Some suffering is intrinsic to God's love as it comes to expression in a world plagued by sin and evil which actively oppose God.[51] But God in Jesus saves not only by participating in the suffering of creation, but also by overcoming it, partially in history, proleptically in Jesus' resurrection, and finally in the eschaton. To do this God must be transcendent to suffering and its causes.

The repetition in time and space of the divine life of the immanent Trinity in the atoning work of Jesus happens in encounter with sin and evil. This does not change the nature of God's love, but it does change the way it is expressed. In the life of the immanent Trinity there is a continuous expression and celebration of divine beauty and goodness that is transcendent to suffering, sin, and evil. This goodness and beauty is further expressed in history in the economic Trinity through the Word and the Holy Spirit. The suffering of God occurs here as the Word and Holy Spirit encounter sin and evil in history.

This suffering is not intrinsic to God's nature or being. It is part of the difference between the economic and the immanent Trinity. The lives of Jesus and the Holy Spirit in the economic Trinity are marked by joy as well as sorrow. Their activity brings an increase to the person of the Holy Spirit. But in Jesus' public ministry and his death on the cross, and when the Holy Spirit is grieved or quenched, suffering is experienced by the second and third persons of the economic Trinity. Through their further expression of God's goodness and beauty, which includes suffering, God redeems a fallen creation, establishing a relationship to humanity that makes possible a new future for victims and oppressors. This is the suffering of love for the beloved that is freely undertaken for the beloved's sake. It is a suffering of solidarity for the sake of a greater communion that effects a transformation aimed at ending suffering. Through Jesus' suffering and death God enters into the situation of the godforsaken and guilty, establishing a new communion with them that does not depend on their righteousness but solely on what God has done for them.

Christ suffers because God's people suffer and God wills to be with them. Where sin causes suffering one can say that Christ suffers because of it.[52] As God in Christ seeks to enter into communion with those whose

51. Heyward, *Saving Jesus*, 156.

52. "The consequences of moral and other evil have to be born, and this truth

suffering is caused by sin, God must endure the consequences of sin. But not all suffering is caused by sinful actions and there is an element of innocence in all suffering.[53] If one moves from thinking of sin as a specific act to understanding sin as a condition of alienation, one could argue that "sin" in the sense of the distorted or fallen condition of creation is the ultimate cause of suffering, that there is suffering because the world is not yet as God wills it to be. Creation is good and yet in need of redemption. To say that sin in the sense of the fallen condition of creation is the cause of suffering affirms that ultimately suffering is not God's will. Yet within a fallen creation there can be redemptive dimensions to suffering.

One can go further and ask, why is there sin and evil in the first place? Christian theologians have sometimes offered explanations for this, but ultimately there are none. If there were an ultimate reason for sin and evil, then this would be a justification for them[54] and they would not be truly evil. At this point the broken nature of a rationality that recognizes the existence of sin and evil and their ultimate incongruence with the good is superior to one that seeks to comprehend these ultimately incompatible realities in a seamless rational whole.[55] God is opposed to sin and evil. These are not necessary to creation but a distortion of it and an assault upon it. God overcomes the alienating effects of sin and evil in principle through the ministry, death, and resurrection of Jesus. Through Jesus entering into the situation of those suffering from violence or guilt, God overcomes the separation these create between God and God's beloved, in this way overcoming one of the barriers these pose to the fulfillment of God's creation.

The rationality of substitutionary models of atonement becomes clearer when one recognizes how they hold firmly to the reality of sin and evil and the tension this creates between the justice and mercy of God, both of which are expressions of God's love.[56] Attempts to understand Jesus' saving significance or the nature of God that relax this tension, often in the name of an enlightened reason or a sentimental notion of love, may express accurate criticisms of how substitutionary theories of

---

underlies what is valid in the atonement theories;" Williams, *The Spirit and the Forms of Love*, 182–83.

53. Schweitzer, "The dialectic of understanding," 252.
54. Moltmann, *The Future of Creation*, 77.
55. Schweitzer, "The dialectic of understanding," 259.
56. Smiechen, *Saving Power*, 119.

atonement distort the gospel. But they also frequently become less rational than these theories, for in seeking to understand reality with a seamless coherency they exclude crucial aspects of it, such as the reality of evil or the opposition of God's love to it.

Substitutionary theories of atonement, like the Christus Victor theory, see in Jesus Christ a decisive revelation of God in history. What happens in Jesus according to these theories is not just something God does, but a revelation of the divine life, a further expression in history of what God is in eternity. This is a transcendent reality greater than human reason can fully grasp in a technically consistent manner.

THE TRINITARIAN DYNAMICS OF THE DIVINE LIFE IN THE DEATH AND RESURRECTION OF JESUS

The saving work of Jesus is a further communication of God's goodness and beauty in history through the economic Trinity. Jürgen Moltmann has offered an understanding of how this happens in Jesus' death and resurrection that can be summarized as follows:[57] the first and second persons of the Trinity are united in their will to redeem creation. To do this the first person abandons the second, Jesus, who consequently suffers godforsakenness in a unique way in dying on the cross. As this happens the first person of the Trinity suffers the grief of this loss. The two are united in their will to redeem humanity but separated in Jesus' abandonment, which he undergoes in order to enter into and overcome the alienation of suffering humanity from God. The first and second persons of the Trinity bear this mutual yet distinctive suffering, grief, and separation out of love for one another and creation. From their mutual suffering and love there proceeds the Holy Spirit, the bond of unity between them, which remains intact as their love for one another through their separation. The Holy Spirit proceeds from their suffering and reaches out to encompass all of creation everywhere, no matter how separated from God it may seem to be. The pattern is one of undergoing suffering for the sake of communion with the other.[58] Here Jesus' cross

---

57. Moltmann, *The Crucified God*, 243–46.

58. Moltmann's Trinitarian theology continued to develop past this point. For a succinct account of this, see Thompson, "Interpretatio in bonem partem," 159–78. But this pattern of God undergoing suffering for the sake of communion with the other has remained a permanent characteristic of it.

is the way to his resurrection, whereas in Moltmann's earlier *Theology of Hope* Jesus' cross and resurrection stood in opposition to each other. [59]

The great strength of Moltmann's understanding of the Trinitarian dynamics of the atonement is the way it takes seriously the suffering of God in Jesus' death and its understanding of how God is present in and with those who suffer. The weakness is that as this becomes paradigmatic of the divine life it makes suffering intrinsic to it.[60] Moltmann understands God's suffering in Christ to be partly an exercise of virtue for the sake of others, but partly a fate that God lives under. For Moltmann God must suffer in order for God's love to find fulfillment in communion with an other.[61] This overlooks a key aspect of Jesus' resurrection.

Most New Testament witnesses portray Jesus' resurrection as resulting not from God's patient suffering but from God's intervention on Jesus' behalf in opposition to the sin represented by Jesus' cross.[62] God's action in the atonement expresses God's being as love but also God's freedom and transcendence to sin and evil.[63] God must suffer in the Word and Spirit in the economic Trinity if God is to enter into the condition of suffering humanity. But God does so out of moral necessity, not ontological necessity, and God's suffering alone does not overcome the cosmic powers of sin and evil.

God's suffering in Jesus' death is an excellence, a virtue freely exercised,[64] in part because the immanent Trinity is beyond suffering, sin, and death, and undergoes this freely as a result of the divine will, not necessarily due to a restriction or deficiency of the divine nature. This transcendence of God to suffering, sin, and evil is key to God being a source of hope for the final overcoming of sin and evil. Because God is greater than suffering, sin, and evil, God can rescue creation from it.[65] But how is God transcendent to sin and evil? In Moltmann's *Theology of Hope* Jesus' resurrection was described as "a new totality which annihilates the total nihil" of his death.[66] Here God's being was portrayed

59. Moltmann, *Theology of Hope*, 197–202.

60. Schweitzer, *Contemporary Christologies*, 80–81.

61. Schweitzer, "Aspects of God's Relationship," 9–14.

62. For example, Acts 2:23–24.

63. Barth, *Church Dogmatics* IV/1, 529.

64. Johnson, *She Who Is*, 266.

65. Ibid., 268.

66. Moltmann, *Theology of Hope*, 198.

as actively overcoming sin and evil through a new and decisive exercise of God's creative power. In Moltmann's description of the Trinitarian dynamics of Jesus' death and resurrection in *The Crucified God*, God's transcendence lies in God's ability to endure suffering rather than in God's power to actively resist it.[67] As God's suffering became key to Moltmann's understanding of the Trinitarian life, the conceptualization of God's transcendence in his theology was undermined in certain respects.[68] Drawing on the doctrine of the Trinity developed in chapter 4, we will attempt to describe somewhat differently how "the doctrine of the living God and the doctrine of the atonement coincide."[69]

As Moltmann argues, Jesus' death and resurrection represent two different dynamics or moments in the divine life. For Moltmann the first dynamic, the suffering of the first and second persons of the Trinity in Jesus' death, gives rise to the second, the resurrection of Jesus and the pouring out of the Holy Spirit. Through the first dynamic suffering and sin are taken up and "integrated" into the being of God.[70] This creates the new relationship in which communion is established in an unshakeable way between God and humanity. From this emerges the second dynamic, the resurrection of Jesus in the Holy Spirit, the pouring out of the Holy Spirit and the joy of the new creation. Here the suffering of love leads to communion with the other and the overcoming of sin and evil.

In the doctrine of the Trinity sketched in chapter 4, the first dynamic of the divine life is the expression of God's goodness and beauty in Jesus Christ. The second is the mutual rejoicing of the first and second persons of the Trinity in this, their celebration of their love for each other that generates the Holy Spirit. The ministry of Jesus and his subsequent suffering and death can be seen as further communications of God's goodness and beauty that repeat this first dynamic in history. This further expression of God's goodness and beauty differs from the eternal generation of the Word in that this takes place in the Holy Spirit, which prepares the way for the work of Christ and empowers Jesus to fulfill it.

---

67. Moltmann, *The Crucified God*, 248–49.

68. As Thomas Thompson notes, Moltmann continues to affirm God's transcendence to creation and to suffering, sin and evil in certain ways; Thompson, "Interpretatio in bonem partem," 170–77. But as Thompson notes, statements indicating that suffering is intrinsic to God's being also continue to appear in Moltmann's later Trinitarian theology; ibid., 173, 176.

69. Tillich, *Systematic Theology* Vol. II, 175.

70. Moltmann, *The Crucified God*, 246.

It also takes place in encounter with evil and sin. This further expression takes place in Jesus' person and ministry along two trajectories, both culminating differently in his death on the cross. The first trajectory of Jesus as a person inspired by the Holy Spirit culminates in his execution by Roman soldiers. The second trajectory, the reaching out of God's love in Jesus to the godforsaken and sinners, also culminates in Jesus' cross, which symbolically represents the nadir of human existence.

The expression of God's goodness and beauty along the first trajectory in Jesus' ministry does not depend upon Jesus suffering. He suffers from the rejection and violent response that his ministry provokes, but he does not effect this ministry by suffering. The healings, exorcisms, and acceptance of sinners by Jesus are an assertion of God's being that "drives out of creation the powers of destruction, which are demons and idols, and heals the created beings who have been damaged by them."[71] While Jesus' public ministry drives these idols and demons out of creation, his suffering and death overcome the separation they have created which still exists between God and God's people. Each trajectory is a different way of expressing God's goodness and beauty so as to overcome a different kind of suffering and alienation from God. Though Jesus' death was a catastrophic end to his public ministry that shattered his person and the hopes and beliefs of the community gathered around him, it was also the means by which he overcame the separation that suffering and guilt create between God and creation.

In the immanent Trinity the expression of God's goodness and beauty in the Word gives rise to a second dynamic of mutual joy and celebration between the first and second persons of the Trinity. From this proceeds the Holy Spirit. This second moment or dynamic is expressed definitively in history in Jesus' resurrection and the pouring out of the Holy Spirit. This relates dialectically to the occurrence of the first movement in history, in particular to Jesus' death. The second movement affirms and celebrates the goodness and beauty expressed in the first, yet it judges and overcomes the sin and evil that Jesus' cross represents.

On one hand Jesus' resurrection signifies and celebrates "the permanent, redeemed, final and definitive validity of the single and unique life of Jesus who achieved the permanent and final validity of his life precisely through his death in freedom and obedience."[72] In this respect

71. Moltmann, *The Way of Jesus Christ*, 104.
72. Rahner, *Foundations*, 266.

there is an intrinsic relationship and profound unity between Jesus' death and his resurrection. The love and faithfulness shown in his living and dying as a human being responsive to God reach their goal of final and definitive expression in and through his death. As Jesus' resurrection is God's affirmation of the expression of God's love and love for God in his life, and as his death is the definitive expression of this, Jesus' death leads to his resurrection. There is also a unity and intrinsic relation between Jesus' death and resurrection along the second trajectory outlined above. The expression of God's love in Jesus' death laid the basis for a new relationship to God for suffering and sinful humanity. Jesus' resurrection made this actual. In these respects Jesus' resurrection affirms what happened in his death.

But Jesus' cross was also a crushing end to his public ministry, a violent assault on his person, on God's love and creation. While God's love and Jesus' love of God reach their highest expression in his faithfulness and obedience unto death, both were also refuted and destroyed by his death. Jesus' resurrection affirms the first aspect of his death but negates and overcomes this second aspect. As much as Jesus' resurrection affirmed his faithfulness in dying, it also liberated him from the violent death he suffered.[73] In this second respect Jesus' resurrection occurs not as a result of his suffering and death, but in opposition to it, as a reassertion of the transcendence of God's beauty and goodness in relation to the sin and evil that Jesus' cross represents. This element of opposition between Jesus' cross and resurrection must always be acknowledged.

In the immanent Trinity the Holy Spirit proceeds as the bond of unity from the love and joy that the first and second persons of the Trinity have for each other. But in the economic Trinity, as this second movement occurs definitively in history in Jesus' resurrection, the Holy Spirit is already present. It has been at work in Jesus' ministry all along. Some New Testament traditions attribute an active role to the Holy Spirit in Jesus' resurrection,[74] but others hesitate to do so.[75] This suggests that Jesus' resurrection cannot be attributed to the Holy Spirit alone. The Holy Spirit plays a role in it, but Jesus' resurrection as a definitive communication of God's goodness and beauty is an event parallel to creation out of nothing (Rom 4:17). The resurrection of Jesus results from his

73. Sobrino, *Christ The Liberator*, 80.

74. Käsemann, *Romans*, 11–13.

75. Dunn, "Towards the Spirit of Christ," 14–15.

affirmation and vindication by the first and third persons of the Trinity. But this affirmation reasserts the goodness and beauty he incarnated to such an extent that it is a re-creation of Jesus' person, a transformation that constitutes him as the Christ in a new and ultimate way. The dialectical relationship of their affirmation to his death issues in the continuity and discontinuity of the risen Christ with the historical Jesus. It is Jesus who was crucified who is risen. Yet the destructive power of sin and evil is repudiated and overcome as he is risen to new life beyond death. The risen Christ is a promise of the final overcoming of the violence his cross represents and is not bound by the limitations of Jesus' historical era.[76] The resurrection of Jesus is thus not simply an affirmation or rescue of his person and message. It is also an exaltation and transformation of it.

If one follows the second trajectory of the expression of God's love in Jesus' suffering and death, or if one focuses on the virtue of Jesus shown in the first trajectory, one sees the continuity between his death and resurrection. But if one focuses on his person, how Jesus was broken and executed as one of the numberless victims of violence and empire in history, one sees the opposition of his resurrection to his cross. God's love, having expressed itself in Jesus' ministry and faithfulness unto death, expressed itself again in a new and ultimate way in his resurrection. Jesus' resurrection makes both trajectories of expression ultimately decisive, at once negating and affirming his cross. There is a dialectical relationship between Jesus' death and resurrection because there are elements of sin and evil in Jesus' death that his resurrection can only oppose and overcome.

Substitutionary theories of atonement like Anselm's that focus on how Jesus' death creates a new relationship for humanity to God through Jesus' satisfying God's wrath or paying the debt sinners owe God through his death typically leave out this ineradicable opposition between Jesus' cross and resurrection. They overlook how Jesus' death was something that happened to him[77] that destroyed his person and was an outrage to God's love. Feminist and womanist critiques of substitutionary theories of the atonement point this out and insist that "theologians must remain cognizant of the sinful horrors of the cross."[78] Overlooking this leads to Jesus representing only God's mercy and the first person of the Trinity

76. Cone, *God of the Oppressed*, 223–24.

77. Pannenberg, *Jesus—God and Man*, 277.

78. Tanner, *Christ the Key*, 252.

representing only God's judgment. To prevent this it is necessary to see Jesus' resurrection as a further expression of God's goodness and beauty that affirms Jesus' ministry and death, revealing hidden meaning in the latter, yet also overcoming the primary destructive meaning of Jesus' death and transforming his person so that it becomes the basis of a new relationship between God and humanity, in which both victims and the guilty can find comfort, hope, and the courage to love.

GUILT

Substitutionary theories of atonement have traditionally addressed issues of guilt and judgment resulting from the opposition of God's love to sin. In sinning people act against God's love. As we do this, "we do have God against us,"[79] though God does not cease to love us. The idea of God's judgment or wrath needs careful retrieval. There can be no going back to the God who demands punishment or the death of an innocent victim to atone for the offense of sin to God's honor. But if God's love is to be a source of hope for the overcoming of sin and evil then it must judge and oppose these. "God isn't wrathful in spite of being love. God is wrathful *because* God is love."[80]

> The wrath of God in the sense of righteous anger against injustice is not an opposite of mercy but its correlative. It is a mode of caring response in the face of evil, aroused by what is mean of shameful or injurious to beloved human beings and the created world itself. Precisely because Holy Wisdom cares with a love that goes beyond our imagining, the depths of divine anger are likewise immeasurable. . . . The religious symbol of divine wrath discloses God's outrage at the harm done to those she loves; this should not be.[81]

God's wrath and judgment arise from the nature of God's love as a universal principle of justice. Where it is violated, regardless of by whom, it expresses itself as judgment and wrath. Yet God's wrath is also an expression of God's abiding love for the sinner.[82] The wrath of God

---

79. Barth, *Church Dogmatics* IV/1, 221.

80. Volf, *Free of Charge*, 138–39.

81. Johnson, *She Who Is*, 258.

82. "The opposite of love is not wrath, but indifference," Moltmann, *The Crucified God*, 272.

kindled by the harm that sin does is not meant to destroy the sinner. It is meant to stop the evil they do and to deliver the sinner from their own evil deeds.

God's justice is essentially creative and transformative, working towards the establishment of the reign of God.[83] Substitutionary theories of atonement should articulate one way in which this justice is effected through Christ. In these theories God does not give the sinner what they deserve, but joins them in their sinful condition and so changes it. By entering into their condition Christ reconciles them with God. This creates the possibility for them to be reconciled with others and themselves. This is in some ways an extension of the dynamic of the mercy code in the Hebrew Bible, which was intended to continually create the possibility of those rendered marginal or excluded from society through lack of economic means being able to re-enter it and become active members of it again.[84] This dynamic finds contemporary expression in the preferential option for the poor, which seeks to guide thought and action so that those excluded by poverty and oppression can be reintegrated as respected and productive members of society. In each case God's justice meets people where they are, regardless of how they got there, and seeks to move them to where they should be. In a parallel fashion but in relation to a different form of alienation, the goodness and beauty of God expressed in substitutionary atonement seeks to enable those burdened by guilt or banished from the community because of their crime to be reaccepted into it so that they too can once again contribute to it. Anselm tried to articulate how this happens using feudal notions of honor. Calvin tried to do the same using legal terms. In light of the critiques of substitutionary theories of atonement outlined above, some contemporary theologians reconceptualize how this happens in spatial terms.

A first step towards this is to realize that God's judgment is in part the withdrawal of God's presence from sinners.[85] As sin provokes God's judgment it creates a place of alienation, "a spiritual, psychological space of pain and anguish and sense of separation from God."[86] Sin separates one from God, from others and from whom one should be. Some Hebrew prophets conceived God's wrath as expressing itself through

83. Tillich, *Love, Power and Justice*, 65.

84. Welker, "Security of Expectations," 252.

85. Moltmann, *The Crucified God*, 272.

86. Placher, *Jesus the Savior*, 141.

disasters visited on the sinful people, either through natural plagues or conquering armies, so that the ensuing suffering would lead the sinful people to repent and turn back to God. Similarly, the withdrawal of God's presence as an expression of God's judgment is intended to lead people to repent of their sin and turn back to God. But as one seeks to return to God an awareness of one's sin brings the realization that one cannot do so of one's own accord. Atonement must be made as much as possible to the victims of one's sin. But this can never repair the rupture that sin creates. The movement of a sinner from alienation to reconciliation with God requires a bridge that only God can build.

God atones for human sin by crossing the divide separating the sinner from God. God does this through the Word assuming human nature in Jesus. By means of this God in Christ "steps into our place,"[87] enters into history and descends to its depths.[88] This divide is the experience of God's absence created by God's wrath in response to sin. God in Jesus takes this wrath upon Godself by entering into the sinner's condition of separation from God. This is what God in Jesus did on the cross. God did not punish Jesus on the cross. Those who crucified him did that. But reflecting on the cross, Paul and other New Testament authors saw that in dying this way Jesus symbolically[89] entered the place of the guilty (Gal 3:13), dying as one condemned by God's justice. Jesus' cross symbolizes the suffering of those who seem godforsaken. It also symbolizes the absence of God that the guilty suffer. In dying on the cross Jesus symbolically entered the spiritual place of people who experience themselves as separated from God by their sin.

By entering the condition of those who experience God's judgment as guilt, Jesus goes beyond the moral dimensions of God's love. In light of his resurrection, his suffering and death give definitive expression to the transmoral dimensions of God's goodness and beauty. Instead of leaving people in their guilt, God in Jesus enters into their condition. As Jesus does so he endures the pain that this entry into alienation from God brings. Jesus who is not guilty suffers representatively for the sake of

87. Tanner, *Christ the King*, 258.

88. Hayes, *The Hidden Center*, 199.

89. Symbolically here means representatively. Jesus enters into a place that represents the experience of guilt. But symbolically also means that Jesus really participates in what this place represents. On the cross he experienced the absence of God.

those who are.[90] He endures the condition of the sinful in order to bring God's presence to them. The moral dimension of God's love remains in force and yet in Jesus God's love goes beyond this. God does not ignore sin. To do so is ultimately to fail to love the victims of sin and also the sinner. Yet God's love does not give up on the sinner either. Instead God in Jesus symbolically goes to where sinners are, to their place of self-created isolation, and through this bestows upon them a new, complex identity of being at once a sinner and yet loved and accepted by God in spite of this. Through this the sphere of God's presence is enlarged without its moral dimensions collapsing. Jesus' death and resurrection create a new spiritual space of communion with God that includes those who know themselves to be sinners.[91] In this way it carries forward Jesus' acceptance of sinners in his public ministry and the teaching in parables of Luke 15.[92] Regardless of their historical circumstances, people can live "in Christ" and know by faith that their ultimate identity is determined not by their moral failings but by God's love in Jesus. Jesus' resurrection, as it vindicates his person and message, affirms that it was indeed God in Jesus who made this journey. As it does so it promises that sinners will not remain in their complex identity forever. Jesus' resurrection promises that this second movement will end with them wholly in God's presence, moved from their alienation into unbroken communion with God.

This spatial understanding of how Jesus effects atonement breaks with traditional notions of substitutionary atonement in some respects. It understands Jesus as dying in the place of sinners not in the sense of taking their place and receiving their punishment, but in the sense of entering their condition. Yet, in continuity with substitutionary theories of atonement stretching from Paul through Anselm to the present, it understands Jesus as doing this so that "the other can keep on living."[93] The notion of substitution for Paul can also mean "substantial union and identification,"[94] as understood here. Through faith people participate and share in what God in Jesus has done, and in what Jesus as the Christ

---

90. Pannenberg, *Systematic Theology* Vol. 2, 426–27.

91. Becker, *Paul*, 418.

92. The parable of the lost sheep, Luke 15:1–7; the woman and the lost coin, Luke 15:8–10; the parable of the prodigal son, Luke 15:11–32.

93. Becker, *Paul*, 409.

94. Ibid.

is. People's destinies are ultimately determined by what God has done in Jesus, not by their own failures or misdeeds.

In light of this, substitutionary theories of atonement like Anselm's point toward universal salvation.[95] In Anselm's *Cur Deus Homo?* Anselm's dialogue partner Boso, having heard Anselm expound the saving significance of Christ's death, exclaims:

> And I receive such confidence from this that I cannot describe
> the joy with which my heart exults. For it seems to me that God
> can reject none who come to him in his name.[96]

To this Anselm replies, "Certainly not, if he come aright."[97] Anselm himself is reported to have expected that not many people would be saved. Yet as the words of Boso indicate, the logic of Anselm's position points toward God rejecting none. It also points beyond Anselm's own caveat, for if one does not come "aright," will that not be forgiven as well?

LAW AND GOSPEL

This understanding of how Jesus creates a complex identity for sinners in which their sin is acknowledged and yet they are reconciled to God in spite of it has important ethical potential. It can be extended beyond forgiveness of sin to play a role in a person's journey to selfhood and a society's journey towards justice and peace.

To be a self involves living within a moral framework and striving to be more than one is. This striving also takes place in relation to one's moral framework. One strives both to better fulfill one's moral goals and to have a more adequate set of moral goals. But this striving for more adequate moral goals is carried out within a sea of relativity, a world containing myriad different goods and different ways of actualizing the same good. The relentless imperative for self-transcendence within a sea of relativity can become destructive of the self. As one becomes self-critical and strives to participate in a higher good, the relativity of all achievements and the impossibility of ever finally knowing which good one should strive for and how one should strive for it can lead into the dark night of the soul. The call to seek the reign of God, which "never

---

95. Haight, *Jesus*, 230.

96. Anselm, *Anselm: Basic Writings*, 285.

97. Ibid.

leaves anyone in peace,"[98] can become cause for despair if it turns into an endless road that can never be traversed and one's identity depends upon reaching the end. Once the imperative for self-transcendence is awakened and the journey towards selfhood begun, one needs to en- counter a radical transcendence that can give one both orientation and a sense of self-worth amidst the ambiguity of history.[99] If one does not experience a transcendent identity that comes to one as a gift, even now in one's imperfect state, seeking an identity based on one's own actions can become a hopeless task.

Here God's transmoral acceptance of the self can be important. The self dedicated to self-transcendence and seeking social justice needs an identity independent of its own achievements if self-justification is not to replace the goal of achieving social justice. Substitutionary theories of atonement can provide this. The experience of the moral valuation of the self, its demand for self-transcendence, and the transmoral goodness of God that substitutionary theories of atonement articulate can work to- gether to help constitute the self.[100] Jesus awakens a demand for self and social transcendence through his teachings and moral influence. His unconditional acceptance of the self enables one to pursue this without being consumed by it. Together these two dynamics of law and gospel can give the self and the church an identity characterized by "bounded openness."[101] The self and the church community are bounded by the teachings, example, and person of Jesus, which give them orientation. Yet they can remain open to self-transcendence and to others who are different through the transcendent identity they have in Jesus Christ. As people's identities are secure in Christ, this can enable them to acknowl- edge their faults and errors and help them to be truth-seeking com- munities open to critique.[102] The complex identity that substitutionary theories of atonement provide can thus help one to be open to correction by others, to self-criticism, and able to accept those who are different.

It can also help sustain individuals and churches whose identities have been compromised by their own actions. The Anglican, Presby- terian, Roman Catholic, and United churches in Canada are currently

98. Sobrino, *Spirituality of Liberation*, 131.

99. Schrag, *The Self after Postmodernity*, 124.

100. Ibid., 144.

101. Jones, *Feminist Theory and Christian Theology*, 171–72.

102. Williams, *The Spirit and The Forms of Love*, 178.

struggling to come to terms with their past involvement in running residential schools. First Nations children, sometimes as young as six years old, were taken, if need be by force, from their parents to live in schools run by churches at the behest of the Canadian federal government. These schools were generally characterized by an ethos in which First Nations children were vulnerable to violence, abuse, neglect, and illness. The last of these were closed in the 1970s.[103] Jessie Oliver, a white woman, worked at one of these, the Alberni Residence in Port Alberni, British Columbia. Without her knowing it at the time, a number of students there were sexually abused by one of her coworkers. Reflecting on this thirty years later, she describes feelings of shame, resentment, and guilt.[104] As Oliver notes, many of her coworkers were "fine, dedicated folk . . . who cared for the children,"[105] whose work was an expression of their Christian faith. Oliver was one of these, yet she now sees her work there as something for which she needs forgiveness.

How does one continue to seek justice and resist evil, to love one's neighbor, after discovering how the best efforts of many in this regard resulted in much harm? The church now has very different missions goals. But it is not enough to say that the church now knows better. The history of residential schools as a lesson from the past reveals a disturbing truth about the present and the future. Ernst Bloch once said, "In the citizen of the French Revolution the bourgeois was hidden: God have mercy on us, we cannot tell what may be hidden in the comrade."[106] Seeing now some of the cultural imperialism and harm that was then hidden in the residential school system, one can only wonder what may be hidden in contemporary notions of Christian love and discipleship. This thought can paralyze one. Yet if one has the means to care and does not act, one becomes guilty in another way. In such a setting the complex identity mediated by substitutionary theories of atonement can empower one to act responsibly,[107] giving one the courage to love even though one's

103. For histories of Residential Schools in Canada, see Miller, *Shingwauk's Vision*; Milloy, *A National Crime*. For a personal account of life in a residential school, see Johnston, *Indian School Days*.

104. Oliver, "The Bitter Teardrops Fall," 12.

105. Ibid.

106. Quoted from Moltmann, *Religion*, 28.

107. For Bonhoeffer's understanding of this, Tödt, *Authentic Faith*, 161–64.

actions may incur guilt. In this way it can help sustain a commitment to peace and justice that otherwise might falter or become fanatical.

The complex identity that substitutionary theories of atonement present can also be an important ethical source in social conflicts. A great weakness of these theories is that their focus on the universality or condition of sin as opposed to the concrete differences in power and suffering between victims and their oppressors can lead into the moral equivalent of "the night in which all cats are grey."[108] Yet this obliviousness to moral specifics can also make them an important moral source. The "doctrine of the universality of human sin can also lead to an insight into a solidarity which goes beyond all boundaries because it is boundless."[109]

The injustices that give rise to social conflicts and the violence occurring during them often lead to social divisions that perpetuate violence. Substitutionary theories of atonement present a moral vision that can help arrest this. In these theories victims "and perpetrators stand together before the cross, all in need of atonement. Yet injustice and oppression are taken with absolute seriousness."[110] The other who has sinned against one has been accepted by God for the sake of Christ, just as God has accepted oneself. Christ has died for the other just as Christ has died for oneself. As Christ has accepted them in spite of their sin, one can accept them too. The other remains a sinner. The injustices they have perpetrated are not ignored. Yet their identity to which one must relate is not finally determined by what they have done, but by what God has done for them and for oneself in Christ. Substitutionary theories of atonement thus provide a "vision of reconciliation that cannot be undone,"[111] as it has been accomplished once and for all by Jesus Christ. This presents a metaphysical warrant for the difficult work of seeking reconciliation with one's enemies. The irrevocable reconciliation of all that is effected on a metaphysical level in Christ must find "nonfinal"[112] historical expression in law, politics, and culture. Christ's acceptance of all calls and empowers one to seek this.

---

108. Moltmann, *History and the Triune God*, 45.

109. Ibid.

110. Wells, "Theology for Reconciliation," 11.

111. Volf, *Exclusion and Embrace*, 110.

112. Ibid.

MARGINALITY

Substitutionary theories of atonement can also address the condition of marginality in a saving way. Marginality can be defined as a condition of permanent and enforced liminality.[113] Liminality is a state of in-betweenness, of being out of social structure, which is often a source of creativity and transition to a new state or identity. But when liminality is made permanent and enforced by powers beyond one's control, it becomes the soul-destroying alienation of marginality, of never belonging or being accepted as one is by the society in which one lives. Marginality is primarily about status, the recognition accorded one by surrounding society.

Marginality is created in part by the shared values and norms of a society's ethos. These are in many respects shared by a society's members. But they must also be imposed and enforced by "the dominant forces in society"[114] partly because they inevitably suppress other values and exclude certain members from full participation in society. Every moral code, every struggle for justice, every understanding of the reign of God inevitably suppresses some values and oppresses some people. No society, no church, no person can live without a moral code. Yet every code marginalizes some through no fault of their own.

Marginality, a lack of belonging that cannot be overcome by any virtue or effort on one's own part, is experienced by members of social groups who by reason of their race, culture, physical makeup, or sexual orientation fail to conform to what society values as normative. Because they stand out as different from prevailing social norms they are never fully accepted by dominant social groups as belonging to the society in which they live. This lack of acceptance is communicated, often unwittingly, by members of the dominant group in personal encounters and by mass media geared to the dominant group's values.

Asian Americans experience this marginality in America,[115] as do Mexican Americans.[116] The chronically ill and differently abled also often experience a sense of not belonging fully to society, sometimes through the way accounts of Jesus' healing miracles are expounded.[117]

113. Lee, "Pilgrimage and Home," 52. What follows on liminality and marginality is drawn substantially from Sang Hyun Lee's work.

114. Baum, *Religion and Alienation*, 172.

115. Lee, "Pilgrimage and Home," 49–51.

116. Elizondo, "Elements for a Mexican American Mestizo Christology," 4.

117. Betcher, *Spirit and the Politics of Disablement*, 70.

Expressions of compassion extended towards the differently abled frequently express a commitment to normalcy that functions to marginalize those who cannot be "normal." Marginality can only be overcome through social/political struggle that seeks to change the presenting exclusions of society's values and practices. But insofar as marginality is a matter of status, substitutionary theories of atonement can function to strengthen and empower people as they endure it. As Ada María Isasi-Díaz notes, when sung by the marginalized, the Kyrie Eleison becomes a cry not for forgiveness, but for recognition by God in the face of social exclusion.[118]

Substitutionary theories of atonement mediate a complex sense of identity in which a person experiences themselves as at one judged and found wanting in light of a moral code and yet accepted and valued by God in spite of this. They communicate that the fullness of one's person, one's capacities, one's value, and one's future are not perceived by society's moral codes.[119] Though judged and found wanting by these, one is nonetheless accepted and valued by God. The marginalized person's identity, damaged by the lack of recognition from dominant social groups, is nonetheless strengthened and upheld by this recognition from a divine perspective that transcends and judges society.[120] Being accepted and valued by God bestows a dignity upon people that disregard and disdain from others cannot take away. From this recognition can come the courage and strength to creatively struggle to overcome one's marginalized status, to accept oneself in spite of it while continuing to work against it.

When the marginalized are strengthened in this way, the liminality of their marginal status can once again become a source of creativity and prophetic insights and movements towards a more just and inclusive society. Conversely, as noted earlier, the message of substitutionary atonement can enable those who belong to the dominant group to recognize the fallibility of their society's and their own moral codes. It can create within them an openness to the other that affirms relative moral goods without these becoming final judgments on those who differ.

118. Isasi-Díaz, "Identifícate con Nosotras," 38.

119. Welker, "Security of Expectations," 250.

120. Ibid., 251.

CONCLUSION

Substitutionary theories of atonement address forms of alienation involving one's status before God, within one's society, and before oneself. This is an important dimension of life that the gospel must address, for people do not live by bread alone (Luke 4:4). These forms of alienation cannot be finally overcome by the exercise of brute force, but only by the communication of recognition and acceptance from a source of ultimate value. Substitutionary theories of atonement do this by mediating a complex identity that can acknowledge different aspects of human identities as sinner and/or as victim while restating one's overriding identity as loved by God. These theories, which see God as coming to be with suffering humanity irrevocably through Jesus' death on the cross, will always be potentially dangerous. Yet they communicate an essential element of Jesus' saving significance and address an important dimension of human life. Reconfigured as something God does for humanity rather than as describing what God demands of humanity, and supplemented and corrected by other theories of atonement, they can continue to play an important role in enabling people to follow the way of Jesus Christ.

Part III

Introduction to Part III

PART I OF THIS book developed an understanding of the person of
Jesus Christ. Part II examined some different forms of his saving
significance. Here in part III the final four chapters will look at aspects
of Jesus' relationships to other people, other movements and ideas in
history, other religions, and people who believe in him as the Christ.
Christianity today exists in a globalized world where different religions
constantly interact with each other. This raises the question of Jesus' relationship to other religions with a new urgency. As well, the emphases
in process and feminist theologies on the relational nature of reality and
human life[1] have renewed questions of how Jesus relates to others and
how his work as the Christ includes others. As a result, Jesus needs to
be understood as the Christ in terms of his relationships as well as his
person and work.

Chapter 9 begins by looking at the intrinsic relationality of Jesus,
how his person is partly constituted by his relationships to others. As
a human being, Jesus exists in relationships with others and is shaped
by them. This is also true of his presence in history as the risen Christ.
Chapter 10 then looks at how Jesus provides a center by which people
can orient themselves to other religions, movements, and events in history. As such, Jesus has a formative influence on who they are. Chapter
11 then examines how Jesus Christ relates to four other religions in the
present: Judaism, Islam, Hinduism, and the traditional religion of the
Rock Cree of northern Manitoba. Chapter 12 looks at how Jesus Christ
relates to Christians in their prayer life. Jesus' relationships are part of
who he is as the Christ, and part of his saving significance.

---

1. Suchocki, *God—Christ—Church*, 5-8; Johnson, *She Who Is*, 225.

9 The Sociality of Jesus Christ

A person's identity is constituted partly by their relationships and historical circumstances. People are able to reflect on these and so gain some critical distance on them. This can alter their influence on a person but it does not remove it. Dietrich Bonhoeffer used the term "sociality" to describe this, how people exist as individuals only in relationships with others.[1] This chapter will examine the sociality of Jesus Christ, how his person was formed partly through his relationships with others during his earthly life and how it continues to be formed by his relationships with others in the present. There is a social dimension to Jesus Christ as a person and pivotal event in salvation history.[2] This includes Jesus' relationships to other persons in history and to the other "persons" of the Trinity. These divine and human socialities intermingle. The Holy Spirit works through other people and their relationships to Jesus to prepare the way for and to help constitute his being as the Christ. The Holy Spirit also works through his relationships to others in subsequent history and the present to constitute his presence as the risen Christ in history. When people receive Jesus as the Christ, the risen Christ finds a new body in history, a new form of historical existence as "church-community."[3] The goodness and beauty of God that he incarnated finds further expression through this.

The revelation of God in Jesus Christ leads to understanding God as also having a twofold sociality. There is a social dimension within the Trinity in the perichoretic relations of the Trinitarian "persons." Jesus' person as the Word of God, the second person of the Trinity, is constituted through his relations to the first and third persons of the Trinity, and they through their relations to each other and him. Also, as argued

1. Green, *Bonhoeffer*, 36.

2. "The event 'Jesus as the Christ' is unique but not isolated; it is dependent on past and future, as they are dependent on it" (Tillich, *Systematic Theology*, 3:147).

3. Bonhoeffer, *Sanctorum Communio*, 190.

in chapter 4, God's being is internally related to humanity and creation. As the goodness and beauty of God find further expression in history through Jesus Christ and the Holy Spirit, the being of God in the person of the Holy Spirit is quantitatively increased. The identity of God is in a limited but still real way at stake in God's relationships to humanity and creation.

Who Jesus was as a person in history was constituted partly by his relationships to others. After his death Jesus was constituted as the Christ in a definitive way through his resurrection.[4] As the risen Christ Jesus gained a new sociality, formed in part by the memory of his historical sociality but extending in history beyond this through the existence of church-communities.[5] The historical presence of the risen Christ also extends beyond the church into its surrounding cultures in manifest and latent ways.[6] The risen Christ also has a transcendence undergirding his presence in history that points towards his still outstanding future. Therefore the sociality of Jesus Christ must be examined in terms of his past, present, and future.[7] His relationships in the past that helped form his person and work help shape his relationships in the present. If the latter are authentic they will be continuous with his past but not limited by them. Together his past and present relationships work towards the coming of his future, which in turn will be continuous with but not limited to these.

THE SOCIALITY OF THE HISTORICAL JESUS

In looking at Jesus as a person formed partly by his relationships to others, we begin with Jesus as a Palestinian Jew, steeped in the traditions of Second Temple Judaism. Jesus' sense of himself and his calling arose out of the matrix of his Jewish heritage, the circumstances of his upbringing and his life as a Jewish peasant carpenter in Nazareth. This Jewish heritage was appropriated in different ways in Jesus' day by the Pharisees, Sadducees, Essenes, Zealots, and Qumran community[8] and movements

4. Dupuis, *Jesus Christ*, 142.

5. Bonhoeffer, *Sanctorum Communio*, 140.

6. The notions of the manifest and latent church are presented in Tillich, *Systematic Theology*, 3:152–55.

7. Cone, *God of the Oppressed*, 130.

8. For an overview of these groups and others in Jesus' time, Meier, *Marginal Jew*, 3:289–613.

that formed around charismatic leaders like John the Baptist. Jesus located himself within this milieu by being baptized by John. John's followers were drawn mostly from lower social strata.[9] John's interpretation of Judaism and his understanding of his calling appear to have significantly influenced Jesus.

John the Baptist

In the quest for the historical Jesus it is taken as historical fact that Jesus was baptized by John. Jesus may have been one of John's followers, though for how long no one can say. Baptism by John indicates that Jesus affirmed John's eschatological outlook and call to repentance. As a follower of John, Jesus would have lived "in an environment of charismatic prophecy."[10] John may have been a mentor to Jesus, someone from whom Jesus learned before embarking on his own path of charismatic prophecy. Much of John's person and message remained present in Jesus' public ministry.

> Even after the Baptist's arrest and execution, Jesus was never entirely "without John" . . . he carried John's eschatology, concern for a sinful Israel facing God's imminent judgment, call to repentance, and baptism with him throughout his own ministry, however much he recycled and reinterpreted this inheritance.[11]

This suggests that John functioned as someone who inducted Jesus into a way of being and seeing the world, who helped him acquire a language for speaking about God and who was pivotal for Jesus' self-definition and understanding. John probably remained a figure in relation to whom Jesus had to define himself during his public ministry.[12] His influence on Jesus appears to have been continuing and deep and helped constitute who Jesus was as the Christ. Yet Jesus cannot be reduced to a disciple or extension of John.[13] There was an irreducible novelty to Jesus as he defined himself in his public ministry by the symbolic actions he

9. Stegemann and Stegemann, *Jesus Movement*, 184–85.

10. Ibid., 196.

11. Meier, *Marginal Jew*, 2:176.

12. "[H]aving emerged from John's circle with some of John's disciples, Jesus would find it necessary to explain to interested Israelites and potential enemies alike how he continued yet differed from the Baptist's preaching and praxis" (ibid.).

13. For new elements in Jesus' public ministry in relation to that of John, see ibid., 126–27.

carried out, the message he proclaimed, his healings and exorcisms, his eating with tax collectors and sinners, and his focus on the poor.

Jesus and Other Movements in First-Century Judaism

In the course of his public ministry Jesus came into contact with members of other Jewish religious parties or movements, such as the Pharisees, the Sadducees, the Zealots, and possibly the Essenes. None of these were as influential on Jesus as John the Baptist. Jesus appears to have had the most contact with the Pharisees. In Jesus' time they had lost political power and like him were focused on winning the common people to their vision of Jewish life. The Gospels describe adversarial interactions between Jesus and the Pharisees during his public ministry, but also more collegial moments.[14] Though the Pharisees were probably Jesus' main sparring partners in public debate they do not appear to have played a role in his death.[15] Jesus seems to have had little direct contact with the Sadducees, who were located in Jerusalem, controlled "institutional religious power in Palestinian Judaism,"[16] and probably counted Caiaphas the high priest among their number. Apart from the role some Sadducees may have played in Jesus' death, it is difficult to say how much influence this or other groups had on Jesus. He was an eschatological prophet proclaiming a message, not a scholar specializing in debate with other religious authorities. The great majority of Jews in his time shared "a broad consensus on what was religiously important"[17] but belonged to none of the groups mentioned above.[18] Jesus focused his attention on these people and on the poor in particular.

Jesus and the Movement around Him

In his public ministry Jesus consciously sought to gain followers and develop a movement with a discernible identity centered on his person and message. He called people to be his disciples and "used certain

14. Luke 7: 36–50; John 3:1–2.

15. Meier, *Marginal Jew*, 3:639.

16. Ibid., 637.

17. Fredriksen, *Jesus of Nazareth*, 62. Fredriksen describes this consensus as consisting of a focus on "the people, the Land of Israel, Jerusalem, the Temple, and Torah. Behind these concepts and subsuming them stood . . . [a] unique commitment to the imageless worship of the one God of the universe" (ibid.).

18. Ibid., 64.

distinguishing practices to form"[19] and give them identity as such. The movement around him was one of a number of "Jewish eschatological groups with radical lifestyles, fervent hopes for Israel's future, and tense or hostile relations with the priestly establishment in Jerusalem,"[20] the ruling powers of Rome and King Herod. John Meier suggests that it was composed of three concentric circles of followers with different levels of closeness to Jesus: the crowds, the disciples, and the Twelve.[21]

The "crowds" who came to hear and see Jesus included some of the wealthy, powerful and privileged but were mostly made up of the poor. Jesus concentrated on the poor but his message was addressed to all of Israel.[22] The crowds were interested in Jesus, often enthusiastic but not deeply committed to him. Their size made Jesus a public figure who could be threatening to the ruling power of Rome and the temple authorities. The "crowds" were not the "sinners" that Jesus was known to fraternize with. These "sinners" seem to have been Jews who did not observe the Jewish Law.[23] Jesus' openness to them and association with them characterized his person and ministry as directed to all of Israel[24] and not just to the virtuous. Through the crowds that he attracted, his welcome of sinners, his message of the imminent coming of God's reign, and his healings and exorcisms, Jesus gained a public profile that brought him to the attention of Caiaphas and Pilate as he arrived in Jerusalem when it was filled with people who had come to celebrate the Passover. Many would have been "vocally enthusiastic" about Jesus; others would have been hostile.[25] Passover tended to heighten tensions around religious and political issues in Jerusalem. It was likely as a result of Jesus' public profile and this tense atmosphere that Jesus had his decisive confron-

---

19. "The practice of baptism, the rejection of voluntary fasting yoked with festive meals celebrated with the outcasts of Israel, the rejection of divorce . . . the special prayer we call the Lord's Prayer, the fierce demands made on those who followed him literally on his itinerant ministry, the inner circle of the Twelve symbolizing eschatological Israel, the mission of the Twelve and perhaps other disciples to Israel—all these incipient structural elements shaped the contours of a clearly distinguished group of disciples" (Meier, *Marginal Jew*, 3:251).

20. Ibid., 532.

21. Ibid., 245.

22. Ibid., 28.

23. Wright, *Jesus*, 266.

24. Becker, *Jesus of Nazareth*, 160.

25. Fredriksen, *Jesus of Nazareth*, 256–57.

tation with Pilate and the Sanhedrin.[26] This led to a defining moment for his person and work, his death on the cross. As the crowds helped make Jesus a public person, a social presence that religious and political authorities were compelled to reckon with, they had a constitutive role in his being as the Christ.

The crowds Jesus attracted made him a public figure but the movement around him really began with his disciples. Between them and the crowds lay the threshold of commitment. Discipleship to Jesus meant an active reception of his message, commitment to his cause of the coming reign of God, and often sacrifice and suffering for its sake. The crowds gave Jesus a public profile. The disciples gave him an identity as a charismatic prophet and ultimately as the Christ. Within the disciples four subgroups can be discerned: (a) disciples who followed Jesus around and extended his ministry by participating in it, (b) sedentary followers who provided a support system for Jesus and those who traveled with him, (c) women who did both, and (d) the disciples who formed the group known as the Twelve.

The crowds listened to Jesus, but the disciples were expected to follow him and exhibit behavior appropriate to the coming reign of God that Jesus called all Israel to adopt.[27] A basic feature of discipleship was being called by Jesus to follow him.[28] The disciples physically accompanied Jesus during his ministry. Probably they were a somewhat fluid group, with some coming and going as new members were called and others becoming no longer able or willing to travel with Jesus. They formed "a small group of men and women in which Jesus of Nazareth played the central role."[29] However, discipleship was a reciprocal relationship. It arose "from a particular social interaction: the decision and command of Jesus to call certain people to follow him and their obedience in answering his call."[30] Both Jesus' call and people's assent were intrinsic to his being the Christ. Jesus could not have been the Christ without those who received him and his message as such. He only be-

---

26. Ibid.

27. Becker, *Jesus of Nazareth*, 233–34.

28. Meier, *Marginal Jew*, 3:51.

29. Stegemann and Stegemann, *Jesus Movement*, 102.

30. Meier, *Marginal Jew*, 3:51.

came the Christ through the unity of both sides of this interaction; his call and his disciples' response.[31]

Jesus formed the disciples into a movement partly through creating practices that functioned as identity badges expressive of his message and self-understanding. These included baptism, a prohibition of voluntary fasting, a practice of feasting, often with "the social and religious lowlife of the day," and what has come to be known as the Lord's Prayer.[32] Through Jesus' leadership the disciples formed an identifiable movement that helped give substance to his message and person. The reign of God was becoming present in history through Jesus' ministry but also through the ministry of his disciples who were sent out in his name. It was present in their ministry and in the community they formed around Jesus.[33] The disciple community thus had a constitutive role in Jesus' ministry and extended it beyond his physical presence.

In addition to the disciples who traveled with Jesus there were sedentary adherents who did not travel with him but who formed a support system for him and those who did.[34] These people, such as Mary, Martha, and Zacchaeus, were not called disciples as they did not literally follow Jesus about. But their material support enabled Jesus and others to undertake his public ministry. Their mention in the Gospels indicates a practical aspect of reciprocity existing between Jesus and those committed to him. Jesus could not have carried out his ministry alone. In order to give to others through his public ministry, Jesus also had to receive. In addition to these sedentary supporters there were women who did travel with Jesus, most notably Mary Magadalene (Mark 15:40–41). Some of these women are remembered as having been present at Jesus' cross and as the first to discover the empty tomb. These women are never named as disciples, yet in the Gospels of Mark and John and in Acts, they are remembered as apostolic witnesses, exemplary models of discipleship.[35] Through the recovery of their presence by twentieth-century feminist scholarship, the memory of these women now plays a formative role in how many perceive Jesus.

31. Tillich, *Systematic Theology*, 2:99.

32. Meier, *Marginal Jew*, 3:627, 626–27.

33. Lohfink, *Jesus and Community*, 69.

34. Meier, *Marginal Jew*, 3:631.

35. Schüssler Fiorenza, *In Memory of Her*, 320–21, 326.

Finally there was the group within the disciples known as the Twelve. Their presence with Jesus was intended to symbolically begin the regathering of the twelve tribes and signal that Jesus was reconstituting Israel as the people of God. The Twelve seem to have formed an inner circle about Jesus. The inclusion in their number of a Zealot (Simon the Zealot) and a toll collector (Levi), who would have been enemies in public life, may have been intended to signify the inclusiveness of Jesus' intention to reach out to all of Israel.[36] As a symbolic group, their presence with Jesus helped define and proclaim what he was about.

Jesus' Relationships: Reciprocal, Asymmetrical, Dialogical and Dialectical

Jesus' relationships to the people in the movement around him were reciprocal. Jesus touched them through his message and call. They in turn embodied his message, participated in his ministry, and enabled it through their support. It was through this reciprocity that Jesus became the Christ. However, while this reciprocity was genuine, the Gospels portray it as asymmetrical. There is a uniqueness to Jesus in this movement such that after his death no one stepped forward to take his place. Instead, through his resurrection and the pouring out of the Holy Spirit, his followers and subsequent converts understood themselves as living in him. Jesus played a central, catalytic role in this movement that can be compared to that of leaven in bread dough.[37] He would not have been the Christ without the movement around him. Others were constitutive each in their own way of Jesus' being as the Christ. Yet there was a distinctiveness to Jesus as such. It is he who is the Christ, not he and others. It was Jesus who was crucified and risen, not Jesus and Mary or Jesus and Peter. Jesus "is the firstborn among many sisters and brothers, and yet all are one" in him as the Christ.[38] Jesus is one of them, yet more than that. "In all his singularity Jesus Christ never was or is or will be isolated."[39] He could not be who he was and is apart from others, yet they "are not identical with Him and never will be."[40] It was through Jesus' person and

---

36. Meier, *A Marginal Jew*, 3:628.

37. Taylor, *Remembering Esperanza*, 171–72.

38. Bonhoeffer, *Sanctorum Communio*, 142.

39. Barth, *Church Dogmatics* IV/2:519.

40. Ibid., 521–22.

his relations with others that the reign of God became present in history. Others play a role and participated in this through faith, but it was his person and his relationships with them that were the major factor.

Various New Testament witnesses stress the asymmetrical character of these relationships to indicate that though Jesus being the Christ occurred through his reception as such by others, it was ultimately a result of God's transcendent grace. The accounts of the virgin birth in Matthew and Luke can be read this way. For instance, in Luke's account of this, from Jesus' inception on, "there is no point at which Jesus is not κύριος."[41] Jesus' being as the Christ results from a special divine initiative. Yet these same accounts indicate that this did not happen apart from the exercise of human freedom. The biblical witness poses a great challenge for human thought here in its attestation that salvation results from God's grace and its accompanying affirmation that human freedom has a role to play in it. The Bible is the story of two freedoms, that of God and that of humanity. The first is infinite. The second is finite. Both are real. Jesus' resurrection is the great act of divine freedom that establishes him as the Christ in a decisive and final way. New Testament traditions like those of the virgin birth insist that the uniqueness of Jesus' relationship to God was present all along. The salvation experienced through Jesus has its origin and basis in God, as does his person. Yet the concreteness of his person in his public ministry took shape through his relationships with others. Insisting that human freedom enters into the identity of Jesus Christ in the sociality of his person is in keeping with the Chalcedonian Definition of Jesus as fully human. It must also be noted that Jesus was fully divine, and that salvation results from the unity of these two natures in his one person. The divinity of Jesus provides the assurance of salvation. His humanity means that his relationships to other people helped shape the form his person took as the Christ, even if these relationships were asymmetrical.

While the relationships that help constitute Jesus' identity as the Christ are asymmetrical, they are also dialogical in the sense of being characterized by the shared agency of those involved.[42] Jesus Christ is not a static entity who remains essentially the same while giving to others and receiving from them. Rather, Jesus became the Christ through his interactions with others and was shaped as such partly by

41. Rowe, *Early Narrative Christology*, 44.

42. For this understanding of dialogical action see Taylor, "Dialogical Self," 311.

their initiatives and responses to him. This continues wherever people receive him as the Christ.

The Gospels of Matthew and Mark give a striking record of this in their accounts of Jesus' encounter with a Syro-Phoenician woman.[43] The historicity of this account is debatable, but it "addresses an issue that Jesus too must have been faced with in his own life" and during his travels in the location where it is set and it likely records the manner in which he responded to the question of his relationship to Gentiles.[44] A Gentile woman asks Jesus to cast a demon out of her daughter. Jesus rebukes her with an insult, saying that what he has to give is meant for children and should not be thrown "to the dogs" (Mark 7:27). His response indicates that she is excluded from those to whom his ministry is directed. She replies "'Sir, even the dogs under the table eat the children's crumbs'" (Mark 7:28). Through her respectful response to Jesus' insult and her persuasive reasoning and appeal on the basis of her understanding of "the availability of God's power that surprises even the Markan Jesus,"[45] she is remembered as having moved Jesus to grant her request. What is germane here for this discussion is the way Jesus' being as the Christ is portrayed as being shaped by her interaction with him. Jesus' mission appears to have been directed originally to all of Israel, but the movement he began "came to see the Gentile mission as a logical extension of itself."[46] The attribution of the saying in Mark 7:28 quoted above to the Syro-Phoenician woman can be taken as "a sign of the historical leadership"[47] women may have had in broadening the parameters of Jesus' mission to include Gentiles. While God's saving power was

---

43. Mark 7:24-30; Matt 15:21-28.

44. Freyne, *Jesus*, 90. According to Gerd Theissen, "the cultural context reveals that the story is probably Palestinian in origin. It presupposes an original narrator and audience who are acquainted with the concrete local and social situation in the border regions of Tyre and Galilee. As a result, it now appears more difficult to trace the origins of the story exclusively to early Christian debates about the legitimacy of the gentile mission—debates we read about in Jerusalem, Caesarea, and Antioch. Something more concrete is at stake. In principle we cannot exclude the possibility that the story has a historical core: an encounter between Jesus and a Hellenized Syrophoenician woman" (Theissen, *Gospels in Context*, 79).

45. Malbon, *Mark's Jesus*, 84.

46. Sanders, *Jesus and Judaism*, 220.

47. Schüssler Fiorenza, *In Memory of Her*, 138.

available through Jesus, women like this may have played a formative role in broadening the circle of those to whom it was available.

There is a dialectical moment in this encounter of the Syro-Phoenician woman with Jesus. The "final word of this story . . . does not conform to the boundaries imagined by Jesus for his ministry."[48] Her acknowledgment of the presence of God's power to free her daughter from demonic possession in Jesus and her "no" to his restricted understanding of who this was available to "safeguarded the inclusive discipleship of equals called forth by Jesus"[49] by negating his parochial understanding of its limits and expanding its scope. This dynamic of affirming yet negating aspects of previous understandings of Jesus becomes repeatedly necessary following Jesus' resurrection, as the church journeys through history and enters into new social contexts in which the forms of sin and evil threatening creation may vary greatly from previous eras. Jesus always remains the Christ. But as the face of "evil changes from age to age,"[50] the church has to repeatedly ask, "Who is Jesus Christ for us today?,"[51] and its understanding of his saving significance must often change in order to remain faithful to him. In light of this one must anticipate that "an irreducible hybridity"[52] will be intrinsic to Christology as the agency, needs, and context of those who receive Jesus as the Christ enter into his public person and risen presence within history, at times, as is illustrated in the periscope of the Syro-Phoenician woman, in dialectical ways.

THE SOCIALITY OF JESUS IN THE PRESENT

For the early Christian communities that produced the New Testament, Easter transformed Jesus from being a deceased, defeated, and discredited Jewish rabbi/charismatic leader to being the Savior who could only be adequately described in mythic terms.[53] Those who believed in Jesus' resurrection often experienced the Holy Spirit in powerful new ways. Experiences of Jesus' resurrection and the outpouring of the Holy Spirit

48. Perkinson, "Canaanitic Word," 70.

49. Schüssler Fiorenza, *In Memory of Her*, 138.

50. Baum, *Religion and Alienation*, 188.

51. Feil, *Theology of Dietrich Bonhoeffer*, 92.

52. Perkinson, "Canaanitic Word," 82.

53. Käsemann, *New Testament Questions*, 51.

presented the early church with the challenge of understanding who Jesus was, who they were, and how they related to surrounding society in light of this. The diversity of Christologies in the New Testament show that this challenge was met in a variety of ways. This pluralism of Christologies in the early church gave rise to a need for criteria to judge their relative adequacy.

The memory of Jesus' public ministry emerged as a crucial criterion in this regard. Paul primarily referred simply to Jesus' cross, but this still anchored his understanding of the risen Christ in Jesus' historical existence. What could be remembered of Jesus' life and public ministry was considered essential for authentic understandings of Jesus Christ because the early church believed that Jesus who was crucified and the risen Christ were one.[54] Then as now, this memory is only available through the witness of faith, for only those who believed in Jesus as the Christ were concerned to remember who he had been and what he had done in his public ministry. But this memory as preserved in the New Testament and investigated by the quest for the historical Jesus is sufficient to give Jesus a relative autonomy in relation to those who believe in him.[55]

As the risen Christ, Jesus finds a new "body" in those who believe in him as such. Peoples' beliefs in Jesus and understandings of him as the Christ are in some respects always responses to their perceived needs in their contemporary circumstances.[56] The relationship of Jesus to those who believe in him as the Christ is thus reciprocal. Jesus gives assurance, guidance, strength, and hope to the church. Through the church he gains a continued historical presence. This relationship is also asymmetrical. A Christian's ultimate identity is determined by Jesus Christ, not by themselves. It is Jesus who is the Christ and not the church. As Christians are a people of the book, they carry with them a codified memory of Jesus that provides criteria for determining how he should be received and appropriated. While people always understand Jesus in relation to their perceived needs, still the recollection of him in the New Testament has a concreteness that helps create a critical distance between Jesus and those who believe in him. As a result, Jesus never simply meets peoples' needs. As he does this he also brings a call to discipleship, a challenge for people to become more than they are, to play a role in the further expression of

54. Käsemann, *Essays on New Testament Themes*, 33–34.

55. Käsemann, *New Testament Questions*, 63.

56. Taylor, *Remembering Esperanza*, 220–21.

God's beauty and goodness in history. A person's relationship to Jesus is thus characterized by justification and sanctification. As Carter Heyward puts it, because of Jesus "we Christians are stretched beyond what we might have been without these stories and images of a radically faithful brother."[57] And as Heyward emphasizes, this stretching is twofold.

The church and its varied influences on the societies it lives in, the "living remembrance of Jesus as the Christ, are part of the full identity of Jesus."[58] As Jesus saw himself to be playing a decisive role in salvation history, the historical influence of his message and person can be said to have been intended by him. The honorific titles that the church gives to Jesus, as they are appropriate, make explicit what was implicit in his own self-understanding[59] and extend it. As people believe in Jesus Christ and remember him in the way they live, aspects of their life circumstances, their hopes and fears, enter into the historical identity of Jesus Christ. The witness of Christians points to Jesus who is always to some extent other to them. Yet it also identifies and defines who Jesus is and what he means in a given time and place. Thus there is a dialogical aspect to the living remembrance of Jesus. Through their interpretations of Jesus in terms of their perceived needs, the hopes, insights, and creativity of people enters into the identity of Jesus. As Heyward puts it:

> And because of us, his sisters and brothers, the images of JESUS are stretched way beyond the horizons that we, or those who have gone before us, could have envisioned.
>
> In this way, we and all who have preceded us, including authors of the Bible, have shaped JESUS, making him what he is today. Moreover, through the Bible and Christian history, we have shaped not one, but many, images of the same historical person.[60]

An example of this stretching and shaping can be found in how Jesus became the Black Christ through the struggles, faithfulness and creativity of the black church and its theologians.[61] Here the agency of African-

---

57. Heyward, *Saving Jesus*, 3. This sanctifying work of Jesus can also be described as Jesus giving people what they need. Together with justification it is part of the work of redemption by which Jesus moves people and creation towards the fulfillment of their divine destiny.

58. Schillebeeckx, *Christ*, 802.

59. Ibid., 802–3.

60. Ibid.

61. Douglas, *Black Christ*.

Americans who believed in Jesus, their "story" as they understood it and the circumstances they lived in entered into Jesus' identity in the present.

All of this illustrates how through this process Jesus becomes more than he was as a historical person. He becomes the Christ who enters into the life stories of people all over the earth. Their stories become a part of his and his becomes part of theirs. As this happens, the stories of Christians in different times and places also become part of each other's stories.[62] As Jesus became the Black Christ, the story of African-American Christians became part of the story of white North Atlantic Christians in a new way, challenging, complicating, enriching and transforming their sense of self and their understanding of Jesus. Through this dialogical aspect of people's relationship to Jesus they assist in his transformative work.

Yet they may also hinder and deface it. As Jesus is received by people in faith, he is stretched to become more than he was before. But through their reception of him, he may also become less. As mentioned in the previous chapter, in Canada during the late 1800s and up until the 1960s, faith in Jesus who welcomed little children became part of the motivation for taking First Nations children away from their parents to residential schools, where they were often separated from other members of their families, susceptible to severe discipline, sexual abuse, and often punished for speaking their own language.[63] While this is not the whole story on residential schools, it is a searing part of it that cannot be evaded. It is important to note that many of the white people involved in running residential schools believed that their work was a form of faithful discipleship to Jesus Christ. Members of the denominations that ran these schools cannot distance themselves from this history by saying, "They sinned but we know better." On one level this is true. But on another level, as pointed out in the previous chapter, many of the Christians involved in running these schools were doing exactly what many Christians are doing today: trying to live their faith in Jesus as best they can in the circumstances in which they find themselves and in light of prevailing myth and knowledge that they take for truth.

---

62. Niebuhr, *Meaning of Revelation*, 115–18.

63. For a history of the residential school system, see Miller, *Shingwauk's Vision*. For some repercussions of this for contemporary Christian ethics, see Schweitzer, "Legacy of Residential Schools," 11–14.

The history of residential schools in Canada illustrates how people who believe in Jesus Christ are "disturbed sinners."[64] Though faith in Jesus has a transformative effect on people, those who believe in Jesus Christ remain sinners. Their sin influences their appropriation of Jesus Christ and factors into the way Jesus is present in their church communities. Through the sociality of Jesus in the past and present the conflict between sin and grace enters into his identity as the Christ. Jesus Christ becomes himself a site of struggle between sin and grace.

As a result people's relationships to Jesus are characterized by justification and sanctification on two levels. On one level, every understanding of Jesus Christ brings assurance to believers and a challenge to live their faith more fully. Yet on a second level, because a believer's sin inevitably enters into their understanding of Jesus Christ, the canonical memory of Jesus and the Holy Spirit also work to sanctify this understanding. Ultimately, people are saved by Jesus, not by the accuracy of their understanding of him. Justification extends to false beliefs as well as sinful actions. But people are called by Jesus not only to live their faith more fully, but also to apprehend Jesus more truthfully, to be "transformed by the renewing" of their minds (Rom 12:2).

This transformation can be coming to understand one's beliefs more fully. Or it can have a dialectical character, as one comes to believe in Jesus differently than one used to. As the account of Jesus and the Syro-Phoenician woman suggests, Jesus may have had this kind of experience with his own self-understanding. As people come to have faith in Jesus Christ a dialogue ensues between their perceived needs, their self-understanding, and the good news of Jesus Christ as encountered by them. Through this dialogue they may come to a new understanding of their perceived needs and with this a new understanding of Jesus Christ. Furthermore, a person's relationship with Jesus always takes place within a social context. Significant changes in this may require dramatic changes in one's understanding of Jesus Christ in order to remain faithful to him. As Gregory Baum notes,

> evil changes from age to age. The forces that threaten human life depend on many cultural, political, and personal factors. In every period of history, the de-humanization operative in society has a different face.[65]

64. Barth, *Church Dogmatics* IV/2:524.
65. Baum, *Religion and Alienation*, 188.

When a significant cultural change happens as with the rise of the environmental crisis, or when the church enters into a new cultural context as when missionaries brought the gospel to India, a continued adherence to previous understandings of Jesus Christ may block perception of the presenting evil in the new context and hinder the church's response to it. When a significant cultural change causes the presenting evil to assume a new form different from the past, the church can only respond faithfully to Jesus through the Holy Spirit helping it understand him in a new way appropriate to its changed context.[66] The Holy Spirit may challenge the church from without and thus trigger a dialectical process of development that moves the church to a new understanding of Jesus Christ.[67] Or charismatic leaders may arise within the church who proclaim and embody a creative new understanding of Jesus in response to the evil of the day. Archbishop Oscar Romero of El Salvador was an example of this.[68] As this happens, a struggle usually ensues over who Jesus was and who he is in the present.

This struggle is always ongoing, though in times of cultural transition or fragmentation it may become much more acute and divisive. Within a given cultural context people continually work to understand Christ better. The dialogical element in a person's relationship to Christ means that no one is ever finished in the quest to know and follow Jesus. Jesus always has something more to say to us and always seeks a more faithful response from us. This quest to know Jesus more fully may involve many conversions, in which one must die to one's previously held understanding of Jesus in order to enter into another. Coming to understand Christ better may be a joyful and largely pain-free process of growth in knowledge. But frequently, because Christians are disturbed sinners, coming to know Christ better involves a dying to one's old self and image of Jesus as one comes to understand him anew in a more faithful way. This process thus includes elements of the way of the cross.[69] In this respect Jesus Christ is the object of Christian faith but also a model of how one comes to know him. He is a person one believes in, but also a road that Christians must follow, practically and in terms

---

66. Neville, *Symbols of Jesus*, 150.

67. Baum, *Credibility of the Church*, 151–76.

68. Sobrino, *No Salvation outside the Poor*, 109–28.

69. Baum, *Man Becoming*, 155.

of their understanding of him.[70] Christian theology is always a theology on the way, a theology that must continually seek to know Jesus more adequately in recognition that those who do it are always disturbed sinners. This recognition is drawn from one of the meanings of Jesus' cross, developed in the preceding chapter. Building this into the self-understanding of Christian theology makes it a theology of the cross[71] that recognizes that Christians continually need to repent and discover who Jesus is again and again. Yet in this ongoing pilgrimage Christians are able to rest and celebrate in the faith that, however fragmentary their knowledge of Christ may be, Christ's knowledge of them is full, and they have been accepted by Christ once and for all.

In the history of Christianity there have been figures like Francis of Assisi, Julian of Norwich, or Archbishop Romero who have functioned as exemplars of what it means to have faith in Christ.[72] These people make a particular contribution to the sociality of Jesus Christ. They draw from the church's memory of him something new that makes Jesus present in history with a new and vital immediacy. They offer striking and empowering interpretations of Jesus' person and meaning that affect the church's memory of Jesus as a whole, so that people read the Gospels and understand Jesus differently in light of them. Like the Syro-Phonecian woman, such people leave their mark on the sociality of Jesus.

The entry of the creativity, experiences, culture, and wisdom of those who believe in Jesus Christ into his identity means that there will be a plurality of Christologies in the present, just as there are in the New Testament. Because peoples' understandings of Jesus are always shaped by their historical, geographical, and social location, there will always be a historical specificity to how Jesus is understood. As the Holy Spirit leads people to believe in Jesus Christ, it does so in terms of the particular culture, time, and place in which they live.[73] Even within one culture there will be different Christologies depending on the various social locations of Christians within it. Christology needs to be pluralistic "because Jesus Christ must be interpreted and culturally appropriated by particular communities today even as he was in the formation of the

---

70. Moltmann, *Jesus Christ for Today's World*, 47.

71. Moltmann, *On Human Dignity*, 105.

72. For Romero, see Sobrino, *No Salvation outside the Poor*, 122, 126.

73. Del Colle, *Christ and the Spirit*, 199; Haight, *Jesus*, 427.

New Testament."[74] Through this pluralism the Holy Spirit can correct, supplement, and enrich the faith life of different churches by their contact with each other. Christ provides a unity that spans these differences and criteria by which each can critically relate to others.

But a recognition of the necessity and inevitability of a pluralism of Christologies does not imply a relativism in which each community defines the truth of Jesus for themselves.[75] The pluralism of Christologies always exists on the basis of certain commonalities: the canonical memory of Jesus in the biblical witness, the witness of the Spirit in the present, and the supporting witness of church tradition, both its teachings and exemplary figures. At times situations develop that demand a binding confession of Christ that cuts across the pluralism of Christologies present in the church. In some Protestant traditions this can give rise to what is known as a *status confessionis*, a statement by a church body declaring that a present circumstance requires a particular confession of faith on the part of all those who believe in Jesus Christ.[76] A *status confessionis* states that regardless of variations in their understandings of Jesus Christ, all must join in confessing this declared meaning of Jesus in relation to this issue. To those issuing the declaration failure to do so means separating one's self from Jesus Christ. Recent examples of a *status confessionis* are the declarations by the Lutheran World Federation in 1977 and the World Alliance of Reformed Churches in 1982 that "any theological defense of apartheid" was heresy.[77] A *status confessionis* recognizes an extreme situation in which the starkness and gravity of the presenting issues requires a particular response on the part of Christians. Just as the variations in historical context and within a historical context mean that Christ will take form in a variety of ways, so the concreteness of the church's memory of Jesus means that, on occasion, Jesus can only

74. Haight, *Jesus*, 426.

75. Here I follow a distinction that Gregory Baum finds in the thought of Karl Mannheim between relativism and relationism: "Relativism is the approach that recognizes that all knowledge is socially dependent, bound to the location of the thinker, and reasons from this to the inevitable relativity of all human truth. Relationism, on the other hand, is the approach that also acknowledges the social dependency of knowledge but refuses to use this principle reductively as an argument for the relativity of all truth" (Baum, *Truth Beyond Relativism*, 36). The truth of Jesus Christ is relational. The next chapter will discuss this distinction further.

76. TeSelle, "How Do We Recognize?," 78

77. Ibid., 75.

be faithfully confessed in one way, and is only truly present in communities that do so.

THE SOCIALITY OF JESUS IN THE FUTURE

"The meaning of Jesus Christ for us today is not limited to his past and present existence."[78] This is because the promise of Jesus' praxis and resurrection extends beyond these. This promise extends not simply to an increase of present realities or a continuation of historical trends, but to the arrival of a reality that is new in respect even to Jesus' presence in history. As noted above the sociality of Jesus in the present is always ambiguous. It extends his liberating praxis into the present but also incorporates the sin of his followers and sometimes the limitations of Jesus' own historical person. The difference between Jesus' contemporary presence and his promised future can also be traced along other lines. For the oppressed, the present reality of Jesus often resembles his cross.[79] His promised future involves the reversal of present injustices and an end to the suffering they cause. This difference can also be traced in terms of how Jesus' person and work is conceived. Jesus' gathering of twelve disciples was a prophetic sign signifying that he was regathering the twelve tribes of Israel. The sociality of Jesus in the present falls short of this, yet also reaches far beyond it. The future of Jesus will include all peoples and all of creation, but what this will look like cannot be foreseen. All this indicates how the future sociality of Jesus has a dialectical relationship to the present. It can be anticipated and prepared for on the basis of what is revealed in Jesus and how he is understood in the present.[80] But it will transcend what can be presently imagined. It will be both a dramatic reversal and a fulfillment of history. It will be a reversal in that forces of sin and evil that assault and destroy life will be overcome. It will bring a fulfillment in that creation will be brought to an eschatological wholeness. The sociality of Jesus in the future is not the sociality of Jesus ten years from now, but the sociality that is anticipated in eternity on the basis of the future that has been manifested historically in Jesus, the movement around him, his death and resurrection, and the work of the Holy Spirit that followed. It is not extrapolated from

78. Cone, *God of the Oppressed*, 126.

79. Sobrino, *No Salvation outside the Poor*, 3–4.

80. Moltmann, *Way of Jesus Christ*, 304.

the present, but anticipated on the basis of the biblical witness, experiences of the Holy Spirit, and the experiences and insights of people in the past and present.[81]

The past and present socialities of Jesus point towards an inclusive future characterized by diversity and harmony that can only be mythically or symbolically conceived. It is anticipated in worship, particularly in the celebration of Communion, and in acts of love and hope. It is a future that confronts the present with comfort and hope[82] and contradicts present suffering and sins with what ought to be. It is not a timeless myth but a future that seeks to become present, that can be denied but that yet keeps appearing in history. It is anticipated, yet its concrete features change as the imaginations of disturbed sinners are continually further disturbed by God's grace in manifold ways.

As the risen and exalted Christ, Jesus has an objectivity that undergirds his presence in history and points towards his still outstanding future. The subjectivity and particularities of people that factor into his past and present will be part of his future sociality. Yet the coming of this future does not depend on the virtue and faithfulness of people. It will not come without this. But its principle of expectation lies not in peoples' responses to Jesus, but in the objectivity of Jesus as the crucified and risen Christ.[83] The future sociality of Jesus will be asymmetrical, just as his past was and present is. But it will include the subjectivity and particularity of people, the whole breadth of history, transformed by grace and reconciled to God.

CONCLUSION

Jesus was and is a person in relationships. These helped constitute who he was, who he is, and who he will be. Jesus cannot be reduced to a product of his relationships. There was an irreducible uniqueness to him, as there is to every person. Part of his uniqueness is that he is the Christ, the person in whom the reconciliation of God and creation took place, in whose resurrection the future of creation appeared. Still, the reign of God that appeared in his person extends beyond him to include others,

---

81. Moltmann, *Future of Creation*, 46–48.

82. Ibid., 29–31.

83. Moltmann, *Crucified God*, 263–66.

their agency, creativity, and insights. While Jesus is the Christ, he is never this in isolation and others help constitute his being as such.

In turn, as the Christ, Jesus helps constitute the personhood of those who believe in him. The next chapter will examine one way in which he does this, by providing a center through which people are able to orient themselves in relation to other social movements and ideologies in history.

10 Jesus Christ as the Center of History

The previous chapter discussed how the identity of Jesus Christ is constituted partly by his relations with others. This chapter also focuses on the relationality of Jesus Christ but reverses the point of view. It looks at how Jesus Christ helps constitute the identities of those who believe in him by giving them a point of reference and an orientation in life. Chapters 5–8 looked at how Jesus helps constitute people's identities through his teaching and other saving significances. This chapter examines a sixth saving significance relating to the dimension of life called "history."[1] Jesus Christ has saving significance as the center of history for those who believe in him. He gives people an orientation in life through his teaching and moral example. But there are many teachers and moral examples. Jesus gives more than this. As the Christ he provides a transcendent point of reference by which to understand, evaluate and relate to the many other teachings and developments that appear in history. People "need some center from which to view the plurality"[2] of religions, social movements and events in society. By providing this Jesus helps constitute the identity of those who believe in him.

WHAT IS A CENTER?

A center can be defined as "a point, area, person, or thing that is most important or pivotal in relation to an indicated activity, interest, or condition."[3] It can also mean the "source from which something originates."[4] Jesus Christ is the pivotal person and event by which Christians should orient themselves in history and the source from which this orientation comes.

1. Tillich, *Systematic Theology*, 1:67.
2. Cobb, *Transforming Christianity*, 57.
3. *Webster's New Collegiate Dictionary*, s.v. "center."
4. Ibid.

A number of Psalms state that it is characteristic of human life to exalt and praise something.[5] If God is not praised something else will be. Linked to this are two related ideas: (1) that human life finds its fulfillment in praising God, and (2) that the exaltation of someone or something else in place of God leads to the destruction of life.[6] Human life inevitably has a center that is exalted and praised and that provides guidance for living. Yet not any center will do. These ideas help form the background for belief in Jesus Christ as the center of history.

The title "Christ" is a Greek equivalent to the Hebrew term "Messiah." In Jesus' time this meant someone anointed by God for a special task.[7] There were various understandings of what this would be. Jesus' public ministry presented an implicit claim that he was playing a decisive role in salvation history, but he seems to have been ambivalent toward the messianic expectations of his followers and the crowds who heard him. His public ministry led some to believe that he would fulfill these expectations. After his death and resurrection his disciples attributed this title and role to him and "in a very general sense it corresponded to his own view of himself."[8] But Jesus during his public ministry seems to have been reticent to explicitly proclaim himself the messiah and some of his actions seem to have been intended to transform the messianic expectations of his followers and the crowds.[9] His death and resurrection complicated things further as they did not fit with any messianic expectations of his day.[10] Jesus was proclaimed the Christ by the early church, but the meaning of this term was reinterpreted in light of his life, death, resurrection,[11] and subsequent experiences of the Holy Spirit connected to them.

Early Christian interpretation of Jesus' resurrection in light of passages like Psalm 110:1 led to the belief that God had exalted Jesus "to a unique heavenly status."[12] Most of the early church praised the risen Christ for this and his decisive saving significance. As a result Jesus became for them the center of history. Reality was to be understood in light

---

5. Westermann, *Praise and Lament*, 159.

6. Ibid., 160–61.

7. Sanders, *Historical Figure of Jesus*, 241.

8. Ibid., 242.

9. Theissen and Merz, *Historical Jesus*, 538–40.

10. Ibid., 540.

11. Dahl, *Jesus the Christ*, 38–40.

12. Hurtado, *Lord Jesus Christ*, 72.

of what had happened in and through him. Paul expresses this understanding of Jesus' significance in 2 Corinthians 5:16–17:

> From now on, therefore, we regard no one from a human point
> of view; even though we once knew Christ from a human point
> of view, we know him no longer in that way. So if anyone is in
> Christ, there is a new creation: everything old has passed away;
> see, everything has become new!

These verses are situated in a larger passage (2 Cor 2:14—6:10) in which
"Paul defends his apostleship by various arguments, all of which refer
to the turn of the ages"[13] that has occurred in Jesus Christ. For Paul and
in the Gospels Jesus' death and resurrection form the decisive event in
salvation history that determines how one should understand and relate
to other people, other religions, and reality in general.

To call Jesus the Christ was to attribute to him a definitive, saving,
and normative significance. It meant to exalt him in one's own life as the
center of history in response to God's exaltation of him in eternity. As
the center of history Jesus Christ is the basis on which Christians evaluate historical events, movements, and ideas, including their own.

The notion that human life must have a center is intrinsic to the
idea of human agency. To be a living human being active in the world is
to have a sense of identity formed by a moral framework by which one
makes qualitative evaluations between different ways of life and different
courses of action.[14] Human identity is partly a matter of one's genetic and
cultural heritage, time and place of birth, social location, and so forth.
But it is also a matter of the beliefs and values one becomes committed
to. The moral framework that forms the basis for one's decision making
and evaluation of events helps constitute one's identity and character.
Any moral framework prioritizes some values over others and in its own
way celebrates them, praising them as worthy of being actualized over
other possibilities.[15] Thus every moral action implicitly declares some
values, persons, or events to be normative and points towards a center
by which actions should be guided.

13. Martyn, *Theological Issues*, 91.
14. Taylor, *Sources of the Self*, 27.
15. Goffman, *Presentation of Self*, 35–36.

As Jesus Christ is the "medium and focus of a Christian's faith in God,"[16] he functions as the normative center of history and personal life for Christians. This does not mean that Jesus' life occurred in the midpoint of time. Jesus Christ is "the qualitative center" of salvation history that, in quantitative terms, "proceeds from an indefinite past into an indefinite future."[17] The history that precedes and follows him is to some extent always both a preparation for him and a reception of what he incarnates,[18] as the event of Jesus being received as the Christ by the early church is paradigmatic for what happens in every era in which the church continues and in every Christian's life as Jesus becomes the center of their history. As such Jesus Christ is the criterion by which God's presence in the Holy Spirit is discerned in history. He is the incarnation of the goodness and love that is the Holy Spirit's source.

HOW IS JESUS CHRIST A CENTER OF HISTORY?

To say that Jesus Christ is the normative center of history is to claim that what is revealed in him has an ultimacy, "a validity which cannot be qualified or conditioned by any end or limit, which cannot be contested, questioned or transcended, which constitutes a threat"[19] to other claims to ultimate validity, such as those of empires. By itself this first aspect of Jesus Christ as the center of history poses a threat to other religions that raises the specter of religious violence and cultural oppression. But there is a second aspect to Jesus Christ as the center of history that must also be noted. In the resurrection of Jesus, which establishes his person as the center of history for Christians, the end of history has dawned within time but only in a preliminary form.[20] Christians in history never know Jesus completely. What Christians perceive in Jesus is that through him God knows them in a final way and that there is an ultimacy to the goodness, beauty, and love that he reveals. Nothing can separate them from it. But the transcendence of this beauty, goodness, and love means that there is always more for Christians to learn about it.

---

16. Haight, *Jesus*, 406.

17. Tillich, *Systematic Theology*, 3:147.

18. Ibid., 364.

19. Barth, *Church Dogmatics*, IV/3.1:160.

20. Pannenberg, *Basic Questions in Theology*, 2:24.

Paul declared that a new creation had come into being in Jesus Christ, but not that he lived "completely and exclusively" therein.[21] Jesus' cross was followed by his resurrection but not replaced by it.[22] Jesus' cross remains indicative of where he is to be found as the risen Christ and how he is to be known in history. It indicates that the present is not continuous with the eschatological future promised in his resurrection. Between the two lies the transformation that awaits every Christian and all of creation, exemplified in the transformation of the crucified Jesus in his resurrection. In the mean time there is the pilgrimage of creation and the church, which involves celebration of this coming future and its presence in the Holy Spirit, service in love that seeks to anticipate and work towards its coming, and openness to ongoing conversion to a deeper understanding of who Jesus Christ is.

This transformation will affect all aspects of human existence, including every Christian's knowledge of Jesus. Paul speaks of this as follows:

> For now we see in a mirror, dimly, but then we will see face to face. Now I know only in part; then I will know fully, even as I have been fully known.[23]

For Paul full knowledge of Jesus Christ lies only in the eschatological future.[24] Until this arrives the cross of Jesus remains the norm by which one recognizes the presence of the Holy Spirit in history, for the Holy Spirit "is none other than the Spirit of the crucified Christ."[25] Jesus Christ as the center of history is thus the key to discerning the Holy Spirit's presence at work in the world. Christians know Jesus Christ as the center of history, but they know him as such by faith. By faith they know there is an ultimacy to what Jesus reveals. But they also know that their knowledge of this is not final, that in faithfulness to him it must remain open to correction and enhancement.

The portrayals of Peter's confession of Jesus as the Christ in the gospels[26] also convey the understanding that there is an ultimacy to Jesus Christ that makes him the center of history, but that the church's

---

21. Martyn, *Theological Issues*, 108.

22. Ibid., 109; Moltmann, *Theology of Hope*, 198–201.

23. 1 Cor 13:12; see also 2 Cor 3:18.

24. Conzelmann, *1 Corinthians*, 228.

25. Martyn, *Theological Issues*, 108.

26. Mark 8:27–30; Matt 16:13–20; Luke 9:18–20; John 6:60–71.

understanding of him is always from within history and never final. For instance, in Mark's Gospel Peter's confession is portrayed as fitting but limited.[27] It is fitting in that Jesus is the Christ and not a prophetic figure like Elijah or John the Baptist. But Peter's understanding of Jesus as the Christ, representative of that of the disciples and the church, is limited. Peter is portrayed as correct in naming Jesus as the Christ but as not fully understanding what this means. He will learn this more fully and his false notions will be corrected only by following Jesus and through the event of Jesus' death and resurrection. In this Peter is paradigmatic of all Christians. The truth of Jesus Christ must be continually sought and gained through a sometimes painful pilgrimage of following him, of being willing to relinquish aspects of one's previous understanding of him, in order to come to a more adequate and appropriate one. The church does not live at present fully in the eschatological future where it will know Jesus in a final way. It lives now within history, where it knows the ultimacy of Jesus in a fallible way. If it is to be faithful to Jesus what it claims to know about him must always be open to revision in light of his transcendence as the Christ.

Jesus Christ is the center of history and thus normative for Christian life because of his transcendence as the Christ. But as this discussion of some New Testament texts indicates, a Christian's awareness of Jesus Christ's transcendence should include an awareness of his transcendence to one's own understanding of him. A true grasp of Jesus' transcendence includes an awareness of the continuing mystery of his person and saving significance even to those who believe in him as the Christ.[28] This, coupled with the realization that what one has encountered in Jesus is also present in the lives of people belonging to other religious traditions or social movements, means that faith in Jesus Christ as the center of history can be the basis for an openness to dialogue with other religious and nonreligious traditions and learning from them. Faithfulness to Jesus means to be open to being creatively transformed "by the new possibilities given by God"[29] in a particular time and place. Jesus as the center of history must be related to the events, forms of knowledge and experience, social movements, and other religions in it. Some of this happens simply through negation, even of some movements claiming to

27. Malbon, *Mark's Jesus*, 105–6.

28. Haight, *Jesus*, 408.

29. Cobb, *Transforming Christianity*, 45.

be Christian.[30] Faithfulness to Jesus Christ means upholding him as the center of history in ways appropriate to what he reveals of God against attempts to put other figures, centers, or distorted understandings of him in his place. But when aspects of what Jesus reveals of God are present in other religions or philosophies, then this relating should include dialogue, which may transform the church's Christology. The Barmen Declaration, largely composed by Karl Barth in 1934, is a famous example of Jesus Christ being held up as the center of history against an attempt to put another in his place. It states that "Jesus Christ, as he is attested to us in Holy Scripture, is the one Word of God whom we have to hear, and whom we have to trust and obey in life and in death."[31] But as Barth later acknowledged, there are other true words to which the church should listen, which can "lead the community more truly and profoundly than ever before to Scripture."[32] Jesus Christ as the center of history mandates openness to dialogue with others that functions in this way, unless a situation develops in which a *status confessionis* must be declared. Then dialogue must give way to resistance.

WHAT IS HISTORY?

The word "history" refers to "the set of events that have occurred and the set of reports on these events."[33] The first meaning designates the overarching context of temporality in which human life and all creation exist. History in this broadest sense begins with creation. Jesus is the center of the creative process that gives rise to history. As the Word of God he is central to its origin, as history exists for the further expression of the goodness, beauty, and love that he incarnates. As the incarnation of the Word he is also the culmination of creation, the reason for its being, and the basis for its redemption.

In a more restricted sense "history" refers to human history, the events involving people that occur within time. All life occurs within time. This is the historical condition of creation and humanity. No one can survey history by rising to a vantage point above it.[34] As human

30. Ibid., 183.

31. Online: http://www.ucc.org/beliefs/barmen-declaration.html.

32. Barth, *Church Dogmatics* IV/3.1:115.

33. Ricoeur, *Memory, History, Forgetting*, 305.

34. Ibid., 284.

thought and action always take place within time, they are always historically conditioned. Situated within the history of creation and redemption, human history is a sequence of events perpetrated and experienced
by people interacting with their environment, with others, and with God.

As human agents people not only exist in history, they also help
make it. This making occurs on two levels: through people acting in time
and through people creating histories of such actions. There is the history people live in and help make, and there are the histories they write
describing this. The origin of the second kind of action lies partly in the
self-reflective capacity people have of cognitively distancing themselves[35]
from their immediate surroundings in order to understand and evaluate
them. Paul Ricoeur describes this critical reflection as an "upsurge" that
"is always current and always already there."[36] People thus exist in history on two dialectically related levels. They live within (1) the passage
of time and within (2) various interpretations of this passage of time.
The passage of time raises the question of its own meaning and leads
people to interpret it. In turn these interpretations become the basis of
actions that make history. Jesus Christ shares this twofold relation to
history. He is an answer to the questions and the search for salvation that
arise within history. Yet, as an object of faith, Jesus Christ also inspires
people to make history by their response to him.

The critical reflection that gives rise to history writing is occasioned
by an existential dimension of human life that Martin Heidegger called
"care."[37] Care arises from the critical capacity of persons to make moral
judgments, their limited but real freedom to act on these, and their sense
of the significance of doing so. "Care" means that persons are never neutral to their world. The nature of it and the question of how one should
relate to it always concern people.[38] This human characteristic of care
gives rise to the disposition described in a number of the Psalms to always exalt and praise something. It means that people are always "strong
evaluators"[39] who make moral judgments about the value and appropriateness of different ways of life or courses of action. Thus people always

35. Ibid., 139.
36. Ibid.
37. Heidegger, *Being and Time*, 237–39.
38. Ibid., 238.
39. Taylor, *Human Agency and Language*, 16–21.

implicitly exalt certain values, persons, institutions, or events and point to a center of history by their moral judgments and actions.

History is thus partly the interplay of the many affirmations of different centers to it. Each affirmation reflects the historically relative nature of human thought. History is always understood from a point of view reflecting the location and orientation within history of its author.[40] The "upsurge" of critical reflection that seeks the truth of history never fully transcends the limitations of human thought resulting from its historical condition. Thus, though critical reflection seeks an understanding transcending history, it always remains limited by its place within it. Yet to assert the relativity of all interpretations of history in light of this is self-contradictory.[41] To do so would be to present a transcendent perspective on history which one claims is impossible. Asserting such a claim would show that the person doing so does not accept the relativity of all interpretations of history that they claim is true. A center of history is always implied in every account of it. Accounts denying that there is any center and proclaiming the relativity of all interpretations of history present themselves as the center where the truth of history is to be found.

The historical nature of all accounts of history means that the identification of any person or event as the center of history is ultimately a matter of faith,[42] not empirical demonstration. It also means that though such identifications are necessary they are all potentially oppressive. They are necessary because all responsible human action implies one. They are potentially oppressive because any identification of a center to history "can only be shored up by strategic exclusions, by declaring opposition where there is complicity, by denying the possibility of randomness, by proclaiming a provisional origin or point of departure as ground."[43] The identification of a center of history seeks to express the truth of the whole on the basis of limited experience and knowledge. This limitation, combined with an element of self-interest that is always present in the interpretation of history, means that the identification of a center of history inevitably expresses the ideology of one group or person over against that of others.[44]

40. Pannenberg, *Basic Questions in Theology*, 2:20.

41. Ricoeur, *Memory, History, Forgetting*, 304.

42. Barth, *Church Dogmatics*, IV/3.1:80.

43. Spivak *Critique of Postcolonial Reason*, 147.

44. Niebuhr, *Nature and Destiny*, 1:182.

However, that all interpretations of history are influenced by their social location does not mean they are all relative, but that they are relational.[45] This means that the truth gained or available from any one perspective or religious tradition "stands in need of complementation, correction and expansion" and so should always "retains an openness to other socially defined viewpoints."[46] Consequently the truth about history or Jesus Christ "cannot be discovered by one tradition of thought alone nor from a single cultural perspective."[47] What is available in one tradition must be supplemented by what is found elsewhere. The church recognized this implicitly when it accepted four gospels into the canon of Scripture. The need for truth to be supplemented in this way gives it a dynamic quality. Truth is available, yet it continually needs to be discovered again, reinterpreted in relation to new forms of knowledge and experience. In the Reformed tradition of Christian theology this dynamic aspect of the truth is recognized in the formula that the church is "reformed and always in need of reform."

The affirmation that Jesus Christ is the center of history expresses a critique of relativism[48] and affirms instead a relational understanding of truth. The claim that Jesus Christ is the center of history should acknowledge that all perspectives on history or Jesus Christ need to be complemented through dialogue with those coming from other religious traditions, cultural heritages, and social locations. The limited nature of any Christian's knowledge means that full knowledge of Jesus Christ lies in the future towards which Christians journey.[49] Part of this journey is dialogue with other Christian traditions, other religions, and other forms of knowledge and experience. Faithfulness to Jesus Christ as the center of history thus demands openness to dialogue, correction, and learning from others.[50] However such dialogue always takes place within the conflicts of history and seldom on a level playing field. As "true dialogue takes place only among equals,"[51] faithfulness to Jesus requires that openness to dialogue be accompanied by a "commitment

45. For this distinction see Baum, *Truth beyond Relativism*, 36.
46. Ibid., 38.
47. Ibid., 24–25.
48. Tillich, *Systematic Theology*, 3:364.
49. Cobb, *Transforming Christianity*, 45.
50. Ibid.
51. Baum, *Truth beyond Relativism*, 43.

to emancipation"[52] of the marginalized and oppressed. Faithfulness to Jesus Christ as the center of history thus calls Christians to dialogue with others and to exercise a preferential option for the poor in struggles for justice and peace.

These two mandates can lead to the kind of conflict that many Western Christians currently experience between their calling to be in dialogue with Jews and in solidarity with Palestinians.[53] The implication of centuries of Christian supersessionism in preparing the ground for the Holocaust demands that Christians enter into dialogue with Jews, for many of whom the existence of the state of Israel has profound religious meaning. But the oppression of Palestinians demands a solidarity from Christians that often leads to criticism of the state of Israel, which is interpreted by many Jews as "a manifestation of . . . Christian supersessionism that makes genuine dialogue virtually impossible."[54] At times dialogue must give way to a stance of resistance and opposition to what is perceived to be unjust. In doing so Christians, like others, must be willing to accept the guilt that may accrue as a result of their attempts to act responsibly within their limited understanding. At other times resistance to evil must be paired with or give way to dialogue. When and where either must happen is an ethical judgment that cannot be fully determined in advance. Yet the call to dialogue and to solidarity with the oppressed is never finally opposed. Both arise from recognition of the other as a person. The call to dialogue means that even in resistance to others one must retain a recognition of them as persons and an openness to reconciliation with them once liberation is achieved.

JESUS CHRIST AS THE CENTER OF CREATION AND ITS HISTORY

The affirmation of Jesus Christ as the center of history points beyond itself to the place of Jesus in creation and to the Word in the Trinity. The noetic basis of these affirmations lies ultimately in Jesus' resurrection. It was this that overcame the scandal of his death and gave rise to

52. Ibid., 44.

53. For an account of this "acute bind" see Cobb, "Theological Response," 195–96.

54. Marmur, "United Church and Jews," 32. However, in a recent article analyzing Jewish voices of dissent against the state of Israel that call for an end to the occupation of Palestinian lands, Gregory Baum concludes that designating "opposition to the Occupation as antisemitic has lost all meaning" (Baum, "Is Denouncing Antisemitic?," 5).

a renewed understanding of him as the Christ. But Jesus Christ as the center of history must also be understood along the lines of a descending Christology that begins with his place in the doctrine of the Trinity. The ontological basis for Jesus being the center of history and creation lies in the kind of claim found in the first part of the prologue to John's Gospel (John 1:1–5), where Jesus is identified as the incarnation of the divine Word through which the world was created.[55] Jesus Christ is the center of history and creation and the telos or end for which creation and history exist.

The reason for the existence of creation and history lies in the self-expressive dynamics of the triune life of God. As God is living, "God is eloquent and radiant."[56] This eloquence and radiance arises from the self-diffusive nature of God's goodness, beauty, and love, which is infinitely expressed in eternity in the Word, the second "person" of the immanent Trinity. The infinite and eternal expression of this in eternity is repeated in time and space through the creation of the world and its history, which culminates qualitatively in the incarnation. The further expression of God's beauty, goodness, and love in history happens definitively in Jesus Christ, but also in the lives of others; Christians who follow Jesus, Jews who lived before and after him, and members of other religions and of none whose lives express the love, goodness, and beauty that one sees in Jesus. It also happens in non-human realms of creation.

The world is created through the Word and for its further expression in time and space. Seen from this perspective, "Jesus is not the great exception to terrestrial life but its fulfillment."[57] Jesus Christ is the reason for creation and the goal of evolution. As such Christ is present in the ongoing processes of creation as the drive towards more complex and beautiful forms of life. But evolution is distorted by the fall and shares in the ambiguity of creation and history. As a result the "history of every form of progress has its other side in the history of its victims."[58] This means that the empirically discernible course of evolution cannot be simply identified with Christ. Jesus Christ relates to evolution as its goal and its redeemer. Between the empirical course of evolution and creation's eschatological future lies the redemptive transformation

---

55. Smith, *John*, 51–52.

56. Barth, *Church Dogmatics*, IV/3.1:79.

57. Delio, *Christ in Evolution*, 171.

58. Moltmann, *Way of Jesus Christ*, 296.

symbolized in Jesus' resurrection. Jesus Christ crucified and risen is "the symbol of what is intended for created reality,"[59] the promise of the transformation and glorification of creation that will take place in the coming of its eschatological future. But evolution in its historical form alone does not lead to the coming of Jesus or to his eschatological future. The cross does not lead directly by itself to Jesus' resurrection. Between the present and the eschatological future stands the transformation of reality into a new creation by God. Christ is the goal and drive of evolution insofar as it leads to a more diverse and harmonious creation and further expressions of God's goodness and beauty. But Christ is also the redeemer of evolution in its historical ambiguity. The cross of Jesus means that the diversity of creation will be extended in its eschatological future to include the victims as well as the victors in evolutionary processes. This locates the risen Christ in history also among the victims of evolution and historical and technological progress.[60] Jesus Christ is not the center of a purely immanent progress in history, but of a transcendent process of creation and redemption that embraces creation and history and points beyond both to the coming of a new creation.

JESUS CHRIST AS THE CENTER OF HUMAN HISTORY

According to Bonaventure it "is the eternal Word, who lies at the center of the mystery of God . . . who becomes incarnate in Jesus of Nazareth, thus assuming a central place in the created universe and its history."[61] But Bonaventure identified "the cross of the incarnate Word"[62] as the heart of this center, seeing the humble love exemplified here as the form appropriate for God's love amidst "the fallen condition of humanity."[63] Jesus Christ is the incarnation of the eternal Word, but Bonaventure's understanding is one-sided in its emphasis on humility as a virtue and pride as a sin. As Bonaventure saw, Christ has "paradigmatic significance

---

59. Delio, *Christ in Evolution*, 171. "What happens in Jesus, therefore, anticipates the future of humanity and of the cosmos; not annihilation of creation but its radical transformation through the power of God's life-giving Spirit" (ibid., 40).

60. Moltmann, *Way of Jesus Christ*, 269.

61. Hayes, *Hidden Center*, 14.

62. Ibid., 24.

63. Ibid., 182.

for understanding the nature and direction of human life."[64] Following Christ in a world plagued by sin, evil, and suffering is always in some respects a following of the way of the cross. But as the center of history Jesus Christ is not only a call to humility to the proud, but also a sign of hope to the marginalized and oppressed and a source of dignity to the denigrated. According to Martin Luther, people should have "a most holy pride" in their calling and in what Christ has accomplished for them and others in the cross.[65] Pride is not necessarily sinful,[66] but can be the source of virtuous moral commitments, and certain forms of pride can follow from faith in Jesus Christ.

The cross has saving meaning only in relation to Jesus' public ministry and his subsequent resurrection. It is all three together in their reciprocal relationships that constitute Jesus as the center of history, not the cross alone. Jesus' public life demonstrates openness to others and to correction on occasion, but also adamant resistance to evil and a courageous commitment to the coming of God's reign. His cross is a sign of humble love that undertakes suffering for others, of ultimate obedience to God, but also of the power of God's love to "overcome evil, hatred and suffering."[67] His resurrection brings hope to struggles for justice within history, hope for life beyond death, and hope for the transformation and glorification of all creation. It also brings hope for the church that the light it bears witness to cannot be permanently put out, that through God's creative power it will continue to shine and that sin, evil and suffering will not overcome it.

Jesus Christ as the Word of God expresses the ecstatic self-transcending nature of God's goodness. God is not content to remain alone in eternity but seeks to further express God's own beauty and love in time and space through creation, the incarnation and the redemption of the world. Humanity created in the image of God has a self-transcending inclination corresponding to the self-diffusiveness of God's goodness. The self-transcendence of God in the incarnation and the self-transcendence of humanity authentically conceived and lived both glorify God by further expressing God's beauty, goodnesss, and love.[68]

64. Ibid., 40.

65. Luther, *Luther's Works*, 26:21.

66. Schweitzer, "Pride as Sin and Virtue."

67. Baker-Fletcher, *Dancing with God*, 97.

68. Lonergan, *Method in Theology*, 116–17.

This human capability of self-transcendence functions on two levels. On the first level, human life always exalts and expresses some values. On a second level there is the "upsurge" that leads people to transcend their present state through critical reflection on history and an attempt to discern a center or purpose to it, and then to give this purpose further expression in their own lives. This second level of self-transcendence began when someone first asked about the meaning of life. It begins again in each person's life as they ask this question for themselves. Human life with its dimension of "care" and its capacity for critical reflection can thus become a "radical question about God."[69] This question is asked by humanity but involves all of creation. It arises in each individual's life and from history as a whole. The histories of religions and cultures can be seen as histories of how this question has been asked and answered. In a Christian perspective this question arises from the presence of the Holy Spirit in every human life. It results from common grace, the Holy Spirit working through and assisting natural principles and faculties to fulfill their intended potential apart from faith in Jesus Christ. Through asking this question people can become open to receive what Christ brings. Jesus Christ is the center of human history as he is the ultimate and irrevocable answer to this question in its many forms.

Jesus is the center of history through his proclamation of the coming reign of God, his death and resurrection. The coming of the reign of God will involve the fulfillment of life in all its dimensions.[70] The all-encompassing nature of his proclamation of the reign of God in relation to creation and history and the exaltation of his person that was perceived by the early church in his resurrection impart an ultimacy to Jesus Christ. Subsequent reflection on his person by the early church in light of this led to the affirmation of the doctrine of the Trinity and the Chalcedonian Definition that Jesus was fully human and fully divine. At every stage of reflection the church saw the resurrection and exaltation of Jesus as an action by God that was eschatological in nature and significance. What happened and is communicated in him is irrevocable. His public ministry and death were not simply actions inspired by God, but actions undertaken and experienced by God in the second person of the Trinity.

69. Rahner, *Foundations*, 225.

70. Tillich, *Systematic Theology*, 3:359.

As questions about the meaning of creation, life, and history seek the presence of what they ask about, they presuppose both an inspiration and an alienation from God. In the person of Jesus Christ this alienation of humanity and creation from God was proleptically overcome. The movement of God towards humanity and humanity towards God that had been occurring through human history reached its goal in principle in his person.[71] Jesus in his person and practice of the reign of God was "the kingdom of God in person, and the beginning of the new creation of all things."[72]

As the center of history Jesus stands in a long line of leaders, prophets, and saints inspired by the Holy Spirit extending in time before and after him. Those that preceded him among the people of Israel prepared the way for him. From a Christian perspective Jesus is the culmination of the development they represent. Jesus is continuous with them, taking up traditions of Second Temple Judaism even as he transformed them, being shaped himself by his interaction with John the Baptist and others. Human capacities of reason and will are expandable under the influence of God's grace.[73] Salvation history from a Christian perspective is partly the history of how these capacities were expanded through the traditions, practices, and messianic expectations of Judaism developing over time to create the possibility of Jesus coming and being received as the Christ.[74]

Yet as the center of history Jesus also transcends this long line of saints and prophets who appeared before and after him. While Jesus is fully human like these and all others, he was also something they were not. Like them he is inspired by the Spirit, but unlike them he is inspired by it without limit. In Chalcedonian terms, he is fully divine even as he is fully human. This claim is an inference from the "unusual capacity"[75] of Jesus to act in God's name, and from his resurrection and the new experiences of the Holy Spirit connected to him. All this led the early church to proclaim him as the Christ. The experience of salvation experienced through faith in him has continued to lead others to do

---

71. Rahner, *Foundations*, 169–70

72. Moltmann, *Way of Jesus Christ*, 149.

73. Tanner, *Christ the Key*, 37–40.

74. Tillich, *Systematic Theology*, 3:365. For attempts to trace this expansion, see Moltmann, *Theology of Hope*, 95–229; Whitehead, *Religion in the Making*, 13–44.

75. Tanner, *Christ the Key*, 56.

the same. Thus there is continuity between Jesus and those who precede and follow him, but also discontinuity. Jesus Christ as the center of history belongs within this line of saints and prophets yet he also transcends it as the criterion for discerning the presence of the Holy Spirit that inspired them. He was inspired by the same Holy Spirit that inspired them, but as the risen Christ he is also its source and the key to discerning its presence.

THE ETHICAL TRANSCENDENCE OF JESUS CHRIST AS THE CENTER OF HISTORY

Jesus is the center of history for Christians because he is the unique incarnation of the Word of God. But his transcendence must also be articulated in terms of its ethical qualities and function.

> Divinity is transcendent when it actually judges the existing order, condemns the injustices of the social system, and empowers those unjustly treated to struggle for the remaking of society according to greater justice. According to the sociology of knowledge, a doctrine of God is an ideological defense of the status quo and bespeaks no transcendence whatever, unless it is open to totality and based on a commitment to universal liberation.[76]

The meaning of Jesus Christ cannot be exhausted by an analysis of his ethical function. But Jesus Christ cannot be the transcendent center of history if he does not function as a moral source that can move people to seek a greater justice and a deeper peace.

Here it is important to distinguish between what Jesus makes available and how this has been historically lived out by Christians and others. Jesus Christ, like the centers of other religions and moral views, is not invalidated as a moral source simply because people have done terrible things in his name.[77] How Jesus has inspired people and what he has inspired them to do have to be critically examined. But for Christians the ultimate criterion by which this happens is what is revealed in Jesus Christ himself. The witness to Jesus Christ in the Scriptures gives his person a historical concreteness that prevents this from being a tautology. The church's communal memory of Jesus Christ as recorded in Scripture retains a critical transcendence in relation to the church. The

---

76. Baum, *Truth beyond Relativism*, 68.
77. Taylor, *Sources of the Self*, 519–20.

church was the source of this witness and continually interprets it, but the church also stands under it. The written nature of this witness gives it a public character so that it has a relative independence to the practice and proclamation of the church. The church confesses Jesus Christ, but its confession is open to scrutiny in light of its basis in him as witnessed to in Scripture. Conversely, in light of its understanding of Christ or new knowledge, the church may overrule particular injunctions of Scripture.[78] Scripture gives a concrete witness to Jesus Christ, but the Christian life is ultimately authorized by Jesus Christ, not Scripture.

Jesus Christ also has a relative transcendence to contemporary society that can help people come to a conscious awareness of suffering and injustice in the world and empower them to resist it. The world has become a place "where capital and goods, information and images, pollution and people, flow across national boundaries with unprecedented ease."[79] As a result many current ethical problems lie "beyond the reach of the individual"[80] and can only be adequately dealt with through political and public action. At the same time differences among the religious and moral communities involved can make developing the communal will to address these issues difficult. As a result the suffering of others is easily forgotten or ignored. The "care" that is central to being human easily becomes restricted, diffuse, weak, and distracted. Against this diffusing and weakening of care the ethic of Jesus calls for love that is "in principle, unlimited"[81] through its focus on relieving the suffering of others and standing in solidarity with the victims. Jesus Christ as the center of history also provides a moral framework in which the meaning of such efforts does not depend on the gratitude of those who are aided or the effectiveness of one's efforts, but on the beauty, goodness, and love revealed in him. Christians will always express the beauty and love they see in Jesus in culturally relative terms. Yet Jesus Christ as the center of history is transcendent to the cultures in which he is received through his provocation to these to seek a greater justice and a deeper peace.[82]

78. Wells, *Christic Center*, 227–31.

79. Sandel, *Democracy's Discontent*, 338.

80. Metz, *Love's Strategy*, 168.

81. Ibid., 170.

82. This has recently been argued in terms not specific to Christianity in Habermas, "Awareness of What Is Missing," 18–19.

Jesus' proclamation of the reign of God is key to his ethical transcendence as the center of history. The petition for its coming in the Lord's Prayer makes hope for it intrinsic to Christian identity. The reign of God that he proclaimed and that Christians pray for has transhistorical and inner-historical sides.[83] It cannot be fully realized within the conditions of history. In this it points to a final fulfillment for creation that lies beyond history. But it also has an inner historical side that makes a decisive contribution to Jesus Christ being the center of history. The reign of God was present in an initial way in Jesus' public ministry. Aspects of it continue to be realized in history through movements for human fulfillment, healing, justice and peace, and environmental preservation. Jesus' proclamation of the reign of God is crucial to how Christians should understand and relate to such movements.

> Although the Kingdom of God cannot be achieved on this earth, the ideal of the Kingdom serves to measure, on principle, how much of the Kingdom there is in particular social developments; it also serves to avoid all such developments appearing infinitely remote from the Kingdom by the standards of the Kingdom. The Kingdom certainly relativizes them, but it also grades them, and this is supremely important.[84]

Jesus' proclamation of the reign of God and his death for its sake embeds traditions of Second Temple Judaism as taken up by him in his person as the center of history. As a result Jesus has a dialectical relationship to these and to present-day Judaism. They remain a basis for critique of understandings of his person. Because Jesus cannot be understood as the Christ apart from his proclamation of the reign of God, the Jewish "no" to Christian faith in Jesus as the Messiah must be taken up into Christian understandings of Jesus Christ as the center of history. The Jewish "no" to faith in Jesus Christ is based on the recognition that continuing realities of injustice, evil, sin, and suffering in the world[85] show that the reign of God has not yet come in fullness. Christians take this realization up into their understanding of Jesus Christ when they see these continuing realities as a scandal that they should mourn and work to overcome in light of Jesus' message and resurrection. When Jesus Christ is seen as the center of history in this way, he, his message,

83. Tillich, *Systematic Theology*, 3:357.

84. Sobrino, *Jesus the Liberator*, 115.

85. Moltmann, *Way of Jesus Christ*, 32–34.

and the future promised in him can empower the marginalized and oppressed to struggle for freedom and justice.[86]

As the center of history Jesus Christ is an answer to questions about the meaning and purpose of creation and human life that arise from historical existence. But this second aspect of his transcendence means that he also makes history by moving people to act in it. The goodness, beauty, and love expressed in Jesus Christ give rise to a sense of mission that makes history through the actions it inspires.[87] The mission arising from faith in Jesus Christ includes ethical struggles but also evangelism and dialogue. This meaning that Jesus has as the center of history is dynamic. It not only moves people to act, but what it moves people to do "can be altered, corrected, and improved over time to suit changing circumstances."[88] The work of Jesus as the Word of God is always surrounded by that of the Holy Spirit, which works to prepare the way for his coming and then to actualize in history the new relationship to God that he makes possible. This pattern of preparation and actualization is repeated in the lives of Christians as the Holy Spirit moves them to new understandings of Jesus Christ in relation to new circumstances.

A change in the way Christians understand Jesus can happen through dialogue between Christians and those belonging to other religious traditions or none, or when the gospel is received or pondered in cultures strongly shaped by other religious traditions. When the latter happens other religious traditions come to stand in a similar relationship to Jesus as the center of history as Judaism. As they prepare the way for him through their traditions and prophetic criticism and how these have shaped a given culture, they influence how Jesus is received as the Christ. This introduces diversity and a wealth of critical insights into the Christian church that it otherwise would not have.[89] Jesus Christ is the center of history but not the whole of it. His person and meaning are always partly informed by the history that he is the center of, by the events, traditions, and cultures present in it, and in the lives of those who believe in him.

---

86. Russell, *Household of Freedom*, 20.

87. Moltmann, *Theology of Hope*, 288–91.

88. Tanner, *Christ the Key*, 280.

89. For an example of this influence, see the discussion of the Christology of Jacques Dupuis in Schweitzer, *Contemporary Christologies*, 115–23.

JESUS CHRIST AS A SOURCE OF BOUNDED OPENNESS
IN THE NEW UNITY OF HISTORY

"Time, so to speak, runs ahead toward the new, the unique, the novel, even in repetitions."[90] In the twentieth century this creative aspect of time has brought a new unity to history through the development and use of modern technologies.[91] Faith in Jesus Christ has always asserted a unity to history. While nations, peoples, species, places, and individuals have their own histories, Jesus Christ is the center of a history that in principle includes all. But the development and application of the ever-increasing powers of modern technologies to travel, communications, agriculture and industry, commerce and war in the second half of the twentieth century have given history a new negative unity encompassing humanity and creation. As the productive capacities of modern technologies have increased, so have the incalculability of risks associated with them. For example, the risks accompanying the use of nuclear power as an energy source or herbicides, pesticides, and genetic engineering in agriculture "are no longer tied to their place of origin," and by "their nature . . . endanger all forms of life on this planet."[92] Climate change resulting from global warming is indiscriminate and unpredictable in its effects. Usually it is the poor and the marginalized who suffer most when these negative possibilities are actualized. Yet the extent of the dangers they pose levels social and national boundaries. All people and forms of life are exposed to the global risks that the increasing power and application of modern technologies have created.[93] As a result, while peoples continue to have different pasts, they now have a common future with creation of either surviving these dangers together or being destroyed by them.[94]

This negative unity is accompanied by a new positive unity of history and an increased fragmentation of societies. Globalization, the compression of time and space in terms of its meaning for human relationships and action, has intertwined the individual histories of peoples and places to an unprecedented degree, thus giving history a new unity. Modern technology now makes it possible for individuals, social

90. Tillich, *Systematic Theology*, 3:319.

91. Ibid., 341.

92. Beck, *Risk Society*, 22–23.

93. Ibid., 48.

94. Moltmann, *God in Creation*, 136. "Ever since Chernobyl in 1986, all life has been in deadly danger, not just human life" (Moltmann, *God for a Secular Society*, 242).

agencies, and governments to cross boundaries that formerly separated peoples, to meet the urgent needs of others living on the other side of the world and on a scale previously unimaginable.[95] Societies have become increasingly interdependent, even those separated by great cultural or geographical distances. The "expansion of the media of communication, not least the development of global TV, and of other new technologies of rapid communication and travel, has made people all over the world more conscious of other places and of the world as a whole."[96] Though the consciousness of millions of people remains relatively unaffected by this, still these developments have created a heightened "sense of the world as being one."[97]

With this new unity to history has come an increased fragmentation of cultures and societies. Peoples, nations, communities, and individuals continue to have distinctive identities and desires. But the distant is now near and the local is often different and unknown. Societies that have not undertaken ethnic cleansing have become increasingly pluralistic. This has at times helped give rise to xenophobic forms of "introverted nationalism."[98] The world remains culturally, ethnically, racially, sexually, nationally, and religiously differentiated within the new unity of history. As a result the human condition has become cosmopolitan.[99] People remain rooted in and oriented by the ethical visions of the particular and bounded communities they belong to, but they are constantly involved with moral issues extending beyond the limits of these and are constantly interacting with people near and far belonging to other communities.

As the risks created by the use of modern technologies cross the borders of particular nations and communities, they can only be adequately addressed by the coordinated action of peoples belonging to different religions, cultures, and denominations. For the sake of their common future people belonging to one community have to communicate and work with people belonging to others. The positive unity of history means that such action is in theory possible and in some ways already happening.

95. Schweitzer, "Food as Gift," 10.

96. Robertson, *Globalization*, 184.

97. Ibid.

98. Beck, *Cosmopolitan Vision*, 4.

99. Ibid., 2.

To act responsibly in this context Christians need a center giving them norms and guidance in relation to the events, developments, and pluralism of religions and human communities in history. They also need openness to the wisdom and insights of other sources of knowledge and experience so they can learn from these and cooperate with people belonging to other communities in seeking justice and resisting evil. The notion of having a center that gives one guidance is sometimes seen as opposite to being open to other worldviews and religions. The argument of this chapter has been that Jesus Christ is a center of history that gives one an identity bounded by ethical norms yet open to learning from and cooperating with those who live by others. The new unity of history situates Christians within a postmodern trilemma of needing "to acknowledge tradition, to celebrate plurality, and to resist domination—all three together."[100] Jesus Christ as the center of history has saving significance in relation to this by giving people an identity of "bounded openness,"[101] an identity characterized by ethical norms and definition yet also fluid, open to revision, and affirmative of pluralism.

The identity Jesus Christ offers is bound to him; his proclamation and practice of the coming reign of God, his death and resurrection. It requires acknowledgement of the tradition stemming from him, its life-giving forms, it distortions and fallible nature, its need of constant critique and correction. The Christian community is bound by Jesus Christ in that he is its judge and hope, the ultimate basis for its action and critique. He is the center from which it understands itself and relates to others.

The centrality of the reign of God to Jesus Christ means that this identity should include resisting domination of all kinds. In the present context it is also oriented to celebrating plurality, acknowledging what it has learned from others, seeing in other religions, social movements, and institutions aspects of the goodness that it seeks to exemplify. Jesus Christ as the center of history gives one an identity that is defined but also fluid; open to reformation, dialogue, and cooperation with others. Faith in Jesus Christ as the center of history can thus give people and communities an identity characterized by the bounded openness that the new unity of history and its cosmopolitan condition requires.

100. Taylor, *Remembering Esperanza*, 40.

101. Jones, *Feminist Theory*, 135, 170.

CONCLUSION

Jesus Christ as the center of history sets one to working "half in and half out of what is at hand."[102] He binds one to the received Christian tradition yet with openness to what is outside it. He calls one into the church but also to move beyond its present form in seeking the coming reign of God. He puts one into the world with commitment to it yet with hope for justice and peace beyond what it presently offers. He gives one a sense of identity within history that transcends the present. He evokes commitment coupled with humility. The cosmopolitan nature of the human condition at present requires this kind of center that is open to revision. What does it look like in practice? The next chapter will examine this in relation to some other religious traditions.

102. Spivak, *Critique of Postcolonial Reason*, 110.

11 Jesus Christ and Other Religions

The last chapter concluded that Jesus Christ is a source of bounded openness, an orientation in the world bounded by a vision of hope, a sense of identity as loved and accepted by God, and a call to discipleship. This is an orientation open to others and carried by its own commitments into dialogue with other religions, social movements, institutions, and developments in surrounding society. Faith in Jesus Christ thus gives rise to a dialogical relationship to the world and the many forms and visions of life within it. As noted in previous chapters, the boundedness of this orientation may at times necessitate a shift to protest and resistance. Dialogue is not an appropriate relationship to radical evil.[1] But this same boundedness frequently mandates openness and dialogue.

This chapter continues this line of thought by examining how Jesus Christ relates to other religions. Some general parameters of these relationships will be explored and then aspects of the relationship of Jesus Christ to Judaism, Islam, Hinduism, and traditional religion[2] of the Rock Cree in northwestern Manitoba will be discussed. This twofold approach is taken because it is necessary first to articulate a general understanding of how Jesus Christ relates to other religions. A definition of "religion" adequate to all of what goes by this name is difficult to offer.[3]

---

1. Cracknell, *In Good and Generous Faith*, 161.

2. Some Cree use the term "spirituality" rather than "religion." As I am dependent upon the work of anthropologist Robert Brightman in this section, I follow him in using the term "religion."

3. John B. Cobb argues that "There is no such thing as religion. There are only traditions, movements, communities, people, beliefs, and practices that have features that are associated by many people with what they mean by religion" (Cobb, *Transforming Christianity*, 63). But he goes on to note that all the great religious traditions "can be thought of as a way of ordering the whole of life" (ibid.). Cobb's point is that there is no underlying essence common to all religions.

For purposes of dialogue and comparison I follow Hans Küng's suggestion that religion can be defined as that which "provides a comprehensive meaning for life, guarantees supreme values and unconditional norms, creates a spiritual community and home."[4] As there are significant differences between religions, the relationship of Jesus Christ to specific ones must also be examined. Therefore a general overview of how Jesus Christ relates to other religions will be presented, then fleshed out in relation to four specific religions.

In the past the relationship of Jesus Christ to other religions was sometimes studied to demonstrate the superiority of Christianity to other religions. That is not the approach intended here. Every person speaks from out of some tradition and context and in doing so states truth claims. The transcendent nature of religious truth suggests that it is more adequately arrived at through a dialogical approach recognizing a plurality of different perspectives on it, each having some validity, than through a monological approach positing one perspective as true in opposition to all others that are false.[5] In confessing their faith churches have to say who Jesus Christ is in their context. But their truth claim should be arrived at through dialogue with different voices, some enshrined in the canon of Scripture, others speaking from the history of its reception, and some from other traditions. The inclusion of more than one gospel in the canon suggests that a dialogical approach is intrinsic to knowledge of Jesus Christ. A dialogical approach states a truth claim, but recognizes that there are others and that interaction with these is essential to arriving at and understanding one's own position. Certain aspects of the person, work, and relationships of Jesus Christ can only be discovered through dialogue with other religions. Such dialogue may lead Christians to appropriate their "own tradition in a new way." [6] It is only through dialogue with "the other that we become aware of what we ourselves are, and sure of our own identity."[7]

Religions are comprehensive belief systems that orient life in the midst of history by their symbols, practices, and truth claims. The purpose of interreligious dialogue is primarily to explore these and build

4. Küng, "Toward Dialogue," xvi.

5. I have drawn the terms "dialogical" and "monological" from Bakhtin, *Problems of Dostoevsky's Poetics*.

6. Baum, *Tariq Ramadan*, 164.

7. Moltmann, *God for a Secular Society*, 228.

relationships of mutual understanding between members of different religions. Second, as noted in the previous chapter, there is always an element of mystery to Jesus Christ. Interreligious dialogue is a way of exploring this and, at the same time, exploring the understanding of reality found in other religious traditions. The knowledge gained through this is a good in itself. Through dialogue with each other, people of different religions can draw closer to what they each worship and love. Through this can also come greater understanding between members of different religions that bears practical fruit. As the human condition has become cosmopolitan different religious traditions are increasingly interacting with each other. Mutual understanding can help this occur in cooperative, respectful, and mutually beneficial ways, thus helping people of different faiths live together in peace. Finally, interreligious dialogue can help move Christians and our understanding of Jesus Christ closer to the coming future that Jesus proclaimed. While there are no permanent gains in history, many Christian churches have been transformed in their self-understanding and understanding of Jesus Christ in relation to denominational diversity within Christianity. Ecumenical dialogue has largely replaced the violent conflicts between churches that have occurred in Western history. The challenge today in North Atlantic societies is to take this transformation further by developing a fruitful understanding of "the relation of Christianity to other religious communities."[8]

Who Jesus is as the risen Christ in history is determined partly by how he is seen to relate to other religions. These relationships help constitute the "social meaning"[9] of Jesus Christ. Interreligious dialogue is partly a way of discerning this and so of coming to know Jesus Christ more fully.

THE TENSION BETWEEN COMMITMENT TO JESUS CHRIST AND AFFIRMING RELIGIOUS PLURALISM

Jesus Christ rarely relates to other religions in only one way. Typically faith in Christ separates one from people belonging to other religions in some ways and unites one with them in others. For instance, faith in Jesus Christ generally leads to understanding God in Trinitarian terms. This separates most Christians in their understanding of God from most

8. Cobb, "Introduction," 10. This is not to suggest that ecumenical dialogue and relations have achieved their goals and are no longer important.

9. Yoder, *Jewish-Christian Schism Revisited*, 57.

Muslims and Jews, as Judaism and Islam typically repudiate Trinitarian understandings of God.[10] Yet faith in Jesus Christ may lead Christians to stand with Muslims and Jews in defense of religious liberty in secular societies when religion is attacked. Faith in Jesus Christ is a commitment to God as revealed in Jesus and to Jesus Christ as the center of history as opposed to other possible centers. But the nature of Jesus Christ means that commitment to him implies love and respect for others, seeking to know and do the truth wherever it may be found, honoring and acknowledging God's love but also God's transcendence, even to one's own faith tradition. Faith in Jesus Christ leads to the recognition that wherever there is love, there is God.[11] It thus commits one to Jesus and to recognizing the presence of God wherever aspects of the love Jesus revealed appear.

This dual commitment springing from faith in Jesus Christ creates a tension between affirming "the enriching facts of cultural and religious plurality, and 'commitment' as a clear advocacy of the distinctive symbols and perspectives of the Christian tradition centered in Jesus the Christ."[12] In the context of globalization "[t]here could hardly be a more salient tension for Christian theologians."[13] This tension has been present in Christian faith since its beginning. One finds it in Paul's attempt to understand the relationship of Judaism to Christianity in Romans 9–11. One finds it in the letter-journal of the early-1800s Anglo-Canadian fur trader George Nelson, as he struggled to reconcile his commitment to Jesus Christ with his experience of Ojibway and Rock Cree religious traditions and practices. Nelson found himself compelled to judge the character of First Nations people formed by these traditions as in some ways superior to that of people formed by his own culture and religion. Yet some aspects of these traditions and practices seemed to him to result from the "agency of the Devil."[14]

The tension between commitment to Jesus Christ and affirming religious pluralism is always shaped by its context. For Nelson, it was shaped partly by his circumstances in the fur trade. When he needed to

10. Ochs, "God of Jews and Christians," 59; Al-Jifri, "Loving God and Loving Neighbor," 83.

11. Bulgakov, *Comforter*, 337.

12. Taylor, "Introduction," 32.

13. Ibid., 33.

14. Brown and Brightman, "Introduction," 23–24.

know "the whereabouts of delayed employees and missing supplies," he commissioned a conjuring session involving a "shaking lodge," a ritual of the Rock Cree in his time, because he believed this could tell him what he needed to know.[15] Nelson believed that affirming Rock Cree religious beliefs and practices conflicted with his Anglican Christianity, yet he experienced these beliefs and practices as at times having beneficial aspects when judged from his Christian perspective.

In contemporary interreligious dialogue this tension tends to run along doctrinal and ethical lines. Doctrinally, religions differ in their conceptions of ultimate reality and how humanity should relate to it. But discussions of doctrinal similarities and differences happen in historical contexts where religions are wrestling with or implicated in social conflicts. Commitment to Jesus Christ thus frequently calls for recognition of the grace and truth present in other religions and critique of their involvement with injustice. It frequently also calls for a critique of Christian faith itself. In each of the four specific relationships examined in this chapter, Christian faith struggles to renew itself in the wake of involvement with profound injustices against the other religious traditions involved.

On one level, interreligious dialogue is not new. Christian churches have almost always lived in proximity to other faith communities. While relationships with these were sometimes competitive, polemical, and violent, there were also exchanges of ideas and intellectual stimulation between Christianity and other religions. Anselm developed his understanding of the atonement partly in response to challenges from Islamic and Jewish thinkers. Martin Luther discussed and drew upon the work of Jewish exegetes in his lectures on Genesis.

However, the contemporary realization that commitment to Jesus Christ calls for dialogue with other religions is mostly a post–World War II phenomena that has developed partly out of struggles to recover and renew Christian faith from its involvement with various forms of oppression and evil. Shock over events like the Holocaust and the implication of Christian anti-Semitism in preparing the way for it[16] has had a revelatory effect on many Christian churches, triggering what can be described

15. Brown and Brightman, "Northern Algonquian," 147.

16. The "anti-Jewish teaching and symbols present in the Christian tradition had created a cultural world in which the anti-Semitic language and sentiment of the Nazis were able to spread so rapidly and where people had a vague feeling that the destruction coming upon the Jews was a providential punishment" (Baum, *Theology and Society*, 141).

as a learning process. The shock the Holocaust produced helped give rise to a critique of inherited Christian supersessionism[17] and a rereading of Scripture in search of an understanding of Jesus Christ that points towards a different future. The impact of this extends beyond issues relating to the Holocaust.[18] This shock became a negative communications media[19] conveying a message about the implication of Christian faith in evil that broke through the self-referentiality of churches and societies, giving a new priority to Jewish-Christian dialogue in particular and interreligious dialogue in general, and helping to create openness to voices of the oppressed and marginalized. This was part of a wide-ranging movement in Western churches during the twentieth century that has led to Jesus' commandment to love being understood as a call to universal solidarity and compassion for all.[20] At the same time, the growth of Christian populations in Asian and Africa amidst other religious communities and the increasing religious pluralism of Western societies have helped create contexts in which interreligious dialogue has become imperative for Christian faith.

One lesson learned from the Holocaust is that when a religion achieves cultural dominance, its "symbols of power and domination" will become objective social factors leading to the oppression of those described as other, in this case Jewish communities, which no amount of love on the part of individual Christians can prevent.[21] In light of this, Christian faith had to submit itself to an ideology critique and reformulate some key doctrines and teachings.

In recent decades this emphasis has been counterbalanced by another focused on the subject location of those inhabiting religions. Subject location refers to the place of a person in their historical context. As the meaning of a religion is always socially grounded, it frequently varies depending on social factors such as whether a religious community

17. A classic text in this regard is Ruether, *Faith and Fratricide*.

18. This shock is present in a guiding question of Jürgen Moltmann's book *The Crucified God*: "What does it mean to recall the God who was crucified in a society whose official creed is optimism, and which is knee-deep in blood?" (Moltmann, *Crucified God*, 4). For an account of the shock of the Holocaust and the critique and rereading of Scripture this engendered, see Baum, *Theology and Society*, 141–56.

19. Beck, *Power in the Global Age*, 104.

20. For an account of this development in the Roman Catholic Church, see Baum, *Compassion and Solidarity*, 11–30.

21. Baum, "Introduction," 8.

is a social minority, its self-perception, and what kind of influence and power it has.[22] A religious symbol or tradition does not always have the same meaning for all persons in all places. An understanding of Jesus Christ along the lines of the Christus Victor theory of atonement may enable a concrete and efficacious naming of the sinners, the sin, and what Christian hope entails in a context of racial oppression.[23] Yet this form of Christology risks a dualistic demonizing of the oppressors that in other contexts may incite violence against innocent victims.[24] Every Christology is vulnerable to the danger that its salvific meaning will be distorted into a source of oppression. While it is important to reread Scripture and reinterpret Jesus Christ in light of the shock from events like the Holocaust, this alone is not sufficient. Such an approach can give rise to an understanding of Jesus Christ that points to a future different from the past, but it cannot give rise to a Christology free of moral ambiguity.[25] As a Christology or any other religious teaching makes a strong claim to religious truth there is always an inherent moral ambiguity to it.[26] All human knowledge has an ideological taint.[27] Therefore so will every Christology. While there are better and worse Christologies, none completely transcend the ambiguity of history. Therefore rethinking Christology in light of Christianity's involvement in different injustices must be matched by attention to the subject location of those holding a Christology and the meaning it has for them there.

The shock of the Holocaust and other great horrors of the twentieth century have helped create a new cultural context in which many people appropriate the meaning of Jesus Christ and relate to those belonging to other religions differently from the past. For instance, in the wake of the Holocaust, for many Christians faith in Jesus Christ no longer mandates seeking the conversion of Jews to Christianity but instead warrants interreligious dialogue with them.[28] In this new cultural context the demand for explicit reformulation of doctrine has given way in some theological circles to Jewish and Christian theologians instead openly

22. Michel, *Christian View of Islam*, 55.

23. For instance, Cone, *God of the Oppressed*, 232.

24. Ray, *Deceiving the Devil*, 126–27; Baum, *Signs of the Times*, 42–44.

25. Pinnock, "Atrocity and Ambiguity," 505–7.

26. Taylor, *Sources of the Self*, 518–19.

27. Niebuhr, *Nature and Destiny*, 1:194.

28. For one example of this, see *Bearing Faithful Witness*.

acknowledging differences and participating in respectful dialogue.[29] This is partly because for many people it is their identification with morally ambiguous traditions like Christianity that makes them concerned with the safety and well-being of members of other religions. The result has been a shift among Jewish and Christian theologians to attention to how doctrines do and should function in a given cultural context rather than seeking to reformulate them. Still, as noted above, when religions become culturally dominant, their teachings of contempt will become objective social factors that no amount of respect and dialogue can counterbalance. This means that at times the church must explicitly reformulate its Christology in faithfulness to moral commitments arising from its faith in Jesus Christ.

Discussions concerning the relationship of Christianity to other religions and interreligious dialogues have themselves been learning processes. In the twentieth century a typology of exclusivism, inclusivism, and pluralism developed, denoting three different ways of understanding the relationship of Christianity to other religions.[30] Exclusivists emphasize the uniqueness of Jesus Christ and generally take a critical attitude towards other religions. Inclusivists stress the unsurpassable nature of Jesus Christ, yet acknowledge that elements of what is present in Christ can be found in other religions. Pluralists stress that there is no objective place from which to assess the strengths and weaknesses of religion and tend to affirm that each is a path towards the one ultimate reality.

The presence of aspects of the wisdom found in Jesus Christ in other religions has discredited the exclusivist negation of them.[31] It has also discredited the inclusivist notion that Jesus Christ is the fullness of what other religions have only in part. While elements of what is revealed in Jesus Christ can be found in other religions, these have their own integrity and cannot be seen simply as incomplete revelations of what is fully revealed in Jesus Christ. Attention to the uniqueness of different religions has also undermined the pluralist option of either positing a common essence to religion by which all religions can be judged or accepting a conceptual relativism. Any understanding of the essence of religion reflects a particular religious tradition and cultural heritage.

---

29. Pinnock, "Atrocity and Ambiguity," 505–6.

30. For an overview of these three approaches see Wells, *Christic Center*, 182–84.

31. Cobb, *Transforming Christianity*, 80.

There is no essence of religion common to all. Conversely, faith in Jesus
Christ warrants respect for other religions but not conceptual relativism.

Out of his experiences of interreligious dialogue, John B. Cobb Jr.
notes:

> One enters dialogue both as a believer convinced of the claims
> of one religious tradition and as a human being open to the pos-
> sibility that one has something to learn from representatives of
> another religious tradition. Furthermore, this duality of attitudes
> is often united. In many instances, precisely as a believer one is
> open to learn from others, believing that the fullness of wisdom
> goes beyond what any tradition already posseses.[32]

Religions tend to claim that their particular teachings have universal
value. Yet they also tend to teach humility in terms of their members'
understanding of the ultimate reality they worship. It was Cobb's commitment to Jesus Christ that has led him into interreligious dialogue.[33]
Interreligious dialogue is partly an expression of the high moral standards of universal compassion, solidarity, and respect taught by Jesus.
High moral standards require strong moral sources to maintain them.[34]
These moral sources demand an overriding commitment. Paradoxically,
it is commitment engendered by a particular religion and its universal
claims that can sustain the solidarity and respect towards others that
warrants interreligious dialogue.

For these reasons the tension between commitment to Jesus Christ
and recognition of religious pluralism continues, but the goals of this
commitment for Christians are now understood in light of the shock of
events like the Holocaust. This shock is best seen not as a call to move
beyond religious differences, but rather to live these out differently from
the way they were in the past, in part through "probing and respectful
communication"[35] between different religions and, when necessary, critique of their implication or one's own in injustice and evil. Jesus Christ
as the center of history is the source of this tension with other religions
but is also key to negotiating it. Faith in Jesus Christ gives rise to the doctrine of the Trinity, which recognizes God as revealed in Jesus Christ,
but also as present and at work throughout creation in the Holy Spirit.

32. Ibid., 66.
33. Ibid., 72, 79, 83.
34. Taylor, *Sources of the Self*, 516.
35. Pinnock, "Atrocity and Ambiguity," 506.

Interreligious dialogue can be one of the ways in which Word and Spirit work together to lead the church and the world to a greater understanding and better doing of the truth.

GENERAL PRINCIPLES FOR LIVING WITHIN THIS TENSION

Faith in Jesus Christ in the cultural context created by the shock of events like the Holocaust gives rise to a number of general principles for living in the tension between commitment to Jesus Christ and affirming religious pluralism by participating in interreligious dialogue.

A *first principle* is to recognize that one cannot overcome this tension and therefore should not try to. Instead it must be accepted and taken into Christology and faith in Jesus Christ. Jesus Christ enables one to live in this tension by enabling one to accept it. As those who know themselves to be justified by grace through faith in Jesus Christ, Christians are able to accept the ambiguity of the tension between commitment to Jesus Christ and religious pluralism and dwell therein, knowing in Christ that this ambiguity is not the last word. Also, Christ brings the hope that in this dwelling there can be sanctification, both in movement towards greater understanding of the truth and movement towards peace and understanding between Christians and members of other religions. As the light that enlightens every person, Christ brings the hope that through interreligious dialogue people can come to a deeper understanding of God and each other. In light of Jesus Christ this tension is not an iron cage from which one cannot escape, but a challenging condition presenting possibilities for spiritual growth and further expressions of God's goodness and beauty in history.

A *second principle* is that the love Jesus models involves reciprocal recognition and respect for members of other religions.[36] One should extend to members of other religions the hospitality and recognition that one would wish for one's self. This leads to a *third principle*. Members of a religion must be able to recognize their faith in the presentation of it in interreligious dialogue.[37] A *fourth principle* is that the internal pluralism of religious traditions must be respected. There are distinct traditions and movements[38] in every religion. This "makes it difficult to make general

---

36. Moltmann, *God for a Secular Society*, 235.

37. Küng, "Toward Dialogue," xv.

38. Baum, *Tariq Ramadan*, 73.

statements about a religion and even more difficult to make comparisons between different religions."[39] This means that interreligious dialogue must often be conducted selectively and with the recognition that the religions involved extend beyond the dialogue participants. When this happens the reasons for dialoguing with one tradition or movement rather than another should be made clear.

A *fifth principle* is that while interreligious dialogue is a good in itself, one must always attend to its effect in the context in which it occurs. Dialogue between religious communities can have "a tranquillizing effect on things as they actually are,"[40] if conducted without attention to social conflicts in its context. Christian participation in interreligious dialogue should have hope for and commitment to the coming of God's reign as a guiding horizon. This means that concern for how interreligious dialogue affects the ways in which life is threatened in the context where it occurs must enter into the dialogue itself. With these principles in mind we turn to examine aspects of interreligious dialogues between Christianity and Judaism, Islam, Hinduism, and the traditional religion of the Rock Cree.[41]

JESUS CHRIST AND JUDAISM

In the background of contemporary Jewish-Christian dialogue in North Atlantic countries lie "two decisive events of the twentieth century: the Holocaust and the founding of the modern state of Israel."[42] As the overwhelming evil of the first gained theological attention in the 1960s and early 1970s, it forced churches and theologians to begin confronting the

---

39. Ibid.

40. Moltmann, *God for a Secular Society*, 228.

41. Judaism has been chosen because of its shared heritage with Christianity, the involvement of Christianity in the persecution of Jews culminating in the Holocaust and the presence of a significant Jewish population in Canada. Islam has been chosen because of its size, its prominence in Canada at this time and because it too shares some heritage with Judaism and Christianity. Hinduism has been chosen partly because my brief experiences of India have exposed me to it as a significant dialogue partner to Christianity. The traditional religion of the Rock Cree has been chosen because of the importance of First Nations communities, many of them Cree, in the immediate context of Saskatchewan where I live and partly because of its accessibility through the scholarly work of anthropologists like Robert Brightman.

42. Braaten and Jenson, "Introduction," vii.

effects that Christian supersessionism[43] and the teaching of contempt[44] towards Judaism have had on the social meaning of Jesus Christ for Jews. These have made the cross a sign of evil to them.[45] Conversely, the Shoah or Holocaust taught Jews that they needed their own nation-state to ensure their survival. For many contemporary Jews this makes the state of Israel "central to the very existence of Judaism,"[46] a meaning that Gentiles often may not fully appreciate.

In the foreground stand statements from Christian and Jewish communities. The first was *Nostra Aetate*, affirmed by the Roman Catholic Church at Vatican II.

> Nostra Aetate rejected all forms of anti-Semitism as sinful; repudiated the accusation of Jewish collective guilt for the death of Jesus, both at the time of Jesus and through the ages; and affirmed God's ongoing love of his people, and the church's spiritual bond with Jews.[47]

It "may be considered the Magna Carta of the Roman Catholic Church's new approach to its relation with the Jewish people."[48] Similar statements from Protestant churches began to appear in the 1970s and have proliferated to the point where the leadership and official statements of most Christian churches have repudiated traditional supersessionist views of Judaism. This was recognized in a groundbreaking statement signed by Jewish theologians and religious leaders representing most forms of Judaism in September 2000, entitled *Dabru Emet: A Jewish Statement on Christians and Christianity*.[49] This acknowledged that Christianity had changed dramatically since the Holocaust, that Christian churches have repudiated traditional supersessionism, that Jews and Christians worship the same God (through different understandings), and that Nazism "was

43. For a definition of supersessionism see below.

44. The phrase "teaching of contempt, " coined by Jules Isaac, refers to the view that as a result of not believing in Jesus Christ, Jews have been rejected by God and that their persecution is God's punishment for this (Fleischner, "Jews and Christians," 50).

45. Ibid., 43; Langer, "Liturgy and Sensory Experience," 193.

46. Marmur, "United Church and Jews," 32. For a dissenting view, see Ellis, *Judaism Does Not Equal Israel*.

47. Fleischner, "Jews and Christians," 71.

48. Ibid.

49. *A Jewish Statement*. Jewish-Christian dialogue tends to involve Jews from the Reformed and Conservative branches of Judaism. But representatives of Orthodox Judaism were among the co-signers of Dabru Emet.

not a Christian phenomenon,"[50] and it called upon Jews and Christians to work together for justice and peace. These developments have set the stage for contemporary Jewish-Christian dialogue.

Though traditional supersessionism has been repudiated by most churches, issues underlying this teaching remain important for Jewish-Christian dialogue. Christian supersessionism can be defined as "the theology that sees the putative new revelation [in Jesus Christ] as transcending and surpassing the old [in the Hebrew Bible], rendering it obsolete."[51] The idea that the Hebrew Bible is obsolete was rejected by the early church when Marcion was excommunicated in 144 CE. Marcion's thought was characterized by the assertion of a radical discontinuity between the gospel and the Hebrew Bible. For Marcion, Jesus did not fulfill the latter but abolished it.[52] Marcion's creation of a canon excluding the Hebrew Bible clashed with early Christianity's fidelity to it.[53] In excommunicating Marcion the early church declared that this exclusion was injurious to the Christian faith,[54] that the gospel was continuous with the Hebrew Bible, and that the latter continued to be revelatory and authoritative for Christians. Consequently Christianity and Rabbinic Judaism, two traditions that emerged from Second Temple Judaism "at

50. The quote is from a paragraph heading in Dabru Emet. The paragraph reads as follows:

> Without the long history of Christian anti-Judaism and Christian violence against Jews, Nazi ideology could not have taken hold nor could it have been carried out. Too many Christians participated in, or were sympathetic to, Nazi atrocities against Jews. Other Christians did not protest sufficiently against these atrocities. But Nazism itself was not an inevitable outcome of Christianity. If the Nazi extermination of the Jews had been fully successful, it would have turned its murderous rage more directly to Christians. We recognize with gratitude those Christians who risked or sacrificed their lives to save Jews during the Nazi regime. With that in mind, we encourage the continuation of recent efforts in Christian theology to repudiate unequivocally contempt of Judaism and the Jewish people. We applaud those Christians who reject this teaching of contempt, and we do not blame them for the sins committed by their ancestors (A Jewish Statement, xvii).

51. Levenson, "Did God Forgive Adam?," 151.

52. Pelikan, Christian Tradition, 1:76.

53. Ibid., 70. Marcion's canon also excluded significant parts of the New Testament.

54. Following Augustine's definition of heresy, see ibid., 69.

roughly the same time,"[55] remain joined by their common heritage of the Hebrew Bible.

However, Christian theologians and churches continued to teach that Jesus Christ rendered Judaism obsolete. In the early church this was partly polemic fueled by competition between Jewish and Christian communities. It was also an answer to questions arising from the relationship of Christianity to Judaism: "[i]f the preceding order was altogether adequate, why should a new one have come into existence and why should anyone adhere to it?"[56] These questions remain pertinent because, as David Novak argues, while there is a great deal of overlap in their teachings at a penultimate level, "Jews and Christians have to recognize that [at an ultimate level] their truth claims are not only different, they are mutually exclusive."[57] The Jewishness of Jesus' ministry and person anchors Christianity in history and makes the Hebrew Bible a defining part of its story.[58] Yet the proclamation that Jesus is the Christ distinguishes Christianity from Judaism. Because of Jesus Christ Christians must acknowledge both their common heritage and their differences with Judaism.[59] This means that supersessionism cannot be transcended "once and for all."[60] While Christians have predominantly repudiated traditional supersessionism that declared Judaism obsolete, the relationship of Christianity to Judaism remains a central issue for Jewish-Christian dialogue.

At this point Novak introduces a distinction between a "harsh" supersessionism declaring Judaism obsolete and respectful supersessionism that upholds Christian truth claims but does not denigrate Judaism. According to Novak, "Christian supersessionism need not require condemnation of Judaism, no more than Judaism requires condemnation of

---

55. Novak, *Talking with Christians*, 20.

56. Levenson, "Did God Forgive Adam?," 151.

57. Novak, *Talking with Christians*, 29; see also 159–60. Novak also notes that there is significant overlap, agreements and commonalities in many teachings of Judaism and Christianity.

58. Neuhaus, "Salvation is From the Jews," 72.

59. There are Messianic Jews or Jewish Christians who combine faith in Jesus Christ with Jewish practices. For information on their beliefs and organization, see http://www .iamcs.org/WhatWeBelieve.php. From a Christian perspective their faith in Jesus Christ suggests they are a Christian denomination. From a Jewish perspective they remain Jews who have converted to a different faith (Novak, *Talking with Christians*, 218–28).

60. Cartwright, "Afterword," 231.

Christianity—although on both sides there will be strong critiques."[61] He portrays this respectful Christian supersessionism as the mirror image of the "Jewish view that Christianity, while 'a valid gentile relationship with the Lord God, . . .' is in many ways a grave distortion of Torah."[62] In this portrayal of their relationship, Judaism and Christianity retain their truth claims and critiques of each other, but in a context of mutual respect and commitment to dialogue. This respectful supersessionism recognizes the commonalities between Judaism and Christianity. There is agreement and similar understanding and concerns in Judaism and Christianity in many areas. It also recognizes the differences between the two, "the Church's development of doctrine and Rabbinic Judaism's ability to define its own boundaries,"[63] and that each can benefit from dialogue and cooperation with the other.

In this view Christianity and Judaism have a dialectical relationship. At the center of this is Jesus Christ. Jesus' Jewish heritage means that "Christianity speaks a language that is largely Jewish, a language most of whose vocabulary and grammar come from the same sources that living Judaism draws upon—namely, the Hebrew Bible and the Judaism of the late Second Temple period."[64] Yet this language and grammar were reshaped and transformed as they were appropriated by Jesus and used to interpret his ministry, death, and resurrection.[65] This dialectical relationship continues in the present. "What binds Christian worship to Judaism is the language and imagery of Christian prayer; what sets it apart is the person of Christ, who is present in both parts of the Christian liturgy."[66]

This relationship has been destructive for much of Western history partly because the Christian "no" in this dialectic overshadowed its "yes" and prevented Christians from recognizing Jews as people they were commanded to love and respect. The shock of the Holocaust has helped correct this. In coming to terms with the role that Christian anti-Semitism played in helping prepare the way for the Holocaust, most churches have rejected the notion of Judaism as legalistic and affirmed

---

61. Ibid.

62. Levering, *Jewish-Christian Dialogue*, 15.

63. Ibid., 3.

64. Novak, *Talking with Christians*, xiii.

65. Dahl, *Jesus the Christ*, 180.

66. Wilken, "Christian Worship," 199.

its continuing validity as a response to God's grace, as a tradition of faith that Christians need to be in dialogue with, and as a sign of God's faithfulness and continuing presence in the world.

Overcoming the denigration potentially present in even the mildest supersessionism requires that Christians develop "a deeper understanding of creation and providence,"[67] one in which the continued witness of Judaism is seen to be willed by God. Jewish theologian Irving Greenberg has formulated this as follows:

> Humans cannot keep the covenantal tensions in perfect balance. The key to upholding the totality of covenant and the fullest realization of the goal is that there be multiple communities working on many roads toward perfection, and that there be mutual, loving criticism to keep standards high.[68]

To undergird this kind of relationship it helps to note that even protest can be a form of communion. In disagreeing about Jesus Christ, Jews and Christians can find that they agree about the importance of faith in God and in many of their beliefs. Jewish-Christian dialogue can be a discovery of communion and common responsibility, a communion that for Christians is rooted in Jesus Christ but not limited to those who believe in him. Walter Kasper describes the parameters of this as follows:

> Jews and Christians—for so long adversaries when not merely indifferent to each other—should strive to become allies. They have a great common heritage to watch over: the common image of the human person, its unique dignity and responsibility before God, the understanding of the worlds as creation, the concept of justice and peace, the worth of the family, and the hope of definitive salvation and fulfillment.[69]

One result of Jewish-Christian dialogue has been the discovery of this communion, which for Christians extends in various ways and degrees to other religions as well. This has been a discovery of one meaning

---

67. Levering, *Jewish-Christian Dialogue*, 3.

68. Greenberg, "Judaism and Christianity," 156. Robert Jenson argues that the "church and the synagogue are together and only together the present availability to the world of the risen Jesus Christ" (Jenson, "Toward a Christian Theology," 13). This seems to me to veer to close to making Judaism a part of Christianity, and to not sufficiently respect the distinction between Judaism and Christianity that many Jewish participants in Jewish-Christianity dialogue wish to make.

69. Kasper, "Paths Taken," 10–11.

of the ancient story of Cain and Abel (Gen 4:1–16); that deep as religious differences may be, deeper still is the responsibility human beings have for each other.[70] This awakening to the humanity of those who belong to other religions has brought Christians a new awareness of their own humanity, a new humility in relation to other faiths, a changed understanding of Jesus Christ, and a loss of false innocence. One of the lessons for Christians from Jewish-Christian dialogue is that faith in Jesus Christ has not been an unmitigated good for all people. Christians are responsible for seeing that Jesus Christ is not a cause of suffering or a name to fear among members of other religions.

In the twentieth century Jewish philosophers and theologians like Martin Buber, Franz Rosenzweig, and Abraham Heschel who adopted this kind of dialectical relationship to Christianity have significantly influenced Western Christian thought, helping theologians and churches negotiate the possibilities and pitfalls that Western modernity poses to Christian faith. Greenberg articulates this way of understanding of Jesus from within Judaism as follows:

> From this perspective, Jesus is no false Messiah, that is, a world-be redeemer who teaches evil values. Rather, when Christianity, in his name, claims absolute authority and denigrates the right of Judaism or of Jews to exist, then it makes him into a false Messiah. Short of such claims, however, Jews should recognize Jesus as a failed Messiah. This recognition would allow Jews to affirm that for hundreds of millions of people, Christianity has been and continues to be a religion of love and consolation.[71]

The Jewishness of Jesus and the (to Jewish minds unacceptable) proclamation that Jesus is the Christ tie Judaism and Christianity together and yet distinguish them so that they can productively challenge and stimulate each other.[72] The Jewish "no" to Jesus as the Christ is partly "based on the experienced and suffered unredeemedness of the world."[73] It need not rule out the experience many Christians claim of reconciliation in Christ, but it does mean that Christians must "talk about the total and universal redemption of the world only in the dimensions of a future

---

70. von Rad, *Genesis*, 104–6.

71. Greenberg, "Judaism and Christianity," 156.

72. Ochs, "God of Jews and Christians," 58.

73. Moltmann, *Way of Jesus Christ*, 32.

hope, and a present contradiction of this unredeemed world,"[74] so that Christian faith remains "open for the messianic future of Jesus,"[75] which remains outstanding. This future will be in continuity with Jesus Christ, but it will also be something new that Christians will discover partly through dialogue and cooperation with members of other religions.

In recognizing that Jesus Christ does not abolish Judaism, churches have made a second correction in their relationship to it, equal to the early church's repudiation of Marcion's deletion of the Hebrew Bible from the canon. Jesus Christ is still seen as the center of history. But now the line separating sin and grace is no longer seen to run between the church and the world, but through each religious community and every people,[76] the church included. Partly through the shock of the Holocaust and interreligious dialogue, Christians now understand Jesus Christ as "the Great Protector of humans, who stood against all the forces of death."[77] Christ's saving power is seen to be present "in the lives of those who stand up for victims in the midst of social oppression,"[78] regardless of their religious affiliation. This understanding emphasizes the continuity of Jesus Christ with the teachings and practices of other religions that also oppose injustice and violence.

This changed understanding of Jesus Christ draws Christians into dialogue with Jews but can also separate them over issues concerning the Israeli-Palestinian conflict.[79] The Holocaust poses a double challenge to Christians: "'Speak out against social evil,' and 'Examine your own complicity in this social evil.'"[80] This has led many Christians to defend the existence of the state of Israel and at the same time demand "human rights for Palestinians and . . . [recognition of] their claim to a homeland."[81] This has strained some Jewish-Christian relations. For some Jews and Christians unquestioned support for the state of Israel has become "a kind of litmus test for the trustworthiness of Christians

---

74. Ibid.

75. Ibid., 33.

76. Baum, *Signs of the Times*, 42.

77. Baum, *Theology and Society*, 142.

78. Pawlikowski, "Christ Event," 120. A biblical warrant for this is found in Matt 25:41–46.

79. Fleischner, "Jews and Christians," 76–81.

80. Baum, *Theology and Society*, 143.

81. Ibid., 146.

after Auschwitz,"[82] and Christian criticisms of the state of Israel are seen as a continuation of supersessionism by another name and/or a veiled form of anti-Semitism. On occasion this criticism has shaded into the latter.[83] However, the Jewish community in Israel and abroad is also divided over issues of justice for Palestinians and some actions of the state of Israel.

Understanding Jesus Christ as the protector of human life rules out any fundamental dualism between Jew or Palestinian. The legacy of the Holocaust demands solidarity "for all victims in the world, non-Jews as well as Jews."[84] It also demands that Christians in North Atlantic countries continue to examine how "their own history of centuries of Christian anti-Judaism" has helped make security such a pressing and legitimate question for Jews.[85] Finally, Christians living outside the Middle East should respect the complexity of the Palestinian-Israeli conflict. Solidarity for Palestinians and criticisms of actions and policies of the state of Israel are best done in conjunction and consultation with Palestinian and Jewish organizations working for peace in the Middle East.

In the wake of the Holocaust Christians have rediscovered the Second Temple Jewishness of Jesus. This has drawn them closer to contemporary Judaism. Yet part of Jesus' Jewish heritage was a prophetic demand for justice. In relation to the suffering of Palestinians from the occupation of their lands by Israel, the latter tends to separate Christians from some Jewish communities. It can also provide an opportunity for anti-Semitism, intended or otherwise. Jesus Christ places Christians into this tension. Faithfulness to him requires that Christians stay there.

JESUS CHRIST AND ISLAM

Islam is not part of the Western cultural heritage in the way that Judaism and Christianity are. This is an important factor in the background of Muslim-Christian relations in Western countries. Judaism, Christianity, and Islam are religions of revelation with many similarities. But Muslim-Christian dialogue in the West is in many respects an exercise in bridging cultural differences that have been the site of conflicts leaving deep

---

82. Pollefeyt, "Between a Dangerous Memory," 136.

83. Genizi, *Holocaust*, 147–52.

84. Pollefeyt, "Between a Dangerous Memory," 137.

85. Ibid., 140.

divisions in many places between these two faiths. The history of the Crusades, Western colonialism in Muslim countries, and more recent military, economic, religious, and cultural assaults on Islam and Islamic countries have led many Muslims to believe that North Atlantic countries are intent on destroying Islam.[86] As a result, "Muslims cannot view Christianity today simply as the teaching of the holy prophet Jesus, but rather as a contributing element in a comprehensive system of oppression and cultural destruction that caused suffering and violated the dignity of their people."[87] Out of this history has arisen a desire on the part of Christians and Muslims for dialogue between their communities as part of a way towards peace between them.[88] This is of broader importance in light of the size of each faith community. As Muslim religious leaders and scholars have observed,

> Christianity and Islam are the largest and second largest religions in the world and in history. Christians and Muslims reportedly make up over a third and over a fifth of humanity respectively. Together they make up more than 55% of the world's population, making the relationship between these two religious communities the most important factor in contributing to meaningful peace around the world.[89]

Muslim-Christian dialogues have been ongoing in North Atlantic countries for the past thirty years.[90] These received renewed impetus from the tragic events of September 11, 2001, and the increase in discrimination against Muslims in Canada and the United States that followed.[91] These factors led churches in Canada and elsewhere to seek to enter into dialogue with Muslim communities and support them against denigration in the mass media and government sanctioned discrimination.[92]

86. Michel, *Christian View of Islam*, 64.

87. Ibid.

88. Relations between Muslims and Christians have not always been conflictual in the past, nor are they necessarily so in the present. As Thomas Michel notes, "Muslims and Christians, when issues of power and influence do not separate them, do not find it difficult to live and work together, either as individuals or as social groups" (ibid., 56).

89. "Open Letter," 4.

90. Michel, *Christian View of Islam*, 61.

91. Baum, *Signs of the Times*, 18.

92. Committee on Inter-Church and Inter-Faith Relations, *That We May Know Each Other*, 61.

Also in the foreground of Muslim-Christian dialogues is the exchange of open letters triggered by Pope Benedict XVI's address at the University of Regensburg on September 12, 2006. Here the pope quoted some derogatory statements about Islam from a dialogue about Islam and Christianity in the late fourteenth century and contrasted differences in Islamic and Christian understandings of the relationship between the nature of God and reason. [93] The pope's unfortunate remarks triggered outrage in Muslim communities, violent responses against Roman Catholics, and a subsequent expression of sorrow on the pope's part and a clarification of his views on Islam. Thirty-eight Muslim religious leaders and scholars responded to the pope's address "in a spirit of dialogue and reconciliation," [94] on October 12, 2006, with an "Open Letter to His Holiness Pope Benedict XVI," correcting some of the pope's false impressions of Islam and expressing appreciation for his subsequent clarifications and assurances of good will. [95] This was followed a year later by "A Common Word between Us and You," an open letter addressed to the pope and other church leaders, signed by numerous Muslim intellectuals and religious leaders. This restated a commitment to peace based on mutual understanding between Muslims and Christians and argued that the basis for this lies in two foundational principles common to both faiths: love of God and love of neighbor. [96] Christian responses to this include the Yale Response, "Loving God and Neighbor Together: A Christian Response to 'A Common Word between Us and You,'" [97] and "A Common Word for the Common Good," by Archbishop of Canterbury Rowan Williams. [98] In the years since September 11, 2001, a number of churches have also produced study documents and statements on Christian-Muslim relations.

Muslim-Christian dialogues, like other interreligious dialogues, can be divided into four categories:

> a) the dialogue of life, "where people strive to live in an open and neighbourly spirit"; b) the dialogue of action, "in which Christians and others collaborate for the integral development

93. Benedict XVI, "Faith, Reason and the University," 2–4.

94. Baum, "Proclamation or Dialogue?," 4.

95. "Open Letter."

96. "Common Word," 28.

97. "Loving God and Neighbor Together," *New York Times*, November 18, 2007.

98. Williams, "Common Word."

and liberation of people"; c) the dialogue of theological exchange, "where specialists seek to deepen their understanding of their respective religious heritages"; and d) the dialogue of religious experience, "where persons rooted in their own religious traditions share their spiritual riches."[99]

The dialogue of theological exchange is examined here.

What this dialogue makes clear is how Jesus Christ divides and unites Muslims and Christians. Both esteem him, but in different ways. According to "A Common Word between Us and You,"

> Muslims recognize Jesus Christ as the Messiah, not in the same way Christians do (but Christians themselves anyway have never all agreed with each other on Jesus Christ's . . . nature), but in the following way: . . . *the Messiah Jesus son of Mary is a Messenger of God and His Word which He cast unto Mary and a Spirit from Him* . . . (Al-Nisaʾ, 4:171).[100]

In Islam Jesus is seen as a messenger from God, but his message is seen as preliminary to that of Muhammad.[101] Conversely though, there is seen to be a basic continuity between their messages. As the authors of the "Open Letter to His Holiness Pope Benedict XVI" note,

> the Prophet never claimed to be bringing anything fundamentally new. . . . Thus faith in the One God is not the property of any one religious community. According to Islamic belief, all the true prophets preached the same truth to different peoples at different times. The laws may be different, but the truth is unchanging.[102]

From an Islamic perspective, what divides Christians from Muslims in terms of belief is not Jesus' teaching, but Christians' understandings of Jesus' person and the way this has led Christians to understand God as triune.

Tawhid, which means the oneness or unity and the transcendence of God, is the first principle of Islamic faith. To associate anything else with God, to worship anything else is shirk, an error and betrayal of human nature that causes personal and social disorder.[103] The idea that

99. Williams, *Common Word*, 15. These category descriptions are taken from the 1991 Vatican document *Dialogue and Proclamation*.

100. "Common Word," 48.

101. van Ess, "Islamic Perspectives," 6.

102. "Open Letter," 3–4.

103. Murata and Chittick, *Vision of Islam*, 47–52.

God became incarnate in Jesus Christ is seen as a violation of *tawhid*, a failure to acknowledge divine transcendence and incomparability and the fundamental error of Christian belief. As a Muslim speaker at the Yale Common Word Conference stated: "We do not believe that God . . . can be divided, nor do we believe in divine incarnation (*hulūl*) or hypostatic union (*ittihād*)."[104] This repudiation highlights the distinctiveness of the Christian belief that through becoming incarnate in Jesus Christ God assumed human nature and shared human suffering, so that one can look to Jesus on the cross and know that God is with one and shares one's loneliness, sorrow, and pain.

Yet as Jesus Christ separates Muslims and Christians in one way, he can bring them together in another. The belief that in Jesus Christ God has acted in a unique way, becoming incarnate in Jesus, experiencing death on the cross and overcoming this in principle in Jesus' resurrection is perhaps where Christian faith clashes most with the "philosophically enlightened self-understanding of modernity."[105] These beliefs about Jesus Christ put Christians into a dialogical relationship to Western modernity. Islamic faith does the same for many Muslims.[106]

The relationship of Christian faith to Western societies is itself an issue in Muslim-Christian dialogues. Some Muslims take a critical view of the individualism and secularism of Western liberal societies. In Islam, faith in God must be performed publicly.

> For Muslims, it is God who is the center of the universe, at the heart of human life and every human activity. Any way of life that reduces faith to private morality and ritual is unacceptable, an affront to God's majesty and holiness. They regard modern Christians' easy acceptance of secular society and humanist ethics as a compromise with the essence of religious faith.[107]

This emphasis on practice and obedience in Islam illuminates subtle differences in the meaning of faith between the two religions. For Islam, to have faith is to practice it. But in Christianity, while faith should give rise to works, it cannot be restricted to this. For many it is fundamentally trust in God and confession of belief (Rom 10:9). This difference

---

104. Al-Jifri, "Loving God and Loving Neighbor," 83.

105. Habermas, "Awareness of What Is Missing," 16.

106. Baum, *Tariq Ramadan*, 117.

107. Michel, *Christian View of Islam*, 107.

is related to the Christian view of Jesus Christ. In most New Testament traditions, Jesus does not just bring a teaching that should be practiced. He also brings a new reality that Christians enter and participate in first of all by faith. For Christians, the eschatological future is present in the risen Christ and received through faith, regardless of one's obedience. A weakness of this emphasis in Christianity on salvation through grace received in faith is that it can devalue the ethical dimensions of faith, particularly in the public sphere. The Muslim critique noted above can help Christians rediscover the public meaning of Jesus Christ. Faith in Jesus is connected to hope for the coming reign of God by one of the petitions of the Lord's Prayer (Luke 11:2; Matt 6:9–10). It needs to find public expression.[108]

However, this critique needs to be balanced by another concerning how Christian faith has been publicly expressed. The Yale Response to "A Common Word between Us and You" included the following apology:

> Since Jesus Christ says, "First take the log out of your own eye, and then you will see clearly to take the speck out of your neighbor's eye" (Matthew 7:5), we want to begin by acknowledging that in the past (e.g., in the Crusades) and in the present (e.g., in excesses of the "war on terror") many Christians have been guilty of sinning against our Muslim neighbors. Before we "shake your hand" in responding to your letter, we ask forgiveness of the All-Merciful One and of the Muslim community around the world.[109]

This paragraph acknowledges and repents of the fact that "the cross of Jesus Christ has become to many Muslims (and, for that matter, to many Jews) not a symbol of good news, self-sacrifice, and salvation, but of military conquest and oppression."[110] The secularism of liberal Western societies developed partly as a response to religious pluralism, as a means of protecting people from religious coercion, persecution, or discrimination. From a Christian perspective it is an ambiguous phenomenon that cannot be adequately judged from only one perspective.

These two Muslim critiques remind Christians that the relationship of Jesus Christ to modern Western societies must be dialectical. On one hand, secularism, as a social structure institutionalizing respect for others regardless of their religious views, can be an expression of

---

108. Boff, *Lord's Prayer*, 50.

109. "Loving God and Neighbor," 52.

110. Volf et al., "Commentary," 63.

the love for others that Jesus taught and modeled. On the other hand, it can represent a severe restriction of the meaning of Jesus Christ to the private life of individuals. The first critique is a reminder to Christians that in saying the Lord's Prayer they ask for and commit themselves to seeking the sanctification of all of society and creation. There is no realm to which the love of Christ should not extend. But the second critique raises the question of how that love should be extended and what love means in a religiously pluralistic world. Together these two critiques remind Christians that in many respects Jesus does not fit into the liberal ethos of Western societies. The reign of God that he proclaimed cannot be simply equated with Western style democracy. "The bourgeois virtues of autonomy, stability, competitive struggle and performance" cannot replace "the messianic virtues of repentance, compassion and unconditional love for the 'least of the bretheren.'"[111] The first critique is a reminder that the holy seeks to embrace and heal everything. The second points out that as people seek to participate in this, their means must be as holy as their ends.

The relationship of Jesus Christ to the various traditions within Islam is inevitably dialectical on most topics. As a result Muslim-Christian dialogue can help to keep the person, meaning, and teaching of Jesus Christ fresh and alive for Christians. As Thomas Michel notes,

> When a Christian reads the Qur'anic teaching on nature, it is like going to one's storehouse and finding things old and new. Some images are new and vivid and invite the reader to a renewed examination of our indifference or irreverence toward the divine message found in nature. Other emphases can awaken in the heart of the Christian reader a sense of respect for God's creation and a greater awareness of the seriousness of our sins against the natural world.[112]

This dialectical relationship stems from Islam and Christianity being different religions that believe in the same God.[113] As the exchange of open letters between Muslim and Christian leaders and intellectuals has clarified, the "yes" of each to the other is based on two principles upon which Muslims and Christians should be in wholehearted agreement. Both see that at the heart of Islam and Christianity there is a call to love

---

111. Schüssler Fiorenza, "Introduction," xiv.

112. Michel, *Christian View of Islam*, 173.

113. Baum, *Tariq Ramadan*, 160.

God and other people. The same concern for unconditional love and obedience to God is present in the Torah, in the teaching and preaching of Jesus, and in the message of in the Qur'an.[114] All three also teach the necessity of love for others.[115] These two teachings are inextricably linked, as the first is expressed through the second.

Christian understandings of Jesus Christ separate Christians from Muslims. Yet part of what Jesus Christ taught and represents, the unity and necessity of unconditional love for God and others, is also taught by Islam. This provides a common ground on which these two religions can meet in mutual respect, so that their differences over Jesus Christ become a stimulus to conversation, not conflict. The conflict that Jesus came to initiate on earth (Luke 12:49–53) runs between righteousness and injustice, not between Islam and Christianity, both of which call people to love God and others.

JESUS CHRIST AND HINDUISM

There are no central texts or religious figures common to all forms of Hinduism such as one finds common in virtually all forms of Judaism, Christianity, and Islam. Characteristic of Hinduism is an acceptance of a diversity of paths to the divine. Hinduism is by nature radically pluralistic in this regard compared to Judaism, Christianity, and Islam. Underlying this pluralism is a belief that all religions share "a broad intentional unity, insofar as all religions are trying to open up a path for human beings to God (or to the ultimate reality, to the Absolute) and to salvation, however defined."[116] Consequently Christian claims about the divinity of Jesus Christ are not a major issue in dialogue with Hinduism in the way that they are with Jews and Muslims. "[M]any Hindus do not find it difficult to acknowledge the divinity of Christ."[117] There are a number of avatars or divine mediators in Hindu traditions. Jesus Christ is just one more. However, the implications of Christian claims about Jesus Christ for understanding God and the nature of salvation, and Christian claims about the uniqueness of Jesus Christ, are major points of division between Christianity and influential Hindu traditions.

114. Küng, "Christian Response," 63.

115. "Common Word," 46.

116. von Stietencron, "Hindu Perspectives," 144.

117. Samartha, *One Christ—Many Religions*, 19.

Hindu-Christian dialogue is not limited to India, but any discussion of it should take into account what is happening there.[118] The cultural power of Hinduism and the political power of Hindu communalism in much of India give this dialogue existential dimensions for Indian Christians that it does not have for Christians elsewhere.[119] Here the Hindu-Christian dialogue is also a dialogue within the church about inculturating the gospel in Hindu terms and a dialogue in civil society about the legitimacy of Christianity as a religion in India.

In the background of Hindu-Christian dialogue in India lies the history of Western colonialism here. British colonial rule ended in August 1947 when India became an independent nation, but Western nations still exert colonializing influences on India. Tradition has it that Christianity first came to India when St. Thomas, one of Jesus' disciples, went there after Jesus died. The Thomas Christians in the state of Kerala trace the existence of their church to him. They form a unique social group that in 2004 formed almost one fifth of the state's population.[120] In the 1500s Christian missionaries began to arrive in India from Europe.

> [They] came with merchants, under the patronage of kings and the protection of soldiers. The society they came from fused religious and political authority into a complex whole, even if the sources of power for each were different.[121]

As a result, Indians often viewed Christian missions as part of Western imperialism. Christian missionaries often shared this view.

In the more immediate foreground lie issues of nation building and national identity. India's achieving political independence was part of a movement to make India a modern nation-state. Against this background, Jesus Christ and the church are evaluated in India in terms of their contribution to the nation's well-being. But since independence India has been the site of ongoing debate and at times violent struggle over whether it is a Hindu or a secular state. Against the backdrop, a central question is whether Christianity is a religion foreign to India and whether it belongs here.

Finally, three theological developments in India and Asia have influenced Hindu-Christian dialogue here. First, in the late 1800s the Indian

---

118. Ibid., 25.

119. Carman, "Christian Interpretation," 237.

120. Fernando and Gispert-Sauch, *Christianity in India*, 61.

121. Ibid., 108–9.

Christian theology movement began, which demanded that the gospel be expressed in terms indigenous to India. In the 1970s a second movement gained prominence, as Asian Christian theologians influenced by Latin American liberation theology began to relate the gospel to issues of poverty and economic oppression. Then in the 1980s Dalit theology appeared, a liberation theology indigenous to India. Each represents an ongoing moment in the dialogue with Hinduism about Jesus Christ.

Missionaries who came to India to convert people to Christianity tended to see Jesus Christ and Hinduism as dichotomous. An important change came with the initiative of Roberto de Nobili (1577–1656), a Roman Catholic. Most Christian converts were Dalits or of lower caste. In order to enter into dialogue with Brahmins, high-caste Hindus who regarded Dalits as polluting, de Nobili adopted a Brahmin's dress and lifestyle. His pioneering attempt to live the gospel in terms indigenous to India[122] ignored caste oppression but recognized that Jesus Christ is distinguishable from Western cultures and can be followed in non-Western ways.

A second important moment in this dialogue was the Hindu Renaissance, begun by the Bengali Hindu reformer Raja Ram Mohan Roy (circa 1772–1833). Sometimes called "the father of modern India," Roy sought to reform Hinduism and Indian culture by opening both to select Western ideas while remaining rooted in Hindu traditions. He translated the New Testament into Bengali with the help of Baptist missionaries and published a collection of Jesus' ethical teachings. Key figures of the Hindu Renaissance like Roy, Keshub Chander Sen, and Mahatma Gandhi rejected claims that salvation was only available through Jesus Christ, but were deeply influenced by Jesus' life and ethical teachings. Their interest in Jesus and reforming activity made Hinduism more concerned with social causes and the welfare of the poor. Through their work Jesus Christ had an impact on Hinduism and Indian culture.[123] Conversely, Christian worship inculturated in a Hindu context can give Western Christians a new experience of the transcendence and mystery of God.[124] This illustrates how "spontaneous fecundation"[125] of religions and cultures can occur through their contact and dialogue with each other.

122. Ibid., 97–100.

123. For a study of this see Thomas, *Acknowledged Christ.*

124. Johnson, *Quest for the Living God,* 173.

125. Panikkar, "Can Theology Be Transcultural?" 15.

Hindu interpretations like Ram's "provided the impetus, inspiration and confidence for Indian Christians to develop their own indigenized portrayals of Jesus."[126] This was a third moment in this dialogue; the development of Indian Christian theology, which sought to understand Jesus in terms indigenous to India. As Hinduism is a predominant influence on much of Indian culture, this means trying to understand Jesus Christ in Hindu terms. Pandipeddi Chenchiah (1886–1959) stated the reason for this as follows:

> To the Indian Christian, Hinduism is the heredity, the living past, the memory content, the organ of spiritual vision and not merely an outside creed. This has to be understood to realize the tremendous importance and fascination of the problem of interrelation of religions to the Indian Church. It comes to us with an urgency hardly intelligible to Christians in the West who had no past but the Christian.[127]

It was believed that interpreting Jesus in Hindu terms would aid in communicating the gospel in India, distance Christianity there from its Western associations, and resist Western cultural imperialism. However, there was also a christological rational for this.

As Hinduism is a formative cultural influence in much of India and as culture helps constitute a person's identity,[128] Hinduism is a formative element in the identity of many Indian Christians. As Chenchiah stated, for many it is not an "outside creed" but part of who they are. A guiding principle of christological developments in the patristic era was that in order to effect salvation the second person of the Trinity in becoming incarnate had to assume all aspects of human nature except sin.[129] Patristic theologians applied this on an ontological level. Indian Christian theologians apply it on a cultural level,[130] in recognition of the role culture plays in the formation of a person's identity. Because the human nature Jesus assumed always exists in some cultural terms, his soteriological significance always leads sooner or later to the gospel becoming inculturated, consciously or otherwise.

126. Sugirtharajah, "Interpretative Foreword," 3.
127. Chenchiah, "Wherein Lies Uniqueness?" 83.
128. Benhabib, *Another Cosmopolitanism*, 60.
129. Gregory of Nazianzus, *On God and Christ*, 158.
130. For selections of such interpretations, see Boyd, *An Introduction*.

Indian Christian theologians brought the dialogue between Jesus Christ and Hinduism into the church. Their concern to inculturate the gospel reveals that they have two loyalties: one to Indian culture, shaped as it is by Hinduism, and one to Jesus Christ.[131] Christians in other contexts also have dual loyalties as people always "live out of more than one story."[132] One of the stories that form people's identities is that of the ethnic community or country that they belong to.[133] The dual loyalty of Indian Christian theologians stands out because they have had to distinguish Jesus from the theological understandings shaped by the Western cultures in which he was brought to them.

Western Christians also have a dual loyalty, but because Christianity is part of Western cultural heritages, their dual loyalty may seem to them to be simply loyalty to Jesus Christ. Through questioning the Western forms in which Jesus has been understood as the Christ, the Hindu-Christian dialogue in Indian Christian theology can help uncover and demythologize "cultural and philosophical accretions" that have become axioms of Western Christologies, so that Western Christians can better recognize the difference between fidelity to Jesus Christ and self-congratulation.[134] Being Christian does not necessarily mean being Western.

However, the inculturation of Christology in Hindu terms is contentious because central to Advaita ("not two") Hinduism, one of the most prominent Hindu traditions in India is the notion that

> ultimate reality, Brahman, is unchanging and that only that which is beyond change is ultimately real. The result of maintaining this axiom is the corollary that the experienced world of change must be characterized as unreal.[135]

This clashes with the "theological density" that the Gospels attribute to Jesus' life, death, and resurrection.[136] Here history is seen as the site and the medium of the drama of salvation. Events occurring within it bring a relative but still real increase to God's being.

---

131. Panikkar, "Can Theology Be Transcultural?" 15.

132. Baum, *Essays*, 59.

133. Taylor, *Religion, Politics*, 49. As Taylor notes, people "almost everywhere are born into existence with a sense of belonging to places, times, and groups" (ibid.).

134. Clooney, *Comparative Theology*, 113.

135. Thatamanil, *Immanent Divine*, 23.

136. Dupuis, *Jesus Christ*, 33.

Several observations can be made here. *First*, while the gospel affirms the theological density of history, it also relativizes much of it. The doctrine of justification by grace through faith asserts that the reality of most of history is relative to that of Jesus Christ. This is not the same as the understanding of history as *maya* (unreal) in Advaita. But both see that meaning is found in history by looking to the divine that transcends it.[137]

Second, Jesus Christ reveals God to be both absolute and involved in history. Conceptualizing this can lead to a panentheistic understanding of divine infinity in which God radically transcends creation, but creation exists in God, so that in a sense God and creation are understood as "not two"[138] in a way with some similarities to what Advaita teaches. Advaita Hinduism and Christianity are not simply incompatible. They can illuminate each other.

Third, while theologians debate the possibility of inculturating the gospel in a Hindu cultural context, on a popular level inculturation has been ongoing in India for some time, and has created hybrid understandings of Jesus Christ that incorporate elements of Christian faith and Hinduism.[139] Jesus Christ cannot be simply interpreted in the worldview of Advaita because Christ, as "an actual, decisive divine intervention in history,"[140] requires that history be understood as more than unreality and illusion. But this does not mean that inculturation is impossible. Using Hindu terms to understand Jesus will involve "an understanding of those elements different from that of the Hindu believer."[141] But it can also produce hybrid understandings of Jesus Christ that are new to the church and new in salvation history.[142] Using Hindu terms to understand Jesus Christ "opens up the sluices for the living waters"[143] of Indian culture to flow into Christology. As with every major inculturation of the gospel, this brings the danger of domesticating the gospel

---

137. "All of these religions are convinced that without God man (*sic*) remains a torso, a fragment, a *homo in curvatus*, a creature warped in upon itself, as Augustine and Luther kept stressing" (Küng, "Christian Response," 240).

138. Schweitzer, "Jonathan Edwards" 50–52.

139. Bauman, *Christian Identity*, 243.

140. Dupuis, *Jesus Christ*, 33.

141. Carman, "Christian Interpretation of 'Hinduism,'" 239.

142. For instance, Soares-Prabhu, *Dharma of Jesus*.

143. Panikkar, "Can Theology Be Transcultural?" 17.

to the terms of the new culture. It also brings the possibility of gaining new insights into the person, work, and relationships of Jesus Christ, as happened with the development of the doctrine of the Trinity when the gospel was inculturated in a Hellenistic context.

A fourth moment in Hindu-Christian dialogue began as secular humanisms became influential in India during the twentieth century. These made the contributions of Hinduism, Christianity, and Hindu-Christian dialogue to the creation of a just, peaceful, and pluralistic community a pragmatic criterion by which they were evaluated. This changed the understanding of Jesus Christ here in two ways. First, Christians responded by recognizing that Christ could be present though hidden in Hinduism that was contributing to personal salvation and the common good.[144] The historical cross of Jesus remains the criterion for discerning where Jesus is present in this way.[145] Second, the pragmatic concerns of secular humanisms stimulated a shift from focusing on "Jesus Christ as the revelation of God to Jesus Christ as the revelation of the new creation of God in human history."[146] The "unique humanity of Jesus crucified and risen as the power of being human and the source of renewal for historical existence" became Christianity's most important contribution "to the dialogue of religions and secular ideologies."[147] Jesus Christ and Hinduism are seen here as partners in a dialogue about the common good.

A fifth moment began in 1985 with the development of Dalit theology. Central to Hinduism is the notion of caste, which teaches that a person's social status and place is determined by their birth. Hinduism has four main castes, with many subdivisions. The Brahmins are the highest caste. Beneath all castes are the Dalits, who are regarded as polluting to higher-caste people and existing to serve them. Caste designation has been the basis for the social marginalization and oppression of Dalits. It has made them vulnerable to violence and injustice at the hands of higher-caste people and trapped many in poverty. From the 1870s to the 1920s there were a series of mass conversions of Dalits to Christianity.

---

144. Thomas, *Risking Christ*, 77. Raimon (Raimundo) Panikkar made an important contribution to this with his pioneering work, *The Unknown Christ*.

145. Thomas, *Risking Christ*, 115.

146. Ibid., 101.

147. Ibid., 110.

Today Dalits comprise more than half the Christians in India, but a common complaint is that caste discrimination continues in the church.[148]

In 1985 Arvind Nirmal inaugurated Dalit theology with a groundbreaking paper, "Towards a Christian Dalit Theology."[149] Nirmal charged that Indian Christian theology, obsessed with relating the gospel to Brahmanic Hindu traditions, had failed to relate it to the caste oppression of Dalits. The Dalit Christian experience was one of exodus from Hinduism to Jesus Christ.[150] Rather than understanding Jesus as the embodiment of Brahmanic ideals, Dalit theology interprets Jesus as a Dalit. The term *dalit* means "broken, split apart, down trodden, crushed, manifest, displayed."[151] The dalitness of Jesus is most evident in his death on the cross.[152] Here Jesus revealed the dalitness of God.

This was an important moment in the ongoing Hindu-Christian dialogue in India in two respects. First, it added Christian voices to those of the many Hindu critics of the caste system. Dalit theology is a Christian critique of the massive injustice of caste oppression, Hinduism's legitimation of this, and Indian Christian theology's failure to address it. But Dalit theologians have also taken up Indian Christian theology's tradition of engagement with Hinduism by engaging with the Hindu traditions of Dalit communities. Dalit theologians have drawn upon Dalit Hindu myths and rituals to understand the death of Jesus.[153] The Dalit Christian experience is one of exodus from caste oppression and Brahmanic Hinduism authorizing this. But it is not an exodus from the Hindu traditions of Dalit communities that have formed Dalit identities in empowering ways.

Each of these five moments in the Hindu-Christian dialogue continues in India. This dialogue reveals how Jesus Christ has an innate tendency to become inculturated wherever Christians live. In India this inculturation has taken the forms of demand for conversion, inspiration for non-Christians, interpreting Jesus in Hindu terms, dialogue about the common good, and the demand for liberation from caste oppression. While each moment has some validity, none is complete in itself.

148. Fernando and Gispert-Sauch, *Christianity in India*, 188.

149. Nirmal, *Heuristic Explorations*, 138–56.

150. Ibid., 148.

151. Ibid., 139.

152. Ibid., 155.

153. Clarke, "Re-Imaging the Death of Jesus," 187–217.

This history and diversity of this Hindu-Christian dialogue suggests that it is unlikely to ever be finished. Through their dialogue and contact with each other and interaction with other forms of thought and experience, Jesus Christ and Hinduism stimulate and enrich each other. As they do so, each evolves and Christians and Hindus continue to have more to talk about.

JESUS CHRIST AND ROCK CREE RELIGION

A comparison of Jesus Christ with Rock Cree religion is also a cross-cultural exercise that takes place against a historical background of Christian implication in Western imperialism. Settlers from Europe and their descendents encountered First Nations peoples in Canada first as indispensable allies and then as obstacles to be removed to make way for the building of a nation and the progress of Western civilization. First Nations resistance to this grew during the twentieth century and experienced a significant victory when Elijah Harper, a member of the Manitoba Provincial Legislature, consulting with other Manitoba First Nations leaders, blocked passage of the Meech Lake Accord in June 1990.[154] Since the 1970s some Canadian churches have attempted to be allies with First Nations peoples in their struggles for justice and have apologized for their participation in colonizing strategies of Canadian governments, particularly for their roles in running residential schools, which involved First Nations children being taken from their parents and educated in ways intended to assimilate them to British values and Christian religion.

These apologies, important as they are, are "a beginning, not an end."[155] Seeking right relations with First Nations peoples includes respecting their spiritual heritages. These have often been "systematically ridiculed and attacked"[156] by white newcomers to Canada. Entering into dialogue with the traditional religion of the Rock Cree is hopefully a small step towards reversing this.

The Rock Cree are found in northern Manitoba and Saskatchewan, mostly in the Churchill River drainage basin.[157] Roman Catholic priests

154. Miller, *Skyscrapers*, 302.
155. Miller, "'We Are Sorry,'" 5.
156. Brightman, *Grateful Prey*, xi.
157. Ibid., 4–8.

came here in the late 1800s and gained converts. Today some Rock Cree practice no religion, many are Roman Catholic, and many have synthesized elements of Rock Cree religion with Roman Catholicism.[158] Rock Cree religion consists of narratives, rituals, and beliefs that continue to be told, practiced, and believed to some extent. While few still participate in rituals like the shaking lodge, enough "is still known and believed of this religion within the community to provide the basis for its reemergence in the future."[159]

There is significant overlap between Rock Cree teachings of respect for nature and generosity towards others[160] and contemporary understandings of Jesus Christ. Rock Cree religion and Jesus Christ could be compared in many ways. What follows will focus on Wīsahkīcāhk and what comparing him to Jesus Christ illuminates about the latter.

Wīsahkīcāhk is an important figure in Rock Cree religion. Stories involving him "are related in households and in the bush for entertainment, instruction, and philosophical reflection."[161] Wīsahkīcāhk is a trickster-transformer whose actions in the primordial era helped shape the present environment and animal characteristics. He remains active as a spirit-guardian. In 1823, George Nelson described Wīsahkīcāhk and his relationship to the Rock Cree thus:

> He is uncommonly good and kind, addresses them and talk[s] to them as to children whom he most tenderly loves and is extremely anxious for. Thus far everything is very well, and is perhaps a better idea than many of the vulgar christians can give; but on the other hand again their Mythology, or stories relating to him, are many of them absurd and indecent in the highest degree: reducing him to the level of his creatures, and not unfrequently making him their dupe; . . . This one they love, they love him a great deal, and are by no means afraid of him, because he always addresses them, "My Little Children, &c", and all the rest of his character is of a piece with this.[162]

Writing in 1989, Thomson Highway, a Cree from Brochet, Manitoba, describes Weesageechak as

158. Brightman, *Traditional Narratives*, 138.
159. Brightman, *Grateful Prey*, 27.
160. Ibid., xii.
161. Ibid., 7.
162. Brown and Brightman, *"Orders of the Dreamed"*, 36.

the being who inhabits that area of our dream world, our sub-
conscious, where we connect with the Great Spirit, . . . who exists
to teach us about the nature and the meaning of existence on the
planet Earth.[163]

Stories involving Wīsahkīcāhk describe him as re-creating the world after a flood, tricking animals so that he can kill and eat them and changing
the features of plants or animals to their present form. In these stories
"Wīsahkīcāhk is clearly aligned with the interests of human beings."[164]
These and other stories also describe him as marrying his daughter, being defecated upon, being tricked by animals and acting foolishly.[165]

In some respects Wīsahkīcāhk is an integrative figure like Samson
in the Book of Judges, who communicates a sense of identity and
gives guidance through both moral failings and heroic exploits.[166] But
whereas Samson is ultimately a tragic figure, Wīsahkīcāhk is comic.
Robert Brightman notes that telling Wīsahkīcāhk stories usually occasions "great hilarity" and that as they were told to him "both narrators
and audience were, on many occasions, nearly incomprehensible with
laughter."[167] What light does this aspect of Wīsahkīcāhk shed on Jesus
Christ?

The laughter Wīsahkīcāhk engenders is what Mikhail Bakhtin called
"festive laughter . . . the laughter of all the people . . . universal in scope;
. . . directed to all and everyone."[168] It is laughter that sees the world "in
its droll aspect, in its gay relativity."[169] There is debilitating and vicious
laughter that mocks life with cruelty or in despair. But festive laughter is
different. Festive laughter mocks, but in a spirit of joy, celebration, and
acceptance. Festive laughter sees life as it is, as falling short of ideals of

163. Highway, "Foreword," viii.

164. Brightman, *Grateful Prey*, 73.

165. "Certain features are repeatedly emphasized when Rock Crees discuss
Wīsahkīcāhk. Of these, the most important appears to be his ability to transform into
other organic and inorganic forms. His ability to converse with animate and inanimate
objects, his trickiness, his foolishness, his use of the ubiquitous nisimy 'younger sibling'
in address, his sexual voracity, his continual hunger, and his modification of the environment are all emphasized. Most of these abilities are related to his possession of . . .
extraordinary power" (Brightman, *Traditional Narratives*, 53).

166. For Samson as this kind of integrative figure, see Welker, *God the Spirit*, 65–74.

167. Brightman, *Traditional Narratives*, 7.

168. Bakhtin, *Rabelais*, 11.

169. Ibid.

what it could and should be, but instead of seeking to punish a person for this, accepts them anyway. Festive laughter creates a transcendence to reality so that one can see beyond what is to what might be. Festive laughter does not so much flaunt moral ideals as acknowledge that they have not been fully achieved and with this, creates a space for seeking to fulfill them in new ways.[170] It is an aspect of creative effervescence that is both a source and celebration of liberation from the need to constantly strive to achieve as much as possible.

Festive laughter is one of Wīsahkīcāhk's gifts to people as a spirit-guardian. Through laughing at Wīsahkīcāhk one experiences laughter's liberating power, its role in celebrating life, in helping people accept their humanity and rejoice in it. One is liberated from the deadening weight of the struggles of life by laughing with and at him. Laughing at Wīsahkīcāhk helps one take life seriously and still laugh at one's self.

Unlike Wīsahkīcāhk, Jesus brings an eschatological hope for the final overcoming of sin, suffering, and evil. This makes Jesus Christ more a redemptive than an integrative figure. Jesus helps people endure conflictual situations, but his call is to transform these if possible, to seek the reign of God by imitating him. There is potential humor in Jesus' public ministry, for instance in the disciples repeated failure to understand him in Mark's Gospel. But the call of Jesus to discipleship creates a great seriousness. As respect for God, for the value of life and the goodness of creation, this seriousness is a good thing grounded in reality. But if Jesus only brings a call to high moral ideals, self-sacrifice, and great seriousness, he becomes an external lawgiver whose effect on human life is as alienating and destructive as it is beneficial.

The seriousness of Jesus' call to discipleship cannot be abandoned. Jesus' cross was not a joke and neither are the crosses of those who have followed him. These are not sources of festive laughter. But Easter changes things.

> Easter is an altogether different matter. Here indeed begins the laughing of the redeemed, the dancing of the liberated and the creative game of new, concrete concomitants of the liberty which has been opened for us, even if we still live under the conditions with little cause for rejoicing.[171]

170. Ibid., 122–23.
171. Moltmann, *Theology and Joy*, 50.

Jesus' resurrection is a source of festive laughter and celebration as a release from the permanency of loss, guilt and death, through the hope of eternal life. It enables joy, celebration, and self-critical humor in spite of the continuing realities of sin and evil. Christians do celebrate this aspect of Jesus Christ.[172] But it is often forgotten or ignored. Wīsahkīcāhk can help Christians better appreciate it.

In contemporary understandings of Jesus Christ oriented towards liberation and social justice, there is a tremendous demand for moral achievement and great seriousness of purpose. It should not be otherwise. But the high moral demands of contemporary understandings of Jesus cannot be sustained without aesthetic delight and festivities.[173] Without these moral seriousness tends to collapse into cynicism and despair or harden into fanaticism. The failure of human life to ever fully reach the high moral ideals that people strive for can give rise to a hatred for both these ideals and human life. Festive laughter recognizes the value of these ideals, how life fails to achieve them, and the worth of life nonetheless. Life is not whole without festive laughter. Ethical seriousness needs it so that it does not become dehumanized by the sin and evil it struggles against. Jesus brings a hope for the overcoming of life's negativities that Wīsahkīcāhk does not. But this hope can become a relentless spirit-killing demand if not accompanied by the kind of laughter Wīsahkīcāhk evokes. Festive laughter that recognizes the inadequacies of those who follow Jesus, the incongruity between their high calling and their capabilities, helps sustain commitment, enabling people to remain serious without becoming intolerant of human weakness. Festive laughter arises from the joy of Easter and can also reconnect one to it, by reframing the present in relation to it. It is part of the play and creativity needed to sustain movements for social justice and keep them humane.

The festive laughter Wīsahkīcāhk gives rise to illuminates an aspect of Jesus' person and work that is easily forgotten in Western achievement-oriented societies. Jesus' resurrection enables one to laugh at oneself, at the church, at Jesus even, in a festive way. Stories of Wīsahkīcāhk[174] can help one see this. Discovering this can enable commitment to Christ

172. For instance, the lyrics to the hymns "O Laughing Light" by Sylvia Dunstan and "Give to Us Laughter" by Walter Farquharson celebrate this. These hymns are numbered 434 and 624, respectively, in *Voices United*.

173. Taylor, *Executed God*, 161.

174. Brightman, *Traditional Narratives*, 9–48.

to remain open to others, to be simultaneously self-critical and self-accepting, and to be tolerant while deeply serious.

CONCLUSION

The relationship of Jesus Christ to other religions is typically dialectical. Through comparisons between them, new light falls on Jesus Christ and his relationship to them. Sometimes this relationship is confrontational. In the name of Jesus Christ, Hindu caste divisions and the oppression they give rise to must be opposed. But often Christians find that faith in Jesus Christ brings them together with members of other religions. Across the divides of religion and culture they encounter the Spirit of Jesus, present and at work, where Jesus is not worshipped. Through these other religions, and through the cooperation and dialogue of Christians with members of them, the beauty and goodness of God that Jesus reveals can be further expressed.

12 Jesus Christ and Christian Prayer

This third section of the book, focused on Jesus Christ's relationships with others, concludes with this chapter looking at Jesus' relationship to Christians in their dialogue with God in prayer. Prayer is a crucial part of the larger dialogue with God[1] that occurs through worship and Bible study, participation in church life, outreach, solidarity, and dialogue with others. Jesus is at the center of a Christian's relationship to God in prayer. Jesus' relationship to Christians in their prayer life is also at the heart of who he is as the Christ. When people come to have faith in him, his person and work affects their prayer life. It is partially through prayer that Jesus Christ enters into the actions, words, and character of Christians and so takes form in history as "church-community."[2]

WHAT IS PRAYER?

Prayer can be broadly defined as turning to the divine.[3] As such it is part of most religions in one form or another. In his study of prayer predominantly in the Hebrew Bible, Patrick Miller concludes that there is "something universal"[4] in prayer that is common to humanity. If human minds have an innate awareness of divinity, as John Calvin argued,[5] then this combined with the beauty of the world and the fragility of life might be one reason why this is so.

---

1. According to Bonhoeffer, "prayer is the heart of Christian life" (Bonhoeffer, *Barcelona, Berlin*, 577).

2. Bonhoeffer, *Sanctorum Communio*, 190.

3. Oberlies, "Prayer/Curse," 1486.

4. Miller, *They Cried to the Lord*, 31.

5. Calvin, *Institutes*, 1:43.

Prayer can be said to be common to humanity in another way. According to Mikhail Bakhtin, every human utterance is addressed to a second party,[6] some person or persons. But as people make truth claims in speaking, they presuppose a third party that they also address. Each "dialogue takes place as if against the background of the responsive understanding of an invisibly present third party who stands above all the participants in the dialogue."[7] Bakhtin describes this third party as "a higher superaddressee . . . , whose absolutely just responsive understanding is presumed, either in some metaphysical distance or in distant historical time."[8] Bakhtin deduces this from "the nature of the word, which always wants to be heard, always seeks responsive understanding, and does not stop at immediate understanding but presses on further and further (indefinitely),"[9] until heard in an ultimate way. Bakhtin acknowledges that there are words that fear "the third party and . . . [seek] only temporary recognition (responsive understanding of limited depth) from immediate addresses."[10] Human life is comprised of both kinds of words and of words that do both.

As prayer is a dialogue involving speech addressed to God, Bakhtin's analysis suggests that there is an element of it in every human life. Not every word is a prayer. But in every human life there are words implicitly and ultimately addressed to God, even if not consciously uttered as prayer. In this respect prayer as speech addressed to God is intrinsic to human life.

PRAYER IN THE HEBREW BIBLE

Many prayers in the Hebrew Bible have motive clauses that articulate reasons why God should answer them.[11] These typically draw attention to the character of God, the situation of the person praying, or God's relationship to them.[12] Descriptions of the petitioner's situation explain why they need God's help. The reasons for expecting this lie ultimately

6. Bakhtin, *Speech Genres*, 99.

7. Ibid., 126.

8. Ibid.

9. Ibid., 127.

10. Ibid.

11. Miller, *They Cried to the Lord*, 114–15.

12. Ibid.,116.

in God's character and relationship to the petitioner. The fundamental reason for expecting God's help is typically the character of God, who is revealed in events like the exodus to be responsive and attentive to the needs of God's people.[13] Two fundamental characteristics of prayer in the Jewish and Christian traditions arise from this. First, prayer is understood to have a dialogical character.[14] "[T]he one who prays can truly engage the deity" to the extent that the "mind and heart of God are vulnerable to the pleas and the arguments of human creatures."[15] Prayer is an event in which God and humanity both participate and which can affect both. Second, though, the plea for God to act appeals to the moral transcendence of God. It asks God to act in accordance with God's steadfast love, goodness, and faithfulness. While prayer seeks to move God, it does so by appealing to God to act in accordance with God's character and nature.[16] While the biblical witness attests that prayer can affect God, it also teaches that authentic prayer acknowledges God's moral transcendence and subordinates the petitioner's desires to this.

The basic modes of prayer in the Hebrew Bible are prayers for help and prayers of thanksgiving and praise. There are also prayers of lament, confession, intercession, blessings, and curses. Prayer in the Hebrew Bible has holistic dimensions. There are cultic sites, places set aside for prayer, but prayer can happen anywhere. Prayer can be limited to words, but it can also include the body through gestures such as outstretched hands or prostration. Prayer is part of a dialogue with God that includes the whole person. A second holistic dimension of prayer stems from the nature of the God to whom prayer is directed. The moral transcendence of God means that prayer cannot be detached from one's relationships with one's neighbor.[17] Petitions to or praise of the God of justice contain truth claims concerning one's relations to others. The fifth petition of the Lord's Prayer as found in Matthew's Gospel is an example of this: "forgive us our debts as we have forgiven our debtors" (6:12). Asking for God's forgiveness implies the truth claim that God is merciful. As God's mercy extends to others as well, those who ask for God's forgiveness must exercise mercy

---

13. Ibid., 102.

14. Ibid., 46, 133.

15. Ibid., 126.

16. Ibid.

17. Ibid., 226.

in their relation to others.[18] This means that while prayers may be uttered in private, there are usually two communal dimensions to prayer. The God one prays to is the Creator and Redeemer of one's neighbor. God's care and concern extends to them as well. Prayer to God thus puts one into community with all of humanity and creation and binds one to one's neighbor. Secondly, while one may pray privately, one is rarely the only person praying. Even when praying alone, one prays as part of a worshipping community, using words that have been shaped by its history.

These two holistic dimensions of prayer lead to a third. As prayer can involve the whole person and as it makes a claim upon all aspects of their person, one can extend the notion of prayer to encompass the whole of a person's life. As the prophets pointed out, appropriate prayer is not simply a matter of words, but involves how one lives, the shaping of one's life according to God's will.[19] While prayer as a turning to God involves specific rituals and genres of speech, these exist in a dialectical relationship to the rest of life. The events of daily life lead people to explicit prayer. Conversely, the subject and object of authentic prayer seeks to find expression in daily life, so that all of one's life comes to express what one verbalizes in explicit prayer. As this happens, the whole of one's life becomes a turning to God, an address to God of petition and praise.

The dialogue of prayer in the Hebrew Bible includes silence on the part of the person praying and with this, waiting on God (Ps 37:7). This silence and waiting upon God requires self-discipline that represents a moral achievement on the part of the person praying.[20] In Christian prayer, silence is said to be needful because the Word of God continues to speak and dwell within a person after it has been heard.[21] The silence that is part of the dialogue with God in prayer can include the silence of God.[22] Waiting on God in silence and listening to the silence of God can help move a person, sometimes in a painful way, towards greater spiritual maturity, so that they gain a greater awareness of God and their life comes to express more fully the faith their prayers verbalize.[23]

---

18. Betz, *Sermon*, 404.

19. Heschel, *Man's Quest*, 132.

20. Weiser, *Psalms*, 318.

21. Bonhoeffer, *Life Together*, 84–85.

22. Craigo-Snell, *Silence, Love*, 42–54.

23. Kraus, *Psalms 1–59*, 405.

In the Hebrew Bible the dialogue of prayer often has a rhythm or structure of moving through lament, petition, confession or intercession, to thanksgiving and praise in response to God's answer. Petition, confession, and intercession look forward to praise after being heard and responded to by God. Praise is part of this "continuing dialogue,"[24] that often begins with petition. In this sense it is the conclusion that God is moving individual dialogues and history as a whole towards.

However, praise is not limited to being a response to God's answer to a petition. It frequently bursts forth in spontaneous response to God's goodness shown in creation. This points to an important aspect of prayer in the Hebrew Bible and New Testament. "The focus of prayer is not the self."[25] Ultimately it is the goodness of God. A situation of human need is not necessary to begin the dialogue of prayer. God's goodness alone is sufficient. Both petition and thanksgiving focus on this goodness. Though the dialogue of prayer typically moves through petition to praise, its fundamental beginning lies in the communication of God's beauty and goodness through God's address to humanity. God takes the initiative in the dialogue of prayer, in Christian terms, through the Word by which the world was created and through which God becomes "familiar to us and opens the door for us."[26] Prayer may begin experientially as a turning to God in time of need. But once it becomes a regular practice, one recognizes that prayer begins not with one's self, but with the self-communication of God's goodness in Jesus Christ and the Holy Spirit, through creation and redemption.

A human word is never the first word in a dialogue, including the dialogue of prayer. It is always uttered in the midst of an ongoing conversation, as a living rejoinder to the word of another.[27] Human words of prayer are always in some way a response to a preceding address by the Word of God, which may come in a hidden, inner way.[28] The dialogue of prayer begins ultimately with the procession of the Word in the immanent Trinity. This eternal procession leads to the creation of the world, the incarnation of the Word and the history of redemption. All

---

24. Miller, *They Cried to the Lord*, 223.

25. Heschel, *Man's Quest for God*, 15.

26. John Calvin, quoted in Hesselink, "Introduction," 5.

27. Bakhtin, *Dialogic Imagination*, 279.

28. For the Word being present in history and peoples' lives in a hidden, inner way, see Baum, *Truth beyond Relativism*, 55–56, 75–78.

this stems from the self-diffusive nature of God's goodness and God's yes to its communication that the Word expresses. The dialogue of prayer is ultimately a response to this goodness as expressed in the Word, and as further expressed and celebrated in the Holy Spirit. Through the dialogue of prayer one participates in the expression and celebration of God's goodness that makes up God's Trinitarian life.

Prayer is also something demanded by God in the Hebrew Bible. As prayer is a dialogue capable of affecting how God responds, it becomes clear in some prophetic literature that "God expects a prophetic voice to stand forth and plead for the people,"[29] even as the prophet proclaims God's judgment against them. This points to a second rhythm in the dialogue of prayer. Prayer frequently runs through a first rhythm of petition, waiting for God's answer and then thanksgiving in response to it. But it also stands in a second rhythm with proclamation. The role of the prophet is both to proclaim God's judgment and to intercede in prayer for those against whom it is directed. This trajectory of interceding for a sinful people who act in opposition to the prophet is continued in the New Testament; for instance, in the injunction to Jesus' disciples and Christians to pray for their enemies and those that persecute them,[30] and in Jesus' lament over Jerusalem (Luke 13:34–35).

There is a third rhythm to prayer in the Hebrew Bible. The prophet can only continue to proclaim God's Word as their prophetic activity is empowered, guided, and sustained by prayer. Prayer and prophetic activity are not opposites or detached from one another, but reciprocally related.[31] The moral transcendence of God places moral demands on people that can only be sustained through an active prayer life. The prophet who undertakes to proclaim these needs the empowerment of regular communion with God in prayer. The Gospel of Matthew describes this rhythm as central to Christian discipleship.[32]

---

29. Miller, *They Cried to the Lord*, 276.

30. Matt 5:44. Prayer in this rhythm can be intercession for those to whom God's Word is directed or thanksgiving for their receptive response. The Word that is proclaimed need not only be one of judgment. It can be one of comfort. What is striking in this second rhythm is that those to whom judgment is proclaimed are also those for whom intercessory prayers are offered.

31. For this as a significant theme in the praxis of Martin Luther King Jr., see Baldwin, *Never to Leave Us Alone*, 4, 43–44, 60–61, 85.

32. Luz, *Mathew*, 389.

Finally, in "the late Old Testament literature (e.g., Dan 6:12) and continuing on in Judaism at the time of the New Testament,"[33] prayer is presented as a spiritual discipline that people need to receive instruction in and practice regularly. This leads us to the teaching of Jesus about prayer and his own practice of it.

JESUS AND PRAYER

Various New Testament traditions portray Jesus as practicing the rhythms of prayer and proclamation mentioned above. In the New Testament, particularly the Gospels and Hebrews, Jesus is presented as a model and teacher of how to pray. In light of his resurrection he becomes a basis of Christian prayer. However, Jesus, as a prophet of eschatological renewal, is also depicted as depending upon prayer, his own and others, to sustain and guide his ministry.[34]

This sustenance has a self-involving side. A petition for the coming of the reign of God, the central theme of his proclamation, is prominent in the prayer that, according to Luke, Jesus taught his disciples in answer to their request. Subsequent petitions, such as "give us each day our daily bread" (Luke 11:3), may reflect the need his followers experienced for daily food. Those who walked with Jesus in his itinerant ministry could not take the provision of their daily bread for granted. No one should, for food ultimately always is a gift in certain respects.[35] The point here is that, for Christians, prayer and discipleship go together. Following Jesus requires trust in God and prayer to sustain it. Conversely, to pray in Jesus' name is to grant him an authorizing role[36] in one's life and so to accept his teaching and proclamation as a guideline for one's own words and actions. Discipleship and prayer are tied to the other. Here and earlier in the Hebrew Bible, prayer emerges as a way of being in contact with God as a transcendent moral source. Prayer is a means of empowerment to and purification of ethical action. Conversely the tie between prayer and discipleship means that Christian prayer should lead one to listening to the Word of God and engaging in the praxis of love.[37]

33. Miller, *They Cried to the Lord*, 312.

34. Catchpole, *Jesus People*, 126.

35. Schweitzer, "Food as Gift," 3–4.

36. Keck, *Who Is Jesus?*, 163–69. Keck defines "authorizing" as "authority exercised, not as coercion but as generating, energizing, legitimizing influence" (164).

37. Sobrino, *Christology*, 175.

Jesus' teaching and example regarding prayer reflect a piety at home in Second Temple Judaism. Most of what has been discussed above about prayer in the Hebrew Bible underlies Jesus' teaching and example and subsequent teaching about prayer in the New Testament.[38] It is difficult to know exactly how much of the specific injunctions in the gospels regarding prayer can be traced to Jesus and how much reflect the early Christian communities that produced them.

Jesus does seem to have departed from one prayer practice found in some parts of the Hebrew Bible, that of cursing.[39] The teaching of Jesus ruled out cursing others from the prayer life of his followers.[40] The attitude of love for enemies was to be expressed in prayer so that, instead of cursing their enemies and those who abuse them, Jesus' followers should pray for them and bless them. Prayer for ones' enemies does not rule out resistance to their assaults. But it does prevent one from demonizing them.

Persistence in prayer, praying with confidence, refraining from ostentatious prayer in public, and brevity of expression are all teachings found in the Synoptic Gospels that may not stem directly from Jesus but that are in tune with the central teaching of Jesus concerning prayer. This central teaching is found in what is known as the Lord's Prayer. A shorter version of this is found in Luke 11:2–4, slightly longer versions in Mathew 6:9–13 and the *Didache*.[41] It has often been argued that the Lukan version "is more original in the number of petitions and in the address, but Matthew in the wording."[42] Luke portrays Jesus as offering this prayer in response to the disciples' request, "Lord, teach us to pray, as John taught his disciples" (Luke 11:1). It is possible that this portrayal has a basis in history. As "religious groups were distinguished . . . by their

38. Soares-Prabhu, *Dharma*. 210.

39. For a brief discussion of curses in the Hebrew Bible, for instance in 2 Samuel 3:39 as "a form of prayer for the justice of God" (Miller, *They Cried to the Lord*, 302).

40. For an argument that the teaching "Love your enemies, do good to those who hate you, bless those who curse you, pray for those who abuse you" (Luke 6: 27–28) stems from Jesus, see Catchpole, *Jesus People*, 127–29. Catchpole notes that "the expression of love in the form of prayer for the opponent or enemy . . . is not alien to the spirit of Judaism" (130).

41. *Didache* 8:2. The *Didache* is a brief document in Greek from the early church, probably dating from the end of the first or beginning of the second century.

42. Luz, *Matthew 1–7*, 370.

characteristic prayers," the disciples may have asked Jesus for a form of prayer appropriate to his specific message and movement.[43]

The Lord's Prayer is essentially "a summary of the fundamentals of Jesus' proclamation"[44] that probably goes back to Jesus in its basic features.[45] In Christianity it has functioned as an important teaching on how to pray and as a central feature in worship. It is the prayer of a community, as the petitions relating to bread, debts, and forgiveness indicate.[46] Matthew's version stresses this by having it begin "with a communal 'our' rather than just an individual 'my.'"[47]

The nature of God and the believer's relationship to God signified by the address of God as "Father" are part of the basis of Christian prayer. A patriarchal understanding of this divine name is an error blocking the access of many to the God Jesus proclaimed.[48] This address to God is also open to a false infantilizing interpretation that is "an evasion of the suffering of this world."[49] Within Jesus' context of Second Temple Judaism this address was intended to signify the caring nature, ability to provide, and accessibility of God in prayer. In effect, this address denotes God's goodness and willingness to act on this. The petitions that follow reinforce this by showing that "God's concerns are not alien to those of human beings, and their concerns are not foreign"[50] to God. Addressing God as "Father" or "Our Father" was intended to establish the relationship between God and believers on the basis of which they could follow Jesus with hope and joy. While many continue to use this gendered address today, other forms of address expressing the same kind of relationship can alternatively replace or supplement it.

The Lord's Prayer is frequently divided into two halves. The first is comprised of the first two (Luke) or three (Matthew) petitions relating directly to God. The second is comprised of petitions concerning

43. Jeremias, *Prayers of Jesus*, 77.

44. Ibid.

45. Catchpole, *Jesus People*, 135.

46. These speak of "our daily bread," "our debts," rather than that of an individual (ibid., 133).

47. "The prayer is certainly 'personal,' but personal-in-community rather than personal-in-privacy. You may certainly pray it alone, but you are never alone when you pray it" (Crossan, *Greatest Prayer*, 47).

48. Lochman, *Lord's Prayer*, 20.

49. Boff, *Lord's Prayer*, 37.

50. Ibid., 6.

human need. A profound unity of concern underlies the different emphasis of each.

The petitions in the first half are linked by what they ask for. "God's name cannot be hallowed except through the coming of God's kingdom, which results in God's eternal will being done on earth."[51] These petitions establish the guiding horizons of a Christian's outlook upon the world; what they can and should hope for, pray for, and seek. The hallowing of God's name, the coming of God's reign, and the doing of God's will are transcendent and never fully attainable goals to which Christians, as they utter this prayer, commit themselves. These petitions recognize that salvation consists partly in one's life and will becoming adjusted to the nature and will of God. The Lord's Prayer begins by asking that God's name be hallowed by one's own life and the rest of the world being brought into conformity with God's will, rather than God being reduced to conformity with one's own will. Thus while the address of "Our Father" is open to an infantilizing interpretation, the first three petitions of the Lord's Prayer work against this. When prayed attentively they lead to greater spiritual maturity, moving one beyond childish images of God that center around oneself towards a worldview centered on God, God's goodness, and the coming of God's reign. They also work to critique idolatrous notions of race and nationalism by implicitly acknowledging how God and God's reign transcend the limits of nationalities and nation-states. They explicitly acknowledge God's otherness. Together with the opening address of "Our Father," they characterize God as near and loving yet radically transcendent.

The request that God's name be hallowed implies a recognition of the fallen nature of the world and a desire for its redemption.

> [H]uman society has been corrupted both in its structure and in
> its functioning. . . . The discovery of this basic shortcoming gives
> rise to a desire that bursts forth in the form of a supplication: thy
> name be hallowed![52]

The first two (Luke) or three (Matthew) petitions of the Lord's Prayer position the coming of God's reign as its central theme. God's name is hallowed and God's will is done as God's reign is established. The phrase "the reign (or kingdom) of God," as used by Jesus, had various meanings. Part

---

51. Crossan, *Greatest Prayer*, 141.
52. Boff, *Lord's Prayer*, 43.

of what the petition for its coming in the Lord's Prayer refers to "was an intervention in the history of the Jewish people that would come soon."[53] This petition places widespread, deeply entrenched, and deadly evils such as racism and economic oppression within the horizon of hope for the coming reign of God. "In this way it relativizes them, robbing them of their final validity."[54] Their massive evil remains, but the fatalism they can engender is overcome, in part by Jesus' cross and resurrection, and in part by his proclamation and this petition, which sees the coming of God's reign to be the will of God whose love was revealed in Jesus' resurrection to be ultimately more powerful than sin and death. The opening address of God, "Our Father" (Matthew) or "Father" (Luke) is further delineated by this petition and the nature of God's reign is likewise delineated by this opening address. The reign of God that is prayed for is the reign of the loving, transcendent, yet accessible God of life.

The placing of the petition "Your will be done" in Matthew's version (Matthew 6:10) ahead of the petitions for daily bread, etc., means that "the will of God takes priority over all other petitions"[55] even though the asking of these other petitions is expected and taught. This petition works to critique the pretensions of those who play at being God. It relates to the first of the Ten Commandments (Exod 20:3) and is often linked to the prayer attributed to Jesus in the Garden of Gethsemane, "yet not my will but yours be done" (Luke 22:42). Here Jesus is portrayed as praying that he be spared suffering the cross but also that God's will be done, and accepting that this suffering may be God's will.

> Jesus' prayer is for deliverance, but Jesus accepts the possibility that God's will may be otherwise. He subordinates his own will to God's, a dimension of the prayer for God's will to be done that is implicit in the Lord's Prayer but is now made explicit.[56]

When this petition is read in light of Jesus' prayer in Gethsemane and Paul's account of his prayer for deliverance from suffering that was not granted (1 Cor 12:8), one can see a theology of the cross implicit in it.[57] But it is crucial to note that the suffering Jesus accepts in praying that

53. Catchpole, *Jesus People*, 138.

54. Lochman, *Lord's Prayer*, 62–63.

55. Miller, *They Cried to the Lord*, 321.

56. Ibid., 322.

57. Ibid., 323–24.

God's will be done is suffering for the sake of God's coming reign. It is not suffering per se. Suffering can only be accepted as God's will concretely, on a case-by-case basis. The suffering that should be accepted as God's will is suffering that moves creation closer to the coming of God's reign. This serves as a criterion to distinguish what suffering should be accepted and what not. Acceptance of suffering can be part of "a yes to life as a whole,"[58] and thus a yes to God, as long as it serves the coming of God's reign. God is glorified by love that seeks the well-being of humanity and creation. When such love involves suffering then God may be glorified by it. God is not glorified by suffering that does not in some way do this. It is a question of who and what suffering serves.[59]

The truth claim in the petition "Thy will be done" can work in several ways. The prayer that God's will be done so that God might be glorified can foster resistance to empires that glorify themselves by or-daining suffering for others.[60] But conversely, God's will may involve the temporary acceptance of empire rather than squandering one's life in futile resistance to it. This petition does not relieve Christians of seeking to discern God's will amidst the ambiguities of history. It commits one to God and so frees one to resist or accept worldly powers, depending on what seems to be God's will in a given context.

The next petition, "Give us each day our daily bread,"[61] "marks a turning point in the Lord's Prayer"[62] from a focus on God and the coming of God's reign to humanity and its needs.

> In the first part of the prayer, God's concerns are dealt with; in the second part, human concerns. Both belong in the prayer.[63]

This observation highlights how the two are intricately linked. While the first part seeks the conformity of human wills to God's, the petitions in the second part indicate that human well-being is a fundamental con-cern of God. Both parts of the prayer, each in their own way, are extrapo-lations from the opening address in Matthew's version, "Our Father who

---

58. Soelle, *Suffering*, 108.

59. Ibid., 134–35.

60. Lochman, *Lord's Prayer*, 71.

61. Luke 11:3; Matt 6:11.

62. Boff, *Lord's Prayer*, 74.

63. Ibid.

art in heaven," and belong together. When God's reign comes and God's will is done, all will have their daily bread.

"Daily" probably refers to the bread needed for the present day. According to Ulrich Luz,

> The fourth petition of the Lord's Prayer belongs to a situation of social urgency in which the nourishment for the following day could not simply be taken for granted. "Bread" as the most important food in the Semitic idiom can stand as pars pro toto for "nourishment" as such, but should not be extended beyond this to any sort of necessities for life. One may perhaps think of the situation of a day laborer who does not yet know whether he will find work again on the next day so that he can live with his family. "Bread for tomorrow" implies at the same time a limitation: It is a question, not of riches, but only of being able to survive.[64]

However, others note that "bread" here has an expansive quality. It can be taken to include "all our bodily requirements,"[65] as well as a person's aesthetic needs for occasional celebration.[66] Still the sense of restraint remains. The petition is for the bread one needs to live on, not for luxury items and the excesses of conspicuous consumption.

The bread asked for here "is bread that must be shared."[67] This is particularly true now that famine results as much from food not being made available to the hungry as from natural causes.[68] This petition for the bread that is needed puts the question of justice into the Lord's Prayer[69] and the prayer life of Christians. It implicitly critiques distortions in global and regional economies concerning food, where many suffer from overeating while others starve. With this petition the Lord's Prayer takes on an intercessory aspect as well as that of direct petition. When Christians pray for their daily bread they also implicitly pray for others, that all might be fed. This petition has political dimensions. Leonhard Ragaz (1868–1945), a Swiss Lutheran theologian and a founder of Christian Socialism in Switzerland, "pointed out that in asking for daily bread we ask for a change in the modern social order,

64. Luz, *Matthew 1–7*, 382–83.

65. Gregory of Nyssa, *Lord's Prayer*, 70.

66. Schweizer, *Good News*, 154.

67. Lochman, *Lord's Prayer*, 96.

68. Schweitzer, "Food as Gift," 10–13.

69. Lochman, *Lord's Prayer*, 96.

which rests on exploitation and profit."[70] In the present age this petition is a request for some form of socialism and deliverance from the ravages of neoliberal economics.

The wording of Matthew's version of the next petition, "And forgive us our debts," seems more original than Luke's "And forgive us our sins."[71] Like "bread," "debt" here is an expansive term. It can refer to material debts,[72] but its primary reference is to moral wrongs and sins understood as unfulfilled and unfulfillable obligations to God.[73] This petition asks God's forgiveness for the moral failings of the praying community and of the rest of the world. Just as prayer and prophetic activity go together, so do the request for daily bread and this petition for forgiveness. The one is not more important than the other. The need of others or oneself for daily bread often gives rise to the need for forgiveness. The following clause, "as we also have forgiven our debtors" (Matt 6:12), expresses the self-involving nature of prayer. One's practice cannot be divorced from one's prayers. If one prays for the forgiveness of one's sin, one must also be prepared to forgive the sin of others. Praying for forgiveness is also a vital part of prophetic activity. It recognizes the moral transcendence of God, and how even though one speaks in God's name, one may frequently sin.

> In solidarity with the world, Christians are aware of their own debts and their own need of forgiveness, always, everywhere, by all. Before God the communion of saints is never a fellowship of creditors but always a fellowship of debtors.[74]

These petitions of the Lord's Prayer are requests for certain things to happen, but also express recognition that the human condition is one of fundamental need that only God can meet. The Lord's Prayer inculcates a spirituality characterized by both gratitude and yearning, in which life is seen as a gift and a needy condition, God as both a mystery and a friend, and evil and temptation things to be resisted. The Lord's Prayer inculcates a sense of human responsibility but also trust and reliance upon God.

70. Ibid., 98.

71. Matt 6:12, Luke 11:4. Luke's use of "sin" instead of "debts" "eliminates the Semitic religious connotation of 'debt,' which may not have been comprehensible to his Gentile Christian readers" (Fitzmyer, *Gospel according to Luke*, 897).

72. Crossan, *Greatest Prayer*, 159–60.

73. Betz, *Sermon on the Mount*, 400–403.

74. Lochman, *Lord's Prayer*, 121.

This relation to the divine is not portrayed here as a limitation keeping one in a state of infancy, but as a source of empowerment. Prayer here is a connection, a living relationship to a transcendent source of hope and consolation that enables one to live creatively, responsibly and joyfully, with love for others and a sense of one's own dignity. As well, the human condition is not understood here as simply one of needing physical necessities; it involves an equal need for God's forgiveness.[75] A theology of justice underlies the Lord's Prayer.[76] Its radical nature leads to recognition of a need for God's grace. Thus, while the Lord' Prayer is capable of an ethical reading, the ethical imperatives in it demand a religious reading, an entering into a relationship of prayer with God based on a recognition of one's need for God and God's nature as the Creator and Redeemer who is very near and who answers prayer. This recognition is clearly expressed in the final petition, which is the climax of the preceding ones.[77]

This petition, "do not bring us to the time of trial" or temptation (Matt 6: 13a), "seems to suggest that God is the one who leads into temptation."[78] The underlying presupposition here is that God is the ultimate power in creation and therefore the ultimate "cause of everything."[79] A critique of extending this to making God the source of temptation is present in James 1:13–15, which locates the source of temptation not in God but in human weakness and perversion. The Lord's Prayer does not offer this kind of solution to the theoretical tension its presuppositions create, nor does it offer an answer to the question of theodicy. It simply presumes the goodness and ultimate power of God, and the existence of evil. It does not require one to see God as willing both good and evil. God can be said to be the source of temptation "by allowing evil to persist,"[80] evil being understood here as the deficiencies named in the first three petitions: "the lack of sanctification of God's name, the absence of the kingdom of God on earth, and the resistance by humanity against the will of God."[81] The existence of these deficiencies is present in the Lord's Prayer as a mystery that cannot be rationally harmonized with the nature

75. Betz, *Sermon on the Mount*, 403.

76. Ibid., 404.

77. Ibid., 405.

78. Ibid., 406.

79. Fitzmyer, *Gospel according to Luke*, 906.

80. Betz, *Sermon on the Mount*, 411.

81. Ibid.

of God. The radical nature of the presuppositions of the Lord's Prayer points in the direction of what today is called a protest theodicy, which affirms the contradiction between God's goodness and ultimate power and the realities of suffering, sin, and evil without relinquishing either.[82]

"[R]escue us from evil," the other half of the last petition, is a positive restatement of the first part. God rescuing people from evil by bringing in God's reign means that people are not led into temptation.[83] Evil here can be a physical suffering, an inner lack of the good or an external threat.

> On the basis of the Jewish texts it is suggestive to think of every-day experiences: illness, affliction, evil people, the evil impulse. The Matthean concluding petition thus contains an intensification and generalization of the temptation petition and rounds off the Lord's Prayer through a positive formulation.[84]

The establishment of God's reign means the deliverance of God's creation from evil.

By the end of the second century CE, the phrase "for yours is the kingdom and the power and the glory" had been added to the Lord's Prayer in some versions of Matthew's Gospel and the *Didache*. For the early church praise was intrinsic to prayer. This may have led to this doxology, which has similarities to 1 Chronicles 29:11, being added to the Lord's Prayer.

Numerous commentators have seen in the Lord's Prayer a "compendium of Christian doctrine."[85] This is not completely wrong as it expresses central themes of Jesus' proclamation. Yet it is presented in

82. For examples of this approach to the problem of evil, see Roth, "A Theodicy of Protest"; Beker, *Suffering and Hope*.

83. Interpreters are divided as to whether the Greek word for "evil" in Matt 6:13 is masculine, denoting the "evil one," or neuter, simply denoting evil. According to Ulrich Luz, the "neuter interpretation is supported by the majority of the Matthean and New Testament examples, the parallelism to the temptation petition, the oldest probably interpretations of the petition in 1 Tim. 4:18 and Did. 10:5 as well as the Jewish parallels—in Judaism "the evil one" as a designation for Satan is not found" (Luz, *Matthew 1–7*, 385).

84. Ibid. Hans Dieter Betz argues much the same: "The petition, then, 'Deliver us from evil,' sums up the state of incomplete salvation and the demand to complete it. If God would grant he first three petitions (vss 9b–10c) he would simultaneously also grant the sixth petition. Consequently, vs 13b not only interprets vs 13a but also the Lord's Prayer as a whole" (Betz, *Sermon on the Mount*, 412).

85. Luz, *Matthew 1–7*, 387.

Matthew and Luke's Gospels not as a statement of doctrine but as a model prayer for Christians. Its themes show that preaching, doctrine, and practice had a formative influence on it. The Lord's Prayer bears the "impress" of Jesus, his proclamation and praxis.[86] As a model prayer it has influenced the prayers and lives of countless Christians.

The teachings of Jesus regarding prayer recorded in the New Testament exhort people to prayer and instruct and model how to pray, but they do not dispel the mystery of prayer. Prayer has both mysterious and enigmatic aspects.[87] Why some prayers are answered and some are not is part of the enigma of prayer. The mystery of prayer is the openness of a radically transcendent God to being genuinely engaged by the prayers of people. The Lord's Prayer presupposes both the mystery and enigma of prayer. It understands prayer as an act of faith, not a mechanical exercise. Its final petition presupposes that some prayers for deliverance from suffering and evil are not answered. It's teaching work against the rationalizing and distortion of prayer. It does not answer questions such as why some prayers are answered and why some are not. Instead it teaches one how to pray in such a situation.

"PRAY WITHOUT CEASING"

Jesus influences Christian prayer through the teaching attributed to him in the gospels of Matthew and Luke. He also influences it through his being as the Christ. To those who receive him as such, Jesus mediates the presence of God and salvation. The coming of Jesus Christ is both the basis of Christian prayer and the assurance of its answer. The net effect of this is a response of joy and thanksgiving on the part of Christians, and a desire to reflect in their own lives what God has revealed in Jesus. This second influence is found throughout the New Testament. A particularly prominent example of it is in Paul's exhortation to the Thessalonian Christians to "pray without ceasing" (1 Thess 5:17). This injunction is part of a "single unit of thought"[88] that includes exhortations to "rejoice always" and "give thanks in all circumstances." In 1 Thessalonians Paul describes Jesus Christ as both a gift that is a source of great joy, a cause for rejoicing and thanksgiving, and a promise of things to come. The

86. Ibid., 386–87.
87. Schweitzer, "Prayer," 12–17.
88. Collins, *Birth*, 105.

gift aspect of Jesus Christ moves Paul to prayers of thanksgiving and the promise aspect moves him to prayers of intercession. Even as Paul urges the Thessalonians to pray without ceasing, he also describes how they are the object of his and his coworkers' prayers (1 Thess 3:9–13). As Paul gives thanks and intercedes for them, he expects them to do the same for himself, for themselves, and for others.[89] From Jesus Christ there thus blooms a buzzing network of prayer, of giving thanks and interceding, each for the other and all to Christ and through Christ to God. Jesus Christ as the Word of God thus triggers a great response of prayer and praise to God.

Paul's emphasis on praying without ceasing is matched by exhortations to pray continuously in Matthew and Luke's Gospels.[90] In the course of its history the church has continued to pray and as it has moved into different cultures and contexts, these have influenced the way it prays. The result has been the development of a rich diversity of prayer traditions. For some, to the dialogical nature of Christian prayer has been added the meditative traditions of Eastern religions. To New Testament injunctions to pray in private, the African American prayer tradition has added an empowering practice of prayer in public worship, carried into the streets in the struggle for justice by people like Martin Luther King Jr.[91] There is a sociality to the church's prayer just as there is to its understanding of Jesus Christ. Just as something of the church's own historical particularity enters into its understanding of Jesus Christ, so it enters into the way it prays in his name and what it prays for. In all of this the teaching, example, person, and work of Jesus remains a stimulus to prayer, to the development of styles of prayer and a criterion of authentic prayer.

PRAYER IN THE PRESENT

At present the practice of prayer has become questionable in secularized North Atlantic societies[92] partly because of the development of a

89. Gaventa, *Thessalonians*, 84.

90. Matt 7:7; Luke 11:5–13.

91. Baldwin, *Never to Leave Us Alone*, 67–89.

92. The term "secularization" can refer to the removal of property, activities or spheres of life from church influence or control, or to the lessening of participation in religion and its influence in society. See Kehrer, "Secularization." What follows refers primarily to the second meaning.

worldview that Charles Taylor describes as the "immanent frame."[93] This worldview presupposes that human life is surrounded by impersonal cosmic, natural, and social orders that operate without reference to the welfare of individual human lives. This frame is immanent in that it only accepts as real what can be grasped by technical reason. It is buttressed by the belief that it represents a moral and technical advance over previous worldviews which often saw people and the natural order as open to, affected, and addressed by transcendent beings. The sense of the immanent frame as an advance over other worldviews renders questionable, for those who inhabit it, "all phenomena which . . . [fail] to fit this framework."[94] This includes Christian prayer. As Taylor notes, "the immanent frame is common to all of us in the modern West."[95] The vast majority of people in contemporary Western societies live their daily lives on the basis of this worldview. What is the meaning and purpose of prayer for life lived in the immanent frame?

For many there is little or none. But Taylor notes, the immanent frame can be lived as open or closed to transcendence.[96] It is frequently presented as closed to transcendence, but this overlooks how the transcendent continues to be present in Western societies, for instance, in the phenomena of "the festive," where large numbers of people come together in a way distinct from their regular routine of life and experience themselves as "tapping into something deeper or higher"[97] than the immanent frame can account for. Also, according to Taylor, it is difficult to account for "the specific force of creative agency, or ethical demands, or for the power of artistic experience, without speaking in terms of some transcendent being or force which interpellates us."[98] Conversely, Taylor notes that a purely secular worldview, what he describes as "exclusive humanism," is rendered unstable by the moral demands for universal compassion and solidarity that it takes on, by experiences of transcendence in human life, and the revolt against humanism in philosophy and art.[99] While prayer cannot be explained by the natural sciences and

93. Taylor, *Secular Age*, 295.

94. Ibid., 288, 288–90; see also 539–43.

95. Ibid., 543.

96. Ibid., 543–44.

97. Ibid., 469; see also 482–83, 516, 715.

98. Ibid., 597.

99. Ibid., 533.

remains opaque in certain respects to secular reason, still it can be understood as a response to the transcendent as this impinges upon people in worship and other domains of experience, such as Taylor elaborates. This response can play an important role in modern secular societies.

While the modern Western emphasis on technical rationality has led to increased productivity and advances in healing techniques, it also tends to imprison people in their own subjectivity.[100] The cessation of prayer that it can lead to can be dehumanizing rather than liberating.[101] Dorothee Soelle argues that living simply within a worldview like the "immanent frame" leads to a "purposeless, empty existence devoid of genuine human relationships and filled with anxiety, silence, and loneliness."[102] This renders one's life and society vulnerable to being colonized by economic forces and advertising pressures. Religion, Soelle argues, is a source of moral empowerment that enables one to find meaning and to seek justice, to live with hope, in a way that the moral sources of a purely immanent worldview cannot.[103] Philosopher Jürgen Habermas has also recently emphasized the importance of religion for the ethical vitality and well-being of Western societies.[104] While religion remains opaque to secular reason, secular reason needs the hope and ethical imperatives that religion can bring if it is to maintain a sense of universal compassion and solidarity.

Prayer becomes understandable in the present in this respect. While it cannot be explained scientifically and clashes in some respects with the immanent frame, it can be understood experientially, as a response to the transcendence that people experience in worship and the proclamation of Jesus Christ. Prayer enables one to reach out to something greater than one's self. It is a key part of a dialogue with God that can release one into what is experienced as a broader and more meaningful space[105] than living solely within the immanent frame. The testimony of many is that, as it does so, prayer helps empower them to seek a greater justice, to resist temptation, to forgive those who have wronged them

100. Rahner, *On Prayer*, 31.

101. Metz, "Courage to Pray," 18, 25–27.

102. Soelle, *Death*, 4.

103. Ibid., 130.

104. Habermas, "Awareness of What Is Missing," 18–19.

105. The notions of reaching something higher and being released into a more meaningful space are drawn from Taylor, *Secular Age*, 577.

and to seek reconciliation with those they have wronged. Prayer in the name of Jesus can be a way of connecting with a transcendent moral source that purifies one's ethical stance, enables one to be more fully human and to live a more meaningful life.[106] In Christian terms prayer is an end in and of itself. Yet even within the terms of the immanent frame of secularized Western modernity, it is not necessarily a retreat to a premodern worldview, an infantile dependency upon childish beliefs. It can be a path and practice towards becoming more fully human.

Every language or form of discourse has both centripetal and centrifugal forces coursing through it.[107] Centripetal forces work to centralize or unify a language or worldview, to homogenize it to one frame of reference. Alongside these there are centrifugal forces working to decentralize and dis-unify a language or worldview. What Taylor describes as the "immanent frame" of Western modernity has both forces present in it. Its centrifugal forces include the continuous discoveries and the explosion of knowledge in the natural sciences and humanities, and the accompanying functional differentiation characteristic of modern Western societies.[108] But it also has centripetal forces. The functional differentiation of society works to form people into a narcissistic type of individuality whose ultimate reference point is their own feelings at any given moment.[109] The intangible risks of the environmental crisis and technologies like nuclear power produce a "numbing addiction" to what modern technologies supply that prevents a rational response to their accompanying dangers.[110] This results partly from the immanent frame being a worldview that can cut people off from transcendent moral sources. Because this immanent frame restricts what is meaningful to what people can explain, control, and do, it can be experienced

> as a limit, even a prison, making us blind or insensitive to whatever lies beyond this ordered human world. . . . The sense can easily arise that we are missing something, cut off from something, that we are living behind a screen.[111]

---

106. Gregory of Nyssa, *Lord's Prayer*, 23.

107. Bakhtin, *Dialogic Imagination*, 271–73.

108. For a brief discussion of this functional differentiation, see Welker, *God the Spirit*, 29–34.

109. Ibid., 35–37.

110. Moltmann, "Praying with Eyes Open," 198, 197–98.

111. Taylor, *Secular Age*, 302.

Against these centripetal forces that limit meaning to what can be immediately grasped or experienced, prayer can function as another type of centrifugal force that decentralizes the immanent frame by connecting one to God as a transcendent source of meaning and hope. Through dialogue with God in prayer one reaches out to a transcendence beyond the limits of the immanent frame. This does not abolish the immanent frame, but it decentralizes and disunifies it, keeping alive within it a language of transcendence necessary to sustain commitments to universal compassion, justice, and solidarity.[112] The immanent frame's pervasiveness in Western societies and its lack of access to transcendent meaning means that religious and secular perspectives tend to continually destabilize each other.[113] Thus prayer in Jesus' name remains an act of faith. It always has an "in spite of" quality to it. It is an act that reaches beyond what one can demonstrate and securely grasp or predict. Yet simultaneously, it is a practice that can open one to something greater than one's self that enables one to be more fully human. How does Jesus factor into this?

JESUS AS INTERLOCUTOR

When Jesus is accepted as the Christ, he becomes an interlocutor in one's life, a transcendent dialogue partner. As such Jesus dialogizes[114] a person's life, putting it into conversation with the record of his life and teachings. These present a transcendent perspective on reality to which one's own life and words become a response. This experience of Jesus Christ calls forth prayer, both praise and petition. It draws from one a response to a transcendence beyond what the values and perspectives of the immanent frame can present.

An understanding of Jesus Christ only comes to full fruition through the responses of worship, prayer, and ethical action. As this happens, the Christian's response also dialogizes Jesus Christ. Jesus ceases to be an external authority and becomes instead a source of "internally persuasive discourse"[115] that enters into a Christian's thoughts, words, and deeds. Prayer is a crucial part of this. Through prayer Christ moves

112. Soelle, *Death by Bread Alone*, 139.

113. Taylor, *Secular Age*, 435.

114. Bakhtin, *Dialogic Imagination*, 46.

115. Ibid., 345–46.

from being an ideal, an image, a representative of values, to being a dialogue partner, a significant other in the sense that one's whole life may become lived in dialogue with him.[116] As one's life becomes a dialogue with Christ, prayer can become an inner dimension of all of it.[117] One's life can become "fashioned by prayer, and prayer" becomes the quintessence of one's life.[118] As this happens, Jesus becomes a formative influence in one's life. One's life as a whole becomes a response to him. This leads to what Origen (c. 185–254) saw as one meaning of Paul's injunction to "pray constantly" (1 Thess 5:17).[119] One's life becomes, in a sense, "a single great prayer,"[120] a response to what God has said and done in Jesus Christ.

THE DIALOGUE OF THE DIVINE LIFE

The Trinitarian life of God can be characterized as a dialogue, the communication and celebration of the divine goodness and beauty among the three "persons" of the Trinity. In the immanent Trinity, the self-diffusive goodness and beauty of God is communicated in the Word, Jesus Christ. From this expression of praise for and joy in God's goodness, and from the first person of the Trinity's joy in the Word, the Holy Spirit is generated, the bond of love and joy between the other two. These three are distinct yet one in the love and joy that they share with each other. The incarnation of the Word in Jesus of Nazareth opens up this Trinitarian unity so that humanity can participate in it.[121] Christian prayer is a response to this invitation presented by the Word of God and a participation in the divine life that it makes possible.

The Holy Spirit prepares the way for the reception of the Word and inspires people's prayerful response to it. In effect, the Holy Spirit, God's own response to the Word, is the source of a person's response to God in prayer.[122] As people receive the Word they receive the Holy Spirit in

116. For this notion of significant other, see Taylor, *Malaise of Modernity*, 33–34.

117. Lochman, *Lord's Prayer*, 6.

118. Heschel, *Man's Quest for God*, 12.

119. Origen, *On Prayer*, 104.

120. Ibid.

121. Watson, "Trinity and Community," 170, 180. While in Christian terms the incarnation is the definitive opening up of the divine life to human participation, this opening up has been present in the history of salvation leading up to it and continuing afterwards, which includes the history of other religions.

122. Rahner, *On Prayer*, 28.

a new way and enter more fully into it as the bond of love between the other two persons of the Trinity. Peoples' praise and joy in response to the communication of God's goodness and beauty through Word and Spirit adds to the communication of love, joy, and praise that constitutes the Trinitarian life of God. This brings a relative but still real increase to Gods' being. At the same time, as people enter into this communion, their own being is increased. Through becoming one with God they become "more entirely at one with"[123] themselves.

The further communication of God's goodness and beauty in history finds its definitive form in the crucified and risen Christ, as it takes place in encounter with sin, evil, and suffering in God's good but fallen world. Similarly, the Spirit inspired response to the Word becomes, as it takes place in history in the prayers of God's people, both petition and praise, petition including lament, intercession, confession, and protest.

As peoples' lives become a prayer in response to God's Word, they become a part of this ongoing dialogue of love and joy that makes up the divine life. Through this the dialogue of the divine life is extended to include new voices that formerly were not part of it. As people's lives become a part and extension of this dialogue, they add new voices to this dialogue, thus enriching it, and are themselves enriched by the address and response of God. The response of prayer that Jesus instigates is thus part of this extension of the communication and celebration of God's goodness and beauty.

123. Ibid., 16.

Conclusion

THIS BOOK BEGAN BY noting the diffuseness of issues that confronts a Christology originating in a Canadian/North Atlantic context. It adopted Mark Lewis Taylor's trilemma as a description of the interrelated challenges facing Christologies here. The need to acknowledge tradition produced a Trinitarian understanding of Jesus Christ that provides a metaphysical framework for understanding his work and relationships. The need to resist domination resulted in a reframing of traditional atonement theories as strong moral sources that empower people to follow the way of Jesus. The need to celebrate plurality and difference lead to a study of the relationality of Jesus Christ that examined how the identity he gives is open to others and yet can empower resistance to sin and evil.

According to Gregory Baum, great world religions are "auto-regenerating movements."[1] From "their essential symbolism" they are able to produce "new and unexpected meaning empowering people to respond, out of their religious heritage, to changed historical conditions."[2] Hopefully this book has been an exercise in this kind of auto-regeneration. It has resulted from reflecting on the New Testament witness with some critical tools of biblical studies, in light of the diffuseness of issues in the present, with a great deal of assistance and stimulation from preceding Christologies. It was called forth by the symbols and narratives that it seeks to interpret as much as by the context in which it was produced.

The auto-regenerating power at work here is an aspect Jesus' being as the Christ. His person continues to call forth new attempts to understand him, in every context in which Christians find themselves. His person and message also continue to call forth people to follow in his

---

1. Baum, *Religion and Alienation*, 257.
2. Ibid.

way. His work continues to empower and sustain people as they respond to his call. His presence in history continues to be partially shaped by their faithfulness or failures in following him. As those who are moved by him succeed in following his way, and sometimes even when it seems they have failed, the love of God that became incarnate in Jesus is perfected, in the sense of reaching its goal of finding further expression in time and space. And as this happens, there is an increase to the being of God in the "person" of the Holy Spirit. There is also a simultaneous increase to the being of those through whom this love is perfected, and often to others as well. And in this communication and further expression of God's love, there is an increase of beauty and goodness in the world that does not perish, but endures through its participation in the eternal being of God.

Bibliography

Abailard, Peter. "A Solution." In *A Scholastic Miscellany: Anselm to Ockham*, edited and translated by Eugene Fairweather, 283–84. Philadelphia: Westminster, 1956.

Adams, Marilyn McCord. *What Sort of Human Nature?: Medieval Philosophy and the Systematics of Christology*. The Aquinas Lecture 1999. Milwaukee: Marquette University Press, 1999.

Al-Jifri, Habib Ali. "Loving God and Loving Neighbor." In *A Common Word: Muslims and Christians on Loving God and Neighbor*, edited by Miroslav Volf, Ghazi bin Muhammad, and Melissa Yarrington, 79–87. Grand Rapids: Eerdmans, 2010.

Albertz, Rainer. *A History of Israelite Religion in the Old Testament Period*. Vol. 2, *From the Exile to the Maccabees*. Translated by John Bowden. Old Testament Library. Louisville: Westminster John Knox, 1994.

Anselm of Canterbury. *Anselm: Basic Writings*. Translated by S. N. Deane. La Salle, IL: Open Court, 1962.

Augustine of Hippo. *Concerning the City of God against the Pagans*. Translated by Henry Bettenson. New York: Penguin, 1984.

———. *Confessions*. Translated by R. S. Pine-Coffin. Harmondsworth: Penguin, 1961.

———. *The Trinity*. Translated by Stephen McKenna. Fathers of the Church, a new translation, 45. Washington, DC: Catholic University of America Press, 1981.

Aulén, Gustav. *Christus Victor: An Historical Study of the Three Main Types of the Idea of Atonement*. Translated by A. G. Herbert. London: SPCK, 1950.

Ayres, Lewis. *Nicaea and Its Legacy: An Approach to Fourth-Century Trinitarian Theology*. New York: Oxford University Press, 2004.

Baker-Fletcher, Karen. *Dancing with God: The Trinity from a Womanist Perspective*. St. Louis: Chalice, 2006.

Bakhtin, M. M. *The Dialogic Imagination: Four Essays*. Translated by Caryl Emerson and Michael Holquist, edited by Michael Holquist. University of Texas Press Slavic Series 1. Austin: University of Texas Press, 1981.

———. *Speech Genres and Other Late Essays*. Translated by Vern McGee, edited by Caryl Emerson and Michael Holquist. University of Texas Press Slavic Series 8. Austin: University of Texas Press, 1986.

Bakhtin, Mikhail. *Problems of Dostoevsky's Poetics*. Edited and translated by Caryl Emerson. Theory and History of Literature 8. Minneapolis: University of Minneapolis Press, 1984.

———. *Rabelais and His World*. Translated by Hélène Iswolsky. Bloomington: Indiana University Press, 1984.

Baldwin, Lewis. *Never to Leave Us Alone: The Prayer Life of Martin Luther King, Jr.* Minneapolis: Fortress, 2010.

Banting, Keith, Thomas J. Courchene, and F. Leslie Seidle. "Conclusion: Diversity, Belonging and Shared Citizenship." In *Belonging?: Diversity, Recognition and Shared Citizenship in Canada*, edited by Keith Banting, Thomas J. Courchene and F. Leslie Seidle, 647–87. The Art of the State 3. Montreal: Institute for Research on Public Policy, 2007.

Barth, Karl. *Church Dogmatics* II/1. Translated by T. H. L. Parker et al., edited by G. W. Bromiley and T. F. Torrance. Edinburgh: T. & T. Clark, 1957.

———. *Church Dogmatics* III/3. Translated by G. W. Bromiley and R. J. Ehrlich. Edited by G. W. Bromiley, T. F. Torrance. Edinburgh: T. & T. Clark, 1960.

———. *Church Dogmatics* IV/1. Translated by G. W. Bromiley. Edited by G. W. Bromiley, T. F. Torrance. Edinburgh: T. & T. Clark, 1956.

———. *Church Dogmatics* IV/2. Translated by G. W. Bromiley, edited by G. W. Bromiley and T. F. Torrance. Edinburgh: T. & T. Clark, 1958.

———. *Church Dogmatics* IV/3.1. Translated G. W. Bromiley, edited by G. W. Bromiley and T. F. Torrance. Edinburgh: T. & T. Clark, 1961.

Baum, Gregory. "Afterword." In *Faith That Transforms: Essays in Honor of Gregory Baum*, edited by Mary Jo Leddy and Mary Ann Hinsdale, 135–51. New York: Paulist, 1987.

———. *Compassion and Solidarity: The Church for Others*. CBC Massey Lectures 1987. New York: Paulist, 1990.

———. *The Credibility of the Church Today: A Reply to Charles Davis*. New York: Herder, 1968.

———. "Cultural Causes for the Change of the God Question." In *New Questions on God*, edited by Johannes Baptist Metz, 48–57. Concilium 76. New York: Herder, 1972.

———. *Essays in Critical Theology*. Kansas City: Sheed and Ward, 1994.

———. "Introduction." In Rosemary Radford Ruether, *Faith and Fratricide: The Theological Roots of Anti-Semitism*, 1–22. New York: Seabury, 1974.

———. "Is Denouncing the Occupation Antisemitic?" *The Ecumenist* 47/3 (Summer 2010) 1–5.

———. *Man Becoming: God in Secular Experience*. New York: Herder, 1970.

———. "Proclamation or Dialogue?: Unresolved Questions in Pope Benedict's Teaching." *The Ecumenist* 44/1 (Winter 2007) 1–4.

———. "Reflections on Resurrection and Eternal Life." *The Ecumenist* 40/2 (Spring 2003) 11–14.

———. *Religion and Alienation: A Theological Reading of Sociology*. New York: Paulist, 1975 (2nd ed., Ottawa: Novalis, 2006).

———. *Signs of the Times: Religious Pluralism and Economic Injustice*. Ottawa: Novalis, 2007.

———. "Structures of Sin." In *The Logic of Solidarity: Commentaries on Pope John Paul II's Encyclical On Social Concern*, edited by Gregory Baum and Robert Ellsberg, 110–26. Maryknoll, NY: Orbis, 1989.

———. *Theology and Society*. New York: Paulist, 1987.

———. *The Theology of Tariq Ramadan: A Catholic Perspective*. Ottawa: Novalis, 2009.

Baum, Gregory. *Truth beyond Relativism: Karl Mannheim's Sociology of Knowledge*. Pere Marquette Theology Lecture 1977. Milwaukee: Marquette University Press, 1977.

Bauman, Chad. *Christian Identity and Dalit Religion in Hindu India, 1868–1947*. Studies in the History of Christian Missions. Grand Rapids: Eerdmans, 2008.

Bearing Faithful Witness: United Church-Jewish Relations Today. Etobicoke, ON: Committee on Inter-Church and Inter-Faith Relations, United Church of Canada, 1998.

Beck, Ulrich. *Power in the Global Age: A New Global Political Economy.* Translated by Kathleen Cross. Malden, MA: Polity, 2005.

———. *Risk Society: Towards a New Modernity.* Translated by Mark Ritter. London: Sage, 1992.

———. *The Cosmopolitan Vision.* Translated by Ciaran Cronin. Malden, MA: Polity, 2006.

Becker, Jürgen. *Jesus of Nazareth.* Translated by James E. Crouch. New York: de Gruyter, 1998.

———. *Paul: Apostle to the Gentiles.* Translated by O. C. Dean Jr. Louisville: Westminster John Knox, 1993.

Beker, Christiaan. *Suffering and Hope: The Biblical Vision and the Human Predicament.* Philadelphia: Fortress, 1987.

Benedict XVI, Pope. "Faith, Reason, and the University: Memories and Reflections." Online: http://www.zenit.org/article-16955?l=english.

Benhabib, Seyla. *Another Cosmopolitanism.* With commentaries by Jeremy Waldron, Bonnie Honig, Will Kymlicka, edited by Robert Post. Berkeley Tanner Lectures. New York: Oxford University Press, 2006.

Betcher, Sharon. *Spirit and the Politics of Disablement.* Minneapolis: Fortress, 2007.

Bethge, Eberhard. *Dietrich Bonhoeffer: A Biography.* Translated by Eric Mosbacher et al. under Edwin Robertson. Revised and edited by Victoria J. Barnett. Minneapolis: Fortress, 2000.

Betz, Hans Dieter. *The Sermon on the Mount: A Commentary on the Sermon on the Mount, Including the Sermon on the Plain (Matthew 5:3—7:27 and Luke 6:20-49.* Edited by Adela Yarbro Collins. Hermeneia. Minneapolis: Fortress, 1995.

Blenkinsopp, Joseph. *A History of Prophecy in Israel.* Rev. ed. Louisville: Westminster John Knox, 1996.

Bloch, Ernst. *Heritage of Our Times.* Translated by Neville and Stephen Plaice. Cambridge, UK: Polity, 1991.

Boff, Leonardo. *The Lord's Prayer: The Prayer of Integral Liberation.* Translated by Theodore Morrow. Maryknoll, NY: Orbis, 1983.

Bonaventure. *Itinerarium Mentis In Deum.* New English translation by Zachary Hayes, edited by Philotheus Boehner and Zachary Hayes. Works of St. Bonaventure 2. Saint Bonaventure, NY: Franciscan Institute, 2002.

Bonhoeffer, Dietrich. *Barcelona, Berlin, New York, 1928-1931,* Translated by Douglas Stott, edited by Clifford Green. Vol. 10 of *Dietrich Bonhoeffer Works.* Minneapolis: Fortress, 2008.

———. *Life Together.* Translated by Daniel Bloesch and James Burtness, edited by Geffrey Kelly. In *Dietrich Bonhoeffer Works,* 5:25-140. Minneapolis· Fortress, 1996.

———. *Sanctorum Communio.* Vol. 1 of *Dietrich Bonhoeffer Works.* Translated by Reinhard Krauss and Nancy Lukens, edited by Clifford Green. Minneapolis: Fortress, 1998.

Boyd, Robin. *An Introduction to Indian Christian Theology.* Rev. ed. Madras: Christian Literature Society, 1975.

Braaten, Carl, and Robert Jenson. "Introduction." In *Jews and Christians: People of God,* edited by Carl Braaten and Robert Jenson, vii-ix. Grand Rapids: Eerdmans, 2003.

Bramadat, Paul, and David Seljak. "Toward a New Story about Religion and Ethnicity in Canada." In *Religion and Ethnicity in Canada*, edited by Paul Bramadat and David Seljak, 222–34. Toronto: Pearson Education Canada, 2005.

Brightman, Robert. *Grateful Prey: Rock Cree Human-Animal Relationships*. Berkeley: University of California Press, 1993.

———. *Traditional Narratives of the Rock Cree Indians*. Regina: Canadian Plains Research Center, 2007.

Brown, Jennifer, and Robert Brightman, "Introduction." In *"The Orders of the Dreamed": George Nelson on Cree and Northern Ojibwa Religion and Myth, 1923*, edited by Jennifer Brown and Robert Brightman, 1–26. Winnipeg: University of Manitoba Press, 1988.

———. "Northern Algonquian Religious and Mythic Themes and Personages: Contexts and Comparisons." In *"The Orders of the Dreamed": George Nelson on Cree and Northern Ojibwa Religion and Myth, 1923*, edited by Jennifer Brown and Robert Brightman, 119–85. Winnipeg: University of Manitoba Press, 1988.

———, editors. *"The Orders of the Dreamed:" George Nelson on Cree and Northern Ojibwa Religion and Myth, 1823* (Winnipeg: University of Manitoba Press, 1988).

Brown, Raymond. *The Epistles of John*. Anchor Bible 30. New York: Doubleday, 1982.

———. *An Introduction to New Testament Christology*. New York: Paulist, 1994.

Buber, Martin. "God and Man." In *The Judaic Tradition*, edited by Nahum Glatzer, 567–73. Rev. ed. Boston: Beacon, 1969.

Bulgakov, Sergius. *The Comforter*. Translated by Boris Jakim. Grand Rapids: Eerdmans, 2004.

Bultmann, Rudolf. "New Testament and Mythology." In *Kerygma and Myth*, edited by Hans-Werner Bartsch, 1:1–44. 2nd ed. London: SPCK, 1964.

Burke, Patrick. *Reinterpreting Rahner*. New York: Fordham University Press, 2002.

Cahill, Lisa Sowle. "Christology, Ethics, and Spirituality." In *Thinking of Christ*, edited by Tatha Wiley, 193–210. New York: Continuum, 2003.

———. "Quaestio Disputata—The Atonement Paradigm: Does It Still Have Explanatory Value?" *Theological Studies* 68 (2007) 418–32.

Calvin, John. *Institutes of the Christian Religion* Vol. 1. Edited by John T. McNeill, translated by Ford Lewis Battles. Library of Christian Classics 20. Philadelphia: Westminster, 1960.

Carbine, Rosemary. "Contextualizing the Cross for the Sake of Subjectivity." In *Cross Examinations*, edited by Marit Trelstad, 91–107. Minneapolis: Fortress, 2006.

Carman, John. "Christian Interpretation of 'Hinduism': Between Understanding and Theological Judgment." In *India and the Indianness of Christianity: Essays on Understanding —Historical, Theological, and Bibliographical—in Honor of Robert Eric Frykenberg*, edited by Robert Fox Young, 235–48. Grand Rapids: Eerdmans, 2009.

Carnley, Peter. *The Structure of Resurrection Belief*. Oxford: Clarendon, 1987.

Cartwright, Michael. "Afterword: 'If Abraham is Our Father . . .'" In John Howard Yoder, *The Jewish-Christian Schism Revisited*, edited by Michael Cartwright and Peter Ochs, 205–40. Radical Traditions. Grand Rapids: Eerdmans, 2003.

Catchpole, David. *Jesus People*. Grand Rapids: Baker Academic, 2006.

———. *Resurrection People*. Macon, Georgia: Smyth & Helwys, 2002.

Chenchiah, P. "Wherein Lies the Uniqueness of Christ?: An Indian Christian View." In *Readings in Indian Christian Theology* Vol. I, edited by R. S. Sugirtharajah and Cecil Hargreaves, 83–92. London: SPCK, 1993.

Clarke, Sathianathan. "Re-Imaging the Death of Jesus: An Indian Interpretation and Inter-Religious Theology of the Cross." In *News of Boundless Riches,* edited by Lalsangkima Pachuau and Max Stackhouse, 2:187–217. Delhi: ISPCK/UTC/CTI, 2007.

Clooney, Francis. *Comparative Theology.* Malden, MA: Wiley-Blackwell, 2010.

Coakley, Sarah. "What Does Chalcedon Solve and What Does It Not?: Some Reflections on the Status and Meaning of the Chalcedonian 'Definition.'" In *The Incarnation: An Interdisciplinary Symposium on the Incarnation of the Son of God,* edited by Stephen Davis, Daniel Kendall, and Gerald O'Collins, 143–63. New York: Oxford University Press, 2002.

Cobb, John B., Jr. *Christ in a Pluralistic Age.* Philadelphia: Westminster, 1975.

———. "Introduction." In *The Dialogue Comes Of Age,* edited by John B. Cobb, Jr. and Ward M. McAfee, 1–8. Minneapolis: Fortress, 2010.

———. *The Structure of Christian Existence.* Philadelphia: Westminster, 1967.

———. "Theological Response." In *The Dialogue Comes of Age: Christian Encounters with Other Traditions,* edited by John B. Cobb Jr. and Ward M. McAfee, 185–211. Minneapolis: Fortress, 2010.

———. *Transforming Christianity and the World: A Way beyond Absolutism and Relativism.* Edited by Paul Knitter. Faith Meets Faith. Maryknoll, NY: Orbis, 1999.

Cobb, John B., Jr., and David Ray Griffin. *Process Theology: An Introductory Exposition.* Philadelphia: Westminster, 1976.

Cohen, Shaye J. D. *From the Maccabees to the Mishnah.* Philadelphia: Westminster, 1987.

Colish, Marcia. *Medieval Foundations of the Western Intellectual Tradition 400–1400.* Yale Intellectual History of the West. New Haven, CT: Yale University Press, 1997.

Collingwood, R. G. *The Idea of History.* Oxford: Clarendon, 1946.

Collins, Adela Yarbro, and John J. Collins. *King and Messiah as Son of God: Divine, Human, and Angelic Messianic Figures in Biblical and Related Literature.* Grand Rapids: Eerdmans, 2008.

Collins, Raymond. *The Birth of the New Testament: The Origin and Development of the First Christian Generation.* New York: Crossroad, 1993.

Committee on Inter-Church and Inter-Faith Relations of the United Church of Canada. *That We May Know Each Other: United Church-Muslim Relations Today.* Toronto: United Church of Canada, 2004.

"A Common Word between Us and You" (Summary and Abridgement). In *A Common Word: Muslims and Christians on Loving God and Neighbor,* edited by Miroslav Volf, Ghazi bin Muhammad, and Melissa Yarrington, 28–29. Grand Rapids: Eerdmans, 2010.

Cone, James. *God of the Oppressed.* San Francisco: Harper and Row, 1975.

———. *Martin & Malcom & America: A Dream or a Nightmare?* Maryknoll, NY: Orbis, 1991.

Constas, Nicholas. "The Last Temptation of Satan: Divine Deception in Greek Patristic Interpretations of the Passion Narrative." *Harvard Theological Review* 97/2 (2004) 139–63.

Conzelmann, Hans. *1 Corinthians.* Translated by James Leith. Hermeneia. Philadelphia: Fortress, 1975.

Copeland, M. Shawn. "The Cross of Christ and Discipleship." In *Thinking of Christ: Proclamation, Explanation, Meaning,* edited by Tatha Wiley, 177–92. New York: Continuum, 2003.

Cracknell, Kenneth. *In Good and Generous Faith: Christian Responses to Religious Plural-ism*. Cleveland: Pilgrim, 2006.

Craigo-Snell, Shannon. *Silence, Love, and Death: Saying "Yes" to God in the Theology of Karl Rahner*. Milwaukee: Marquette University Press, 2008.

Crossan, John Dominic. *Four Other Gospels: Shadows on the Contours of Canon*. Minneapolis: Winston, 1985.

————. *The Greatest Prayer: Rediscovering the Revolutionary Message of the Lord's Prayer*. New York: HarperCollins, 2010.

————. *The Historical Jesus: The Life of a Mediterranean Jewish Peasant*. New York: HarperSanFransisco, 1991.

Cyril of Alexandria. *On the Unity of Christ*. Translated by John McGuckin. Crestwood, NY: St. Vladimir's Seminary Press, 1995.

Cyril of Alexandria. "Scholia on the Incarnation of the Only Begotten." In John McGuckin, *Saint Cyril of Alexandria and the Christological Controversy: Its history, Theology, and Texts*, 294–335. Supplements to Vigiliae Christianae 23. Crestwood, NY: St. Vladimir's Seminary Press, 2004.

Dahl, Nils Alstrup. *Jesus the Christ: The Historical Origins of Christological Doctrine*. Edited by Donald H. Juel. Minneapolis: Fortress, 1991.

Daley, Brian. "'He Himself Is Our Peace' (Ephesians 2:14): Early Christian Views of Redemption in Christ." In *The Redemption: An Interdisciplinary Symposium on Christ as Redeemer*, edited by Stephen Davis, Daniel Kendall, and Gerald O'Collins, 149–76. New York: Oxford University Press, 2004.

Dalferth, Ingolf. "Christ Died for Us: Reflections On The Sacrificial Language of Sal-vation." In *Sacrifice and Redemption: Durham Essays in Theology*, edited by S. W. Sykes, 299–325. New York: Cambridge University Press, 1991.

Davies, Alan. *The Crucified Nation: A Motif in Modern Nationalism*. Portland, OR: Sus-sex Academic, 2008.

De Gruchy, John. "The Dialectic of Reconciliation." In *The Reconciliation of Peoples: Challenge to the Churches*, edited by Gregory Baum and Harold Wells, 16–29. Maryknoll, NY: Orbis, 1997.

De Gruchy, John. *Reconciliation: Restoring Justice*. Minneapolis: Fortress, 2002.

Del Colle, Ralph. *Christ and the Spirit: Spirit-Christology in Trinitarian Perspective*. New York: Oxford University Press, 1994.

Delio, Ilia. *Christ in Evolution*. Maryknoll, NY: Orbis, 2008.

Despland, Michel. *The Education of Desire: Plato and the Philosophy of Religion*. Toronto: University of Toronto Press, 1985.

Dibelius, Martin. *Jesus*. Translated by Charles B. Hedrick and Frederick C. Grant. Philadelphia: Westminster, 1949.

Douglas, Kelly Brown. *The Black Christ*. Bishop Henry McNeal Turner Studies in North American Black Religion 9. Maryknoll, NY: Orbis, 1994.

Driel, Edwin Chr. van. *Incarnation Anyway: Arguments for Supralapsarian Christology*. American Academy of Religion Academy Series. New York: Oxford University Press, 2008.

Duff, Nancy. "Atonement and the Christian Life." *Interpretation* 53/1 (January 1999) 21–33.

Dunn, James D. G. *Christology in the Making: A New Testament Inquiry into the Origins of the Doctrine of the Incarnation*. 2nd ed. Grand Rapids: Eerdmans, 1996.

————. *Jesus Remembered.* Christianity in the Making 1. Grand Rapids: Eerdmans, 2003.

————. "Towards the Spirit of Christ: The Emergence of the Distinctive Features of Christian Pneumatology." In *The Work of the Spirit: Pneumatology and Pentecostalism,* edited by Michael Welker, 3–26. Grand Rapids: Eerdmans, 2006.

Dünzl, Franz. *A Brief History of the Doctrine of the Trinity in the Early Church.* New York: T. & T. Clark, 2007.

Dupuis, Jacques. *Jesus Christ at the Encounter of World Religions.* Faith Meets Faith. Maryknoll, NY: Orbis, 1991.

Dyke, Doris. *Crucified Woman.* Toronto: United Church Publishing House, 1991.

Elizondo, Virgilio. "Elements for a Mexican American Mestizo Christology." In *Jesus in the Hispanic Community: Images of Christ from Theology to Popular Religion,* edited by Harold Recinos and Hugo Magallanes, 3–15. Louisville: Westminster John Knox, 2009.

Ellis, Marc. *Judaism Does Not Equal Israel.* New York: New Press, 2009.

Ess, Josef van. "Islamic Perspectives." In Hans Küng et al., *Christianity and the World Religions: Paths of Dialogue with Islam, Hinduism, and Buddhism,* translated by Peter Heinegg, 5–18. Garden City, NY: Doubleday, 1986.

Evans, Christopher . *Resurrection and the New Testament.* Studies in Biblical Theology, 2nd ser., 12. London: SCM, 1970.

Fee, Gordon. *God's Empowering Presence: The Holy Spirit in the Letters of Paul.* Peabody, MA: Hendrickson, 1994.

Feil, Ernst. *The Theology of Dietrich Bonhoeffer.* Translated by Martin Rumscheidt. Philadelphia: Fortress, 1985.

Fernando, Leonard, and G. Gispert-Sauch. *Christianity in India: Two Thousand Years of Faith.* New Delhi: Viking, 2004.

Fiddes, Paul. *Past Event and Present Salvation: The Christian Idea of Atonement.* Louisville: Westminster John Knox, 1989.

Finlan, Stephen. *Problems with Atonement: The origins of, and Controversy about, the Atonement Doctrine.* Collegeville, MI: Liturgical, 2005.

Fitzmyer, Joseph. *The Gospel According to Luke, X–XXIV.* Anchor Bible 28A. Garden City, NY: Doubleday, 1985.

————. *Romans.* Anchor Bible 33. New York: Doubleday, 1993.

Fleischner, Eva. "Jews and Christians through the Ages: A Troubled Relationship." In *The Dialogue Comes of Age: Christian Encounters with Other Traditions,* edited by John B. Cobb Jr. and Ward M. McAfee, 41–85. Minneapolis: Fortress, 2010.

Fredriksen, Paula. *Jesus of Nazareth: King of the Jews.* New York: Vintage, 1999.

Fretheim, Terrence. *God and World in the Old Testament: A Relational Theology of Creation.* Nashville: Abingdon, 2005.

Freyne, Sean. *Jesus: A Jewish Galilean: A New Reading of the Jesus-Story.* New York: T. & T. Clark, 2004.

Fulkerson, Mary McClintock. *Changing the Subject: Women's Discourses and Feminist Theology.* Minneapolis: Fortress, 1994.

————. *Places of Redemption: Theology for a Worldly Church.* New York: Oxford University Press, 2007.

Fuller, Reginald. *The Formation of the Resurrection Narratives.* New York: Macmillan, 1971.

Gaventa, Beverly Roberts. *First and Second Thessalonians.* Interpretation. Louisville: John Knox, 1998.

Gavrilyuk, Paul. *The Suffering of the Impassible God: The Dialectics of Patristic Thought.* Oxford Early Christian Studies. New York: Oxford University Press, 2004.

Genizi, Haim. *The Holocaust, Israel, and Canadian Protestant Churches.* Montreal & Kingston: McGill-Queen's University Press, 2002.

Gilliss, Martha Schull. "Resurrecting the Atonement." In *Feminist and Womanist Essays in Reformed Dogmatics*, edited by Amy Plantinga Pauw and Serene Jones, 125–38. Columbia Series in Reformed Theology. Louisville: Westminster John Knox, 2006.

Gilson, Etienne. *The Philosophy of St. Bonaventure.* Translated by Illtyd Trethowan and Frank J. Sheed. Paterson, NJ: St. Anthony Guild, 1965.

Gnilka, Joachim. *Jesus of Nazareth: Message and History.* Peabody, MA: Hendrickson, 1997.

Goffman, Erving. *The Presentation of Self in Everyday Life.* Garden City, NY: Doubleday, 1959.

Gouldner, Alvin. *The Dialectic of Ideology and Technology: The Origins, Grammar, and Future of Ideology.* New York: Seabury, 1976.

Green, Clifford. *Bonhoeffer: A Theology of Sociality.* Rev. ed. Grand Rapids: Eerdmans, 1999.

Greenberg, Irving. "Judaism and Christianity: Covenants of Redemption." In *Christianity in Jewish Terms*, edited by Tikva Frymer-Kensky et al., 141–58. Radical Traditions. Boulder, CO: Westview, 2000.

Gregory of Nazianzus. *On God and Christ: The Five Theological Orations and Two Letters to Cledonius.* Translated by Frederick Williams and Lionel Wickham. Crestwood, NY: St. Vladimir's Seminary Press, 2002.

Gregory of Nyssa. *The Great Catechism.* In *Nicene and Post-Nicene Fathers*, 2nd ser., edited by Philip Schaff, revised by Henry Wallace, 10:471–509. New York: Cosimo Classics, 2007.

———. *The Lord's Prayer. The Beatitudes.* Translated by Hilda Graef. New York: Paulist, 1954.

Griffin, David Ray. "Resurrection and Empire." In *The American Empire and the Commonwealth of God*, David Ray Griffin et al., 151–57. Louisville: Westminster John Knox, 2006.

Grillmeier, Aloys. *Christ in Christian Tradition.* Translated by J. S. Bowden. New York: Sheed and Ward, 1965.

Gustafson, James. *Christ and the Moral Life.* Chicago: University of Chicago Press, 1968.

Gutiérrez, Gustavo. *The Truth Shall Make You Free: Confrontations.* Translated by Matthew J. O'Connell. Maryknoll, NY: Orbis, 1990.

Habermas, Jürgen. "An Awareness of What is Missing." In Jürgen Habermas et al., *An Awareness of What Is Missing: Faith and Reason in a Post-Secular Age*, 15–23. Translated by Ciaran Cronin. Malden, MA: Polity, 2010.

Haight, Roger. *Jesus: Symbol of God.* Maryknoll, NY: Orbis, 1999.

Hall, Douglas John. "Christianity and Canadian Contexts: Then and Now." In *Intersecting Voices: Critical Theologies in a Land of Diversity*, edited by Don Schweitzer and Derek Simon, 18–32. Ottawa: Novalis, 2004.

———. *God and Human Suffering: An Exercise in the Theology of the Cross.* Minneapolis: Augsburg, 1986.

———. "The Theology of Hope in an Officially Optimistic Society." *Religion in Life* 40 (1971) 376–90.

———. *Thinking the Faith: Christian Theology in a North American Context.* Minneapolis: Augsburg, 1989.

Hanson, Paul. "A New Challenge to Biblical Theology." *Journal of the American Academy of Religion* 67/2 (June 1999) 454–58.

Hanson, R. P. C. *The Search for the Christian Doctrine of God: The Arian Controversy.* Edinburgh: T. & T. Clark, 1988.

Hayes, Zachary. *The Hidden Center: Spirituality and Speculative Christology in St. Bonaventure.* New York: Paulist, 1981.

Heidegger, Martin. *Being and Time.* Translated by John Macquarrie and Edward Robinson. New York: Harper & Row, 1962.

Hengel, Martin. *Studies in Early Christology.* Edinburgh: T. & T. Clark, 1995.

Heschel, Abraham. "A Hebrew Evaluation of Reinhold Niebuhr." In *Reinhold Niebuhr: His Religious, Social, and Political Thought,* edited by Charles Kegley and Robert Bretall, 392–410. New York: Macmillan, 1961.

———. *Man's Quest For God: Studies in Prayer and Symbolism.* New York: Scribner, 1954.

———. *The Prophets.* Vol. 2. New York: Harper & Row, 1962.

Hesselink, I. John. "Introduction." In John Calvin, *On Prayer,* edited by I. John Hesselink, 1–37. Louisville: Westminster John Knox, 2006.

Heyward, Carter. *Saving Jesus from Those Who Are Right: Rethinking What It Means to Be Christian.* Minneapolis: Fortress, 1999.

Highway, Thomson. "Foreword." In Geoffrey York, *The Dispossessed: Life and Death in Native Canada,* by vii–ix. London: Vintage UK, 1990.

Hilbreath, Bernd Jochen. "Identity through Self-Transcendence: The Holy Spirit and the Fellowship of Free Persons." In *Advents of the Spirit: An Introduction to the Current Study of Pneumatology,* edited by Bradford Hinze and Lyle Dabney, 265–94. Marquette Studies in Theology 30. Milwaukee: Marquette University Press, 2001.

Horsley, Richard. *Jesus and Empire: The Kingdom of God and the New World Disorder.* Minneapolis: Fortress, 2003.

Hurtado, Larry. *How on Earth Did Jesus Become a God?: Historical Questions about Earliest Devotion to Jesus.* Grand Rapids: Eerdmans, 2005.

———. *Lord Jesus Christ: Devotion to Jesus in Earliest Christianity.* Grand Rapids: Eerdmans, 2003.

———. *One God, One Lord: Early Christian Devotion and Ancient Jewish Monotheism.* Philadelphia: Fortress, 1988.

Isasi-Díaz, Ada María. "Identifícate con Nosotras: A Mujerista Christological Understanding." In *Jesus in the Hispanic Community: Images of Christ from Theology to Popular Religion,* edited by Harold Recinos and Hugo Magallanes, 38–57. Louisville: Westminster John Knox, 2009.

Jaffee, Martin. *Early Judaism.* Upper Saddle River, NJ: Prentice Hall, 1997.

Jennings, Theodore, Jr. *Transforming Atonement: A Political Theology of the Cross.* Minneapolis: Fortress, 2009.

Jenson, Robert. "Toward a Christian Theology of Judaism." In *Jews and Christians: People of God,* edited by Carl Braaten and Robert Jenson, 1–13. Grand Rapids: Eerdmans, 2003.

Jeremias, Joachim. *New Testament Theology Part I.* Translated by John Bowden. London: SCM, 1971.

———. *The Prayers of Jesus.* London: SCM, 1967.

"A Jewish Statement on Christians and Christianity." In *Christianity in Jewish Terms,* edited by Tikva Frymer-Kensky et al., xv–xviii. Radical Traditions. Boulder, CO: Westview, 2000.

Johnson, Elizabeth. "Christology's Impact on the Doctrine of God." *Heythrop Journal* 26 (1985) 143–63.

———. "Jesus and Salvation." *Catholic Theological Society of American Proceedings* 49 (1994) 1–18.

———. "Passion for God, Passion for the Earth." In *Spiritual Questions for the Twenty-First Century: Essays in Honor of Joan D. Chittister*, edited by Mary Hembrow Snyder, 118–25. Ottawa: Novalis, 2001.

———. *Quest for the Living God: Mapping Frontiers in the Theology of God*. New York: Continuum, 2007.

———. "Resurrection and Reality in the Thought of Wolfhart Pannenberg." *Heythrop Journal* 24 (1983) 1–17.

———. *She Who Is: The Mystery of God in Feminist Theological Discourse*. New York: Crossroad, 1993.

———. *Women, Earth and Creator Spirit*. Madeleva Lecture in Spirituality 1993. New York: Paulist, 1993.

———. "The Word Was Made Flesh and Dwelt Among Us: Jesus Research and Christian Faith." In *Jesus: A Colloquium in the Holy Land*, edited by Doris Donnelly, 146–66. New York: Continuum, 2001.

Johnston, Basil. *Indian School Days*. Toronto: Key Porter Books, 1988.

Jones, Paul Dafydd. *The Humanity of Christ: Christology in Karl Barth's Church Dogmatics*. New York: T. & T. Clark, 2008.

Jones, Serene. *Feminist Theory and Christian Theology: Cartographies of Grace*. Guides to Theological Inquiry. Minneapolis: Fortress, 2000.

Jüngel, Eberhard. *The Doctrine of the Trinity: God's Being is in Becoming*. Translated by Horton Harris. Monograph Supplements to the Scottish Journal of Theology. Grand Rapids: Eerdmans, 1976.

Käsemann, Ernst. *Commentary on Romans*. Translated and edited by Geoffrey Bromiley. Grand Rapids: Eerdmans, 1980.

———. *Essays on New Testament Themes*. London: SCM, 1964.

———. *New Testament Questions of Today*. Translated by W. J. Montague. New Testament Library. London: SCM, 1969.

Kasper, Walter. *The God of Jesus Christ*. Translated by Matthew O'Connell. New York: Crossroad, 1984.

———. "Paths Taken and Enduring Questions in Jewish-Christian Relations Today: Thirty Years of the Commission for Religious Relations with the Jews." In *The Catholic Church and the Jewish People: Recent Reflections from Rome*, edited by Philip Cunningham et al., 3–11. New York: Fordham University Press, 2007.

Keane, Kevin. "Why Creation?: Bonaventure and Thomas Aquinas on God as Creative Good." *Downside Review* 93 (1975) 100–21.

Keating, James. "Epistemology and the Theological Application of Jesus Research." In *Christology: Memory, Inquiry, Practice*, edited by Anne Clifford and Anthony Godzieba, 18–43. The Annual Publication of the College Theology Society, 2002, vol. 48. Maryknoll, NY: Orbis, 2003.

Keck, Leander. *Who Is Jesus?: History in Perfect Tense*. Studies on Personalities of the New Testament. Columbia: University of South Carolina Press, 2000.

Kehrer. Günter. "Secularization." In *The Brill Dictionary of Religion*, 4:1701–4.

Keller, Catherine. *On the Mystery: Discerning Divinity in Process*. Minneapolis: Fortress, 2008.

Kelly, Anthony. *The Resurrection Effect: Transforming Christian Life and Thought*. Maryknoll, NY: Orbis, 2008.

King, Martin Luther, Jr. *Where Do We Go from Here: Chaos or Community?* New York: Bantam, 1968.

Kraus, Hans-Joachim. *Psalms 1–59: A Commentary*. Translated by Hilton C. Oswald. Minneapolis: Augsburg, 1988.

Küng, Hans. "A Christian Response. [Hinduism]" In Hans Küng et al., *Christianity and the World Religions: Paths of Dialogue with Islam, Hinduism, and Buddhism*, translated by Peter Heinegg, 225–40. Garden City, NY: Doubleday, 1986.

———. "A Christian Response. [Islam]" In Hans Küng et al., *Christianity and the World Religions: Paths of Dialogue with Islam, Hinduism, and Buddhism*, translated by Peter Heinegg, 50–69. Garden City, NY: Doubleday, 1986.

———. "Toward Dialogue." In Hans Küng et al., *Christianity and the World Religions: Paths of Dialogue with Islam, Hinduism, and Buddhism*, translated by Peter Heinegg, xiii–xix. Garden City, NY: Doubleday, 1986.

Kyung, Chung Hyun. *Struggle to Be the Sun Again: Introducing Asian Women's Theology*. Maryknoll, NY: Orbis, 1990.

LaCugna, Catherine Mowry. *God for Us: The Trinity and Christian Life*. New York: HarperCollins, 1991.

Langer, Ruth. "Liturgy and Sensory Experience." In *Christianity in Jewish Terms*, edited by Tikva Frymer-Kensky et al., 189–95. Boulder, CO: Westview, 2000.

Lee, Sang Hyun. "Edwards on God and Nature: Resources for Contemporary Theology." In *Edwards in Our Time: Jonathan Edwards and the Shaping of American Religion*, edited by Sang Hyun Lee and Allen Guelzo, 15–44. Grand Rapids: Eerdmans, 1999.

———. *The Philosophical Theology of Jonathan Edwards*. Princeton, NJ: Princeton University Press, 1988.

———. "Pilgrimage and Home in the Wilderness of Marginality: Symbols and Context in Asian American Theology." *Princeton Seminary Bulletin* 16/1, n.s. (1995) 49–64.

Leon-Dufour, Xavier. *Resurrection and the Message of Easter*. Translated by R. N. Wilson. London: G. Chapman, 1974.

Levenson, Jon. "Did God Forgive Adam?: A Exercise in Comparative Midrash." In *Jews and Christians: People of God*, edited by Carl Braaten and Robert Jenson, 148–70. Grand Rapids: Eerdmans, 2003.

———, Jon. *Resurrection and the Restoration of Israel: The Ultimate Victory of the God of Life*. New Haven, CT: Yale University Press, 2006.

Levering, Matthew. *Jewish-Christian Dialogue and the Life of Wisdom: Engagements with the Theology of David Novak*. New York: Continuum, 2010.

Lincoln, Andrew. "'I Am the Resurrection and the Life': The Resurrection Message of the Fourth Gospel." In *Life in the Face of Death: The Resurrection Message of the New Testament*, edited by Richard Longenecker, 122–44. Grand Rapids: Eerdmans, 1998.

Lochman, Jan Milic. *The Lord's Prayer*. Translated by Geoffrey W. Bromiley. Grand Rapids: Eerdmans, 1990.

Lohfink, Gerhard. *Jesus and Community: The Social Dimension of Christian Faith*. Translated by John P. Galvin Philadelphia: Fortress; New York: Paulist, 1984.

Lonergan, Bernard. *Method in Theology*. Minneapolis: Winston, 1972.

Lossky, Vladimir. "Redemption and Deification." In *The Holy Spirit: Classic and Contemporary Readings*, edited by Eugene F. Rogers Jr., 237–57. Malden, MA: Wiley-Blackwell, 2009.

Love, Gregory Anderson. "In Search of a Non-Violent Atonement Theory: Are Abelard and Girard a Help, or a Problem?" In *Theology as Conversation: The Significance of Dialogue in Historical and Contemporary Theology: A Festschrift for Daniel L. Migliore*, edited by Bruce McCormack and Kimlyn Bender, 194–214. Grand Rapids: Eerdmans, 2009.

"Loving God and Neighbor Together: A Christian Response to 'A Common Word between Us and You.'" In *A Common Word: Muslims and Christians on Loving God and Neighbor*, edited by Miroslav Volf, Ghazi bin Muhammad, and Melissa Yarrington, 52–56. Grand Rapids: Eerdmans, 2010.

Luther, Martin. *Luther's Works*. Vol. 26. Edited by Jaroslav Pelikan and Walter Hansen. St. Louis: Concordia, 1963.

Luz, Ulrich. *Mathew 1–7*. Translation by James E. Crouch, edited by Helmut Koester. Minneapolis: Augsburg Fortress, 1989.

Malbon, Elizabeth Struthers. *Mark's Jesus: Characterization as Narrative Christology*. Waco, TX: Baylor University Press, 2009.

Marion, Jean-Luc. "'They Recognized Him; and He Became Invisible to Them.'" *Modern Theology* 18/2 (April 2002) 145–52.

Marmur, Dow ."The United Church and Jews." In *Fire and Grace: Stories of History and Vision*, edited by Jim Taylor, 29–33. Toronto: United Church Publishing House, 1999.

Martyn, J. Louis. *Theological Issues in the Letters of Paul*. Nashville: Abingdon, 1997.

Marxsen, Willi. *The Resurrection of Jesus of Nazareth*. London: SCM, 1970.

McCormack, Bruce. *Karl Barth's Critically Realistic Dialectical Theology: Its Genesis and Development, 1909–1936*. Oxford: Clarendon, 1995.

McDonnell, Kilian. *The Other Hand of God: The Holy Spirit as the Universal Touch and Goal*. Collegeville, MN: Liturgical, 2003.

McGinn, Bernard. "God as Eros: Metaphysical Foundations of Christian Mysticism." In *New Perspectives on Historical Theology: Essays in Memory of John Meyendorff*, edited by Bradley Nassif, 189–209. Grand Rapids: Eerdmans, 1996.

McGuckin, John Anthony. "Hypostasis." In *The Westminster Handbook to Patristic Theology*, 173–75. Louisville: Westminster John Knox, 2004.

———. "Logos Theology." In *The Westminster Handbook to Patristic Theology*, 207–8. Louisville: Westminster John Knox, 2004.

———. *Saint Cyril of Alexandria and the Christological Controversy: Its History, Theology, and Texts*. Supplements to Vigiliae Christianae 23. Crestwood, NY: St. Vladimir's Seminary Press, 2004.

Meier, John. "From Elijah-Like Prophet to Royal Davidic Messiah." In *Jesus: A Colloquium in the Holy Land*, edited by Doris Donnelly, 45–83. New York: Continuum, 2001.

———. *A Marginal Jew*. Vols. 1–3. Anchor Bible Reference Library. Doubleday: New York, 1991–2001.

———. "The Present State of the 'Third Quest' for the Historical Jesus: Loss and Gain." *Biblica* 80/4 (1999) 459–86.

Metz, Johann Baptist. "The Courage to Pray." In Karl Rahner and Johann Baptist Metz, *The Courage to Pray*, translated by Sarah O'Brien Twohig, 1–28. New York: Crossroad, 1981.

———. *Love's Strategy: The Political Theology of Johann Baptist Metz*. Edited by John K. Downey. Harrisburg, PA: Trinity, 1999.

Meyer, Ben. *The Aims of Jesus*. London: SCM, 1979.

———. "Jesus' Ministry and Self-Understanding." In *Studying the Historical Jesus: Evaluations of the State of Current Research*, edited by Bruce Chilton and Craig Evans, 337–52. New Testament Tools and Studies 19. Leiden: Brill, 1994.

Michel, Thomas. *A Christian View of Islam: Essays on Dialogue.* Edited by Irfan Omar. Faith Meets Faith. Maryknoll, NY: Orbis, 2010.

Milbank, John. *Being Reconciled: Ontology and Pardon.* Radical Orthodoxy Series. New York: Routledge, 2003.

Miller, James. *Shingwauk's Vision: A History of Native Residential Schools.* Toronto: University of Toronto Press, 1996.

———. *Skyscrapers Hide the Heavens: A History of Indian-White Relations in Canada.* Rev. ed. Toronto: University of Toronto Press, 1991.

———. "'We Are Sorry': The Canadian Government Apology for Residential Schooling." *The Ecumenist* 46/2 (Spring 2009) 1–5.

Miller, Patrick. *They Cried to the Lord: The Form and Theology of Biblical Prayer.* Minneapolis: Fortress, 1994.

Milloy, John. *A National Crime: The Canadian Government and the Residential School System, 1879–1986.* Manitoba Studies in Native History 11. Winnipeg: University of Manitoba Press, 1999.

Moltmann, Jürgen. *The Church in the Power of the Spirit: A Contribution to Messianic Ecclesiology.* Translated by Margaret Kohl. New York: Harper & Row, 1977.

———. *The Coming of God: Christian Eschatology.* Translated by Margaret Kohl. Minneapolis: Fortress, 1996.

———. *The Crucified God: The Cross of Christ as the Foundation and Criticism of Christian Theology.* Translated by R. W. Wilson and John Bowden. London: SCM, 1974.

———. *The Future of Creation.* Philadelphia: Fortress, 1979.

———. *God for a Secular Society: The Public Relevance of Theology.* Translated by Margaret Kohl. London: SCM, 1999.

———. *God in Creation: An Ecological Doctrine of Creation: The Gifford Lectures 1984–1985.* Translated by Margaret Kohl. London: SCM, 1985.

———. *History and the Triune God: Contributions to Trinitarian Theology.* Translated by John Bowden. London: SCM, 1991.

———. *In the End—The Beginning: The Life of Hope.* Minneapolis: Fortress, 2004.

———. *Jesus Christ for Today's World.* Translated by Margaret Kohl. Minneapolis: Fortress, 1994.

———. *On Human Dignity: Political Theology and Ethics.* Translated by M. Douglas Meeks. Philadelphia: Fortress, 1984.

———. "Praying with Eyes Open." Translated by Margaret Kohl. In *Loving God with Our Minds: The Pastor as Theologian: Essays in Honor of Wallace M. Alston*, edited by Michael Welker and Cynthia Jarvis, 195–201. Grand Rapids: Eerdmans, 2004.

———. *Religion, Revolution, and the Future.* Translated by M. Douglas Meeks. New York: Scribner, 1969.

———. *Theology of Hope: On the Ground and the Implications of a Christian Eschatology.* Translated by James Leitch. London: SCM, 1967.

———. *Theology of Joy.* Translated by Reinhard Ulrich. London: SCM, 1973.

———. *Theology Today: Two Contributions towards Making Theology Present.* Translated by John Bowden. London: SCM, 1988.

———. *The Way of Jesus Christ: Christology in Messianic Dimensions.* Translated by Margaret Kohl. New York: HarperCollins, 1990.

Murata, Sachiko, and William Chittick. *The Vision of Islam*. Visions of Reality; Understandings of Religions. New York: Paragon House, 1994.

Neuhaus, Richard John. "Salvation Is from the Jews." In *Jews and Christians: People of God*, edited by Carl Braaten and Robert Jenson, 65–77. Grand Rapids: Eerdmans, 2003.

Neville, Robert Cummings. *Symbols of Jesus: A Christology of Symbolic Engagement*. New York: Cambridge University Press, 2001.

Niebuhr, H. Richard. *The Meaning of Revelation*. New York: Macmillan, 1960.

Niebuhr, Reinhold. *The Nature and Destiny of Man*. Vol. 1, *Human Nature*. Gifford Lectures 1939. New York: Scribner, 1941.

Nirmal, Arvind. *Heuristic Explorations*. Madras: Christian Literature Society, 1990.

———. "Towards a Christian Dalit Theology." In *Indigenous People: Dalits: Dalit Issues in Today's Theological Debate*, edited by James Massey, 214–30. ISPCK Context Theological Education Series 5. Delhi: ISPCK, 1998.

Norris, Jr., Richard. "Chalcedon Revisited: A Historical and Theological Reflection." In *New Perspectives on Historical Theology: Essays in Memory of John Meyendorff*, edited by Bradley Nassif, 140–58. Grand Rapids: Eerdmans, 1996.

———. *The Christological Controversy*. Translated and edited by Richard A. Norris Jr. Sources of Early Christian Thought. Philadelphia: Fortress, 1980.

———. "Toward a Contemporary Interpretation of the Chalcedonian *Definition*." In *Lux in Lumine: Essays to Honor W. Norman Pittenger*, edited by Richard Norris Jr., 62–79. New York: Seabury, 1966.

Novak, David. *Talking with Christians: Musings of a Jewish Theologian*. Radical Traditions. Grand Rapids: Eerdmans, 2005.

Oberlies, Thomas. "Prayer/Curse." In *The Brill Dictionary of Religion*, 3:1486–89.

Ochs, Peter. "The God of Jews and Christians." In *Christianity in Jewish Terms*, edited by Tikva Frymer-Kensky et al., 49–69. Boulder, CO: Westview, 2000.

Oliver, Jessie. "The Bitter Teardrops Fall." *Touchstone* 16/2 (May 1998) 12–15.

"Open Letter to His Holiness Pope Benedict XVI, October 12, 2006." Online: http://monasticdialog.com/a.php?id=789&t=p.

Oppy, Graham. *Philosophical Perspectives on Infinity*. New York: Cambridge University Press, 2006.

Origen. *On Prayer*. In *Origen*, translated by Rowan Greer, 81–170. Classics of Western Spirituality. New York: Paulist, 1979.

Panikkar, Raimon. "Can Theology Be Transcultural?" In *Pluralism and Oppression: Theology in World Perspective*, edited by Paul Knitter, 3–22. Annual Publication of the College Theology Society 34 (1988). Lanham, MD: College Theology Society/ University Press of America, 1991.

———. *The Unknown Christ of Hinduism: Towards an Ecumenical Christophany*. Rev. ed. Maryknoll, NY: Orbis, 1981.

Pannenberg, Wolfhart. *Basic Questions in Theology*. Vol. 2. Translated by George Kehm. Philadelphia: Westminster, 1971.

———. "History and the Reality of the Resurrection." In *Resurrection Reconsidered*, edited by Gavin D'Costa, 62–72. Oxford: Oneworld, 1996.

———. *Jesus—God and Man*. Translated by Lewis L. Wilkins and Duane A. Priebe 2nd ed. Philadelphia: Westminster, 1977.

———. *Systematic Theology*. Vol. 2. Translated by Geoffrey W. Bromiley. Grand Rapids: Eerdmans, 1994.

Pawlikowski, John. "The Christ Event and the Jewish People." In *Thinking of Christ: Proclamation, Explanation, Meaning*, edited by Tatha Wiley, 103–21. New York: Continuum, 2003.

Pelikan, Jaroslav. "Chalcedon after Fifteen Centuries." *Concordia Theological Monthly* 22 (1951) 926–36.

———. *The Christian Tradition: A History of the Development of Doctrine*. Vol. 1, *The Emergence of the Catholic Tradition (100–600)*. Chicago: University of Chicago Press, 1971.

Perkins, Pheme. *Resurrection: New Testament Witness and Contemporary Reflection*. Garden City, NY: Doubleday, 1984.

Perkinson, Jim. "A Canaanitic Word in the Logos of Christ; or The Difference the Syro-Phoenician Woman Makes to Jesus." In *Postcolonialism and Scriptural Reading*, edited by Laura Donaldson, 61–85. Semeia 75. Atlanta: Scholars, 1996.

Pinnock, Sarah. "Atrocity and Ambiguity: Recent Developments in Christian Holocaust Responses." *Journal of the American Academy of Religion* 75/3 (September 2007) 499–523.

Placher, William. *Jesus the Savior: The Meaning of Jesus Christ for Christian Faith*. Louisville: Westminster John Knox, 2001.

Plaskow, Judith. *Sex, Sin, and Grace: Women's Experience and the Theologies of Reinhold Niebuhr and Paul Tillich*. New York: University Press of America, 1980.

Pokorný, Petr. *The Genesis of Christology*. Edinburgh: T. & T. Clark, 1987.

Poling, James. "The Cross and Male Violence." In *Cross Examinations: Readings on the Meaning of the Cross Today*, edited by Marit Trelstad, 50–62. Minneapolis: Fortress, 2006.

Pollefeyt, Didier. "Between a Dangerous Memory and a Memory in Danger: The Israeli-Palestinian Struggle from a Christian Post-Holocaust Perspective." In *Anguished Hope: Holocaust Scholars Confront the Palestinian-Israeli Conflict*, edited by Leonard Grob and John Roth, 135–46. Grand Rapids: Eerdmans, 2008.

Psuedo-Dionysius. *Psuedo-Dionysius: The Complete Works*. Translated by Colm Luibheid. Classics of Western Spirituality. New York: Paulist, 1987.

Rad, Gerhard von. *Genesis*. Rev. ed. Original translation by John Marks. Old Testament Library. Philadelphia: Westminster, 1972.

Rahner, Karl. *Foundations of the Christian Faith: An Introduction to the Idea of Christianity*. Translated by William V. Dych. New York: Crossroad, 1978.

———. "Jesus Christ: IV. History of Dogma and Theology." In *Sacramentum Mundi*, edited by Karl Rahner et al., 3:192–209. New York: Herder, 1969.

———. *The Love of Jesus and the Love of Neighbor*. Translated by Robert Barr. New York: Crossroad, 1983.

———. *On Prayer*. New York: Paulist, 1968.

———. *Theological Investigations*. Vol. 1, *God, Christ, Mary, and Grace*. Translated by Cornelius Ernst. London. Darton, Longman & Todd, 1961.

———. *The Trinity*. Translated by Joseph Donceel. New York: Seabury, 1974.

Rasmussen, Larry. *Earth Community, Earth Ethics*. Maryknoll, NY: Orbis, 1996.

Ray, Darby Kathleen. *Deceiving the Devil: Atonement, Abuse, and Ransom*. Cleveland: Pilgrim, 1998.

Ricoeur, Paul. *Memory, History, Forgetting*. Translated by Kathleen Blamey and David Pellauer. Chicago: University of Chicago Press, 2004.

———. *Oneself as Another*. Translated by Kathleen Blamey. Chicago: University of Chicago Press, 1992.

———. *The Symbolism of Evil*. Translated by Emerson Buchanan. Beacon Paperback Ariadne 18. Boston: Beacon, 1967.

Rieger, Joerg. *Christ and Empire: From Paul to Postcolonial Times*. Minneapolis: Fortress, 2007.

Robertson, Roland. *Globalization: Social Theory and Global Culture*. Theory, Culture & Society. London: Sage, 1992.

Robinson, James. "Very Goddess and Very Man: Jesus' Better Self." In *Encountering Jesus: A Debate on Christology*, edited by Stephen Davis, 111–22. Atlanta: John Knox, 1988.

Roth, John. "A Theodicy of Protest." In *Encountering Evil: Live Options in Theodicy*, edited by Stephen Davis, 7–22. Atlanta: John Knox, 1981.

Rowe, Kavin. *Early Narrative Christology: The Lord in the Gospel of Luke*. Grand Rapids: Baker Academic, 2009.

Ruether, Rosemary Radford. "Can Christology Be Liberated from Patriarchy?" In *Reconstructing the Christ Symbol: Essays in Feminist Christology*, edited by Maryanne Stevens, 7–29. New York: Paulist, 1993.

———. *Faith and Fratricide: The Theological Roots of Anti-Semitism*. New York: Seabury, 1974.

———. "What I Have Learned from Buddhism." In *Religious Feminism and the Future of the Planet: A Christian-Buddhist Conversation*, Rita M. Gross and Rosemary Radford Ruether, 145–87. New York: Continuum, 2001.

Russell, Letty. *Household of Freedom: Authority in feminist Theology*. Annie Kinkead Warfield Lectures 1986. Philadelphia: Westminster, 1987.

Samartha, S. J. *One Christ, Many Religions: Toward a Revised Christology*. Faith Meets Faith. Bangalore: SATHRI; Maryknoll, NY: Orbis, 1992.

Sandel, Michael. *Democracy's Discontent: America in Search of a Public Philosophy*. Cambridge, MA: Harvard University Press, 1996.

Sanders, E. P. *The Historical Figure of Jesus*. London: Penguin, 1993.

———. *Jesus and Judaism*. Philadelphia: Fortress, 1985.

Sands, Kathleen. "Uses of the Thea(o)logian: Sex and Theodicy in Religious Feminism." *Journal of Feminist Studies In Religion* 8/1 (Spring 1992) 7–33.

Schillebeeckx, Edward. *Christ: The Experience of Jesus as Lord*. Translated by John Bowden. New York: Crossroad, 1980.

———. *Jesus: An Experiment in Christology*. Translated by Hubert Hoskins. New York: Seabury, 1979.

Schmiechen, Peter. *Saving Power: Theories of Atonement and Forms of the Church*. Grand Rapids: Eerdmans, 2005.

Schnackenburg, Rudolf. *Jesus in the Gospels: A Biblical Christology*. Translated by O. C. Dean Jr.. Louisville: Westminster John Knox, 1995.

Schrag, Calvin. *The Self after Postmodernity*. New Haven, CT: Yale University Press, 1997.

Schüssler Fiorenza, Elisabeth. *In Memory of Her: A Feminist Theological Reconstruction of Christian Origins*. New York: Crossroad, 1983.

———. *Jesus: Miriam's Child, Sophia's Prophet*. New York: Continuum, 1994.

———. "Jesus of Nazareth in Historical Research." In *Thinking of Christ: Proclamation, Explanation, Meaning*, edited by Tatha Wiley, 29–48. New York: Continuum, 2003.

Schüssler Fiorenza, Francis. *Foundational Theology: Jesus and the Church*. New York: Crossroad, 1986.

———. "Introduction." In Johann Baptist Metz and Jürgen Moltmann, *Faith and the Future: Essays on Theology, Solidarity, and Modernity*, xi–xvii. Concilium. Maryknoll, NY: Orbis, 1995.

Schweitzer, Don. "Aspects of God's Relationship to the World in the Theologies of Jürgen Moltmann, Bonaventure, and Jonathan Edwards." *Religious Studies and Theology* 26/1 (2007) 5–24.

———. *Contemporary Christologies*. Minneapolis: Fortress, 2010.

———. "The Dialectic of Understanding and Explanation in Answers to Questions of Theodicy." *Studies in Religion/Sciences Religieuses* 34/2 (2005) 251–68.

———. "Food as Gift, Necessity, and Possibility." *Religious Studies and Theology* 20/2 (2001) 1–19.

———. "The Holy Spirit as Giver, Gift, and Growing Edge of God." *Touchstone* 26/2 (May 2008) 23–34.

———. "Jonathan Edwards' Understanding of Divine Infinity." In *Jonathan Edwards as Contemporary: Essays in Honor of Sang Hyun Lee*, edited by Don Schweitzer, 49–65. New York: Peter Lang, 2010.

———. "Karl Barth's Critique of Classical Theism." *Toronto Journal of Theology* 18/2 2002) 231–44.

———. "The Legacy of Residential Schools as a Legitimation Crisis for Christian Ethics." *The Ecumenist* 38/4 (Fall 2001) 11–14.

———. "The Mystery and Enigma of Prayer." *Touchstone* 17/2 (May 1999) 12–17.

———. "A Place for Aesthetics in Critical Theologies." *The Ecumenist* 44/2 (Spring 2007) 1–5.

———. "Pride as Sin and Virtue." *Studies in Religion/Sciences Religieuses* 20/2 (2000) 167–81.

Schweizer, Eduard. *The Good News According to Matthew*. Translated by David E. Green. Atlanta: John Knox, 1975.

Segal, Alan F. "The Resurrection: Faith or History?" In *The Resurrection of Jesus: John Dominic Crossan and N. T. Wright in Dialogue*, edited by Robert Stewart, 121–38. Minneapolis: Fortress, 2006.

Sellers, R. V. *The Council of Chalcedon: A Historical and Doctrinal Survey*. London: SPCK, 1953.

Slusser, Michael. "The Issues in the Definition of the Council of Chalcedon." *Toronto Journal of Theology* 6/1 (1990) 63–69.

Smith, D. Moody. *John*. Abingdon New Testament Commentaries. Nashville: Abingdon, 1999.

Soares-Prabhu, George. *The Dharma of Jesus*. Edited by Francis Xavier D'Sa. Maryknoll, NY: Orbis, 2003.

Sobrino, Jon. *Christ the Liberator: A View from the Victims*. Translated by Paul Burns. Maryknoll, NY: Orbis, 2001.

———. *Christology at the Crossroads: A Latin American Approach*. Translated by John Drury. Maryknoll, NY: Orbis, 1978.

———. *Jesus the Liberator: A Historical-Theological Reading of Jesus of Nazareth*. Translated by Paul Burns and Francis McDonagh. Maryknoll, NY: Orbis, 1993.

———. *No Salvation Outside the Poor: Prophetic-Utopian Essays*. Maryknoll, NY: Orbis, 2008.

———. *Spirituality of Liberation: Toward Political Holiness*. Maryknoll, NY: Orbis, 1988.

Soelle, Dorothee. *Death by Bread Alone: Texts and Reflections on Religious Experience*. Translated by David L. Scheidt. Philadelphia: Fortress, 1978.

———. *Suffering*. Translated by Everett R. Kalin. Philadelphia: Fortress, 1975.

———. *Theology for Skeptics: Reflections on God*. Translated by Joyce Irwin. Minneapolis: Fortress, 1995.

————. *Thinking about God: An Introduction to Theology.* Translated by John Bowden. Philadelphia: Trinity; London: SCM, 1990.

Soelle, Dorothee, and Luise Schottroff. *Jesus of Nazareth.* Translated by John Bowden. Louisville: Westminster John Knox, 2002.

Spivak, Gayatri Chakravorty. *A Critique of Postcolonial Reason: Toward a History of the Vanishing Present.* Cambridge, MA: Harvard University Press, 1999.

Spong, John Shelby. *Resurrection: Myth or Reality?: A Bishop's Search for the Origins of Christianity.* New York: HarperSanFrancisco, 1994.

Stackhouse, Max. "'All Things to All People': Mission and Providence in a Global Era." In *News of Boundless Riches,* edited by Lalsangkima Pachuau and Max Stackhouse, 2:250–75. Dehli: ISPCK/UTC/CTI, 2007.

Stegemann, Ekkehard, and Wolfgang Stegemann. *The Jesus Movement: A Social History of the First Century.* Translated by O. C. Dean Jr.. Minneapolis: Fortress, 1999.

Stietencron, Heinrich von. "Hindu Perspectives." In Hans Küng et al., *Christianity and the World Religions: Paths of Dialogue with Islam, Hinduism, and Buddhism,* translated by Peter Heinegg, 137–224. Garden City, NY: Doubleday, 1986.

Stroup, George. *Why Jesus Matters.* Louisville: Westminster John Knox, 2011.

Studer, Basil. *Trinity and Incarnation: The Faith of the Early Church.* Edited by Andrew Louth, translated by Matthias Westerhoff. Collegeville, MN: Liturgical, 1993.

Suchocki, Marjorie Hewitt. *God—Christ—Church: A Practical Guide to Process Theology.* New York: Crossroad, 1982.

Sugirtharajah, R. S. "An Interpretative Foreword." In *Asian Faces of Jesus,* edited by R. S. Sugirtharajah, 3–8. Faith and Culture. Maryknoll, NY: Orbis, 1993.

Tanner, Kathryn. *Christ the Key.* Current Issues in Theology. New York: Cambridge University Press, 2010.

Taylor, Charles. "The Dialogical Self." In *The Interpretive Turn: Philosophy, Science, Culture,* edited by David Hiley et al., 304–14. Ithaca, NY: Cornell University Press, 1991.

————. "Gadamer on the Human Sciences." In *The Cambridge Companion to Gadamer,* edited by Robert Dostal, 126–42. Cambridge: Cambridge University Press, 2002.

————. *Human Agency and Language: Philosophical Papers.* Vol. 1. New York: Cambridge University Press, 1985.

————. *The Malaise of Modernity.* Massey Lectures, 1991. Concord, ON: House of Anansi Press, 1991.

————. *Philosophical Arguments.* Cambridge, MA: Harvard University Press, 1995.

————. *A Secular Age.* Cambridge, MA: Harvard University Press, 2007.

————. *Sources of the Self: The Making of the Modern Identity.* Cambridge, MA: Harvard University Press, 1989.

Taylor, Mark Lewis. *The Executed God: The Way of the Cross in Lockdown America.* Minneapolis: Fortress, 2001.

————. "Introduction: The Theological Development and Contribution of Paul Tillich." In *Paul Tillich: Theologian of the Boundaries,* edited by Mark Lewis Taylor, 11–34. Making of Modern Theology. London: Collins, 1987.

————. *Religion, Politics, and the Christian Right: Post-9/11 Powers and American Empire.* Minneapolis: Fortress, 2006.

————. *Remembering Esperanza: A Cultural-Political Theology for North American Praxis.* Maryknoll, NY: Orbis, 1989.

Terrell, JoAnne Marie. "Our Mother's Gardens: Rethinking Sacrifice." In *Cross Examinations: Readings on the Meaning of the Cross Today*, edited by Marit Trelstad, 33–49. Minneapolis: Fortress, 2006.

TeSelle, Eugene. "How Do We Recognize a Status Confessionis?" *Theology Today* 45/1 (April,1988) 71–78.

Thatamanil, John. *The Immanent Divine: God, Creation, and the Human Predicament*. Minneapolis: Fortress, 2006.

Theissen, Gerd. "The Ambivalence of Power in Early Christianity." In *Power, Powerlessness, and the Divine: New Inquiries in Bible and Theology*, edited by Cynthia Rigby, 21–36. Scholars Press Studies in Theological Education. Atlanta: Scholars, 1997.

———. *The Gospels in Context: Social and Political History in the Synoptic Tradition*. Minneapolis: Fortress, 1991.

———. "The Political Dimension of Jesus' Activities." In *The Social Setting of Jesus and the Gospels*, edited by Wolfgang Stegemann et al., 225–50. Minneapolis: Fortress, 2002.

———. *The Religion of the Earliest Churches: Creating a Symbolic World*. Translated by John Bowden. Minneapolis: Fortress, 1999.

Theissen, Gerd, and Annete Merz. *The Historical Jesus: A Comprehensive Guide*. Translated by John Bowden. Minneapolis: Fortress, 1998.

Thomas, M. M. *The Acknowledged Christ of the Indian Renaissance*. London: SCM, 1969.

———. *Risking Christ for Christ's Sake: Towards an Ecumenical Theology of Pluralism*. Geneva: WWC Publications, 1987.

Thompson, Thomas. "Interpretatio in Bonem Partem: Jürgen Moltmann on the Immanent Trinity." In *Theology as Conversation: The Significance of Dialogue in Historical and Contemporary Theology: A Festschrift for Daniel L. Migliore*, edited by Bruce McCormack and Kimlyn Bender, 159–78. Grand Rapids: Eerdmans, 2009.

Tilley, Terrence. *The Disciples' Jesus: Christology as Reconciling Practice*. Maryknoll, NY: Orbis, 2008.

Tillich, Paul. *The Courage to Be*. Terry Lectures. New Haven, CT: Yale University Press, 1952.

———. *Love, Power and Justice: Ontological Analyses and Ethical Applications*. Galaxy Book 38. New York: Oxford University Press, 1954.

———. *Morality and Beyond*. New York: Harper & Row, 1963.

———. *Systematic Theology*. 3 vols. Chicago: University of Chicago Press, 1951–63.

———. *Theology of Culture*. Edited by Robert Kimball. New York: Oxford University Press, 1959.

Tödt, Heinz Eduard. *Authentic Faith: Bonhoeffer's Theological Ethics in Context*. Edited by Ernst-Albert Scharffenorth, translated by David Stassen and Ilse Tödt, English edition edited by Glen Harold Stassen. Grand Rapids: Eerdmans, 2007.

Tracy, David. *Blessed Rage for Order: The New Pluralism in Theology*. Minneapolis: Seabury, 1975.

———. *On Naming the Present: Reflections on God, Hermeneutics, and Church*. Concilium. Maryknoll, NY: Orbis, 1994.

Vermes, Geza. *The Religion of Jesus the Jew*. Minneapolis: Fortress, 1993.

Voices United. Toronto: United Church Publishing House, 1996.

Volf, Miroslav. *Exclusion and Embrace: A Theological Exploration of Identity, Otherness, and Reconciliation*. Nashville: Abingdon, 1996.

———. *Free of Charge: Giving and Forgiving in a Culture Stripped of Grace*. Grand Rapids: Zondervan, 2005.

Volf, Miroslav, et al. "Commentary on the Yale Response." In *A Common Word: Muslims and Christians on Loving God and Neighbor*, edited by Miroslav Volf, Ghazi bin Muhammad, and Melissa Yarrington, 56–75. Grand Rapids: Eerdmans, 2010.

Vries, Hent de. *Minimal Theologies: Critiques of Secular Reason in Adorno and Levinas*. Translated by Geoffrey Hale. Baltimore: John Hopkins University Press, 2005.

Walker, Williston. *A History of the Christian Church*. 3rd ed. New York: Scribner, 1970.

Watson, Francis. "Trinity and Community: A Reading of John 17." *Journal of Systematic Theology* 1/2 (July 1999) 168–84.

Weaver, J. Denny. "The Nonviolent Atonement: Human Violence, Discipleship and God." In *Stricken by God?: Nonviolent Identification and the Victory of Christ*, edited by Brad Jersak and Michael Hardin, 316–55. Grand Rapids: Eerdmans, 2007.

Wedderburn, A. J. M. *Beyond Resurrection*. Peabody, MA: Hendrickson, 1999.

Weinandy, Thomas. "Cyril and the Mystery of the Incarnation." In *the Theology of St. Cyril of Alexandria: A Critical Appreciation*, edited by Thomas Weinandy and Daniel Keating, 23–54. New York: T. & T. Clark, 2003.

Weingart, Richard. *The Logic of Divine Love: A Critical Analysis of the Soteriology of Peter Abailard*. Oxford: Clarendon, 1970.

Weiser, Arthur. *The Psalms*. Old Testament Library. Philadelphia: Westminster, 1962.

Welker, Michael. *God the Spirit*. Translated by John Hoffmeyer. Minneapolis: Fortress, 1994.

———. "Resurrection and the Reign of God." In *Hope for the Kingdom and Responsibility for the World: The 1993 Frederick Neumann Symposium on the Theological Interpretation of Scripture*, 3–16. Princeton Seminary Bulletin Supplementary Issue 3. Princeton, NJ: Princeton Theological Seminary, 1994.

———. "Security of Expectations: Reformulating the Theology of Law and Gospel." *Journal of Religion* 66 (1986) 237–60.

———. "'Who Is Jesus Christ for Us Today?'" *Harvard Theological Review* 95/2 (2002) 129–46.

———. "Wright on the Resurrection." *Scottish Journal of Theology* 60/4 (2007) 458–75.

Wells, Harold. *The Christic Center*. Maryknoll, NY: Orbis, 2004.

———. "Theology for Reconciliation." In *The Reconciliation of Peoples*, edited by Gregory Baum and Harold Wells, 1–15. Maryknoll, NY: Orbis, 1997.

West, Cornel. *Prophesy Deliverance!: An Afro-American Revolutionary Christianity*. Philadelphia: Westminster, 1982.

Westermann, Claus. *Praise and Lament in the Psalms*. Translated by Keith Crim and Richard Soulen. Atlanta: John Knox, 1981.

Whitehead, Alfred North. *Religion in the Making*. Lowell Institute Lectures. New York: Macmillan, 1926.

Wilken, Robert Louis. "Christian Worship: An Affair of Things as Well as Words." In *Christianity in Jewish Terms*, edited by Tikva Frymer-Kensky et al., 196–202. Boulder, CO: Westview, 2000.

———. *Judaism and the Early Christian Mind: A Study of Cyril of Alexandria's Exegesis and Theology*. Yale Publications in Religion 15. New Haven, CT: Yale University Press, 1971.

Williams, Daniel Day. *The Spirit and the Forms of Love*. New York: Harper & Row, 1968.

Williams, Delores. *Sisters in the Wilderness: The Challenge of Womanist God-Talk*. Maryknoll, NY: Orbis, 1993.

Williams, Rowan. *Arius: Heresy and Tradition*. London: Darton, Longman and Todd, 1987.

———. "Between the Cherubim: The Empty Tomb and the Empty Throne." In *Resurrection Reconsidered*, edited by Gavin D'Costa, 87–101, Oxford: Oneworld, 1996.

———. "A Common Word for the Common Good." July 15, 2008. Online: http://www.archbishopofcanterbury.org/media/word/2/j/A_Common_Word_for_the_Common_Good.doc.

Wright, N. T. *Jesus and the Victory of God*. Christian Origins and the Question of God 2. Minneapolis: Fortress, 1996.

———. *The Resurrection of the Son of God*. Christian Origins and the Question of God 3. Minneapolis: Fortress, 2003.

Yoder, John Howard. *The Jewish-Christian Schism Revisited*. Edited by Michael Cartwright and Peter Ochs. Radical Traditions. Grand Rapids: Eerdmans, 2003.

Young, Pamela Dickey. "Beyond Moral Influence to an Atoning Life." *Theology Today* 52/3 (October 1995) 344–55.

Manufactured by Amazon.ca
Acheson, AB

11539697R00185